P9-DEB-640

SIX SIGMA DEMYSTIFIED

SIX SIGMA DEMYSTIFIED

Paul Keller

McGRAW-HILL
New York   Chicago   San Francisco   Lisbon   London
Madrid   Mexico City   Milan   New Delhi   San Juan
Seoul   Singapore   Sydney   Toronto

The **McGraw·Hill** Companies

Copyright © 2005 by McGraw-Hill, Inc. All rights reserved. Printed in the United States of America. Except as permitted under the United States Copyright Act of 1976, no part of this publication may be reproduced or distributed in any form or by any means, or stored in a data base or retrieval system, without prior written permission of the publisher.

2 3 4 5 6 7 8 9 0 DOC/DOC 0 9 8 7 6 5

ISBN 0-07-144544-7

McGraw-Hill books are available at special discounts to use as premiums and sales promotions, or for use in corporate training programs. For more information, please write to the Director of Special Sales, Professional Publishing, McGraw-Hill, Two Penn Plaza, New York, NY 10121-2298. Or contact your local bookstore.

 This book was printed on recycled, acid-free paper containing a minimum of 50% recycled, de-inked fiber.

To Roxy, for her love and spiritual strength, and to my children Jessica, Melanie, Ashley and baby Harry, to inspire them to continually improve and help others.

CONTENTS

INTRODUCTION

There are now many excellent books on Six Sigma. Many of these emphasize the deployment issues of Six Sigma, providing valuable insight into the big picture issues required for successful implementation of Six Sigma at an organizational level. These issues, including management responsibility, resource allocation, and customer focus, are summarized in Chapter 1.

Successful Six Sigma Deployment involves continual success of projects, each incrementally moving the organization closer to its strategic goals of shareholder return and customer satisfaction. Each project, in turn, progresses from its initial definition through the DMAIC cycle to maturity of financial reward. This project evolution requires much attention to detail by the project team, including its Black Belt, Green Belts, and Sponsor. Unfortunately, many Six Sigma books fail to develop the detail of the tools necessary for practical use, or cover only a small handful of the tools required for an organization's projects. Readers are not provided clear benefits for the tools or may wonder if the tools may be applied to their specific processes and projects.

I am often asked by clients, "How does Six Sigma apply to us?" It is almost as if we are all part of the Al Franken generation, from the 1970s-era *Saturday Night Live*, where nothing means anything if it can't be put in the context of your own personal existence. Each different industry tends to approach problems as if no other market segment has ever experienced the same problems, now or ever. Even if the problems were the same, the solutions certainly can't apply across industries.

Some books provide far too much statistical background for the tools. Readers are forced to endure academic derivations of formulas or statistical tests that have limited use in today's computerized world. This tends to force the focus away from the practical use and limitations of the tools.

Demystifying Six Sigma is written to address these needs. It includes a variety of tools useful to Six Sigma teams, each presented within the context of an objective for a particular stage of DMAIC. Since many tools have applications within multiple stages of DMAIC, each tool description includes a "When to Use" section relating to the DMAIC methodology and its objectives. Detailed interpretation of each tool is also provided, with reference to other tools that should be used in conjunction with that tool for full effectiveness. Calculations and assumptions are provided as needed, as are detailed examples of their use in popular software such as *MS Excel, Minitab*, and *Green Belt XL*. To attract interest from the widest audience, many examples are provided for service processes. Each chapter concludes with study guide questions to challenge the reader. Detailed solutions are provided at the end of the book.

This book may be used for training groups of Black Belt and Green Belt or for self-study to master the tools and methodology of Six Sigma. I hope you will find this book useful in your Six Sigma journey.

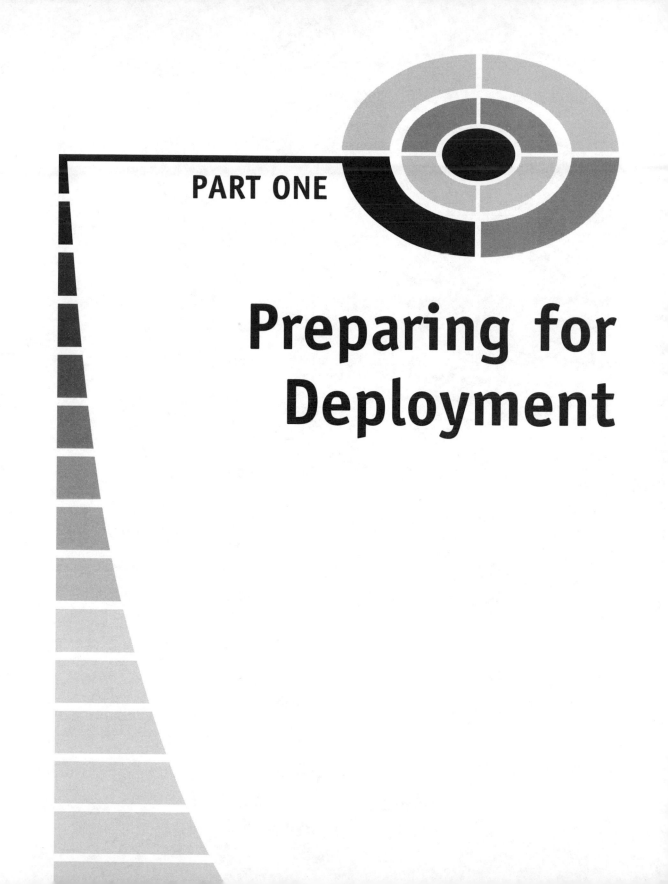

PART ONE

Preparing for Deployment

Deployment Strategy

What Is Six Sigma?

Sigma (σ) is the Greek letter used by statisticians to denote the standard deviation for a set of data. The standard deviation provides an estimate of the variation in a set of measured data. A stated sigma level, such as Six Sigma, is used to describe how well the process variation meets the customer's requirements.

Figure 1.1 illustrates the Six Sigma level of performance for a stable process. The process data is represented by the bell-shaped distribution shown. Using the calculated value of the standard deviation (sigma), the distance from the process centerline to any value can be expressed in sigma units. For example, if the process centerline for the wait time at a bank's teller station is 7.5 minutes, and the standard deviation of the wait time is calculated as 1 minute, then six standard deviations, or six sigma, from the centerline is 1.5 minutes (in the negative direction) and 13.5 minutes (in the positive direction).

Separately, through the use of customer surveys, focus groups, or simple feedback, customer requirements may have been established for the process. In this case, the process is likely to have only an upper specification limit defined by the customers; there is no minimum limit to desirable wait times.

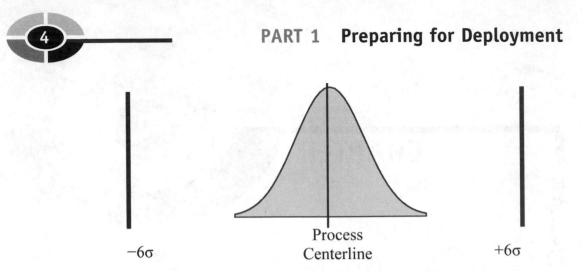

-6σ Process
Centerline $+6\sigma$

Figure 1.1   Six Sigma level of performance for a stable process.

If this upper specification coincides exactly with the plus-six sigma level (i.e., 13.5 minutes), then the process is at the Six Sigma level of performance. The implication is that the customer wait time will only exceed the customer requirements a very small percent of the time.

Although a normal distribution table will indicate the probability of exceeding six standard deviations (i.e., $z = 6$) is two times in a billion opportunities, the accepted error rate for Six Sigma processes is 3.4 defects per million opportunities (DPMO). Why the difference? When Motorola was developing the quality system that would become Six Sigma, an engineer named Bill Smith, considered the father of Six Sigma, noticed external failure rates were not well predicted by internal estimates. Instead, external defect rates seemed to be consistently higher than expected. Smith reasoned that a long-term shift of 1.5 sigma in the process mean would explain the difference. In this way, Motorola defined the Six Sigma process as one which will achieve a long-term error rate of 3.4 DPMO, which equates to 4.5 standard deviations from the average. While that may seem arbitrary, it has become the industry standard for both product and service industries.

These concepts have been successfully applied across a broad range of processes, organizations, and business sectors, with low and high volume, millions or billions in revenue, and even in nonprofit organizations. Any process can experience an error, or defect, from a customer's point of view. The error may be related to the quality, timeliness, or cost of the product or service. Once defined, the Six Sigma techniques can be applied to methodically reduce the error rate to improve customer satisfaction.

Using the curve shown in Figure 1.2 (Keller, 2001), any known process error rate can be directly converted to a sigma level. Most companies, including those with typical TQM-type programs, operate in the three to four

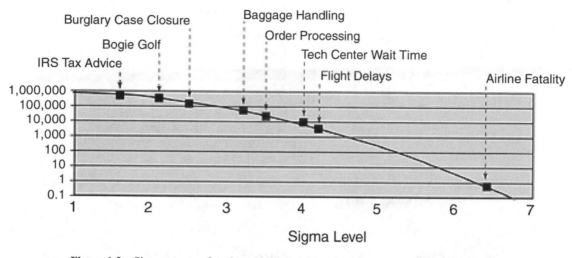

Figure 1.2   Sigma ranges for the activities shown, based on published defect rates.
(Keller, 2001)

sigma range, based on their published defect rates. In Figure 1.2, airline baggage handling, order processing, tech center wait time, and flight on-time performance fall in the general area of from three to four sigma.

Moving from left to right along the curve in Figure 1.2, the quality levels improve. Companies operating between two and three sigma levels cannot be profitable for very long, so, not surprisingly, only monopolies or government agencies operate at these levels.

Notice that the *y* axis, representing DPMO, is logarithmically scaled. As sigma level is increased, the defects per million opportunities decreases exponentially. For example, in moving from three sigma to four sigma, the DPMO drops from 67,000 to 6500, then to just over 200 at five sigma.

It's clear that significant improvement in customer satisfaction is realized in moving from three to four sigma. Moving beyond four or five sigma involves squeezing every last drop of potential improvement. Six Sigma is truly a significant achievement, requiring what Joseph Juran termed *breakthrough thinking* (Juran and Gryna, 1988).

There is some criticism of the DPMO focus, specifically with the definition of an opportunity. In counting opportunities for error in a deposit transaction at a bank, how many opportunities are there for error? Is each contact with a customer a single opportunity for error? Or should all the possible opportunities for error be counted, such as the recording of an incorrect deposit sum, providing the wrong change to the customer, depositing to the wrong account, and so on? This is an important distinction since increasing the number

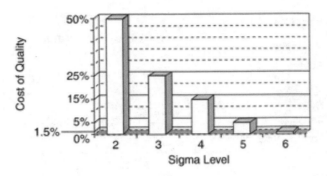

Figure 1.3   Cost of quality as a percent of sales for organizations at specified sigma level. (Keller, 2001)

of potential opportunities in the denominator of the DPMO calculation decreases the resulting DPMO, increasing the sigma level.

Obviously, an artificially inflated sigma level does not lead to higher levels of customer satisfaction or profitability. Unfortunately, there will always be some who try to "game" the system in this manner, which detracts from the Six Sigma programs that estimate customer satisfaction levels honestly.

Since DPMO calculations can be misleading, many successful Six Sigma programs shun the focus on DPMO. In these programs, progress is measured in other terms, including profitability, customer satisfaction, and employee retention. Characteristics of appropriate metrics are discussed further later in this chapter.

The financial contributions made by Six Sigma processes are perhaps the most interesting to focus on. The cost of quality can be measured for any organization using established criteria and categories of cost. In Figure 1.3, the y axis represents the cost of quality as a percentage of sales. For a two sigma organization, roughly 50% of sales is spent on non-value-added activities. It's easy to see now why for-profit organizations can't exist at the two sigma level.

At three to four sigma, where most organizations operate, an organization spends about 15% to 25% of its sales on "quality-related" activities. If that sounds high, consider all the non-value-added costs associated with poor quality: quality departments, customer complaint departments, returns, and warranty repairs. These associated activities and costs are sometimes referred to as "the hidden factory," illustrating the resource drain they place on the organization.

For most organizations, quality costs are hidden costs. Unless specific quality cost identification efforts have been undertaken, few accounting systems include provision for identifying quality costs. Because of this, unmeasured quality costs tend to increase. Poor quality impacts companies in two ways: higher cost and lower customer satisfaction. The lower satisfaction creates price pressure and lost sales, which results in lower revenues. The combination of higher cost and lower revenues eventually brings on a crisis that may threaten the very existence of the company. Rigorous cost of quality measurement is one technique for preventing such a crisis from occurring.

It's not uncommon for detailed quality audits to reveal that 50% of the quality costs go unreported to management, buried in general operating costs. Often these costs are considered "the cost of doing business" to ensure a high-quality product or service to the customer. Reworking, fine-tuning, touch-ups, management approvals, next-day deliveries to compensate for delayed or failed processes, and fixing invoice errors are all non-value-added costs that may go unreported.

As an organization moves to a five sigma level of performance, its cost of quality drops to around 5% of sales. The Six Sigma organization can expect to spend between 1% and 2% of sales on quality-related issues.

How are these cost savings achieved? As a company moves from three sigma to four sigma then five sigma, its quality costs move from "failure costs" (such as warranty repair, customer complaints, etc.) to "prevention costs" (such as reliability analysis in design, or customer surveys to reveal requirements). Consider the increased costs incurred when customers are the ones to detect the problems. A common rule of thumb is that if an error costs $1 to prevent, it will cost $10 to detect in-house, and $100 if the customer detects it. These orders of magnitude provide an incentive to move toward error prevention.

The cost of quality also drops quickly as dollars that go to waste in a three sigma organization (due to failure costs) go directly to the bottom line in a Six Sigma organization, to be reinvested in value-added activities which boost revenue. So while the three sigma organization is forever in "catch-up" or "firefighting" mode, the Six Sigma organization is able to fully utilize its resources. This infusion of capital helps the sales side of the equation, so the cost of quality as a percentage of sales (shown in the Figure 1.3) drops more quickly.

Differences between Six Sigma and Total Quality Management (TQM)

There are four key differences between a Six Sigma deployment and TQM-style implementations (Keller, 2001):

- *Project Focus and Duration.* Six Sigma deployment revolves around Six Sigma projects. Projects are defined that will concentrate on one or more key areas: cost, schedule, and quality. Projects may be developed by senior leaders for deployment at the business level, or developed with process owners at an operational level. In all cases, projects are directly linked to the strategic goals of the organization and approved for deployment by high-ranking sponsors.

  The project sponsor, as a leader in the organization, works with the project leader (usually a Black Belt) to define the scope, objective, and deliverables of the project. The sponsor ensures that resources are available for the project members, and that person builds support for the project at upper levels of management as needed. All of this is documented in a project charter, which serves as a contract between the sponsor and the project team.

  The scope of a project is typically set for completion in a three- to four-month time frame. Management sets criteria for minimal annualized return on projects, such as $100,000. The structure of the project and its charter keep the project focused. The project has a planned conclusion date with known deliverables. And it has buy-in from top management. These requirements, together with the Six Sigma tools and techniques, build project success.

- *Organizational Support and Infrastructure.* As shown in the next section, a proper Six Sigma deployment provides an infrastructure for success. The deployment is led by the executive staff, who use Six Sigma projects to further their strategic goals and objectives. The program is actively championed by mid- and upper-level leaders, who sponsor specific projects in their functional areas to meet the challenges laid down by their divisional leaders (in terms of the strategic goals). Black Belts are trained as full-time project leaders in the area of statistical analysis, while process personnel are trained as Green Belts to assist in projects as process experts. Master Black Belts serve as mentors to the Black Belts and deployment experts to the managerial staff.

- *Clear and Consistent Methodology.* A somewhat standard methodology has been developed for Six Sigma projects, abbreviated as DMAIC (pronounced Dah-May-Ick), an acronym for define, measure, analyze, improve, control. This discipline ensures that Six Sigma projects are clearly defined and implemented and prevents the reoccurrence of issues.

- *Top-down Training.* A properly structured deployment starts at the top, with training of key management. Six Sigma champions, consisting of executive-level decision makers and functional managers, are necessary to align the Six Sigma program with the business objectives through project sponsorship, and allocate resources to project teams. Without committed champions supporting them, Black Belts lack the authority, resources, and business integration necessary for project success.

The result of a properly implemented Six Sigma deployment is data-driven decision making at all levels of organization, geared toward satisfying critical needs of key stakeholders.

Six Sigma deployment doesn't cost, it pays. With minimum savings of $100,000 per project, the Six Sigma training projects will provide financial returns that far exceed the cost of the training. This "reward as you go" deployment strategy has proven beneficial to organizations of all sizes.

If you're still unsure whether a Six Sigma program is the right path for your organization, consider the impact to market share if your closest competitor implemented a Six Sigma program and you didn't.

Elements of a Successful Deployment

Jack Welch, the former CEO of General Electric, said: *This is not the program of the month. This is a discipline. This will be forever* (Slater, 1999).

Six Sigma is primarily a management program. For many organizations, it will fundamentally change the way they operate. It must, to achieve the levels of improvement shown earlier. Consider that moving from three sigma to four sigma means a 91% reduction in defects; from four to five an additional 96%, and from five to six a 99% further reduction. Without strong management and leadership, the time, effort, and expertise of the Six Sigma project team will be wasted, and results will not be achieved.

Program success is based on the following four factors, presented in order of importance:

- Support and participation of top management
- Sufficient resource allocation to improvement teams
- Data-driven decision making
- Measurement and feedback of key process characteristics

MANAGEMENT SUPPORT AND PARTICIPATION

A successful Six Sigma program must be integrated into the organization's business strategy. Active participation by leaders in the organization will ensure program survival.

As with most initiatives he launched as CEO of General Electric, Jack Welch was nearly fanatical about the Six Sigma program. In a January 1997 meeting, only a year after officially announcing the inception of the program to his managers, he challenged them:

> You've got to be passionate lunatics about the quality issue.... This has to be central to everything you do every day. Your meetings. Your speeches. Your reviews. Your hiring. Every one of you here is a quality champion or you shouldn't be here.... If you're not driving quality you should take your skills elsewhere. Because quality is what this company is all about. Six Sigma must become the common language of this company.... This is all about better business and better operating results. In 1997, I want you to promote your best people. Show the world that people who make the big quality leadership contributions are the leaders we want across the business. (Slater, 1999)

To get the most from the endeavor, management must actively support the Six Sigma initiative. Welch urged management to find opportunities to motivate employees to use Six Sigma in meetings, speeches, reviews, and hiring.

Tom Pyzdek, a leading Six Sigma consultant, tells the story of a CEO who was sure he was sending the right message to his management team, but wasn't getting the expected results. Tom had him wear a beeper for a week. The beeper went off at random times during the day, so the CEO could jot down his activities at the time. During the course of the week, the CEO soon realized he was spending very little of his time actually promoting the Six Sigma program. With a little coaching from Tom, he was able to work Six Sigma into his meeting topics and even his impromptu discussions with staff and line personnel.

Jack Welch further challenged his executive vice presidents by tying 40% of their bonus to specific bottom-line improvements from their Six Sigma initiatives (Slater, 1999). He realized that it was critical to move beyond mere words and to demonstrate commitment with leadership and results. This participation from senior management, through integration with their business strategy and practices, marked a key departure from run-of-the-mill TQM initiatives, where leadership was delegated to departments with little authority or few resources.

Here are the key priorities for management leadership:

☑ *Define objectives and goals of the program.* How is program success measured?

☑ *Develop the business strategy based on key customer requirements and market conditions.* Are there market opportunities that build upon the core competencies of the business? Are there competitor weaknesses that can be challenged? By reviewing market, operational, and customer feedback data, areas of opportunity are identified. Which improvements will have the greatest impact on the financial status of the organization? Where are its key losses, the "low-hanging fruit" for the first wave of projects? Some of this data is probably already compiled. A review may reveal gaps in the information, requiring changes to data acquisition methods. Business-level Six Sigma projects provide a sound approach to understanding these issues.

☑ *Define business-level metrics for customer, employee, and shareholder requirements.* Establish baselines and dashboards (measurement standards) for easy synthesis of data needed to gauge the success of the program and highlight hot opportunities. (Metrics are discussed further in the Measurement and Feedback section later in this chapter.)

☑ *Establish project selection, assignment, and approval criteria.* Project selection criteria should be aligned with the business strategy. (This is discussed further in the Project Selection section of Chapter 3.) Define key players for assigning and approving projects.

☑ *Market the program to the organization.* Construct, conduct, and analyze organizational assessment to identify obstacles to deployment within organizational levels. These perceptions are important to understand, so strengths can be built upon and weaknesses addressed. Larger organizations always need this internal buy-in. Many times, smaller organizations do as well. Use an employee-focused dashboard to track progress.

☑ *Select and train deployment team.* Personnel moves send strong signals. By selecting the best and brightest (the A team) for key Black Belt, Champion, and Green Belt positions in the first wave of deployment, management sends a clear signal: This effort is not just important, it is the most important thing we're doing. Training people to do it right sends the message that failure is not an option.

☑ *Develop a human resource strategy to retain Black Belts and motivate middle management to support and contribute to the program.* By giving employees incentives, and ensuring that leadership maintains its priority, management says there is no going back.

RESOURCE ALLOCATION

Organizations need to effectively plan for the human resource needs of the Six Sigma projects. Access to other resources, such as operational processes, will also require difficult prioritization decisions.

Resource allocation is a critical challenge for any organization. You often hear, "Our people already feel overworked." In many smaller organizations, resource allocation is further complicated because employees "wear several hats," usually because each function can't be cost-justified as a full-time position. Furthermore, many of these functions include tasks that are critical to the daily operations, not just the longer-term survival of the firm. Managers may question how they can afford to "lose" key people to the Black Belt role.

The key to resource allocation is the realization that the Six Sigma program will very quickly pay for itself. When the huge amount of waste in a three sigma organization (25% of revenue) is considered, it's clear that there are tremendous opportunities for these organizations. Many of these opportunities exist simply because of resource constraints: people know the problem exists, have a good understanding of potential solutions, yet lack the time to investigate and deploy the best solution. Only by diverting, or adding, resources to the system can waste be reduced and profitability improved.

A mature Six Sigma program usually has about 1% of its work force committed as Black Belts. Once properly trained, these individuals work only on Black Belt projects. In that regard, they are strictly overhead and contribute nothing directly to the everyday operations.

Full-time Black Belts will lead four to seven project teams per year. The teams consist of Green Belts, line personnel, and subject matter experts involved in the process targeted for improvement. These team members maintain their operational roles in the organization and participate only when serving on a project team. Team facilitators are also sometimes needed to help manage group dynamics and build consensus.

In some organizations, Green Belts are designated project leaders, responsible for completing one to five projects per year. Since this can present time-allocation problems, a preferred strategy is for full-time Black Belts to lead projects.

Master Black Belts provide coaching and other expertise to Black Belts. They typically have expertise in advanced statistical analysis methods and change management. One Master Black Belt for every 10 Black Belts is the recommended staffing. In addition, it is useful to appoint a Master Black Belt to assist the executive staff with Six Sigma deployment, technical training development, and technical support for business-level Six Sigma projects.

Smaller companies may have floating Black Belts who provide expertise to a number of Six Sigma teams throughout the organization. Companies of less than a few hundred employees may use key support personnel in part-time Black Belt roles, using consultants as Master Black Belts, particularly for the first year or two of deployment. When part-time Black Belts are used, management assumes a risk in losing project focus to daily operational issues. These resources must be effectively managed by the Six Sigma champions.

Sponsors are middle- to upper-level managers, trained as champions, who authorize, fund, and support the projects through allocation of resources.

Six Sigma project team members will be periodically excused from daily operational duties to work on project-related activities. Other resources (such as equipment and materials) will be diverted from daily operations to gather data. Line managers will need clear signals that upper management not only authorizes this reallocation of resources, but requires it.

Each Six Sigma project should include an estimate of the costs related to deploying the project. These costs are calculated by the accounting department, and include labor, materials, and lost production time. Costs are debited against the financial benefits of the project, which are also calculated by the accounting department.

DATA-DRIVEN DECISION MAKING

Management needs to lead by example. They need to *walk the talk*. Decisions regarding project selections, incentives to sales or production units, resource allocation, and so on, must all be based on sound data analysis. Consider, for example, project selections. If line supervisors had the sole authority to allocate resources for projects, then projects might not be aligned with the strategic direction of the business unit, or the needs of the external customer, simply because line supervisors lack access to that information.

Instead, project selection is a management activity that needs to consider a variety of factors: benefit to customer, probability of success, cost to implement, and time to implement, to name just a few. (See also Project Selection in Chapter 3.) By quantifying these factors, management is able to objectively choose projects that effectively use the company's limited resources.

As projects are deployed, decisions need to reflect the data. Where data does not exist, sponsors need to motivate the project team to acquire sufficient data to justify decisions made at each stage of DMAIC by asking the right questions, for example: Is the project defined for the correct problems? Does the project attack the root cause or just the symptom? Are the best metrics used to gauge project success? Has the data been properly analyzed? Is the improvement plan sustainable?

Business success will be more closely aligned with project success when management consistently integrates this way of thinking into their daily decisions. Rather than reacting to the crisis of the day, management should understand the differences between common and special causes of variation, and react accordingly. Financial incentives to sales or production should be based on metrics encouraging long-term customer satisfaction, business growth, and viability. For example, yield estimates that ignore the hidden costs of rework or customer returns provide poor incentive for production to satisfy external customer needs or longer-term viability.

There is a wealth of data available to management for decision making. Six Sigma projects can be used to define, collect, and synthesize the data necessary for proper decision making.

- Reliable customer data provides the distinction between internal perceptions and actual customer needs. There may be a disconnect between internal perceptions and customer perceptions. To ensure thoroughness, conduct a complete value stream analysis. While site visits are a popular means of collecting this data, they can be costly and may not be necessary. Indeed, their usefulness will certainly be improved if surveys are conducted beforehand. Critical incident surveys, described in Pyzdek's *Six Sigma Handbook* (2003), can also be a great source of customer insight.

- Data mining is sometimes used for discovering opportunities, but is often insufficient for conclusive decision making. Data mining involves the statistical analysis of databases, either to understand the nature of a particular variable (a *directed* analysis) or to search for patterns (an *undirected* analysis). For example, customer data may be mined to look for buying patterns by price and time of year. Because of the nature of this statistical analysis, it is often wise to conduct designed experiments to verify the suspected patterns before committing resources.

- Benchmarking, like data mining, can provide a wealth of ideas for defining direction, but does often not provide sufficient information for direct commitment of resources. Benchmarking can be used to understand best practices and discover new methods. Often the information is readily available from suppliers, books, magazines, and the Internet. Benchmarking helps define the potential for processes, especially those that may represent a new direction, where no internal experience exists in the organization. This information can be used to conduct pilot trials, or experiments, that will serve as valid data collection strategies for decision making.

- Process data is perhaps the most prolific and reliable source of data for decision making, given its relative ease of acquisition and low cost. Unfortunately, process data is often incorrectly analyzed, which can lead to more process degradation than improvement.

It's not uncommon for management reports to use bar graphs or pie charts to represent changes over time. Although bar graphs are certainly easy to interpret, they may not really provide the necessary context for a decision.

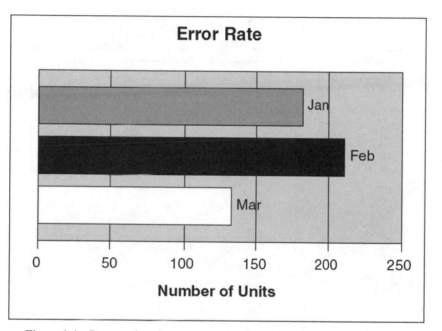

Figure 1.4   Bar graphs often provide misleading analysis of process data.

In the bar graph shown in Figure 1.4, it would appear that the process error rate has decreased in March. Apparently the process change initiated in February was effective in preventing further increases in the failure rate, as observed from January to February.

A proper analysis of the data in Figure 1.5 shows that the process did not significantly change over time. The bar graph in Figure 1.4 is missing context. It does not show how much month-to-month variation is usual or should be expected.

Confidence intervals and hypothesis tests are also incorrect tools to use for this analysis, since (as enumerative statistical tools) they cannot properly detect changes to a process over time. Instead, the analytical control chart shown in Figure 1.5 is the correct tool to estimate process variation over time. Using the control chart, the variation expected from the process (sometimes called the *common cause variation*) can be differentiated from the variation due to process changes (referred to as *special cause variation*).

When all changes to the process are assumed due to special causes (as is done using a bar graph analysis), the process variation can be increased by responding to the natural fluctuation with intentional process changes. This concept is discussed in more detail in Chapters 5 and 6.

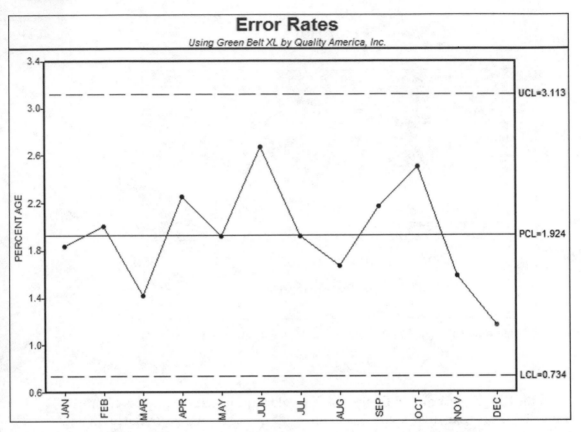

Figure 1.5 The process control chart shows process variation over time.

Obviously, correct analysis of process data is necessary for true improvements to customer service and the bottom line.

MEASUREMENT AND FEEDBACK

Employees need to understand the impact of their processes on customers. It is management's responsibility to establish a continuous flow of information from customer to the process employees. This constant feedback of data enables employees to quickly respond to problems to limit the negative impact on customers.

Metrics provide a quantitative means to assess what is critical to quality, cost, or scheduling. At the business level, these metrics provide feedback from the stakeholders in terms consistent over time and relevant to the business strategy. Six Sigma projects can be used to understand how these critical to quality (CTQ), critical to cost (CTC), and critical to schedule (CTS) metrics correlate with key process variables and controls to achieve systemwide improvements. Project deliverables will be defined in terms of these metrics, and provide an indication of project completion and success.

Appropriate metrics for tracking performance have the following characteristics:

- *A good metric is primarily customer-centered.* If a parameter is important to the customer, it should be important to your operations. Processes that directly impact the customer-centered parameters must be measured and controlled. Conversely, if issues that add no value to the customer experience are the focus, then resources are wasted and the focus should be redirected. Chapter 3 provides techniques for focusing on the customer's needs. Chapter 5 provides flow-down functions (big *Y*, little *y*) for defining process-level metrics that meet business-level customer requirements.
- *It is linked to your organization's strategy so that it can be clearly identified by all as critical.* The dashboard metrics discussed in this section are linked to each of the main stakeholder groups (customers, shareholders, and employees), providing high visibility throughout the organization.
- *The metric is collaboratively developed, assuring buy-in from all parties.* The collaborative development of the metric is realized by the Six Sigma project team in the measure stage, improving buy-in by the stakeholders.
- *It measures performance over time.* The use of the metric to evaluate the process over time is discussed below and further explained in the Metric Definition section of Chapter 5.
- *The metric provides direct information so that it can be applied nearly immediately without further processing.* Immediate feedback allows for quick response to changing conditions.

An effective means of presenting business-level metrics is through the use of dashboards. *Dashboards,* as the name implies, are like the gauges in a car: they provide immediate feedback of system status.

To understand how a car's engine is performing, the most direct method is to open the hood and look. At highway speeds, this can be messy, and even at idle, the results are often less than conclusive. Unless there is catastrophic damage, such as oil or steam shooting from the engine, most problems would be undetected.

So it is with customer feedback. Waiting for feedback from the customer, even requesting direct feedback of unfavorable conditions may provide incomplete, inconclusive, or untimely information.

In most automobiles, gauges, connected to sensors, are provided to constantly measure and report on critical precursors to unfavorable conditions. For example, the temperature gauge, oil pressure gauge, and fuel gauge each provide immediate feedback of impending problems. Better still, today's cars include electronic displays to indicate a drop in coolant level, providing even more advance notice of a potential problem.

Clearly, there are similar metrics available to business processes for measuring real-time precursors to customer problems. These metrics will provide input for data-driven decision making, and they will communicate the status and well-being of the business or process.

Effective dashboards should provide more than just single numbers, or a table of historical values. Instead, dashboards should provide clean and clear graphical displays, where historical context is readily apparent. If the dashboard metric changes, it should be clear whether the change is statistically significant. As discussed in the previous section, a statistical control chart provides the necessary context for this analysis.

From these business-level metrics, drill-down capability to the operations or process levels of the organization will provide further understanding of the variation. For example, if customer satisfaction is trending down, it's important to know which of the key drivers for customer satisfaction is influencing the downward trend.

In a Six Sigma deployment, dashboard metrics should be defined for each of the three main stakeholder groups: customers, employees, and shareholders, as shown by the examples in Table 1.1.

Each of these indices can be measured using representative surveys of the stakeholder groups. As in automobiles, too many dashboard indicators will cause confusion and lack of focus in the short term, and accidents or fatality in the longer term. At the business level, no more than four metrics for each stakeholder type should suffice.

Once these metrics are defined, their performance should be tracked and shared within the organization. The operational drivers for these metrics should be defined and monitored at the lower levels of the organization. For example, if customer satisfaction is closely linked with on-time delivery, customer service response time, and defect rate, then these metrics should be closely monitored at the operational level, with regular feedback provided to operating units. Six Sigma projects should be sponsored to improve performance relative to these metrics.

Table 1.1. Suggested Six Sigma deployment dashboards.

Customers	Shareholders	Employees
Satisfaction score	Earnings per share	Work environment score
Retention rate	Cost of poor quality (as percent of revenue)	Retention rate
Order turnaround time	Working capital turns	Hours of Six Sigma contribution
Sales revenue	Six Sigma project savings	Project completion rate

Chapter 5 provides further discussion of how process metrics relate to the operational and business-level dashboard metrics. Methods for understanding how metrics relate to customer needs are discussed in Chapter 3.

The result of effective measurement and feedback to the organization, when coupled with the other requirements for successful deployment, is empowerment. Rather than waffling with indecision, this data provides the critical link for action for operational personnel and local management. With clear vision forward, and feedback to confirm direction, the elements are in place for a successful journey.

Quiz for Chapter 1

1. Examples of "hidden factory" losses include all of the following *except*:
   a. Capacity losses due to reworks and scrap.
   b. Stockpiling of raw material to accommodate poor yield.
   c. Rush deliveries.
   d. All of the above.

2. Six Sigma methodologies:
   a. Can only be applied to companies who produce goods with large volume.
   b. Concentrate on cost savings rather than customer needs.
   c. Have not been successfully applied to service companies.
   d. None of the above.

3. As an organization's sigma level increases:
    a. The cost of quality increases.
    b. The cost of quality decreases.
    c. The cost of quality is not affected.
    d. None of the above.

4. A criticism of the DPMO metric is:
    a. It doesn't apply to service organizations.
    b. Defects aren't as important as profits.
    c. It can be artificially decreased by increasing the number of defect opportunities.
    d. All of the above.

5. If you estimate your cost of quality as 7% of sales, and your overall DPMO is about 20,000, then:
    a. Your sigma level is about 3.5.
    b. You are probably underreporting the cost of quality.
    c. You should look for evidence of a hidden factory.
    d. All of the above.

6. *Breakthrough*, as applied to improvement, was a term first used by which author?
    a. Mikel Harry.
    b. W. Edwards Deming.
    c. Walter Shewhart.
    d. Joseph Juran.

7. Marketing the Six Sigma program to the organization is important:
    a. So employees understand the program's motives and objectives.
    b. Only for large organizations.
    c. Only for small organizations.
    d. When employees are distrustful of management.

8. In a mature Six Sigma program:
    a. Only a small percentage of the employees are involved, and only for limited times.
    b. There is not much left to be gained by Six Sigma projects.
    c. Nearly everyone in the organization is involved in some way at some time.
    d. The Quality Department is the key customer contact.

9. In many organizations, Black Belts are assigned full-time to projects:
    a. As are Green Belts.
    b. To ensure they have the time necessary for completing projects.

    c. Since a given project will take up all their time for a 3- to 6-month period.

    d. To operate processes for data collection.

10. Data-driven decision making:

    a. Is an integral part of a Six Sigma program.

    b. May slow down some decisions as data is collected and analyzed.

    c. Builds buy-in across the organization.

    d. All of the above.

70%

CHAPTER

Personnel Requirements

Six Sigma is the most important management training thing we've ever had. It's better than going to Harvard Business School; it teaches you how to think differently.

Jack Welch, April 1999 Interview (Slater, 2000)

It's been said many times that a company's most valued resource is its employees, and that is certainly the case in a Six Sigma organization. Employees provide the critical link to customer satisfaction and loyalty and ensure that the organization is constantly aligned with dynamic customer needs. Training provides the means of instructing employees on the necessary practices to meet these needs.

Six Sigma training should begin with the managerial ranks of the organization, so they are prepared to lead the effort. Motorola's director of training and education estimates that they wasted $7 million training from the bottom up. GE learned from this mistake, to Jack Welch's credit.

Initially, Welch required that anyone seeking promotion to a management position be trained to at least Green Belt (if not Black Belt) level. A year later (effective January 1999), all professional employees should have begun Green Belt or Black Belt training. Considering that this directive encompassed 80,000 to 90,000 employees, it sent a clear signal that all levels of management would be leading the Six Sigma effort (Slater, 1999).

Other firms have since adopted this model as an effective way to reinforce the Six Sigma methodology throughout the organization. Studies have shown employees are much more likely to use specific business tools if their direct management uses the tools. Employees want to speak a common language. Conversely, if management won't utilize specific techniques, employees are likely to abandon using them also, feeling they have been discredited or are misunderstood by management.

The overall objective for senior management training should be an understanding of the link between program success and business success. Managers should integrate the program into the business strategy, so that completion of each Six Sigma project leads toward achievement of particular business goals. Likewise, they need to continuously promote and sponsor projects that strive for these goals.

If all levels of management do not see the vision laid out for the Six Sigma program, then deployment will become stagnated or undermined. These are the hidden signals of a doomed Six Sigma deployment. Upper levels of management can help overcome these problems when properly trained as Six Sigma Champions.

Lower levels of management also need to clearly understand the methodology. As first- or second-line department managers and supervisors, they have to see how they and their personnel fit into the deployment scheme. Resource reallocation will have perhaps the greatest impact at their level: personnel will be reassigned from their departments to become full-time Black Belts; many of the remaining employees will be diverted for weeklong Green Belt training, then to participate as project team members; processes will be disrupted for experimentation, data collection, or process redesign.

Departmental managers must not think of themselves as mere "victims" of the Six Sigma deployment. In fact, their functional areas will show measurable improvements through deployment of the Six Sigma techniques, if properly applied. This improvement can only occur through strong leadership at these local levels. Thus, first- and second-line managers (and their functional areas) will benefit greatly from "getting onboard" through Green Belt training, which will offer the deployment skills needed for success. Eventually, all employees should be trained to a Green Belt level, so they can effectively participate in Six Sigma teams.

Developing a Training Plan

A starting point for many organizations is a one-day executive overview, which allows senior executives and managers to understand the deployment strategy and resource requirements necessary to begin a Six Sigma program. Once senior management has decided on the overall strategy, they should train an initial wave of Six Sigma Champions. The first wave of training might follow a schedule similar to this:

- Management training: Week 1.
- Market the program to the organization: Week 3.
- Champion training, including project selection: Week 5.
- Black Belt training: Weeks 9–21.
- Green Belt training: Week 25.

This schedule provides approximately a month between each training session. Realistically, you'll need some lag time between these activities to accommodate schedules. The six months indicated above can be shortened, but the training period is usually seven or eight months in even rapid deployments.

The schedule streamlines the deployment to expedite the training, so projects are quickly completed and savings realized. This immediate payback is a great incentive for management commitment to invest in further projects, including development of the feedback systems necessary to make the program a longer-term success.

Initial projects can be based on internal feedback (bottom-up projects) or well-known customer issues that are prioritized by local Champions as part of their training. There are usually an abundance of potential projects at this stage. As deployment training continues, the following priorities can be implemented:

- Develop the business strategy based on key customer requirements and market conditions.
- Define business-level metrics for customers, employees, and shareholders.
- Develop a human resource strategy.

Training a group of high-profile Champions is a great way to bring exposure to the program. This first wave of Champions will develop and sponsor the first wave of Black Belt training projects. For this first wave of Champions, find managers who are excited about the benefits of Six Sigma, are well respected, and have good visibility across the organization. Their involvement builds credibility, and their success attracts others for subsequent waves.

As discussed in Chapter 1, choose the A team, the best and brightest of employees, for the initial waves of training. This sets a firm tone that success is the priority, and nothing will be spared.

Some organizations prefer to train an initial wave of Green Belts before the Black Belts. In smaller organizations, cost savings can be realized through merging the Green Belt training into the first week of Black Belt training. This provides an additional benefit of a shared experience between the Black Belts and the Green Belts assigned to their teams. By training Green Belts first, team members assigned to the initial projects are exposed to the Six Sigma principles before the projects begin.

As the Six Sigma program matures, new Black Belts, Green Belts, and Champions will need to be trained. Additionally, there may be topics for which Black Belts need refresher courses. Many times, Master Black Belts assume the role of trainer. The program will need established protocol, resources, and budget for this continuing training.

Training Needs Analysis

Since each organization is different, the training plan should reflect the particular needs of the organization, or even groups within the organization. Each organization has a culture that has been established, either by deliberate management intention or from management inattention. Recognizing and responding to these needs will increase the organizational buy-in to the Six Sigma program.

In defining the training needs, it is important to understand the knowledge, skills, and abilities (KSAs) required for each group of participants, notably the Black Belts, Green Belts, and Champions. KSA requirements are covered in detail in the next section. Potential candidates for each group can be evaluated by their peers and through testing of the subject matter. Peer analysis may use confidential surveys or structured evaluations.

The results of these evaluations and the testing can be compiled using matrix diagrams. A gap analysis can be performed on individuals or the summarized results to highlight deficiencies in the current level of the KSAs.

Once an understanding of current KSAs is available, classes can be formed grouping students with similar training needs. For a given group, it's best to target the instruction to the minimum level of KSA. When employees have been exposed to similar training in the past, management may be tempted to assume that additional training on the same topic is unnecessary. Often, however, the prior training may have neglected to focus on one or more of the critical elements necessary for success, which at least partially explains the lack of success of the prior training. Even worse, the organizational environment may not have provided an opportunity for application of the skills, so they were quickly forgotten.

It is important therefore to conduct posttraining assessments to gauge the improvement in KSA. The certification processes discussed in the Black Belt and Green Belt sections below provide a means of evaluating the knowledge acquired. Regular renewal of the certification, such as every three years, evaluates the retention of the material. Of course, testing may never provide the best indication of the true KSA of an individual, since it is difficult, if not impossible, to test the full body of knowledge necessary for qualified personnel. Rather, the true intent of the training is a change in behavior, which can be monitored using employee dashboards as discussed in Chapter 1.

In addition to the KSAs, attitude is often a significant factor to be considered. Organizational assessments provide an indication of the current level of satisfaction and trust among the employees. Even when properly trained, employees with a poor attitude will be unwilling to apply their KSA in a productive fashion, to truly change their behavior. Poor attitude is often a reflection of distrust in management's motives or abilities, resulting from previous real or imagined blunders.

Unfortunately, attitude can be difficult to overcome, especially when it is deeply ingrained from years of neglect. Nonetheless, it is imperative to address these obstacles to build buy-in to the program. Successful approaches for consensus building are discussed in Chapter 4. Employees need to hear a consistent message, so the training of Champions should ensure commitment at all levels of management. Perhaps most important, data-driven decision making must be at the forefront of all policy and procedures, with open communication from and to employees on these decisions. Breaking down these walls takes time and persistence, with the results monitored in employee dashboards.

Champions

Champions are mid- to upper-level management responsible for supporting the Six Sigma program and ensuring it is aligned with the overall business strategy.

KSA REQUIREMENTS FOR CHAMPIONS

The primary role of a Champion is to ensure that organizational systems are in place to support the Six Sigma deployment. Champions are strong, vocal advocates of the Six Sigma program. Because of their standing in the organization at managerial levels, they provide critical exposure of the program to their functional reports and endorsement of the program as a management initiative.

As members of management, Champions bestow authority on the Six Sigma project teams. Through program development, project selection, and resource allocation, Champions ensure that the organizational ground is fertile for project growth and success. Through continuous involvement in the Six Sigma initiative, Champions send a clear signal to the organizational masses that management's commitment is continuous. Dispelling the notion that the program is a flavor of the month is an ongoing but necessary challenge to overcome unproductive subcultures that may exist. Effective Champion training provides an awareness of these roles, responsibilities, and challenges.

The attributes of a Champion can be summarized as follows (Slater, 1999):

- Displays energy and passion for the job
- Excites and mobilizes others
- Relates Six Sigma to customer success and bottom line
- Understands technical as well as financial aspects of Six Sigma
- Delivers bottom-line results, not just technical solutions

In many ways, the first two attributes are inherent to an individual's personality, although they may be dormant from lack of use. In that case, individuals can be nurtured so these qualities surface, providing there is strong upper management commitment and support for the Six Sigma initiative. If support begins to deteriorate, then the excitement expected from Champions will be either short-lived or unaccepted by the masses.

CHAMPION AND MANAGEMENT TRAINING

Champions begin their training with a two- to three-day class, emphasizing their role in program development and as project sponsors. The course material should include the topics presented in Part 1 of this book. A suggested agenda for a two-day session is provided in Table 2.1.

Workshops are a key part of the Champion training, providing an opportunity to build ownership of the Six Sigma program in the

Table 2.1.   Suggested agenda for champion training.

Order	Duration	Topic	Subtopics	Workshop
1	3 hours	Deployment strategy	What is Six Sigma? Comparison to TQM Elements of successful deployment DMAIC problem solving (overview)	Issues contributing to successful deployment
2	3 hours	Personnel and training requirements	Training needs analysis Selecting personnel Training regimen	Understanding training needs Methodology for selecting Black Belts
3	3 hours	Customer focus	Customer requirements Feedback mechanisms	Increasing customer focus
4	3 hours	Project selection and sponsorship	Potential benefits Selection criteria and methods Sponsor responsibilities	Project selection

managerial ranks. The workshops support the key outcomes of the training, including:

- Establishing the understanding and commitment of the managerial role, responsibilities, and project sponsorship necessary for success of the Six Sigma project teams
- Defining of the project selection criteria, aligned with key business objectives
- Selection of suitable Six Sigma projects using the selection criteria

An important component of the Champion training is to get the mid-level managers onboard, since they exercise direct control on the operational resources that will be critical for project success. The project selection exercises will give the managers ownership of the projects and commitment to team sponsorship.

Six Sigma Champions may also attend Green Belt training to learn the basic techniques used by Six Sigma teams. The goal of this training is to foster an awareness of the tools and techniques, so that Champions know the tools' limitations, as well as their strengths. This keeps Champions from pushing for the impossible, while also encouraging them to strive for new possibilities from the project teams. When serving as project sponsors, Champions who are familiar with the techniques can ensure that project teams maintain rigor in their analysis. This serves as a useful checkpoint for sustainability of project successes.

Black Belts

Black Belts are generally full-time change agents, removed from the operational responsibilities of the organization to maximize the resources available for deploying Six Sigma projects.

KSA REQUIREMENTS FOR BLACK BELTS

An important, but not comprehensive, role of a Six Sigma Black Belt is that of technical expert in the area of Six Sigma methods. This expertise allows the Black Belt to understand the link between complex customer needs and the critical internal process elements designed to achieve them.

While Six Sigma Black Belts are generally given credit for their expertise in analytical, statistical, and problem-solving techniques, successful Black Belts must be much more than technical experts. The advancement of an organization from a nominal three sigma to Six Sigma represents a vast organizational (and cultural) change. As such, Black Belts are primarily *change agents*.

Knowledge of company systems and culture is often required for successful change management in an organization. For this reason, many organizations find it better to train Black Belts from within than to hire from the outside. It's not uncommon for experienced Black Belts to later become key operational members of the management team. Their experience working on projects throughout the organization, with customers and suppliers, makes them extremely valuable in strategic positions.

Effective change agents are (Keller, 2001):

- *Positive Thinkers*. Black Belts need to have faith in management and in the direction of the business and its Six Sigma program. They must be upbeat and optimistic about the program success, or they risk undermining management or the Six Sigma initiative. They need to exude self-confidence, without the pitfalls of being overbearing, defensive, or self-righteous. Proper management support and vision allow Black Belts to both believe in and experience their potential as change agents.

- *Risk Takers*. Black Belts need to be comfortable as change agents. While ineffective change agents agonize over implementing change, effective change agents relish it. They enjoy the excitement and challenge of making things happen and "grabbing the bull by the horns." They know that change is necessary for the company's and the customer's sake, and inevitable, given the competitive market. Only by leading the change can its outcome be steered. The effective change agent wants to lead the charge.

- *Good Communicators*. An effective Black Belt needs to be capable of distilling a vast amount of technical material in an easily comprehensible fashion to team members, sponsors, Champions, and management. Many of these personnel will have only minimal training (Green Belt or Champion level) in statistical techniques, if any at all. The Black Belt who can clearly and succinctly describe to the team why, for example, a designed experiment is better than one-factor-at-a-time experimentation will strengthen the team and shorten its project completion time.

  Of course, being a good communicator is much more than just being capable of distilling technical material. An effective communicator must also comprehend and appreciate others' concerns. These concerns must be responded to in a thorough, respectful, and thoughtful manner. Through the use of the Six Sigma statistical techniques, data can be used to predict the merits of various improvement strategies and address these concerns. The effective change agent will enlist those with concerns to participate in these efforts, either as team members or as project sponsors. Through participation, these employees learn to understand the nature of the problem and the most viable solution. Buy-in, a necessary part of sustainability, is greatly enhanced through this participation.

- *Respected by Peers*. It is often said that a title can be either earned or granted, but that true power must be earned. Effective change agents have earned the respect of others in the organization by their hard work and effective communication. Those new to an organization, or those who have not gained respect from others, will find it harder to implement changes.

- *Leaders*. Black Belts will often serve as team leaders; other times they need to show respect to others (and true leadership) by allowing them to assume leadership roles. First-wave Black Belts will also serve as role models and mentors for Green Belts and subsequent waves of Black Belts.

Many of these change agent skills are personality facets, but they can be supported through awareness training, management policy, and coaching and mentoring by Master Black Belts and Champions. The best Black Belts are those individuals who show a balance between these softer attributes and the technical skills discussed elsewhere in this book. Many firms demand demonstration of these change agent attributes, through work history and personal recommendations, as a prerequisite for Black Belt candidates. Depending on the business and functional area, a technical college degree may also be required. For example, a BS in engineering may be required for manufacturing areas, whereas a business degree may be required for sales or business development areas.

BLACK BELT TRAINING

Typical Black Belt training consists of one week per month spread over four months. It integrates classroom learning with hands-on project implementation. Black Belts are assigned a project for this training, which allows them to successfully apply the skills they are taught in training. The trainers, aided by Master Black Belts, serve as coaches for these projects.

A key aspect of Black Belt training is the successful completion of a project. Projects prove training. Projects are only successfully completed when the financials have been certified by the accounting department, and the project has been accepted and closed by the sponsor. In addition to the usual criteria of bottom-line impact and customer focus, training projects are usually selected that will use many of the technical skills in an area of the business in which the Black Belt candidate has some experience (and comfort).

Each Black Belt should arrive for the first week of training with several potential projects, allowing that some of the projects may not meet selection criteria defined by their management (usually as part of Champion training). Workshops are incorporated extensively throughout the training to provide hands-on experience to the attendees. Project data is used in workshops wherever possible.

The flow of the course material roughly follows the DMAIC process, so that the appropriate tools and concepts are taught and applied at each stage of project deployment. The Black Belt training requires the use of suitable Six Sigma software, such as shown in the examples throughout this book. Because of the availability of software, the course material may concentrate on the application and use of statistical tools, rather than the detailed derivation of the statistical methods.

A suggested schedule of training topics is provided in Table 2.2. While there is a credible argument that many Six Sigma projects will require use of only a handful of tools, and that a portion of these will require only rudimentary

Table 2.2. Suggested schedule for Black Belt training.

Week One	Week Two	Week Three	Week Four
Deployment strategy	Measurement systems analysis	Defining the new process	Standardize on the new methods
Managing projects	Value stream analysis, including lean tools	Assessing benefits of proposed solution	Measure bottom-line impact
Teams and change management	Analyzing sources of variation, including statistical inference	Evaluating process failure modes, including FMEA	Document lessons learned
Consensus building methods	Determining process drivers, including designed experiments	Implementation and verification	Customer focus
Project definition			
Process definition			
Six Sigma goals and metrics			
Process baselines, including control charts and process capability analysis			

statistical knowledge, Black Belts nonetheless need to learn these skills. Black Belts should be taught to think critically and challenge conventional thought. Successful breakthrough thinking requires rigorous analysis. Black Belts must be taught to accept ideas and opinions as just that, with their limitations, and use the power of the analytical tools to prove the solutions and their assumptions. This applies equally to manufacturing and service applications. The statistical tools allow Black Belts to prove concepts with minimal data and process manipulation, so that great advances can be made in a short amount of time. Problems that have gone unsolved for years can be attacked and conquered. Data-driven decision making becomes the rule, not the exception.

Six Sigma certification demonstrates an individual's knowledge, skills, and dedication to achieving a high level of competency in the Six Sigma process. The certification criteria are varied. For some companies, completion of a course and a single project suffices. The American Society for Quality (ASQ) applies a rather simple scheme: passing a written exam, with a signed affidavit attesting to completion of either two projects, or one project and three years' experience in the body of knowledge. While the exam offers some proof of the skills learned by the Black Belt, the completion of two projects certifies the successful application of the skills.

The International Quality Federation (www.iqfnet.org) provides an online certification exam that can be used by an organization as part of their certification process. While the ASQ exam prohibits the use of a computer, which seems contrary to the Black Belt's curriculum, the IQF certification mandates its use. The IQF provides a form for use by the employer's certification committee, identifying three main components of certification: change agent skills, application of tools and techniques, and ability to achieve results. It also provides a change agent checklist, which is completed by sponsors and team members and submitted to the committee for review.

Green Belts

Green Belts are employees trained in basic Six Sigma concepts to work as part of a team assigned to a given project.

KSA REQUIREMENTS FOR GREEN BELTS

The role of the Green Belt is to provide local process expertise to the team and to facilitate the brainstorming and data acquisition activities of the team. Unlike Black Belts, who leave their operational duties behind, Green Belts "keep their day job." Likely Green Belt candidates include process supervisors, operators or clerical staff, technicians, or any other individual who may wish to serve on a project team. Eventually, most employees will achieve Green Belt status.

For the initial waves of training, select the Green Belts who can provide the necessary process expertise to the previously selected Black Belt projects.

These Green Belt candidates should be respected by their peers and capable of critical thinking in a positive fashion with a diverse team.

GREEN BELT TRAINING

Green Belts will learn the basics of the tools used by the project team. Their training will be "a mile wide and an inch deep." While they will rely on the project Black Belt for problem-solving skills, it is important they understand at least the need for the tools, if not the general DMAIC problem-solving methodology. For example, as process supervisors, they may be under pressure by the project team to conduct designed experiments to learn about significant process variables. If they have no experience with designed experiments, they may resist these necessary analysis steps.

The Green Belt training is typically a one-week course, providing an overview of the Six Sigma concepts and tools. It allows the Green Belts to speak the language of the Black Belts, so they understand the need and application of the various tools. Perhaps most importantly, Green Belts learn how to function effectively in a team. These team-building skills will ensure the project team stays focused and maintains momentum.

A suggested schedule for Green Belt training is shown in Table 2.3. Workshops are used, rather than detailed instruction, to demonstrate data analysis methods.

Table 2.3.   Suggested training schedule for Green Belts.

Day One	Day Two	Day Three	Day Four	Day Five
Deployment strategy	Managing projects	Data collection workshop	Analyze stage objectives	Improve stage objectives
Project definition	Teams and change management	Process baseline and measurement system analysis workshop	Value stream analysis, including lean tools	Control stage objectives
Process definition	Measure stage objectives		Determining process drivers workshop	

Green Belts can also be certified using a simple evaluation of their KSAs relative to the training discussed above. Rather than having a detailed understanding of the application of tools, Green Belts are only required to recognize the need for such analysis. Being an active member of two or more Six Sigma projects is generally required to demonstrate successful application of the KSA.

Quiz for Chapter 2

1. The preferred plan for training employees for a Six Sigma Deployment is to:
    a. Start at the operational level since these employees have customer contact.
    b. Begin with management personnel.
    c. Train everyone in the organization at the same time.
    d. First train suppliers on changes they will need to implement.

2. It is important for managers to be trained in Six Sigma principles so that:
    a. They understand their responsibilities to the program.
    b. They can effectively discipline their employees if they complain about the program.
    c. Management can prove they are committed to the program.
    d. Operational employees aren't afraid to volunteer for the training.

3. First-wave training projects for Black Belts:
    a. Should be delayed until a complete analysis is done on customer requirements.
    b. Often provide little financial value to the organization, but are necessary for proper training of the Black Belts.
    c. Can effectively target known customer problems.
    d. All of the above.

4. Champion training emphasizes:
    a. Selecting personnel (Black Belts, Green Belts) for the initial deployment.
    b. Defining initial project rating criteria and selecting potential projects.
    c. Methods for communicating program goals and strategy throughout the organization.
    d. All of the above.

5. Personnel selected for initial waves of Black Belt, Green Belt, or Champion training:
   a. Should be the employees needing the training the most.
   b. Should be willing to do the training on their own time so their other responsibilities are not neglected.
   c. Should be the best employees, the ones most valuable to the organization and most capable of succeeding.
   d. Should be randomly selected from each group so favoritism isn't an issue.

6. The best indicator of the effectiveness of training is:
   a. A change in behavior.
   b. High test scores.
   c. Self-evaluation.
   d. Peer evaluation.

7. Successful Champions:
   a. Understand how to develop projects to meet organizational goals.
   b. Motivate others in a positive fashion.
   c. Willingly provide resources to project teams.
   d. All of the above.

8. Successful Black Belts
   a. Are primarily technical experts.
   b. Are well rounded in communication, change management, and problem-solving skills.
   c. Are effective at directing people to do what they say.
   d. All of the above.

9. KSA refers to:
   a. Knowledge, Skill, and Attitude.
   b. Knowledge, Sense, and Attitude.
   c. Knowledge, Skill, and Ability.
   d. Keep It Simple Airhead.

10. In a typical deployment, Green Belts:
    a. Are full-time change agents.
    b. Maintain their regular role in the company, and work Six Sigma projects as needed.
    c. Receive extensive training in advanced statistical methods.
    d. All of the above.

Focusing the Deployment

Customer Focus

When customer requirements are evaluated, internal estimates of customer needs must be replaced with real customer needs. It is not uncommon to discover that many of long-held assumptions are simply wrong. Cost savings and improvement of customer relations are realized through a proper understanding of these needs. Six Sigma projects can even provide financial benefit, and reduced complaints from late deliveries, through *widening* of the internal specifications thought necessary to achieve perceived (but unreal) customer expectations.

All aspects of the customer experience (the value stream) should be considered, including design, use, delivery, billing, etc., and not just the obvious operational processes that are the focus of our business.

When detailed specifications have been provided by customers, they tend to become the focus. Even customer-conscious personnel will define customer needs in terms of specifications: "As long as we meet their requirements,

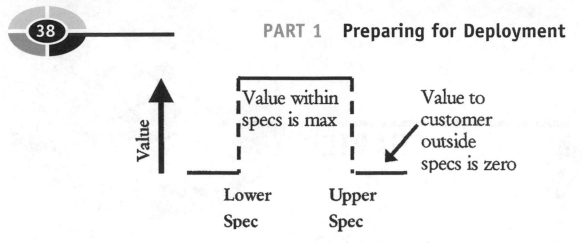

Figure 3.1.   Perceiving customer requirements as goal posts assumes constant maximum value within specs.

we'll be fine." These product specifications are viewed as goal posts: "Anywhere within the requirements is fine." Often, service attributes aren't that important: "The main thing is to deliver what they want, even if it's a bit late."

When customer requirements are perceived as goal posts, as shown in Figure 3.1, there is equal value for all products or services within the specifications, so there is no advantage in improvement beyond this point.

In most cases, the goal post approach does not maximize customer satisfaction, nor does it accurately present the customer's preference. Instead, customers tend to think in terms of optima. The optimal value for the product or service typically lies midway between the requirements, with deviations from that point less desirable. Customers value predictability, or minimum variation, so that their processes are impacted to a minimal degree. This enhances their ability to plan, regardless of their environment. If your organization makes a product, customers want to use your product in a consistent manner, with few adjustments of their equipment to compensate for variation between products. If your organization provides a service, your customers want that service to be consistent so they know what to expect and when to expect it.

These concepts are illustrated in the Kano model (developed by Noritaki Kano) shown in Figure 3.2, where quality is represented on the x axis and customer satisfaction is represented on the y axis. The expected quality is shown on the diagonal line, indicating that an ambivalent level of satisfaction (neither satisfied nor dissatisfied) should be expected when the quality has risen from the basic quality level to the level expected for the given product or service.

Basic quality levels tend to produce dissatisfaction, and satisfaction is only improved above ambivalence as customers become excited about the quality of the product or service.

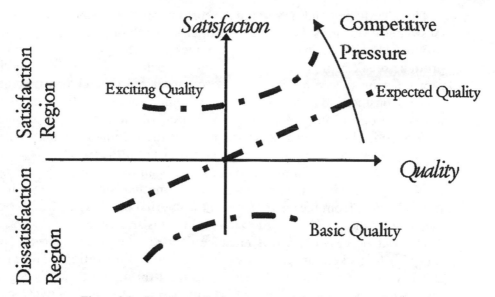

Figure 3.2 Kano model of customer satisfaction and quality.

Competitive pressures tend to move the expected quality line in the upward direction. There are countless examples of this phenomenon, including phone service, home building, computer technology, car safety, and so on, especially when viewed over the course of a generation or more. In each case, a product or service that was once exciting quality became expected quality and then basic quality. Competitive pressures continued to "raise the bar."

The Kano model moves the focus from specifications to real customer needs. When the focus is on specifications and defects, only expected levels of quality will be met, which soon become basic levels of quality in a competitive market.

When the focus is on customers, their business, or even the needs of *their* customers, exciting levels of quality can be delivered through innovation. Consider the lessons of Polaroid: While the company focused internally to become more efficient, its customers switched to digital cameras in place of Polaroid's (once award-winning) products. Lessons like these were not lost on Jack Welch, who remarked that the "best [Six Sigma] projects solve customer problems" (Slater, 1999).

Welch was not suggesting that companies merely reduce defects delivered to the customer or improve the perceived quality of a product or service delivered to the customer. Instead, Welch said that a Six Sigma project should investigate how the product or service is used by the customer and find ways to improve the value to the customer of that product or service.

This clearly demands involving the customer in the business needs analysis. Customer needs must be defined in larger terms than simply product specifications. Understanding how the customer uses the product or service can produce breakthrough changes in design or delivery. While initial design of a product or service process may have considered this, changes in the customer's business may not have been communicated effectively, leaving an unfulfilled opportunity. As additional aspects of the customer's business are understood, changes in that customer's business climate or market, which could upset your business, are appreciated, if not anticipated.

In this way, maintaining customer focus is an ongoing activity. Processes for serving customers must be identified, and mechanisms maintained for real-time feedback from the customer to these internal processes. The metrics and dashboards discussed earlier are integral to this strategy.

Internal process objectives must be defined in customer terms, and the everyday focus kept on the needs of the customer's operations. This visibility is a key aspect of the "lean" techniques used throughout the Six Sigma deployment. The linkage of internal process objectives is effectively mapped using quality function deployment (QFD) techniques. Operationally, we strive to understand how internal processes drive the customer response. To facilitate this understanding, critical to quality (CTQ), critical to cost (CTC), and critical to service (CTS) metrics are measured and tracked on a continual basis. These metrics allow internal estimates, before errors reach the customer and come back as nonconformance reports (or, in the absence of complaints, interpreted as improvement). This proactive approach fosters an ongoing attack on non-value-added (NVA) activities so resources can be shifted to value-added customer *exciters* (in the Kano terminology).

Although there are more current examples using the Six Sigma methods, an interesting and well-documented example is found in the book *Moments of Truth*, written by Jan Carlzon, the former president of SAS Airlines. In the late 1970s and early 1980s, the company was losing vast sums of money as their market had changed drastically with the advent of deregulation. While the most prevalent idea was to cut costs across the board, or cut costs in recoverable expenses such as labor, they instead set an ambitious objective to become the frequent business traveler's first choice for travel. Each expense and resource was evaluated for its contribution toward serving the frequent business traveler. Whole business units and functions were dropped, as were a host of operations and procedures that didn't serve their target market (the business customer). Practices that contributed to the service of the target frequent business traveler were actually expanded, so that a large portion of money saved was reallocated to expand the business. As the company struggled with significant loss in revenue, they spent $45 million to improve their customer service, including projects focused on punctuality, turnaround times, and service quality. They eliminated the detailed marketing reports, which took months to create by staff disconnected from the customers, replacing them with empowerment of the frontline employees who had direct customer contact for analysis and action based on real-time feedback.

The elimination of non-value-added activities is a lean practice used in Six Sigma to concentrate the always-limited resources on the customer. Quick feedback mechanisms using key service metrics is a fundamental Six Sigma approach. Quality function deployment techniques can be used to identify practices that contribute to customer satisfaction.

In any organization, the leadership sets the vision and the strategy. As Carlzon put it: "A leader . . . creates the right environment for business to be done." A soccer coach can neither dribble down court for the team, nor provide constant and immediate instructions to players on shooting, passing, and defense. Instead, the coach needs to develop skills in the players, then empower them to exercise judgment in the use of these skills.

As on the soccer field, responsibility in a customer-focused organization must be delegated down the line. Rather than tightened oversight to achieve adherence to customer requirements, bureaucracy must be reduced and the organizational hierarchy flattened to increase the communication between organizational levels, particularly communication *to* and *from* the frontline personnel with access to the customer.

Through empowerment, the responsibility, focus, and authority of frontline personnel are shifted toward doing what is necessary to win customer loyalty, *without the need for additional management approval.* This empowerment demands flexibility, sharing of information, and an understanding of the business operations, which is afforded by cross-training. The ultimate result is what Carlzon called "moments of truth" in customer relations, where customers realize the commitment of the organization to solving their problem (see Figure 3.3).

A new organizational structure results, where commitment toward the customer is shared across the organization. There may still be a sales force, but they no longer need (or want) exclusive rights to communicate with the customer. (Note that the same can be said of the relationship between suppliers and purchasing agents). As the customer becomes a more critical element of each employee's responsibilities, the relationship between the organization and the customer becomes more of a shared partnership, with mutual benefits.

This real-time data at the point of delivery provides immediate feedback, which empowered employees can act upon. Yet it is not sufficient. Some customers may not be open to sharing information. Others will not even realize dissatisfaction until later, such as where the end user is not the purchaser, or when the product is not immediately used. A call-center client may not

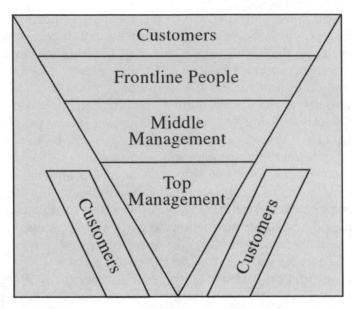

Figure 3.3   The new organizational structure puts customer contact at all levels of the organization. (Pyzdek, 2003)

realize until later that the critical details needed were not provided by the support personnel. Fortunately, there are additional sources of customer data, with varying degrees of usefulness.

Nonconformance reports or complaints are a typical source of customer feedback; however, they often include only a small percentage of all problems. Many problems go unreported. Since the complaints are generally only communicated based on a failure to meet basic customer expectations, they are at most useful for moving to basic or expected quality levels. For some organizations, particularly those at the three sigma level, this is a worthwhile and necessary place to start. These problems cannot be ignored, and their significance to the customer is highlighted by their insistence in reporting them. Prompt analysis of these reports and resulting action sends an important message to the customer. Studies have shown that when customers are made aware of these corrective actions they tend to be more loyal customers, in spite of the initial incident. When analysis indicates systematic deficiencies, these must be addressed, either through management policy changes or process improvement using Six Sigma projects. These persistent problems will undermine even the best attempts of problem resolution.

In many cases broader, more immediate feedback of customer experiences is obtained using simple phone surveys of a random sample of recent customers. More detailed information may be gathered using the critical incident techniques described by Pyzdek (2003). The aim is to define moments of truth in customer terms and qualify key customer perceptions. Even customers who may not take the time to complain may be willing to provide quick feedback in this manner.

Customer surveys provide a useful means for collecting a fair amount of broad-based information. Information gathered from the phone surveys, critical incident interviews, and nonconformance reports or complaints is useful input for survey development. The survey will provide a means to statistically validate the information received from these other sources. They can also be used as a continuous feedback mechanism, particularly for the service aspect of processes. For example, surveys can be sent to all customers, or survey cards can be provided at the point of service.

The construction of a useful customer survey is more science than art. The wording of questions, the topics addressed, the use of open-ended versus multiple-choice responses are but several of the issues that need to be considered. Surveys that lack depth may be useful for feel-good marketing campaigns, but they do little to provide input to Six Sigma operations or process level teams that can use the survey responses to make dramatic improvements in customer satisfaction, retention, and growth. For example, production-oriented businesses may tend to focus on the product in their improvement efforts, failing to realize how important service is to their customers. An effective customer survey can help redirect these efforts.

When dealing with a consumer market, it's useful to provide an incentive to encourage customers with positive experiences to participate, since often only those that are upset about something will take the time to complete the survey cards. Incentives include discounted products or services, entry into a raffle for free products or services, or complimentary dinners for participants. In business-to-business dealings, incentives may be forbidden or even illegal, but generally in this environment the customers are more than willing to provide feedback on what they like and dislike about the product or service. When a broad sample of customers, with both positive and negative experiences, is included in the survey response, then statistical bias can be avoided in the analysis results.

Pyzdek (2003) provides these guidelines for developing the form of the survey questions:

- Format a question based on its purpose. The way the question is asked is relevant to the information required by the survey group.
- Ask only relevant questions. Respect your respondents' time by asking only questions that are truly important. Ask yourself: "How are we going

to use the information from this response?" If you're unsure of the value of the information, don't bother asking.

- Use clear, concise language that is familiar to the respondent. Use the terminology and language level of the respondents so they can provide answers that are truly relevant to the questions.
- Offer complete, mutually exclusive choices. When choices are offered, the list must be complete (all options provided) and mutually exclusive (one choice cannot conflict with another).
- Ask unbiased questions by presenting all (and only) relevant information. Including irrelevant, inflammatory, one-sided, or subjective information will bias the response.
- Quantify response measures. Use a common scale for the question responses, such as the Likert scale, which provides a convenient indication of the strength of opinion (for example, Strongly Disagree, Disagree, Agree, Strongly Agree).
- Order questions in a logical and unbiased way. The survey flow should prevent confusion as to the target of the question. Don't jump around by asking about different topics, as this confuses the respondent.

Site visits to business clients can also show how products are used or service received. In visiting your customers, their customers, and so on, you experience the expressed and latent customer demands that may otherwise be hidden. You may even understand how to solve customer problems, as Jack Welch had suggested.

Competitor analyses are also useful in business level projects because of the competition's inherent influence on sales and profitability. Again, the focus is on the customer as you seek to understand market niches that you currently fill and wish to remain competitive in or new niches that you can take advantage of to increase revenues. Measuring your competitor's strengths and weaknesses, as well as your own strengths and weaknesses, allows you to generate a credible plan of attack.

It's not unusual to find certain issues that can be addressed rather quickly, while others require more detailed strategies. Immediate action represents quick payback for the effort and can often sustain (through improved profitability and morale) the larger effort necessary to achieve further improvements along the path to Six Sigma.

Project Selection

Six Sigma projects are the means by which improvements are realized in a Six Sigma deployment. These improvements are achieved in the areas of quality, cost, or schedule, to address the needs of customers, employees, and shareholders. Six Sigma projects must be clearly defined and managed for these improvements to be realized.

Projects must be directly linked to the strategic goals of the organization. As mentioned earlier, GE's Jack Welch considered the best projects those that solved customers' problems.

What constitutes a Six Sigma project? Juran defines a project as "a problem scheduled for solution" (Juran and Gryna, 1988). Snee (2002) defines a Six Sigma project as "a problem scheduled for solution that has a set of metrics that can be used to set project goals and monitor progress." Snee further differentiates between problems with known solutions, such as the deployment of a manufacturing resource planning (MRP) system, and those with unknown solutions. Snee suggests that projects with known solutions are best led by project managers, while projects with unknown solutions are best defined as Six Sigma projects.

The Snee definition notably adds the concept of quantifiable metrics to projects, which is certainly a useful addition. Organizations need to be able to track the progress of a project, as well as to select those projects that have the greatest potential for the organization. Intrinsic to these metrics is a link to organizational performance. The metrics must provide a tangible measure of benefit to the company, its customers, or its shareholders. Implementing statistical process control (SPC) on a production line, for example, would not directly offer this benefit. While deploying SPC would allow us to understand the nature of the variation in the process, improvement may not be realized to the customer or organization unless, for example, the special causes of variation were eliminated. Although an SPC analysis would provide a useful measure of the before and after performance of a process undergoing a Six Sigma improvement project, the analysis is a means to an end, rather than the end itself.

Since most businesses beginning their Six Sigma program are between three and four sigma level, spending 15% to 25% of their revenue on cost of quality issues, they have ample opportunities for improvement. There are, however, limited resources available for project deployment, as represented by their trained Black Belts and Green Belts. Project selection thus takes on an important role in determining the magnitude of success of a Six Sigma deployment.

Six Sigma projects should be selected based on a suitable cost-benefit analysis. A simple yet effective metric for evaluating projects is the Pareto Priority Index (Pyzdek, 2003).

$$\text{PPI} = \frac{\text{Savings} * \text{Probability of success}}{\text{Cost} * \text{Completion time}}$$

Note that the PPI increases as the probability of success or the dollar savings increases, and decreases as the implementation cost or completion time increases. The units used for each of these terms should be consistent across projects to provide a valid comparison.

The inclusion of the "probability of success" points out a simple fact: not all Six Sigma projects will be successful. Six Sigma projects are usually not tasked for simple problems, but more often for problems that have persisted despite prior attempts at solution. A number of reasons may be behind this lack of success, particularly lack of resources, lack of management commitment or authorization, and lack of sufficient analysis to understand the true causes of the problems (including treating the symptoms rather than the causes). A proper Six Sigma project definition and deployment strategy will address these issues, resulting in a successful project conclusion.

However, other issues can also prevent success. In some cases, the solution is too costly and not justified by the market. In others, the technical knowledge is lacking, and until further research and development is undertaken, a solution is not feasible. It is important that these issues be recognized as soon as possible so that project resources can be redeployed to solvable problems.

The cost to deploy is fairly easy to calculate, including costs such as labor, materials, work stoppage for data collection, etc. Initial estimates documented on the project charter should be updated as the project proceeds to ensure they do not overwhelm the savings. It is the project team leader's responsibility to update these budgets as the project proceeds so the project sponsor can effectively manage the resources.

It is important that the cost and benefit estimates are accepted by the organization as fair and accurate. For this reason, the accounting and finance functions within the organization will be responsible for defining the true costs and benefits for each project, based on predetermined methods of cost estimation. This allows consistency across projects and removes any bias that might be perceived toward the Black Belt or sponsor.

The financial benefit of a given project is sometimes difficult to determine, but potential savings and benefits include:

- Decreased material costs.
- Increased sales due to capacity increase. Note that this only produces a benefit if the process is currently capacity constrained and there is market demand for the increased capacity.
- Decreased labor cost. Note that this benefit is only realized if the process is not capacity constrained and the labor is reassigned.
- Decreased carrying costs for work in process (WIP) inventory, including reworked parts and other parts in common assembly.
- Decreased accidents associated with WIP storage.

- Decreased incidental material usage. This includes the glues, paper, office equipment, coolants, etc., that decrease when the process runs more efficiently.
- Decreased maintenance costs and/or capital expenditure based on decreased material usage. When the process runs more efficiently, new equipment is not needed, additional offices or plants are not needed, and the cost for maintaining the existing infrastructure is reduced.
- Decreased time to deliver to customer, including decreased penalties for late shipment and/or expediting, decreased costs for communicating shipment status to customer, and decreased costs associated with customer dissatisfaction.
- Increased employee morale, with a subsequent decreased employee turnover and training expense.

As a general rule, most companies expect minimum annualized savings of $50,000 to $100,000 from each Six Sigma project. Many projects will yield much higher savings. What may seem surprising is that the per-project savings are not necessarily dependent on the size of the business, so even a $100M company can save $1.5M on a project. Recall that a three sigma company is spending approximately 25% of revenue on cost of quality, so a three sigma company with $100M in sales is spending approximately $25M per year on poor quality. Using a rule-of-thumb measure of 0.5% to 1% of employees as Black Belts, however, the number of projects can effectively scale the total financial return from the Six Sigma deployment for each business.

An example of PPI for a group of potential projects is shown in Table 3.1. Although the first project, PO (purchase order) cycle time, has the lowest projected savings, it is the preferred project, receiving the highest PPI score. This reflects its overall reduced risk (with higher probability of success and lower cost to deploy).

Table 3.1.   Pareto Priority Index calculations.

Project	Saving ($000)	Pr Success	Cost ($000)	Completion Time	PPI
PO cycle time	220	90%	5	3.5 months	11.3
Shipping damage	400	70%	9	6 months	5.2
Design change	770	50%	30	10 months	1.28

Although the Pareto Priority Index is relatively easy to use, it ignores many potential project benefits, such as the ability to meet shipment schedules, reduce inventories, or contribute to strategic business or customer-valued objectives.

A prioritization matrix for selecting projects is shown in Figures 3.4 through 3.6 (courtesy of Quality America's *Green Belt XL* software). A company's project selection committee used customer input to weigh the projects. While customer surveys, interviews, and focus groups could be used to provide valuable input at this point, the company had recently received detailed

Criteria Weighting Matrix

	Qualification of new or revised processes	Design reviews	Incorporation / control of Engineering Changes	Reality-based scheduling	Work procedures / training	Benefit/Cost ratio	Time to Implement	Probability of Success	Row Totals
Qualification of new or revised processes	■	5	1	1	10	1	10	1	29 (0.17)
Design reviews	$\frac{1}{5}$	■	1	$\frac{1}{10}$	10	5	5	1	22.3 (0.13)
Incorporation / control of Engineering Changes	1	1	■	$\frac{1}{10}$	1	$\frac{1}{5}$	$\frac{1}{5}$	$\frac{1}{5}$	3.7 (0.02)
Reality-based scheduling	1	10	10	■	10	5	5	5	46 (0.27)
Work procedures / training	$\frac{1}{10}$	$\frac{1}{10}$	1	$\frac{1}{10}$	■	$\frac{1}{10}$	$\frac{1}{10}$	$\frac{1}{10}$	1.6 (0.01)
Benefit/Cost ratio	1	$\frac{1}{5}$	5	$\frac{1}{5}$	10	■	5	5	26.4 (0.16)
Time to Implement	$\frac{1}{10}$	$\frac{1}{5}$	5	$\frac{1}{5}$	10	$\frac{1}{5}$	■	5	20.7 (0.12)
Probability of Success	1	1	5	$\frac{1}{5}$	10	$\frac{1}{5}$	$\frac{1}{5}$	■	17.6 (0.11)
Column Totals	4.4	17.5	28	1.9	61	11.7	25.5	17.3	167.3

Figure 3.4 Criteria weighting matrix.
(Quality America *GreenBeltXL*)

feedback on its performance from a high-profile client. An internal review of the feedback determined that the client's findings were accurate and fairly representative of some key operational shortcomings. These were summarized as follows:

- Qualification of new or revised processes
- Design reviews
- Incorporation/control of engineering changes
- Reality-based scheduling
- Work procedures/training

The company added three more criteria for project selection: benefit/cost ratio, time to implement, and probability of success. All of these objectives were compared to one another and rated for relative importance by senior management. The results are shown in the criteria weights matrix in Figure 3.4. A value of 1 means the two criteria are equal in importance, a value of 10 implies the row is significantly more important than the column, and a value of 5 implies the row is somewhat more important.

The project selection committee then rated each project relative to these criteria, as shown for one such criterion (reality-based scheduling) in the options rating matrix in Figure 3.5.

A combined score is then summarized, as shown in Figure 3.6, to determine the ability of each project to fulfill the defined business objectives. The matrix rows have been sorted so the project with the best overall benefit, relative to the weighted criteria shown earlier, is the first row: ECO cycle time reduction.

A similar, yet simpler, approach is afforded by the matrix diagram, where each candidate project can be directly compared to the criteria in a single matrix. The assumption for the matrix diagram would be that all criteria are of equal weight. Each of these techniques is discussed in more detail in Part 3 of this book.

DMAIC Problem Solving

The DMAIC problem-solving methodology introduced earlier is typically used for Six Sigma projects. This methodology is designed to:

- *Define* the problem.
- *Measure* the extent of the problem.
- *Analyze* the sources of variation.

Options Rating Matrix for 'Reality-based scheduling' ▼	Cell 12 Scrap Reduction	Proposal Cycle Time Reduction	ECO Cycle Time Reduction	Supplier A Reject Reduction	Row Totals
Cell 12 Scrap Reduction	■	$\frac{1}{10}$	$\frac{1}{10}$	$\frac{1}{5}$	0.4 (0.01)
Proposal Cycle Time Reduction	10	■	5	10	25 (0.59)
ECO Cycle Time Reduction	10	$\frac{1}{5}$	■	1	11.2 (0.26)
Supplier A Reject Reduction	5	$\frac{1}{10}$	1	■	6.1 (0.14)
Column Totals	25	0.4	6.1	11.2	42.7

Figure 3.5 Options rating matrix.
(Quality America *GreenBeltXL*)

- *Improve* the process.
- *Control* the process for sustained improvement.

Readers familiar with quality improvement methods will be reminded of Shewhart's PDCA (plan-do-check-act) and Deming's PDSA (plan-do-study-act). These methods are quite similar in their approach. Both are meant as cycles for improvement, as is DMAIC. Once the final step is completed, it may be repeated for an additional cycle of improvement.

Motorola used the MAIC (measure, analyze, improve, control) acronym. GE and Allied Signal used DMAIC, which has become more of the standard. GE has also varied the methodology for use in product design areas, calling it DMADV, where the second *D* stands for design, and the *V* for verify. This acronym is used in conjunction with the DFSS (design for Six Sigma) nomenclature. The objectives and approach of the design stage are remarkably similar to the improve stage, as is verify to control, making the differences

Summary Matrix									
	Qualification of new or revised processes	Design reviews	Incorporation / control of Engineering Changes	Reality-based scheduling	Work procedures / training	Benefit/Cost ratio	Time to Implement	Probability of Success	Row Totals
ECO Cycle Time Reduction	0.042	0.094	0.013	0.070	0.007	0.019	0.040	0.036	0.321 (0.32)
Proposal Cycle Time Reduction	0.042	0.023	0.005	0.159	0.002	0.002	0.020	0.019	0.272 (0.27)
Cell 12 Scrap Reduction	0.042	0.005	0.001	0.003	0.001	0.053	0.058	0.053	0.216 (0.22)
Supplier A Reject Reduction	0.042	0.008	0.001	0.038	0.000	0.086	0.002	0.002	0.179 (0.18)
Column Totals	0.17	0.13	0.020	0.27	0.01	0.16	0.12	0.11	0.990

Figure 3.6   Summary matrix.
(Quality America *GreenBeltXL*)

between DMADV and DMAIC subtle. Some companies choose to call it DMAIC in either case for ease of implementation.

Some consultants brand the methodology by adding even more steps. Harry and Schroeder added recognize to the front, and standardize and integrate to the end, referring to the product as their "breakthrough strategy," which takes its name from Juran's concept of breakthrough developed years earlier to describe methods for achieving orders of magnitude improvements in quality. A review of Harry and Schroeder's definitions of these additional terms shows similarity to others' descriptions of DMAIC. A casual review of Six Sigma practitioners found the DMAIC methodology to be the one most commonly used. Apparently everyone agrees on what essentially will be done, they just don't agree on what to call it!

Putting these semantics aside, the importance of DMAIC is in its structured approach. This discipline ensures that Six Sigma projects are clearly defined and implemented, and that results are standardized into the daily operations.

The DMAIC methodology should be applied from leadership levels of the organization down to the process level. Whether a project begins at the business level or the process level, the methodology is the same.

Project sponsorship ensures that projects will not be authorized or funded if they fail to provide bottom-line benefits, or are too broadly scoped to be achievable in an agreed-upon timetable. The sponsor provides the functional authority to break organizational roadblocks, and works with other sponsors within the managerial ranks to coordinate projects with the overall business needs.

Business projects are championed at the top level of the organization. They concentrate on vital aspects of business success, such as market share, viability, profitability, employee retention, etc. They may involve purchasing or selling business units, or ways to attract or maintain customer base. Because of the scope of business level projects, the time scale is measured in years, rather than months. Some business level projects may take three to five years to cycle through the Six Sigma process (Harry and Schroeder, 2000), while others are completed in less than a year.

Quiz for Chapter 3

1. In the Six Sigma project methodology acronym DMAIC, the *I* stands for:
   a. Integrate.
   b. Investigate.
   c. Improve.
   d. Ignore.

2. The define stage of DMAIC:
   a. Is linked with the project charter and provides input to the measure stage.
   b. Stands alone in the methodology, but is always necessary.
   c. Is not necessary when the project is mandated by top management.
   d. None of the above.

3. The control stage of DMAIC:
   a. Is only used when you need to define control chart parameters.
   b. Allows the improvements to be maintained and institutionalized.
   c. Is only needed if you have ISO 9000 certification.
   d. None of the above.

4. A top-down deployment of Six Sigma projects:
   a. Is discouraged because projects get delayed by other management commitments.
   b. Undermines the project sponsors.
   c. Emphasizes projects that line workers feel are important.
   d. Ensures that projects are aligned with the top-level business strategy.

5. Which of the following is *not* included in the Kano quality model?
   a. Basic quality.
   b. Expected quality.
   c. Exciting quality.
   d. None of the above.

6. The Kano model is interpreted as follows:
   a. Customer satisfaction is determined solely by the quantity of the product or service delivered.
   b. Customer wants can be determined once and for all and used to design high-quality products and services.
   c. Customer wants, needs, and expectations are dynamic and must be monitored continuously. Providing products or services that match the customer's expectations is not enough to assure customer satisfaction.
   d. Customers will be satisfied if you supply them with products and services that meet their needs at a fair price.

7. Features that distinguish quality-focused organizations from non-quality-focused organizations are:
   a. Larger numbers of employees.
   b. External business focus.
   c. Employees with advanced degrees.
   d. None of the above.

8. Which of the following statements is *not* true?
   a. Customer satisfaction is a value judgment made by a customer.
   b. Quality is an absence of defects and the presence of desirable product or service features.
   c. Quality is one of many factors evaluated by customers.
   d. Customer satisfaction measures service quality.

9. The *customer* for a manufactured item is:
   a. The consumer who uses the product.
   b. The distributor.
   c. The people who package the product.
   d. All of the above.

10. *Customer satisfaction:*
   a. Is synonymous with quality.
   b. Is guaranteed to produce increased revenue.
   c. Results from meeting the customer's needs in a number of key areas.
   d. All of the above.

Exam for Part 1

1. As a company moves from three sigma level of quality to four and five sigma levels of quality, it tends to:
    a. Spend more money on prevention costs.
    b. Spend less money on appraisal costs.
    c. Improve customer satisfaction, which can lead to increased sales.
    d. All of the above.

2. Companies that successfully implement Six Sigma are likely to:
    a. Initially spend a lot of money on training, but receive benefits which might be hard to quantify over the course of time.
    b. Realize decreased quality costs and improved quality.
    c. See a reduction in critical defects and cycle times.
    d. Choices b and c only.

3. A company operating at three to four sigma would spend approximately how much on poor quality?
    a. There is no way to relate sigma level with costs.
    b. 15% to 25% of revenue.
    c. 0.27% of profits.
    d. 15% to 25% of profits.

4. A company operating at three sigma will experience costs of poor quality due to:
    a. Mostly costs of failure.
    b. Mostly prevention costs.

    c. Mostly appraisal costs.

    d. An even mix of failure, prevention, and appraisal costs.

5. Companies moving from three sigma to five sigma experience rapid reduction in costs of quality because:

    a. The awareness of quality costs causes people to improve their work practices.

    b. The five sigma organization spends more on appraisal.

    c. The five sigma organization has forced inefficient workers from its ranks.

    d. The five sigma organization uses its resources more efficiently, causing an increase in revenue.

6. Effective metrics:

    a. Provide timely feedback to process personnel.

    b. Are customer-focused or directly linked to something the customer cares about.

    c. Choices a and b.

    d. None of the above.

7. Dashboards that monitor results of employee surveys:

    a. Can allow an organization to reduce employee turnover.

    b. Provide priorities for improving employee morale.

    c. Must allow for the evaluation of trends over time.

    d. All of the above.

8. Dashboards that monitor feedback from customers:

    a. Can lead to reduced customer complaints.

    b. Provide priorities for improving customer satisfaction.

    c. Must allow for the evaluation of trends over time.

    d. All of the above.

9. Dashboard metrics:

    a. Often tell us directly how to change the organization to drive improvement.

    b. Provide an indication of problems that must be analyzed in more detail.

    c. Are not useful for process improvement.

    d. All of the above.

10. Champions should attend Green Belt training:

    a. To demonstrate commitment to Six Sigma.

    b. To learn the fundamental tools used by the project teams.

    c. To foster ownership of the Six Sigma program.

    d. All of the above.

11. In conducting a training needs analysis:
    a. Employees who have already taken similar training can be exempt from this training.
    b. Employees should be evaluated to measure their current understanding of the material.
    c. It's best to train everyone assuming they don't know any of the material.
    d. Students can test-out if they think they already know the material.

12. The proof of successful Black Belt training is best determined:
    a. Through testing relative to a body of knowledge.
    b. By company certification.
    c. Through successful completion of multiple Six Sigma projects.
    d. By peer evaluation.

13. When evaluating the needs of external customers:
    a. Understanding the needs of the end user is critical.
    b. Distributors and other transfer agents provide the best definition of end-user needs.
    c. Internal customer needs should be considered first.
    d. All of the above.

14. A recognized method of improving customer satisfaction:
    a. Requires feedback from personnel with direct customer contact.
    b. Often requires a total revamping of the organizational structure.
    c. Requires sales and marketing functions to be part of the Quality Department.
    d. All of the above.

15. A customer-focused organization:
    a. Looks for a quick return on their quality improvement efforts.
    b. Realizes that customer needs must be met, even when they don't make sense.
    c. Focuses on detection of problems.
    d. None of the above.

16. A customer-focused organization:
    a. Will often have a lot of turnover, as employees who don't care about quality are let go.
    b. Can afford to take longer in the design and development processes.
    c. Trains employees to improve their value to the customer.
    d. None of the above.

17. Evaluating customer complaints allows an organization to:
    a. Prevent problems.
    b. Focus on all the issues that cause problems.
    c. Exercise recovery skills to win back customer loyalty.
    d. All of the above.

18. The determination to accept a return from a particular customer:
    a. Is based on the profit margin built into the particular order.
    b. Should reflect the long-term value of the customer.
    c. Should be solely based on company policy to prevent any special treatment.
    d. None of the above.

19. To determine the expected value of a particular customer's business:
    a. Sum the revenues over the current year.
    b. Sum the profits for their orders over the expected lifetime of their business.
    c. Calculate the net present value of the profit for their orders over the expected lifetime of their business.
    d. Survey the customer and the sales force to determine their market potential.

20. The management team has decided that there are three criteria for choosing projects, with their relative importance weighting shown in parentheses:
    • Financial benefit/cost ratio (0.3)
    • Perceived customer benefit (0.5)
    • Safety benefit (0.2)

    Four projects have been reviewed relative to these criteria, with the scores for each criterion shown in the following table:

Project	Financial Benefit/ Cost Ratio	Customer Benefit	Safety Benefit
A	120	140	30
B	80	200	25
C	100	100	45
D	140	70	65

Which project should be selected?
a. Project A
b. Project B
c. Project C
d. Project D

21. Which of the following represent project benefits?
    a. Cost savings that are not passed on to the customer.
    b. Cost savings that are passed on to the customer.
    c. Both *a* and *b*.
    d. None of the above.

22. A project to reduce the machining process cycle time is proposed, with expectations that it would reduce the unit labor costs. The labor savings are valid if which of the following conditions are met?
    a. The excess labor is terminated.
    b. The excess labor is reassigned.
    c. An increase in sales, requiring increased capacity that absorbs the excess labor.
    d. Any of the above.

23. A project to reduce the need for rework in a manufacturing process might provide which of the following benefits?
    a. Decreased WIP inventory carrying costs.
    b. Decreased labor costs.
    c. Decreased maintenance costs.
    d. Any of the above.

24. Examples of reasonable Six Sigma projects include:
    a. Reducing cost of product shipments.
    b. Reducing customs delays for international shipments.
    c. Reducing the design cycle for a new product.
    d. All of the above.

25. A process currently operates at a 2.0 sigma level. A reasonable goal for a Six Sigma project is to:
    a. Increase the sigma level to 4.0.
    b. Increase the sigma level to 3.3.
    c. Increase the sigma level to 2.5.
    d. Increase the sigma level to 6.0.

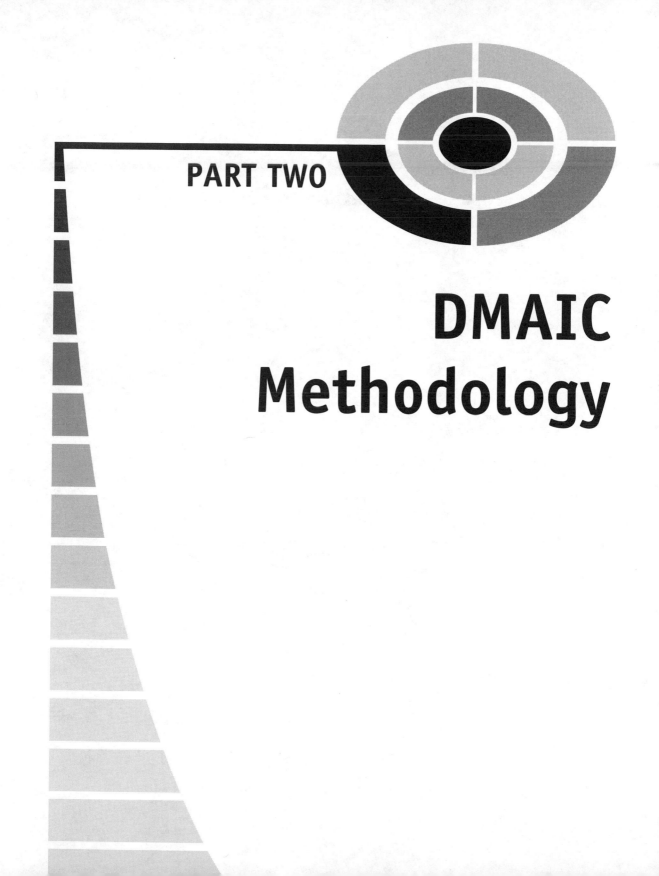

PART TWO

DMAIC
Methodology

4

Define Stage

The starting point for the DMAIC problem-solving methodology is the define stage.

Objectives

The key objectives within the define stage of DMAIC are:

- ☑ *Project Definition*: to articulate the project's scope, goal, and objectives; its team members and sponsors, its schedule, and its deliverables.
- ☑ *Top-Level Process Definition*: to define its stakeholders, its inputs and outputs, and its broad functions.
- ☑ *Team Formation*: to assemble a highly capable team and focus their skills on a common understanding of the issues and benefits of the proposed project plans.

These objectives should be satisfied before the team progresses to the measure stage.

Project Definition

The key project details are documented in the project charter and updated regularly (with approval as necessary) as additional information is uncovered by the team during the DMAIC cycle. The key tasks for developing the project charter can be summarized as follows:

- ☑ Define the problem statement, and the business need for doing the project.
- ☑ Define the project scope, using preliminary data (which usually must be collected and analyzed).
- ☑ Develop deliverables, the useful output of the project, stated in financial terms accepted by finance and management as legitimate estimates.
- ☑ Develop an initial schedule for the project milestones.
- ☑ Define the project stakeholders and assemble a team.
- ☑ Conduct a project kick-off meeting. In this meeting, the team agrees to the project scope, its deliverables, and the schedule.
- ☑ Map the process at its top level.
- ☑ Secure the approval of the updated project charter from the project sponsor.

Project charters provide a means to control and manage Six Sigma projects. They serve as a contract between the project sponsor and the project team. Unlike legal contracts, they are "living documents" in that they are updated as new information is discovered in the DMAIC process. In that regard, they are used to actively manage and continuously focus the project over its life.

Through its sponsorship by the appropriate level of management, project charters help the organization avoid projects that (1) deal with unimportant issues; (2) overlap or conflict with other project objectives; (3) target soon to be obsolete processes or products; (4) have poorly defined or overwhelming scope; (5) study symptoms instead of root causes; (6) provide poorly defined deliverables; and (7) lack management authority and responsibility.

An example project charter is shown in Figure 4.1. Each element of the project charter is described in detail.

Proprietary

SIX SIGMA PROJECT CHARTER
Initiators Name
Date
Draft #: x

TITLE :

PURPOSE :

PROBLEM STATEMENT :

OBJECTIVE / BUSINESS NEED ADDRESSED :

SCOPE :

ROLE AND RESPONSIBILITIES :

Stakeholders :

Sponsors :

Team Members :

RESOURCES (non human) :

MILESTONES / MEASURES :

Project start date :
Planned project Completion date:

How will we know if we are successful?: What are the measurable benefits the project is targeted to deliver?

Figure 4.1   Example project charter form.

PROJECT PURPOSE

The project purpose is a brief statement of the project intent. The project purpose will typically use key metrics of financial benefit, including return on investment (ROI), the underlying metrics of cycle time, or defects per million opportunities (DPMO).

For example:

Decrease purchase order cycle times related to vendor approvals.

BUSINESS NEED ADDRESSED

The business need addressed statement should indicate the business case for implementing the project. This answers the "Why should we care?" question. A good project should be directly linked to the strategic goals of the organization. This *alignment* is critical for program and business success.

Jack Welch commented that the best projects solve a customer problem. An example he cited was invoicing for appliances shipped to Wal-Mart. The initial problem was defined as something akin to "late payments from Wal-Mart," but from the customer perspective, GE was doing a poor job of filling the orders, making it difficult for them to close out the invoice.

For example:

Late orders constituted the number one complaint from customers for FY 2000. Awaiting vendor material was identified as a significant cause of the late orders. When orders are late from the vendor, the traditional response has been an increase in overtime pay for production areas to meet the scheduling demands. By decreasing PO cycle time, we can cut overtime expenses and improve customer satisfaction by decreasing delivery times.

TIP: Use Matrix Diagrams.

PROBLEM STATEMENT

The problem statement summarizes the problems to be addressed. It should also state the current or historical conditions, such as the defect rate or dollars wasted as a result of poor performance.

For example:

PO cycle time is defined as the time from receipt of purchase request until the PO is sent to the supplier. This PO cycle time for unapproved vendors currently averages

27 days, with 95% of orders sent within 45 days. The average time for POs with approved vendors is 7 days, with 95% of orders sent within 11 days. The incidence of overtime pay in Quality and Procurement, who share responsibility for vendor approval, increases as the time goes beyond 30 days.

OBJECTIVE

The objective is a more specific statement of the outcome desired. GE used the following as a guideline:

- If the process is operating at or less than a three sigma level of performance, then the project objective should be a 10 time reduction in defects. For example, if the current DPMO is 10,000, then the goal is for the improved DPMO to be 1,000 or less.
- If the process is operating at greater than three sigma level, then a 50% reduction in defects is warranted. For example, a process operating at 1,000 DPMO should be brought to a level of 500 DPMO.

While DPMO can be useful, it can also lead to somewhat arbitrary definitions of defects and opportunities. Since the Six Sigma deployment effort should be directly related to financial benefits, cost savings provide the most useful indication of project benefit.

For example:

Reduce PO cycle time's three sigma level to below 20 days.

SCOPE

The scope is the specific aspect of the problem that will be addressed. Many projects initially have too broad a scope, such as when: Objectives are too ambitious to reach conclusion in a reasonable time frame; or the impact is too large, affecting too many stakeholders.

As the project cycle time increases, the tangible cost of the project deployment, such as cost due to labor and material usage, will increase. The intangible costs of the project will also increase: frustration due to lack of progress, diversion of manpower away from other activities, and delay in realization of project benefits, to name just a few. When the project cycle time exceeds six months or so, these intangible costs may result in the loss of critical team members, causing additional delays in the project completion. These "world peace" projects, with laudable but unrealistic goals, generally serve to frustrate teams and undermine the credibility of the Six Sigma program.

A critical aspect of a Six Sigma project is that of providing a measurable benefit in terms of cost, schedule, and/or quality. A project whose benefit is not realized in a reasonable amount of time would generally not be acceptable as a Six Sigma project. While this may seem short-sighted, it merely reflects the reality of resource allocation. Since resources for Six Sigma projects are limited, they should be spent on those projects providing the best benefit relative to the cost to deploy.

For these reasons, Six Sigma projects assigned to Black or Green Belts should be scoped for completion in a three- to four-month period. This tight schedule allows team members to commit themselves for the full length of the project. Projects that are too large to be completed in this length of time can usually be divided into several potential projects, whose merits can be compared to other projects competing for project resources.

In many cases, projects can be properly scoped before assignment; however, in some cases the project team, in its problem-solving effort, will uncover a much larger project than initially suspected. In these cases, the team should work with the project sponsor to update the project charter with a redefined project scope, timetable, and deliverable. The newly defined project should then be reevaluated relative to the criteria established for project selection, as outlined in Chapter 3.

For example, a project was developed to reduce the cycle time for a purchase order. A work breakdown structure was used to understand the process dynamics. As shown in Figure 4.2, the process can be broken down into approved and unapproved vendors, then by classification of the purchased items.

Breaking the process into its components forces a recognition of the subprocesses requiring separate improvement strategies. Limiting the project to one or only a few closely related categories will lead to a better chance of project success, given an adequate financial return.

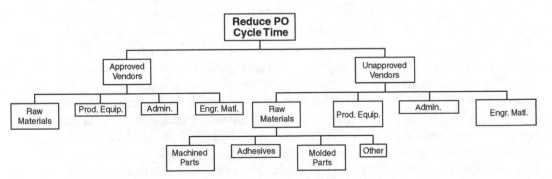

Figure 4.2   Example work breakdown structure.

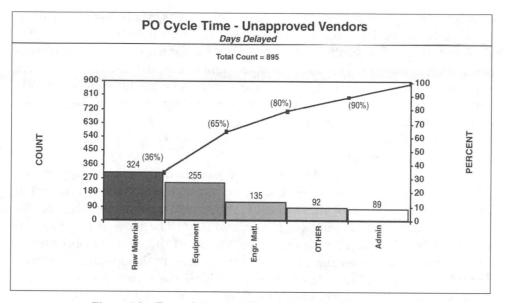

Figure 4.3   Example Pareto diagram for project breakdown.

The Pareto diagram is useful to show the relative impact from each of these subprocesses. The Pareto diagram shown in Figure 4.3 displays the number of days of delay associated with each of the purchased item classifications. Raw materials represent the largest source of delay, followed by equipment purchases, so these categories might represent the best opportunity for improvement. The Pareto diagram can also be displayed with cost data, which might produce a different result. Generally, cost data is more relevant.

For example:

Limited to injection molded parts, which represents 60% of all orders with unapproved vendors.

STAKEHOLDERS, TEAM MEMBERS, AND SPONSOR

The term *stakeholders* refers to the departments, customers, and vendors who will be influenced by the project activities or outcome.

The term *team* refers to the specific members of the stakeholder groups who will play an active role in the project problem solving, data collection, and analysis, including the assigned Black Belts, Green Belts, subject matter experts, operational personnel, and facilitator (if any). Typically, one Black Belt is assigned to a given project. One or more Green Belts may be assigned from a given stakeholder department. Since Black and Green Belts are trained in basic facilitation skills, facilitators should only be needed in exceptional situations, such as if hostility exists between team members. Ad-hoc team members may be identified as such. *Ad-hoc members* are those members who provide assistance, expertise, or background information upon request, but do not regularly participate as members of the team.

These concepts are covered in more detail in the Team Formation section later in this chapter.

The *sponsors* are the middle- to upper-level managers who support the project. Sponsors fund the project, allocate resources, and develop the initial charter. As a member of management, the sponsor builds support for the project in the managerial ranks of the organization. The sponsor's managerial position in the functional area that is the subject of the improvement project helps to build awareness and support for the project in the operational ranks, as well as to clear roadblocks that might inhibit the timely progress of the project. When stakeholders are from different functional areas, the sponsor may be the level above the functional area of management, so that resource allocation and departmental commitment is achieved. In order to prevent the top levels of the organization from sponsoring too many projects, cosponsors from the top ranks of the affected functional areas may also be used.

For example:

Stakeholders: Engineering, Procurement, Quality
Sponsor: Sharon Drew, VP Operations
Black Belt: Bob Hanson
Team Members: Mary Snebly, Accounts Payable; John Schnell, Quality (GB);
Bill Anderson, Procurement (GB); Ann Dodson, Engineering (GB)
Facilitator: Jill Knapp

TIP: Process Map, SIPOC

RESOURCES AND NEEDS

Resources refer to the processes, equipment, databases, or labor (not included as team members) that may be needed to keep the project on schedule and provide the data necessary for conclusive analysis.

For example:

Accounts Payable database, Vendor Quality Records.

DELIVERABLES

Deliverables include all measurable benefits from implementing the project. Properly defined deliverables will answer the question: "How do we define project success and completion?"

For example:

Revised procedure(s), resulting in PO cycle time decrease. Projected savings of approximately $110,000 based on decreased overtime pay. Additional savings of $50,000 based on WIP stoppage.

There are many types of project deliverables:

- Decreased material costs: This applies when the project will reduce product scrap (that product that is unfit for sale).
- Increased sales due to capacity increase: This applies only when the process is capacity-constrained.
- Decreased labor cost: This applies only when the process is not capacity-constrained and labor will be reassigned.
- Decreased WIP carrying costs: This applies whenever work in process is reduced. One often ignored instance of this is when the number of parts reworked is reduced (since there is a WIP cost for the reworked parts); another is WIP cost for the mating parts of an assembly.
- Decreased accidents/losses related to WIP: Work that sits and waits for something or someone can be an accident waiting to happen.
- Decreased incidental material usage: When fewer mistakes are made, less incidental materials (from adhesive to copy paper) are consumed.
- Decreased maintenance costs and/or capital expenditure based on decline in machine use.
- Decrease in time to deliver to customer, resulting in decreased penalties for late shipments and/or costs associated with expediting, customer communication, and customer dissatisfaction.
- Increased employee morale; decreased employee turnover.

Often, project teams are tempted to include some of their analysis results as a deliverable. Even the implementation of SPC control charting in a process is not a deliverable, since it is not itself a direct financial benefit to the organization or customer (although it often provides plenty of indirect benefit through improved product quality).

TIME FRAME

The project charter should list the charter date (i.e., the date approved by sponsor), the start date, and the expected completion date, based on an attached project schedule.

For example:

Date chartered: 07/26/00
Anticipated Completion Date: 10/31/00
See detailed Schedule (attached)

TIP: Critical path and/or PERT analysis techniques are used to develop the completion date.

The project schedule is generally in the form of a Gantt chart, such as from *Microsoft Project*, detailing the activities and milestones associated with the project. The Gantt chart should clearly identify tasks, their precedents, and their required resources. It should allow the project leader to manage the project's critical path.

Each stage of the DMAIC methodology is broken down into activities and milestones. The define stage is broken down into its activities, as are measure, analyze, improve, and control. Milestones are established at the conclusion of each stage, highlighting the opportunity to communicate project status to the sponsor and stakeholders. Figure 4.4 shows a typical DMAIC schedule.

PROJECT STATUS REPORT

The Project Status Report should be provided on a weekly or biweekly basis and at the conclusion of each DMAIC stage milestone. Weekly reports can be provided to the team and its sponsor; milestone reports can be additionally circulated to other stakeholders. As previously mentioned, this communication helps to build buy-in, critical for project success.

In addition to an updated project schedule, and a verbal description of progress, status reports should include the following sections:

- Action Items: issues assigned to specific team members for completion by a stated date.
- Outstanding Items: past-dated action issues.
- Roadblocks: issues that are stalling the project, for which an immediate action item cannot be assigned.
- Conclusions: Findings from each stage of DMAIC, supported with data in its analyzed form.

	Task Name	Duration	Start	Finish
1	⊟ DEFINE	**13 days**	**Mon 8/6/01**	**Wed 8/22/01**
2	Define Project, Develop Charter	7 days	Mon 8/6/01	Tue 8/14/01
3	Team Formation	3 days	Wed 8/15/01	Fri 8/17/01
4	Top-level Process Definition	2 days	Mon 8/20/01	Tue 8/21/01
5	Charter Approval	1 day	Wed 8/22/01	Wed 8/22/01
6	⊟ MEASURE	**16 days**	**Thu 8/23/01**	**Thu 9/13/01**
7	Detailed Process Definition	3 days	Thu 8/23/01	Mon 8/27/01
8	Process Metric Definition	3 days	Tue 8/28/01	Thu 8/30/01
9	Measurement System Analysis	3 days	Fri 8/31/01	Tue 9/4/01
10	Process Baseline Definition	10 days	Fri 8/31/01	Thu 9/13/01
11	Project Status Update	0 days	Thu 9/13/01	Thu 9/13/01
12	⊟ ANALYZE	**20 days**	**Fri 9/14/01**	**Thu 10/11/01**
13	Analyze Value Stream	8 days	Fri 9/14/01	Tue 9/25/01
14	Analyze Sources of Variation	10 days	Fri 9/14/01	Thu 9/27/01
15	Determine Process Drivers	10 days	Fri 9/28/01	Thu 10/11/01
16	Project Status Update	0 days	Thu 10/11/01	Thu 10/11/01
17	⊟ IMPROVE	**20 days**	**Fri 10/12/01**	**Thu 11/8/01**
18	Determine new process operating conditions	10 days	Fri 10/12/01	Thu 10/25/01
19	Estimate benefits from new process	5 days	Fri 10/26/01	Thu 11/1/01
20	Determine and address Process Failure Modes	5 days	Fri 10/26/01	Thu 11/1/01
21	Implement & verify changes at process level	5 days	Fri 11/2/01	Thu 11/8/01
22	Project Status Update	0 days	Thu 11/8/01	Thu 11/8/01
23	⊟ CONTROL	**10 days**	**Fri 11/9/01**	**Thu 11/22/01**
24	Implement plan for Process Owner to control process parameters	9 days	Fri 11/9/01	Wed 11/21/01
25	Implement plan to track monthly savings (financial, time, safety, etc.)	2 days	Fri 11/9/01	Mon 11/12/01
26	Document Lessons Learned	5 days	Fri 11/9/01	Thu 11/15/01
27	Formal Project Completion & Approval	1 day	Thu 11/22/01	Thu 11/22/01

Figure 4.4   Example project schedule.

Communication helps to reduce future problems: when sponsors and stakeholders see progress as it occurs, they understand the direction of the project and can see natural solutions to issues. Reducing surprises is important, since surprises will create confusion and roadblocks, which can slow down or permanently stall a project.

PROJECT CONCLUSION

At the end of the project, in the control stage, the financial benefits are confirmed by the accounting or finance department.

The project sponsor approves the findings and its control strategy. This control plan provides a monitoring scheme for tracking the financial and operational benefits gained and the process-level metrics associated with the project deliverables.

It is also important in this stage to document the "lessons learned" during the project cycle. These often provide valuable input to future projects or to the Master Black Belt responsible for the Six Sigma program deployment. These issues are discussed in further detail in Chapter 8.

Top-Level Process Definition

There are several useful tools available for defining the as-is process.

- Flowcharts have historically been the preferred tool for documenting process activities. The graphical approach is appealing to operational personnel, who may find reading text in paragraph form laborious. The simple branching scheme of flowcharts easily highlights process complexities.
- Process maps have more recently become the preferred choice for documenting process activities, since they provide an additional level of detail (beyond the flowchart) to indicate functional responsibilities for each process step.
- SIPOC (suppliers-inputs-process-outputs-customers) is a tool for identifying the process inputs, outputs, and stakeholders. It is particularly useful at this stage to ensure that all the relevant stakeholders are included in the process.

Generally, these tools will be used in conjunction with one another. The top-level definition of the process provides only a broad view of the process, with little of the details necessary for a complete understanding of the day-to-day process mechanics. At this stage, we are most concerned with the process boundaries and stakeholders to aid in project and team definition. Details on the application and use of each of these tools is provided in Part 3.

Team Formation

Effective team formation is a crucial step for building stakeholder buy-in. After identifying the stakeholders in the project (in the top-level process definition), the stakeholders can be categorized as either key (necessary for success) or nonkey (not necessary for success) stakeholders.

Once the key stakeholder groups have been identified, team members are selected from each of the stakeholder groups. This representative should be credible within each stakeholder group as well as among the other stakeholder groups. These representatives should have the support of local management, be enthusiastic for the change, and be capable and willing to serve on the team. In some cases, a team member skeptical of the change my be selected, if he or she has all the other characteristics, particularly those of credibility and capability. Selection of skeptical representatives is a technique that attempts to build buy-in within the stakeholder group.

Effective teams are generally limited to five to seven full-time members. Larger teams are more difficult to manage, and members may lose a sense of responsibility to the team. Additional team members may be ad-hoc members from nonkey stakeholder groups, who only participate as needed, such as for process expertise.

TEAM MEMBER RESPONSIBILITIES

Team leaders must clearly communicate personal responsibilities to team members in initial meetings and fairly enforce these responsibilities in subsequent meetings.

Each member must take responsibility for the team success or failure. No one should blame the team leader, other members, or the sponsor for failure of the team, nor should anyone take personal credit for a project's success.

Team members need to effectively follow through on commitments in a timely manner. They must contribute to discussions, which includes actively listening, offering constructive and nonjudgmental feedback, and active sharing of ideas. Team leaders can be given feedback regarding what seems to be working and not working.

TEAM LEADER RESPONSIBILITIES

Team leaders must accept their responsibilities for leadership:

- *Keep team focused.* Use the charter's goal, objectives, and scope statements to focus the team. Stick to the DMAIC structure: don't try to analyze or improve until you've defined and measured.
- *Enforce ground rules.* Ground rules provide important protocol to teams, ensuring consistency and fairness for members. Typical ground rules include respectful and inviting communication, consensus-based decision making, and prompt completion of action items.
- *Ensure that conflicts are resolved in a positive manner.* Actively listen to concerns raised by interested parties, then address the concerns. Concerns cannot be ignored or maligned. Data should be collected so concerns can be understood and properly addressed. While this

may take "extra" time, the cost of not addressing these concerns can be lack of project buy-in, which can be fatal to a project's objectives.

- *Schedule, facilitate, and manage team meetings.* Meetings should have a defined agenda, and the leader should ensure that the team sticks to it.
- *Report regularly to project sponsors and stakeholders*, as previously discussed.
- *Ensure that barriers are removed* (if necessary by sponsor). When roadblocks are encountered in a project, it is especially important for the team leader to effectively use his or her consensus-building skills. The project sponsor has the ultimate authority to clear roadblocks, but should only exercise authority to clear roadblocks when all other options have been unsuccessful.
- *Develop team member skills.* Within each stage of DMAIC, use brainstorming tools to expand the team's thinking, followed by data analysis tools to focus on a solution.

In an initial team meeting, the team leader should review and circulate the ground rules. The team should agree (through consensus) on the project purpose and scope, as documented in the project charter. Of course, if the scope changes as the project progresses through DMAIC, the team and sponsor should again reach consensus on the revisions.

The project plan and timeline should be reviewed, and meeting times and locations established. Generally, it's best to meet only when necessary, although default times can be established for meetings to help members allocate time.

Teams require ongoing management to be effective. Ideally, teams should meet only as needed to discuss or resolve issues, or to follow up or assign action items. When meetings become a waste of anyone's time, then the team will begin to lose commitment and momentum. Agendas should be distributed beforehand, so that members are prepared to discuss planned items. Action items should be assigned at the end of each meeting, and they should be reviewed at the start of the meeting for which they are scheduled. The project schedule should be regularly updated to reflect changes as they occur, with regular reports to the project sponsors and stakeholders.

CHANGE AGENTS

To drive change in an organization, you will need to accept a basic fact about human nature: Change scares most people. Organizational change requires adoption of new policies or procedures. Personnel will often need to learn new skills, particularly in a Six Sigma deployment. This is often unsettling to some, nerve-wracking to others. This fear of the unknown is a barrier to change.

To make the matter more complicated, those of us who do not fear change are usually skeptical of it. Change is not always for the better, at least in everyone's eyes. Some will long for the "good old days."

Finally, there are those who know that change could be for the better, but still won't be behind it. Why? They don't believe management is committed to make it happen! "Been there, done that, got the T-shirt. Next!"

Effective change agents will address these concerns, since change cannot occur without buy-in from those responsible for change. The following DMAIC steps are useful to achieve buy-in within the organization:

- *Define* key stakeholders. These are the individuals or groups who can make or break the change initiative.
- *Measure* baseline level of buy-in for each key stakeholder. How committed are they to change?
- *Analyze* buy-in reducers and boosters for each key stakeholder or stakeholder group. Understand the concerns of the stakeholders, which may vary from one stakeholder to another.
- *Improve* buy-in by addressing issues.
- *Control* with a plan to maintain buy-in.

Bear in mind these steps for achieving buy-in may be used several times for different issues within a given project, and even applied informally within a team meeting.

The SIPOC approach to the top-level process definition discussed earlier will allow a clear definition of the stakeholder groups (required to define buy-in). Levels of buy-in (The Forum Corporation, 1996) from a given stakeholder or stakeholder groups can then be assessed, either formally through surveys or informally through team or individual discussions. The lowest level of buy-in, *hostility*, may be the easiest to recognize. The second level, *dissent*, may go unnoticed until stakeholders are questioned (i.e., measured) about the change initiative, such as through discussion or survey. *Acceptance*, the third level, is the lowest level of buy-in that should be considered for proceeding with the change initiative, but often it is not sufficient unless *support* (the fourth level) is achieved from a majority of the critical stakeholder groups. True *buy-in* (the fifth and highest level) is a level above support, in that stakeholders are enthusiastic in their commitment for change. As a team leader, you will want to lead individuals with true buy-in.

To analyze and improve the buy-in reducers, the issues that typically reduce stakeholder buy-in must be clearly understood (The Forum Corporation, 1996: www.forum.com/publications/esub_archive/sales.html).

- *Unclear goals.* The project charter serves as the communication vehicle to clearly present the goals throughout the stakeholder groups.

- *No personal benefit.* Goals, stated in terms that provide a clear link to personal benefits for stakeholders (such as decreased intervention or improved working conditions), should be enumerated in the project charter.
- *Predetermined solutions.* Projects of this type are not suitable for Six Sigma deployment. Adherence to the principles of data-driven decision making prevents subjective solutions from taking root.
- *Lack of communication.* Analyses and results are communicated throughout the stakeholder groups in the project charter.
- *Too many priorities.* The project charter, with its authorized scope, focuses the team on achievable results.
- *Short-term focus.* The linking of the project metrics with business level priorities ensures the long-term benefits of the project.
- *No accountability.* Clearly defined project sponsors, stakeholders, and team members provide accountability.
- *Disagreement on who customer is.* Clearly defined stakeholder groups are required in the project definition.
- *Low probability of implementation.* Formal project sponsorship and approvals provide a clear implementation channel.
- *Insufficient resources.* Project sponsorship by management ensures financial support.
- *Midstream change in direction or scope.* Changes in the project charter must be authorized by the sponsor and communicated to stakeholder groups.

On a personal level, good communication skills can psychologically assist in the buy-in process (The Forum Corporation, 1996). First, show confidence in your ideas by maintaining eye contact and smiling (when appropriate). Second, present your ideas in a direct and concise manner, painting a positive, yet realistic, picture of your idea. Third, show interest in the ideas of others by allowing equal time for all points of view. Ask pointed questions, and use appropriate body language such as sitting up, or leaning forward, or nodding to show you are listening and understand what others are saying (even if you don't agree with them).

Communication should always be respectful and inviting for all members to participate. Toward this end, team members should "leave their badge at the door," meaning that there are no managers or seniority in a team meeting. The team leaders should never consider themselves senior to anyone on the team, nor should they feel as if this is their personal project. Rather, the project is owned by the sponsor, and all team members are serving at the sponsor's request. Leading should never imply seniority or an executive privilege.

Critical to buy-in is establishment of the criteria for team decisions. Consensus is the preferred approach to team decision making. Consensus is a prerequisite for achieving sustained change. Consensus does not mean that everyone is in absolute agreement, nor that everyone thinks the proposal is the preferred approach. Rather, consensus implies that the parties are willing to accept the proposal in spite of the differences of opinion that might exist. A good question to ask the stakeholders in order to gauge the level of consensus is: "Can you live with it?" Differences in viewpoint are accepted, and can be reconciled with Six Sigma's analytical tools. In this way, achieving consensus allows the team to move forward, so the merits of the proposal can be proven through sound data-driven analysis. Alternatives to consensus such as majority voting, arbitrary flipping of a coin, or exchanging of votes for reciprocal votes (bartering) undermine the team's results and must be avoided.

The easiest way to achieve consensus is through the proper use and analysis of data. This so-called *data-driven decision making* removes the subjectivity of decisions. Opinions are replaced by supported facts. Of course, gathering and analyzing data takes time, so management must give teams enough time to be thorough. Fortunately every decision does not require extensive fact-finding, and proper use of DMAIC tools will provide guidance.

Three tools useful for building consensus are:

- *The affinity diagram*, which provides a means to generate a collection of ideas about a proposal, then summarize the ideas in terms of categories.
- *The nominal group technique* is simply a means of reducing a large collection of ideas into a workable number of key ideas.
- *The prioritization matrix* allows us to prioritize our options according to weighted criteria.

Each of these tools helps obtain consensus by systematically reducing a large number of disparate ideas into a smaller group of items that can be managed or analyzed.

TEAM DEVELOPMENT

There are four common stages of team development: forming, storming, norming, and performing.

In the *forming stage*, team members are polite to one another. Procedures and ground rules are emphasized and respected. The team hasn't really gotten into the heart of problem solving, so there is little friction.

In the *storming phase*, the team begins to work on the problems at hand, using brainstorming, data collection, and analysis. At this point, conflicts begin to develop between opposing views. Team members establish roles within the team. This role-playing undermines the authority of the team leader, and circumvents the team's progress. It is important for the team leader to effectively enforce ground rules during this stage. Failure to enforce the ground rules can prevent the team from moving forward to the norming stage, and it can result in project failure.

In the *norming stage*, the team begins to make some progress. Team members allow themselves and each other to reach a stage of independent thinking, which allows them to effectively collaborate on problem solving and analysis.

In the *performing stage*, the team has realized gains and feels confidence and pride as a result. They are performing as a lean, mean team.

Within the group dynamics, it is not uncommon for team members to periodically, even subconsciously, assume counterproductive roles, such as those shown in Table 4.1 (Pyzdek, 2003). The team leader and members should be aware of these easily recognizable roles, which are often prevented through enforcement of the ground rules previously discussed.

Team leaders should concentrate on practicing effective facilitation techniques, particularly when disagreements arise. Emotions must be kept in check. Facilitators must foster respectful communication among the team members. They need to remain neutral, so that they continue to have the trust of all team members. Avoid judgmental language, sarcasm, or nonverbal gestures that

Table 4.1.   Counterproductive team roles.

Role	Description
Aggressor	Attacks values, feelings, or ideas
Blocker	Persists on resolved issues; resists consensus
Recognition-seeker	Boasts
Confessor	Airs personal opinions
Playboy	Shows lack of commitment, jokes around
Dominator	Asserts authority, manipulates
Help-seeker	Evokes sympathy
Special-interest pleader	Shows interest in own group only

might insult or intimidate others. Effective facilitators will ensure that all participants have an opportunity to contribute. Sometimes real effort is required to draw out the quiet participants or to quiet the overbearing participants.

Black Belts learn a variety of focusing tools to lead teams from disarray and disagreement to order and consensus. Focusing on data, rather than opinions, is particularly helpful.

To maintain neutrality when discussion becomes heated, it is sometimes helpful to slow the frenzy and ensure that the points of disagreement are clear to all. In this way, misinterpretation can be resolved or minority voices heard. An effective method of doing this is to help the team develop a clear list of advantages and disadvantages for each option. Keep the focus on the specific problem at hand. Help team members remove opinions and attitudes that cloud or prejudice the issues. At the least, develop a consensus on the points that need to be addressed for the issue to be resolved.

When team authority is not recognized, usually by those outside the team, then the stakeholders may not have been properly identified. Often, team authority is questioned by groups or individuals who feel they are not represented on the team and refuse to contribute as a result. It may be that they are indeed represented, but they have not been brought up to speed on the team's mission. These problems can be prevented through proper communication throughout the stakeholder groups. When stakeholders refuse to contribute or actively block progress, sponsors may need to discuss these issues with the individuals outside of the team setting.

Power struggles can also occur in teams, usually when more senior members of an organization decide to "flex their muscle" or if two groups in the organization have competing interests. The ground rules, discussed at the initial meeting, should be referenced and enforced to prevent escalation of these struggles. Data-driven consensus-based decision making often undercuts these power struggles. Creating an environment where all members participate prevents certain team members from dominating the discussions.

It may sound silly, but too much agreement may be a bad thing. Conflict can be good. A healthy dose of skepticism may find a problem before it becomes a headache. Respectful differences of opinion can help the brainstorming process uncover new methods or discover old problems that haven't been addressed.

In summary, the following issues regarding team development and consensus building should be recognized:

• Projects cannot succeed without a team effort by the affected stakeholders.
• Team members have responsibility to ensure team performance.
• The team leader must establish and enforce ground rules.

- Buy-in is crucial; consensus builds buy-in.
- Responsible team management leads to successful project management.

Recommended Tools

The following tools (discussed in detail in Part 3) are applicable to the define stage of DMAIC:

Project Selection and Definition

- *Matrix diagrams* and *prioritization matrices* are used to select projects that are aligned with the company goals and objectives.
- *Work breakdown structure* is used to define a manageable project scope.
- *Pareto diagrams* help identify significant opportunities.
- *Process maps* provide a visual means to define the process and identify stakeholders.
- *SIPOC* identifies the process activities, key inputs and outputs, and stakeholders.

Project Scheduling

- Activity network diagram calculates a deterministic critical path.
- PERT analysis allows critical path determination assuming variation in time estimates.
- Gannt charts manage the project milestone dates.

Consensus Building

- Affinity diagrams provide a means to generate a collection of ideas about a proposal, then converge on useful categories of issues.
- Nominal group technique reduces a large collection of ideas into a workable number of key ideas.
- Prioritization matrix prioritizes options according to weighted criteria.

Quiz for Chapter 4

1. A Black Belt has been asked to put together a proposal for solving a particular customer problem. In doing so, she determines that the

problem is quite widespread, with many manifestations and causes. As a result, her project plan requires a 15-month deployment, with up to 20 stakeholder groups involved in the team. This project:

    a. Is a good project to raise awareness of the Six Sigma program. It involves many different groups and will have a great impact on the company, its customer relations, and its profitability.

    b. Is way too big. The project should be broken down into manageable projects, each of which can be compared to other proposed projects for funding purposes.

    c. Requires the use of a facilitator to manage the different stakeholder groups.

    d. Both a and c.

2. To break down a large project into smaller, more manageable projects, a Black Belt should use:

    a. An analytical hierarchy diagram.

    b. A flowchart.

    c. A work breakdown structure.

    d. An activity network diagram.

3. Project charters help to prevent the occurrence of which of the following reducers to stakeholder buy-in:

    a. Unclear goals.

    b. No accountability.

    c. Insufficient resources.

    d. All of the above.

4. Joe's project seemed to be going along well until the project team started to implement the solution. At that point, a department that hadn't been involved, but will be affected, starting raising objections and pointing out problems to the proposed solution. This indicates:

    a. The team should immediately get the sponsor involved to settle the disagreements.

    b. The department is afraid of change and needs to be told to accept the team's findings.

    c. The department should have been identified as stakeholders early on and included in the project team or the team's problem-solving sessions.

    d. Choices a and b.

5. Bob, a team leader, is having trouble getting buy-in from various members of the team. In one particular problem-solving meeting, these team members didn't seem to listen to any of Bob's ideas, and were

insistent that their ideas were more credible. Some reasonable advice to Bob would be:

a. Replace the team members with those more willing to work as team players.

b. Work on his communication skills, display interest for others' ideas, and use data to determine which ideas have the most merit.

c. Ask their managers or the project sponsor to convince them to get on board.

d. Choices a and c.

6. Jill is the team leader for a project aimed at reducing the cycle time for invoices. The team has reached an impasse on generating potential root causes of process failure; only a few ideas have been offered by only a few of the team members. As team leader, Jill should:

a. Request that the current team be dissolved, and a new team formed with process experts.

b. Report the impasse to the sponsor, and suggest the team meet again in a month or two when they have a fresh perspective.

c. Use brainstorming tools.

d. End the meeting, and work on developing the list herself.

7. With regard to team dynamics,

a. Initial meetings are generally friendly, with the team leader exercising control.

b. Conflict is common, and can indicate that team members are becoming involved.

c. The team leader should move the members toward thinking independently.

d. All of the above.

8. At the team's third meeting, its leader, John, is starting to feel a bit uncomfortable. He had established ground rules for the team, and some of its members are starting to question those rules. John should:

a. Exercise his authority as team leader and insist that the team follow the rules.

b. Lead the team to establish its own rules.

c. Defer to the team sponsor.

d. None of the above.

9. In team meetings, Jane seems to listen to whoever is speaking, but then has questions for the speaker. John, the team leader, senses that a few team members are frustrated with Jane, thinking she takes up too much time. John should:

a. Politely ask Jane, after the meeting, to try to keep her questions to a minimum.

b. Politely ask Jane during the meeting to try to keep her questions to a minimum.

c. Thank Jane publicly for asking relevant questions of team members, so that issues and opinions are clearly understood.

d. Ignore the frustrations. Personalities don't always mesh.

10. Jim is assembling a team to improve quality of a process with two stakeholder groups that have a history of fixing blame on one another. Jim would like to avoid getting "stuck in the middle" of these two factions. Jim can reduce the likelihood of this by:

a. Asking only one group (the one providing the most value to the team) to be part of the team on a full-time basis, with the other group represented only as needed for input.

b. Asking the sponsor, who oversees both groups, to attend meetings so that she can settle the disagreements.

c. Discussing team ground rules at the first team meeting, and firmly enforcing these rules throughout. These ground rules would include respectful communication between team members and decisions on basis of data (rather than opinion).

d. Asking the two groups to each recommend someone who can colead the team.

CHAPTER

Measure Stage

The objectives of the measure phase are explained and illustrated in this chapter.

Objectives

The objectives of the measure stage include:

- Process definition at a detailed level to understand the decision points and detailed functionality within the process.
- Metric definition to verify a reliable means of process estimation.
- Process baseline estimation to clarify the starting point of the project.
- Measurement system analysis to quantify the errors associated with the metric.

Process Definition

In the measure stage of DMAIC, a detailed process-level map of the current (i.e., as-is) process is developed. This detailed map clearly defines the activities subject to the improvement efforts. The top-level process map developed in the define stage serves as a starting point. While the top-level map shows the general flow of the process, it lacks the detailed decision points that truly characterize the process.

A *process* consists of repeatable tasks, carried out in a specific order. Process personnel responsible for implementing the process on a daily basis should be enlisted to develop the detailed process map. Their perspective on the process is likely to be quite different from their supervisors or the support personnel who originally developed the process flow (if that exists). It's not uncommon to find operational workers have customized the process to address real-world situations they see in practice. This information may not get communicated to all the relevant stakeholders in the process, including their immediate supervision or fellow line workers.

By enlisting the input of these process personnel, their experiences with the process, specifically in the steps they see as necessary and sufficient, are uncovered. At this time, judgment is reserved on whether these are desirable or undesirable customizations. It's likely they are the source of significant variation to the customers, and their effect can be evaluated in the analyze stage. The main concern at this phase is to develop a realistic picture of the as-is process.

The as-is process map can then be used to visualize the decision paths that are encountered in the process. Often much more complexity is built into the process than expected, and much of this complexity is non-value added. This complexity will be reviewed in the analyze stage.

Metric Definition

In general terms, a *process metric* is simply a measured parameter from a process that provides some indication of the process state or condition. For a given process, there may be several metrics useful to operational personnel. Some of these operational metrics may also be useful in Six Sigma improvement projects.

Six Sigma metrics focus on one or more of the following three critical factors: cost, quality, and schedule. Factors critical to cost (CTC) include parameters that impact work in progress, finished goods inventory, overhead, delivery, material and labor, even when the costs can be passed on to the customer. Critical to quality (CTQ) factors are perhaps most familiar to operational personnel since they directly impact the functional requirements specified by the customer. Critical to schedule (CTS) factors impact the delivery time of the product or service.

Recall the earlier recommendations for metrics: the metric should be customer focused, integrated with the business strategy, and collaboratively developed. It should indicate performance over time in a direct fashion, so it can be immediately processed. As discussed earlier in the text immediate feedback is most useful for process control, particularly when employees are empowered to directly respond to the information.

The usefulness of the data, however, is not merely a function of its availability. A reliable, repeatable, and reproducible measurement system is needed, as described in the Measurement System Analysis section of this chapter. The measurements must have sufficient resolution to effectively detect changes in the process and differentiate between real changes and process noise. This point is further discussed in the CTQ Metrics section below.

FLOW-DOWN FUNCTIONS: BIG *Y*s AND LITTLE *y*s

In practice, it is useful to think of metrics as big *Y*s and little *y*s. The little *y*s are the drivers of the big *Y*s. Mathematically:

$$Y1 = \text{function of } \{y1, y2, \ldots, yn\}$$
$$Y2 = \text{function of } \{y1, y2, \ldots, yn\} \ldots$$
$$Ym = \text{function of } \{y1, y2, \ldots, yn\} \text{ for } m \text{ big } Y\text{s.}$$

Big *Y*s and their corresponding little *y*s are defined at each level of the organization: the business level, the operations level, and the process level.

Starting at the business level, then down to the operations level and finally the process level, the little *y*s at each stage become the big *Y*s at the next stage down. While the big *Y*s are useful for tracking, the little *y*s provide the detail necessary for controlling processes and improving the organization.

This flow-down of the metrics from one level to the next provides direct linkage of the operational and process metrics to the key stakeholder big *Y* metrics used in the dashboards at the business level.

For example, the big *Y*s related to the customer stakeholders group may be as follows:

$$Y1 = \text{Satisfaction score}$$
$$Y2 = \text{Retention rate}$$
$$Y3 = \text{Order turnaround time}$$
$$Y4 = \text{Sales revenue}$$

The metrics at this level provide a good high-level stakeholder view, but do not yet provide the details necessary to optimize operations. It would be helpful to drill down on each of these Big *Y*s to understand their little *y* drivers. Conversely, those at the operations or process levels in the organization can drill up to understand how their metrics relate to stakeholder value.

For example, the little ys for the customer satisfaction score ($Y1$) in a restaurant chain might be:

Customer satisfaction = Function of (service quality, culinary satisfaction, restaurant availability, price, ...)

These business level little ys will become the operations level big Ys. Operations level big Ys are useful for Six Sigma project selection criteria, since they are the operational parameters that are perfectly aligned with the business level metrics.

The operational level little ys for service quality of the restaurant chain may be written as:

Service quality = Function of (wait time, friendliness of staff, cleanliness of facility, order accuracy, ...)

Each of the operational level little ys may be further broken down into their components in the process level matrix. For example:

Wait time = Function of (cycle time for cooking, number of staffed registers, time of day, ...)

This resulting function can then be used to:

- Establish conditions necessary for process optimization and/or variation reduction
- Provide process-level Six Sigma project metrics
- Define critical metrics for ongoing process control

These flow-down functions, which relate the big Ys to their corresponding little ys, are determined through regression and correlation analysis. Data is collected through designed experiments, data mining, surveys, focus groups, and critical incident techniques. The functions allow process-level metrics to be linked to both customer requirements and business strategy.

CTQ METRICS

Many production processes are evaluated by their yield, or similarly their scrap rate. *Yield* is calculated for production applications by dividing the amount of product finishing the process by the amount of product that started the process. For example, if 1,000 units started production, and of these 980 units successfully completed production, then the yield is calculated as $980/1000 = 98\%$. The scrap rate refers to the units that could not be sold (in this case, 2%).

Note that once the customer requirements have been determined, any process can be defined in terms of its yield. For example, if 380 clients surveyed in a random sampling of 400 clients of a customer call center indicated that the service level was satisfactory or better, then the yield of the process can be calculated as $380/400 = 95\%$.

A problem with the yield metric is that it does not provide enough detail of the nature of the errors. As an example, consider the following three processes, each with a 95% yield:

- Process A: Of 4000 units started and 3800 completed, 200 defective units each had single defect.
- Process B: Of 4000 units started and 3800 completed, 200 defective units had total of 600 defects.
- Process C: Of 4000 units started and 3500 completed with no defects, 300 units reworked for 420 defects, 200 units scrapped for 580 defects.

These processes have different outcomes, yet the yield metric fails to discriminate between them. In this production process, some units initially with errors can be *reworked* and sold as new. For example, units with unacceptable paint finish might be repaired and repainted. Likewise in a service process, a customer initially dissatisfied with the service may be directed to a manager for repair of the situation, resulting in an ultimately satisfied customer.

In terms of the metric, if the reworked units are treated the same as non-reworked units, information is lost. This simplistic yield metric obscures the "hidden factory" responsible for rework and process variation, resulting in increased process cycle times and costs.

A solution to this limitation is offered in the throughput yield metric. *Throughput yield* measures the ability of the process to produce error-free units (or error-free service): the average percentage of units (or instances of service) with no errors. Throughput yield (Y_t) is calculated by subtracting the defects per unit (DPU) percentage from 100%.

For example, process A (described above) has a DPU of $200/4000 = 0.05$, so its throughput yield is 95%, same as the yield calculated earlier. Process B has a DPU of $600/4000 = 0.15$ (a throughput yield of 85%). In this case, the throughput yield reflects the cost of the multiple errors in some of the sample units. Finally, process C has a DPU of $1000/4000 = 0.25$ (a throughput yield of 75%). In each case, the throughput yield is considerably less than the calculated first-pass yield.

Rolled throughput yield (Y_{rt}) is calculated as the expected quality level after multiple steps in a process. If the throughput yield for n process steps is Y_{t1}, $Y_{t2}, Y_{t3}, \ldots Y_{tn}$, then:

$$Y_{rt} = Y_{t1} * Y_{t2} * Y_{t3} * \ldots * Y_{tn}$$

For example, suppose there are six possible critical to quality steps required to process a customer order, with their throughput yields calculated as .997, .995, .95, .89, .923, .94. The rolled throughput yield is then calculated as:

$$Y_{rt} = .997 * .995 * .95 * .89 * .923 * .94 = .728$$

Thus, only 73% of the orders will be processed error free. It's interesting to see how much worse the rolled throughput yield is compared to the individual throughput yields. As processes become more complex (i.e., more CTQ steps), the combined error rates can climb rather quickly. This should serve as a warning to simplify processes, as suggested earlier in Chapter 4.

Conversely, the normalized yield may be used as a baseline for process steps when a required rolled throughput yield is defined for the process series. The *normalized yield* is calculated as the nth root of the rolled throughput yield. For example, if the desired rolled throughput yield is 73% for a process with six steps, then the normalized yield for each step of the process is $(0.73)^{1/6} = 0.95$, since 0.95 raised to the sixth power is approximately equal to 0.73. The normalized yield provides the minimum throughput yield for each step of the process to achieve a given rolled throughput yield. Of course, if some process steps cannot meet this normalized yield level, then the rolled throughput yield could be less.

From a quality perspective, these throughput yields are an improvement from the simple first-pass yield, but they still lack a fundamental quality: they cannot provide immediate information to prevent errors. Each of these metrics relies upon *attribute* (i.e., count) data, where the numerical value is incremented based on the property of each sample relative to a quality specification. For example, the metric may be the count of errors in a given sample from the process: the count is incremented only when an error is observed. Attribute data has less resolution than measurement (*variables*) data, since a count is registered only if an error occurs. In a healthcare process, for example, the number of patients with a fever (attributes data) could be counted, or the measured temperature of the patient (variables data) recorded. There is clearly more informational content in the variables measurement, since it indicates *how good* or *how bad*, rather than just good or bad. This lack of resolution in attributes data will prevent detection of trends toward an undesirable state.

In addition to the lack of resolution, the data is tainted by the criteria from which it was derived. The count of errors is based on comparison of the process measurement relative to a specification. The customer specification may be unilateral (one sided, with either a minimum or maximum) or bilateral (two sided, with both a minimum and maximum). All values within the specifications are deemed of equal (maximum) value to the customer (i.e., they pass), and all values outside the specifications are deemed of zero value to the customer (i.e., they fail), as shown previously in Figure 3.1.

In most industries, the specifications provide reasonable guidelines, but they are hardly black and white indicators of usability or acceptability of a product or service. As you approach the specifications, the usability becomes gray, and is subject to other mitigating concerns such as delivery dates and costs of replacement. This practicality is not surprising, considering the rather subjective manner in which specifications are often developed. Even in the best of worlds, when frequency distributions are applied to derive probabilistic estimates of requirements, there is uncertainty in the final result. In service industries, specifications are often similar to desirability levels: We may say we want to be seen by the doctor within 45 minutes of arrival, but we're not likely to walk out at that moment if we think service is pending in just a few more minutes. Rather, we'll start complaining after 30 minutes, which will build to irritability then disgust (at least for some of us).

Taguchi (1986) expressed this notion in terms of a loss function, where the loss to society (the inverse of the customer satisfaction) is maximized at some value within the customer requirements, then minimized outside the range of acceptable values. For example, with a bilateral specification, the maximum value of the product or service may be at the midpoint between the specifications. As you move in the direction of either specification limit, the value is reduced in some fashion, typically exponentially as shown in Table 5.1. For example, a five-day delivery is undesirable, but a two-day delivery is preferred over the four-day delivery.

Although the specifications provide reasonable guidelines on acceptability to the customer, they are not absolute. Tainting the data by removing the objectivity of a measured value (or choosing a somewhat subjective attribute data over a more objective measured value) represents a loss in informational content that is not warranted or desired.

Rather, the statistical value of the data improves as the resolution increases, at least until a resolution is reached that can reliably estimate the variation in the data. For a proper statistical analysis, the standard deviation must be estimated, which requires enough information (i.e., resolution) to the right of the decimal point to measure the variation. For example, using the data in the Measure A column of Table 5.1, the standard deviation is calculated as 0.548. The data in this column has been rounded up or down, due to poor resolution of the measurement system. How accurate is this estimate of variation? The data in the Measure B and Measure C columns of the table represent two possible sets of data that, when rounded, would result in the Measure A data. In one case, the variation is overestimated by Measure A; in the other,

Table 5.1. Example of how rounding of data affects results.

	Measure A	Measure B	Measure C
Observation 1	9	9.4	8.6
Observation 2	10	9.8	10.4
Observation 3	9	9.3	9.3
Observation 4	10	10.1	10.1
Observation 5	10	9.7	9.6
Standard Deviation	0.548	0.321	0.704

variation is underestimated. Note that there are many other possible data sets that would result in the same rounded data shown by Measure A, but in all cases the rounding produces an inaccurate result. These inaccuracies would increase the probabilities of rejecting when the hypothesis is true, false alarm, or accepting when the hypothesis is false, failure to detect, errors. Practically, the value of the improved estimates must be balanced with the cost of the increased data resolution.

CTC METRICS

Critical to cost metrics are used to track factors contributing to substantial cost when they vary significantly from their target value. CTC factors may also be critical to quality or schedule.

When considering costs, the true costs of errors in the process, including unreported hidden factory costs, must be included. Examples include:

- Capacity loss due to reworks in system and scrap
- Stockpiling of raw material or in-process material to accommodate poor yield
- Engineering or management approval times
- Rush deliveries
- Lost orders due to poor service or poor quality

Those in service or transactional businesses should not be disturbed by the wording. *Scrap*, *rework*, and *stockpiling of in-process material* occur in these businesses as well. Think of clients who need to come back, call back, or talk to multiple people to get the results they seek. Stockpiling occurs any time orders sit waiting for someone to process them, usually in a batch mode. While boarding in groups may work for the airline, it usually doesn't serve the customer's interest too well.

The cost of quality tends to increase as errors in a product or service move downstream. It bears repeating that if it costs $1 to fix a problem in the design of the product or service, it costs $10 to fix it in manufacturing or service delivery, and $100 after delivery to the customer. Consider the costs due to faulty tires, food poisoning, or software bugs. The sooner problems are detected and resolved, the cheaper the solution.

In this way, failures are low-hanging fruit, providing a quick return on investment. Understanding the causal systems leads to improvement in efforts at appraisal, and eventually, prevention.

While financial metrics such as cost of quality are useful for identifying areas of potential improvements and tracking project savings, there is too much lag in their response to identify process changes requiring action. Instead, critical to cost or critical to schedule metrics are defined that contribute to cost yet are quick to respond to changes in process conditions.

A review of the potential savings and benefits outlined in the Project Selection section in Chapter 3 helps to quantify the costs captured by the response of the particular metric.

CTS METRICS

The most often used metric for critical to schedule issues is the cycle time metric, or some derivation of cycle time such as order processing time, delivery time, or downtime.

As with costs, problems in quality can also impact the schedule. For this reason, process improvement focused on CTQ metrics may also improve CTS issues. Consider the delays associated with rework or the reprocessing of orders after mistakes in a quality parameter have been detected. Preventing the errors by concentrating on the CTQ metrics results in improved CTS response.

In addition to these quality-related issues, there are many other opportunities for improvement of cycle times. In the analysis stage, value stream analysis provides techniques for differentiating between value-added and non-value-added process steps. *Process efficiency* and *velocity* can be calculated, each of which indicates a process's relative value-added cycle time. While these metrics are useful for comparing processes, or for comparing *before improvement* and *after improvement* states of the process, they are not as useful as tracking metrics for identifying changes in process conditions. Calculated values tend to dampen the signal of a cycle time change, and be less intuitive to process personnel who must respond to changes, decreasing their value as metrics for immediate information.

Nonetheless, cycle time metrics are valuable tools in achieving improvement in Six Sigma projects. Even when the focus of the project is on quality or cost, the value stream analysis offers an opportunity for cycle time reduction through elimination of non-value-added activities. As the drivers of a process become clear in the analysis stage, some activities thought necessary for process control will be found to have little effect. These can be eliminated, reducing the total process cycle time.

Process Baseline Estimation

A process baseline provides an estimate of the current state of the process and its ability to meet customer requirements. The baseline estimate typically is the process metric used in operations and accepted within the organization. The baseline will allow the stakeholders to validate the costs associated with the current process performance (as calculated in the previous section).

The context of the process baseline estimate must be clearly understood. How much variation is there between the samples? Would additional samples yield better, worse, or similar results? Do the samples provide a reliable estimate of future samples?

ENUMERATIVE STATISTICS

Classical statistics are enumerative techniques, used to compare samples randomly drawn from populations. Using hypothesis testing procedures, samples can be tested for the likelihood they came from a known population. Similarly, two samples can be compared to gauge the likelihood they came from the same population. The term *population* simply refers to a group of data that meet a defined condition, such as all customers purchasing a specific product. A key assumption is that the samples are each representative of the population. A *representative sample* implies there is no bias in selection of the data: each observation has an equal chance of selection.

In a similar fashion, *confidence intervals* on point estimates may be constructed that will provide bounds (an upper and a lower bound) on the expected value of the statistic based on the data, an assumed distribution (such as the normal, Poisson, or binomial distributions), and a confidence level (usually 95%).

For example, the average error rate can be calculated over a six-month period for a telemarketing process. If this calculation, based on a sample of 5,000 telemarketing calls, indicates an average process error rate of 3.4%, then the lower and upper bounds on the 95% confidence interval can be calculated at 2.9% and 3.9%, respectively (based on techniques described later in this book). If a current sample is taken, and has an error rate of 3.8%, then the current sample could have come from the same population as the prior samples, since it falls within the 95% confidence intervals.

When these classical statistical methods of analysis are applied, the prior data is assumed to be from a fixed population: the population does not change over time. Fixed populations may be graphically represented by a distribution curve, such as shown in Figure 5.1. Note that in this case, a normal distributional curve was assumed for convenience, as is often the case in hypothesis tests and confidence intervals.

ANALYTICAL STATISTICS

A process, however, is different from a population, since it occurs over time. In a process, variation may be due to causes that are persistent or to causes that come and go. A persistent cause, usually referred to as a *common cause*, tends to influence all data in a relatively uniform fashion. Common causes of variation are inherent to the process itself, by design. A given reason (the actual cause) often can't be assigned to a specific amount of variation, but the total level of variation is considered typical for the process due to the influence of these (unknown) common causes. This amount of variation should be expected.

Common causes of variation reflect our ignorance of the process dynamics. So long as the amount of variation is acceptable, the ignorance can be tolerated. Since the variation is persistent, the process can be considered stable, and can be predicted with the appropriate statistical tools.

In contrast, *special causes* of variation are sporadic in nature: they come and go, generally in an unpredictable fashion. This sporadic occurrence causes the process to behave differently in their presence, resulting in process instability. In the presence of special causes, the process outcome cannot be accurately predicted, since the process is not stable.

While logic, reason, or scientific and engineering principles may instinctively be chosen to differentiate between common and special causes of variation in a process, only a properly designed statistical control chart can

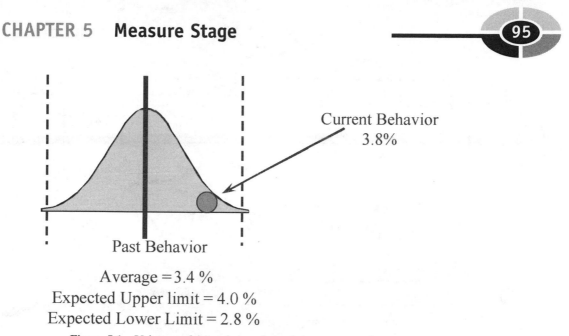

Figure 5.1   Using confidence intervals to detect process changes.

properly offer that insight. A statistical process control (SPC) chart, developed by Walter Shewhart in the 1920s, provides an *operational definition* of a special cause.

SPC uses the element of time as one of its principal axes. Samples are collected over a short period of time. This sample is referred to as a *subgroup*. Each subgroup indicates two things about the process: its current location and its current amount of variation.

Once enough subgroups have been collected over a period of time, the short-term estimates (i.e., the subgroups) can be used to predict where the process will be (its location) and how much the process is expected to vary over a longer time period.

Figure 5.2 displays an SPC chart calculated from the same data used to calculate the confidence interval seen earlier. The control chart reveals something unclear from the distributional curve in Figure 5.1—the element of time. There is a predictable variation inherent to the process evident for the first 40 or so samples. During this period, the process variation was relatively stable.

The most recent sample at 3.8% looks different from these earlier 40 samples, but is much like the seven months immediately prior to it. These last eight samples apparently represent an unknown shift in the process. The "prior defect rate" of 3.4% calculated using the enumerative statistical approach was inflated due to the pooling of this unknown shift in the process with the earlier stable process. The element of time, lacking in the distributional curve and all other enumerative statistical tools, is clearly a critical

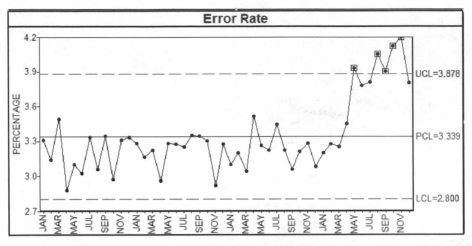

Figure 5.2   Using an SPC chart to detect process changes.

parameter for investigating process characteristics, since processes are by definition occurring over the course of time.

BASELINE ESTIMATES USING ENUMERATIVE OR ANALYTICAL STATISTICS

For Six Sigma projects, it is important to baseline a process using a control chart to investigate whether the process is in a state of statistical control. In at least some cases, out-of-control processes make poor candidates for Six Sigma projects.

Consider a process such as the one shown in Figure 5.3. An out-of-control condition occurs for a period of time, then goes away. This is not at all uncommon in practice, and it might occur for any number of reasons (depending on the metric tracked), including inexperienced personnel filling in for someone on vacation, different material from a supplier, incorrect process settings, change in competitor offerings, etc.

If a control chart were not used in this analysis, the existence of the special cause would remain unknown. The enumerative estimate would include the effect of the special cause as variation in the population. A fundamental error has been made, since the population was not adequately defined. There are actually multiple (or at least two) populations, as evidenced by the special cause.

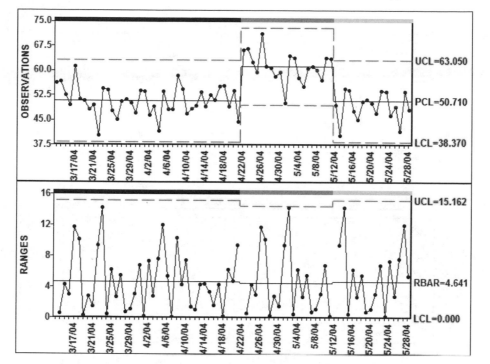

Figure 5.3   Baseline estimates from out-of-control processes will be biased.

Even if no improvement was made to the process, subsequent estimates of the new process would show improvement if the special cause failed to re-appear on its own accord. Furthermore, the "improvements" made were wasted effort, or could even degrade the process performance through tampering (as explained in the SPC Control Charts section of Part 3).

This scenario is likely to have occurred in many historical improvement attempts. When processes are improved and then return to their previous level of performance, a probable cause is a special cause that was not affected by the improvement.

Special causes are often poor candidates for Six Sigma projects because of their sporadic nature. The project investment has an unsure payoff, unlike the predictable nature of common cause variation. Until the underlying root cause of variation is defined, the economic benefit of the improvement is questionable.

The benefit of an improvement on a special cause depends on the underlying process condition at the root of the special cause variation. For example, out-of-control conditions on a control chart can occur when multiple process

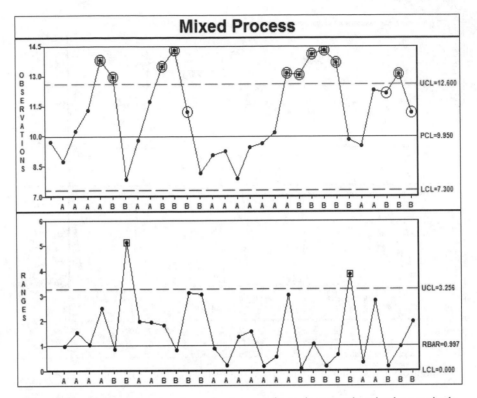

Figure 5.4   Order processing times for two products, improperly mixed on a single control chart.

streams are shown on the same chart. Consider the control chart of order processing times in Figure 5.4. If there are really two underlying processes (one for product A, the other for product B), then out-of-control points can occur if either the average or standard deviation of the order processing times for the two products are different. The severity of the out-of-control condition (i.e., the frequency of out-of-control points) depends on these relative differences, as well as the frequency of occurrence of each product in the process stream. When the products are properly charted (on separate control charts or using short-run standardization techniques), the focus of the Six Sigma project can be properly directed and its financial benefit calculated.

When out-of-control conditions are truly due to sporadic, unpredictable root causes, the financial benefit of improvement can only be known when the root cause of the behavior has been identified in process terms. While historical evidence of the occurrence of similar patterns of behavior may be justification to investigate the process, once an underlying cause is determined an analysis needs to link the cause to the past behavior, since this past behavior may be due to other (unidentified) root causes. Nonetheless, if there is financial burden from the special causes, it would tend to justify a proper investigation, such as a designed experiment as part of a Six Sigma project, into the causes.

Statistically, we need to have a sufficient number of data observations before we can calculate reliable estimates of the common cause variation and (to a lesser degree) the average. The statistical "constants" used to define control chart limits (such as shown in Appendix 6) are actually variables, and only approach constants when the number of subgroups is "large." For a subgroup size of 5, for instance, the d2 value, used to calculate the control limits, approaches a constant at about 25 subgroups (Duncan, 1986). When a limited number of subgroups are available, short-run standardization techniques may be useful.

In order to distinguish between special causes and common causes, there must be enough subgroups to define the common cause operating level of your process. This implies that all types of common causes must be included in the data. For example, if the control chart is developed over a short time frame, such as an eight-hour period, then the data does not include all elements of common cause variation that are likely to be characteristic of the process. If control limits are defined under these limited conditions, then it is likely out-of-control groups will appear due to the natural variation in one or more of the process factors.

DPMO AND SIGMA LEVEL ESTIMATES

When the process is in a state of statistical control, then the process is predictable, and short-term and long-term defect levels can be estimated. Unstable (i.e., out-of-control) processes, by definition, are the combination of multiple processes. Their instability makes prediction of defect levels unreliable.

For controlled processes, the *Process Capability Index* provides a comparison between the calculated process location and its variation with the stated customer requirements.

When the process is unstable (i.e., not in statistical control), or control cannot be established because of lack of data, a *Process Performance Index* may be used as a rough estimate to compare observed variation with the customer requirements. Generally, many more samples are needed to reliably estimate process performance when the process is unstable. Furthermore, as discussed above, there is no reason to believe the process will behave in this same fashion in the future.

The calculated process capability or process performance metric can be converted to corresponding DPMO (defects per million opportunities) and Sigma level using Appendix 8. Let's see how these numbers are derived.

Assuming the normal distribution is an adequate model for the process, the normal probability tables (Appendix 1) are used to estimate the percent of the process distribution beyond a given value, such as a customer requirement (usually referred to as a specification). Z values at $x = $ USL and z_L at $x = $ LSL are calculated, where:

$$z = (x - \mu)/\sigma$$

USL refers to the upper specification limit, the largest process value allowed by the customer. LSL refers to the lower specification limit, the smallest allowed value.

The z value indicates how many sigma (σ) units the x value is from the mean (or average, μ). For example, if the USL for a process is 16, and the process average and standard deviation are calculated as 10.0 and 2.0, respectively, then the z value corresponding to the upper specification is $z = (16 - 10)/2 = 3.0$.

Using the normal tables of Appendix 1, a z value of 3 equals a probability of .99865, meaning that 99.865% of the process distribution is less than the x value that is three sigma units above the mean. That implies that $1 - .99865 = .00135$ (or 0.135%) of the process exceeds this x value (i.e., lies to its right in the distribution). The 0.00135 decimal value may be converted to parts per million by multiplying by 10^6, resulting in 1350 DPMO.

This is shown graphically in Figure 5.5.

Recall that the DPMO to sigma level conversion includes a 1.5 sigma shift. The Six Sigma process is one which will achieve a long-term error rate of 3.4 DPMO, rather than the 2 DPBO (defects per billion opportunities) suggested by a z value of 6. When sigma levels are estimated based on internal process estimates, such as a process capability index, the estimate is termed a *short-term estimate*. External failure rates will actually be higher, due to the longer-term 1.5 sigma process shift.

When sigma levels are estimated based on external process estimates, such as through field data or customer surveys, the observed defect rate already includes the 1.5 sigma shift. These are long-term estimates by their very nature.

Measurement Systems Analysis

Previous sections have discussed the need for adequate data resolution, both in terms of data type (attributes versus variables) as well as precision (lost

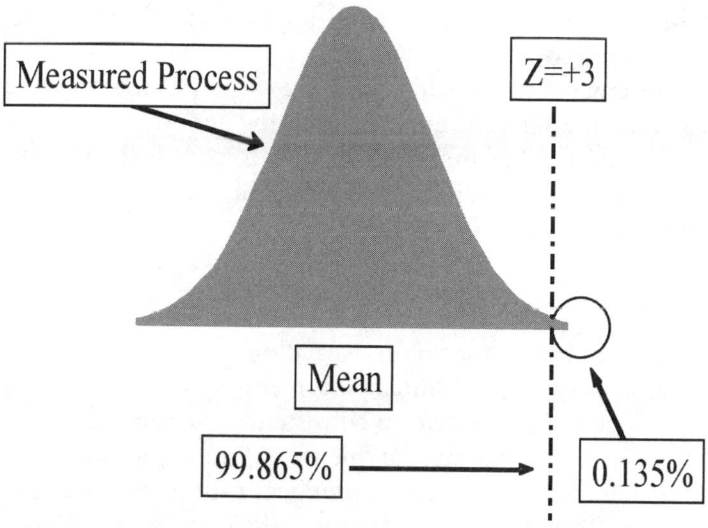

Figure 5.5   A calculated *z* value directly corresponds to a percentile of the normal distribution.

when data is rounded up or down due to the measurement method). Even when a measurement method provides adequate data resolution, the measurement may be subject to significant error due to a number of sources, which can be further quantified in a measurement system analysis. This measurement error affects our estimates of service acceptability, as well as product inspections and dispositions, process stability estimates using control charts, and their resulting effect on our profitability.

A familiar form of measurement error is *bias*, also known as *accuracy*. Bias is an estimate of the systematic error in the measurement system. A measurement system that is purely consistent, with no variation in its estimate for a given unit, may still have bias, since it may be consistently wrong! Bias is a simple, consistent offset in the estimate, and can be corrected through calibration of the measurement system, much like watches are synchronized for accuracy. Measurement systems need to be analyzed for *stability* to ensure that their accuracy does not degrade over time. While this is often not a concern during the short time period of a Six Sigma project, it may become a concern for future control of the process improvements.

Another concern is that of *linearity*: does the measurement system provide the same level of accuracy across its full range of use? If the error is higher for larger measurements, then the estimates of variation in these cases are inflated, which will have an unfavorable effect on improvement and control efforts.

Unfortunately, even a regularly calibrated measurement system may be subject to additional sources of error.

When measurements are taken of a process or population, the variation estimated between the samples includes both the actual variation between the sample units, as well as measurement error. Mathematically, the total variance is composed of the actual variance between the items and the variance, or error, of the measurement.

$$\sigma^2_{\text{total}} = \sigma^2_{\text{item}} + \sigma^2_{\text{measurement}}$$

The measurement error appears as variation between repeat samples of a given sample unit. Bias does not impact this measurement error, since bias alone will cause the measurement system to consistently measure each sample unit.

When the variance of the measurements is known, a gage discrimination ratio can be calculated to provide a practical estimate of the measurement system resolution. The *discrimination ratio* is the number of distinct categories discernible by the measurement equipment. A value of two, for instance, indicates the gage is useful for only attribute analysis, since it can only effectively classify the parts as being in one group or the other (for example, good or bad). A discrimination ratio of eight or more is suitable for statistical analysis of the data.

A primary tool to estimate the variance of the measurements is *R&R analysis*, which categorizes the error as either a repeatability or reproducibility error. *Repeatability error* is associated with the equipment and procedures, while *reproducibility* is associated with the personnel using the equipment. Repeatability is estimated by compare multiple measurements of the same sample unit. Reproducibility is estimated by obtaining measurements of the same sample units by multiple personnel. Categorizing the error in this manner allows us to address and reduce the error.

Considering that the measurement system is used to determine acceptability of the process relative to customer requirements, it should be apparent that as the error increases so does the chance that:

- Products or service truly outside requirements could be measured as being within requirements and subsequently accepted for use.
- Products or service truly within requirements could be measured as being outside requirements and subsequently rejected as unfit for use.

Measurement error also influences control charting and process capability analysis. The calculation of statistical control limits and the estimate of process capability require a sound estimate of the process variation. As measurement error increases, so does the chance that:

- Subgroups from a controlled process will be determined to be out of control.
- Subgroups from an out-of-control process will be determined to be from an in-control process.

In some cases, the most significant source of common cause variation may be the measurement equipment. Some Six Sigma projects have been concluded at the measurement stage with the realization that the perceived process variation was almost entirely due to the measurement system. Of course, the loss to the organization (before this was determined) was quite real, so significant savings were achieved by the project team.

Recommended Tools

The following tools (discussed in detail in Part 3) are applicable to the measure stage of DMAIC:

Process Definition

- *Flowcharts* and *process maps* to define the process level activities necessary.

Process Baseline Estimates

- SPC control charts, including *C, Np, P, U, Individual-X, X-Bar*, and *EWMA charts*, for investigating process stability and evaluating process capability.
- *Histograms* and *stem and leaf plots* to graphically display the process output relative to the requirements.
- *Confidence intervals on mean* and *confidence intervals on proportion* for estimating process performance when the process is not in statistical control.
- *Goodness of fit tests* and *probability plotting* to verify the statistical distributions assumed in the various statistical tools.

Measurement Systems Analysis

- *R&R studies* to quantify the measurement error associated with the equipment, personnel, and procedures.
- *Linearity analysis* and *regression analysis* to understand the measurement system error as a function of measurement size.

- *Design of experiments* for understanding the components of measurement system error.

In addition, the consensus building tools noted at the end of Chapter 4 are also applied, as needed.

Quiz for Chapter 5

1. The process for serving the food at a fast-food restaurant is the subject of a process improvement initiative. All of the following are suitable metrics to baseline the process *except*:
   a. Satisfaction with menu offerings.
   b. Time to process the order.
   c. Percent of items ordered that were delivered.
   d. All of the above are suitable.

2. When calculating the sigma level of a manufacturing process:
   a. The departmental scrap rate reported to management provides a good indicator of the overall DPMO.
   b. The rework rate should not be ignored.
   c. A percent of subgroups out of control on the control chart indicates the defect rate.
   d. All of the above.

3. The yield of a process, calculated as output divided by input:
   a. Is the best estimate of the process performance.
   b. Indicates the effect of the "hidden factory."
   c. Is not sensitive to the complexity of the product or service.
   d. All of the above.

4. If the rolled throughput yield for a four-step process is 95%, then a good target throughput yield for each step of the process is:
   a. 95%.
   b. 99%.
   c. 97%.
   d. 81%.

5. In documenting the current "as-is process":
   a. Talk with the process engineers or managers to understand what is supposed to be done.
   b. Talk with operational personnel responsible for carrying out the process since they may do things differently than specified.

    c. Include all the process stakeholders.
    d. All of the above.

6. Control charts were originally developed by:
    a. W. Edwards Deming.
    b. Walter Shewhart.
    c. George Box.
    d. Lloyd Nelson.

7. What is the relationship between bias and linearity?
    a. Bias is a measure of inaccuracy at a point. Linearity is an evaluation of bias at several points over a range of concern.
    b. Linearity is a special case of bias.
    c. Both a and b above.
    d. None of the above.

8. Accuracy is:
    a. Getting consistent results repeatedly.
    b. Reading to four decimals.
    c. The best measuring device available.
    d. Getting an unbiased true value.

9. Measurement error:
    a. Is the fault of the inspector.
    b. Can be determined.
    c. Is usually of no consequence.
    d. Can be eliminated by frequent calibrations of the measuring device.

10. Gage linearity analysis detects:
    a. Measurement error that changes as a function of the size of the measurement.
    b. Variation between operators.
    c. Variation between different gages.
    d. All of the above.

Analyze Stage

Objectives

The objectives within the analyze stage of DMAIC include:

- Analysis of the value stream, the necessary steps that produce value for the customer.
- Analysis of the sources of variation.
- Determination of the process drivers, the little ys that correlate to the stakeholder requirements and significantly influence the process output.

Value Stream Analysis

Value stream analysis is a key contribution to Six Sigma, borrowed from the lean methodology. (For more details on the lean methodology, refer to that section in Part 3.) The term *value stream* refers to the necessary activities that contribute value to the product or service, as determined by the customer.

Once a process has been mapped, each process step can be categorized as one of the following:

- A step that creates value for the customer.
- A step that creates no customer value but is required by one or more required activities (including design, order processing, production, and delivery). These steps are termed *type 1 waste*.
- A step that creates no customer value and represents the proverbial low-hanging fruit. These steps should and can be eliminated immediately. These are termed *type 2 waste*.

Quality function deployment (QFD) or simpler matrix diagrams are useful tools for comparing the process step's contribution to value, as defined by the customer.

To identify non-value-added activities, it is sometimes useful to ask these questions:

- Is this something the customer is willing to pay for?
- Does the step change form, fit, or function of the product? Or, does it convert input to output?

If the answer to both questions is No, then it is likely the activity does not create value in the customer's eyes. Inspection and review activities, such as monitoring of sales calls or management sign-offs on exceptions, are examples of a non-value-added waste. They do nothing to change the product (or service) and are only necessary to address the poor quality associated with the underlying process. Unfortunately, if their removal would degrade the quality of the delivered product or service, then they are necessary type 1 waste.

Taiichi Ohno of Toyota defined the first five of the following six types of waste. Womack and Jones (1996) added the sixth:

1. Errors requiring rework. Rework refers to any operation required to fix or repair the result of another process step. In service processes, management intervention to resolve a customer complaint is considered rework.
2. Work with no immediate customer, either internal or external, resulting in work in progress or finished goods inventory.
3. Unnecessary process steps.
4. Unnecessary movement of personnel or materials.
5. Waiting by employees as unfinished work in an upstream process is completed.
6. Design of product or processes that do not meet the customer's needs.

REDUCING PROCESS COMPLEXITIES

One common method for decreasing cycle times is to reduce the process or product complexities. The process is simplified by reducing the number of "special items" that are processed. By simplifying to one product, or one type of service customer, then efforts can be concentrated to achieve higher efficiencies. It should be obvious that the more options offered, the higher the process complexity, and the longer the cycle time. By standardizing, cycle time can be reduced.

Henry Ford, in offering the first affordable automobile, realized the efficiency advantages offered by standardization. His motto, "Any color you want, so long as it's black," exemplified the notion of standardization. The modern approach to standardization does not limit options, but instead recognizes the advantages of simplified processes and seeks to remove activities that provide little value at the cost of increased cycle times. For example, the costs of approvals and upset customers may be enough to offset the cost of standardizing on second-day shipments for all orders, instead of only those orders with approval. By grouping parts or services into families, common methods can be applied, thus simplifying processes and reducing overall cycle times.

Decision points and subsequent parallel paths on flowcharts provide indication of process complexities that can sometimes be avoided. The Six Sigma process optimization tools discussed in Chapter 7 provide another method for decreasing cycle times. Rather than simply reducing errors, these tools allow the process to operate at an improved level with respect to customer requirements. For example, the cycle time may be reduced to a point that goes beyond the elimination of complaints to the level of customer delight. These optimization tools include designed experiments, response surface analysis, process simulations, and failure modes and effects analysis (FMEA).

REDUCING NON-VALUE-ADDED ACTIVITIES

Reducing or eliminating non-value-added cycle times often provides the clearest and easiest methods to reduce cycle time and achieve better velocity (see Part 3 for further discussion of velocity). It's not uncommon for more than 50% of a process cycle time to consist of non-value-added activities.

The first step for cycle time reduction should be to identify and eliminate the type 2 waste: the process steps that are simply not necessary. These may include activities such as routine authorizations or approvals or information and data collection that is not necessary or even used. After eliminating these activities, the process flow must often be subsequently redesigned.

Significant cycle time reduction is achieved through a reduction of errors requiring rework. Practices for reducing rework include standardization of procedures, mistake-proofing (using failure modes and effects analysis), and improvement of process capability. (These last two items are discussed in Chapter 7; procedures are discussed in Chapter 8.) As errors requiring rework are eliminated, the non-value-added inspections and approvals currently necessary may be reduced or eliminated.

Unnecessary movement of material or personnel is also a non-value-added activity. Reducing movement typically affects the physical space in which the process takes place: offices may be redesigned, departments moved or reassigned, even entire facilities moved closer to their customers. Movement analysis is aided by the use of spaghetti diagrams. Improvements can be realized through application of the 5S tools, which are discussed in Part 3.

The outcomes of movement and space reduction include:

- Decreased distance from supplier to customer. Both internal and external suppliers and customers are affected. This relocation reduces the wastes of unnecessary movement and wait time associated with the movement.

- Less departmentalization; more multifunction work cells. Within company walls, you may reassign individuals so they work within multifunctional work cells, rather than functional departments. In small companies, cross-training may eliminate the need for some specialized functions. For example, instead of a customer service representative forwarding an order to Accounts Payable, customer service representatives could create and e-mail a completed invoice to the customer while they are still on the phone. This improves the flow of the process (whether a physical product, paperwork, or even ideas), so work is not batched up at each department. Multifunction work cells reduce the waste of waiting and improve visibility of slowdowns, barriers, or inefficiencies that occur in the preceding or following steps.

- Reduced overhead costs and reduced need for new facilities. As space is used more efficiently, overhead costs are reduced, as is the need for new facilities if new equipment or labor is acquired.

Level loading, to match the production rates of the process steps, also reduces non-value-added cycle times. *Level loading* of serial processes will remove all work in progress. The flow becomes batchless, with a shorter cycle time, increased flexibility, decreased response time, and an increase in the percent of value-added activities. *Start an item, finish an item* is the mantra.

Batches are not nearly as efficient, from a systems point of view and a customer's perspective, as they appear. As ironic as it may seem, a major reason processes contain waste is because of historical attempts to drive efficiency. One fallacy commonly accepted is processes become more efficient by creating specialized departments that process work in batches. These departments become efficient from a process standpoint, with economic lot quantities designed to minimize setup time or material delivery costs, but they lack efficiency relative to specific product value streams. Waste is created in waiting for the batch to begin its departmental processing, and waste is additionally created when particular units of product, for which customers are waiting, must wait for the remainder of the batch to be processed.

The attempts to improve the departmental efficiency can create additional waste in the product value stream if the departmental efficiency produces outcomes that do not serve the customer's needs, or requires inputs that increase costs for suppliers without adding value. While standardization of product components makes the individual processes more efficient, this efficiency can come at the cost of customer value. Think about the typical experience of purchasing a new car. You buy "the package," which includes features paid for but not needed, because it is more efficient for the production and delivery processes.

This batch-imposed waste is compounded if changes occur in design or customer needs, as the WIP or final-good inventories require rework or become scrap. Note that these concepts are not limited to manufacturing; businesses in the service sector can also generate waste. Think of the hamburgers cooked in advance, waiting for an order, or checking account statements that come at the end of the month, long after you could possibly prevent an overdraw.

Three common reasons for considering batches are:

- When the cost of movement of material is significant
- When the setup time dominates the per item cycle time
- To accommodate process designed for multiple product or service types

An example of the first case is shipping a batch of items, when the customer really only wants one or a few items. Because of the perceived cost of shipment, the customer has to make the choice of paying for and receiving inventory that will not be immediately (perhaps ever) used, or of waiting to place the order until they need more than one of the items. A remedy for this particular type of waste is to reduce the space between the supplier and the customer, so that shipping charges are reduced. The efficiencies of offshore production may be less than perceived if the true costs of the supplier shipping to consumer, the consumer holding unused inventory, and the consumer waiting for delayed shipments are considered. Perhaps more personally, think of the extra pantry, closet, and freezer space needed since the advent of warehouse shopping.

Some processes are designed to accommodate processing of multiple items. For example, most modern ovens are designed with large capacity. This allows us to cook the turkey, the stuffing, and the potatoes at the same time on Thanksgiving Day. But what if we only want to bake some cookies? We might as well cook a full batch to efficiently use the oven, even though we would really prefer to eat only a few freshly baked cookies tonight, then a few freshly baked cookies tomorrow, and so on. What we would really like is a small oven that could quickly cook only the number of cookies we want to eat *now!* Since we need the same oven for Thanksgiving and for tonight's cookies, we are forced to bake the full batch and eat them before the inventory gets stale (or throw out the unused inventory). Fortunately, the process can be redesigned with smaller batch sizes by using a smaller toaster oven for tonight's cookies.

When setup time dominates a process, it seems natural to process as many items as economically feasible so as to spread the setup costs across the batch. Up until 1990 or so, the printing presses used for producing textbooks required elaborate setup procedures, taking several hours per book title. For this reason, publishers were economically forced to order large quantities to keep the unit price affordable. Often, this resulted in excessive inventories, which served as a disincentive to revise the book with new material. When the setup times were reduced, then smaller batch sizes become efficient, as is now commonly practiced in the book printing industry.

Setup time can be defined as the time to change from the last item of the previous order to the first good item of the next order (George, 2002). Setup includes preparation, replacement, location, and adjustment.

Preparation refers to the tasks associated with getting or storing the material or information needed for the process: Obtaining the raw material from the warehouse, pulling up the process instructions from the computer, moving completed items to the next process step, starting up software needed to process the order, and so on.

Some suitable actions to reduce the time associated with preparation include:

- Convert from departments to work cells to minimize the time required to move the finished product to the next process step.
- Store tools and materials locally, such as advocated by the 5S principles.
- Convert to "always ready to go." Make the software or instructions instantly accessible.

Replacement refers to the tasks associated with adding or removing items or tools. For example, the movement of test fixtures, loading of new material into the hopper, and loading paper in the copy machine. Actions to reduce replacement times include:

- Simplify setups. Reduce the number of steps required, such as through a redesign of fixtures.
- Commonality of setups for product families. When the same setup procedures are established for multiple items, there are naturally less instances of change required, reducing the setup time. This is the 5S principle of standardization.
- The 5S tools of sorting and straightening also help to reduce movement and wait times.

Location tasks are those associated with positioning or placement during setup. Examples include setting temperature profiles for heating, adjusting cutoff length for specific product, and placing the chunk of deli meat in the slicer. Actions to reduce the time associated with location include:

- *Poka yoke* (the Japanese term for mistake-proofing the process), as discussed in Chapter 7
- Commonality of setups as previously mentioned (the 5S tool of standardization)

Adjustment refers to tasks associated with ensuring correct process settings. Examples include monitoring temperature of furnace, checking cutoff length, and proofing copy before printing. A suitable action to reduce adjustment time is process control. If the process is more repeatable, then adjustments are not necessary. Often this is achieved though robust design methods, as discussed in Chapter 7.

A Pareto diagram can be useful to prioritize the setup time categories. In the example shown in Figure 6.1, location and preparation dominate the setup, so are natural targets for improvement.

Michael George (2002) recommends the following four-step approach to reduce setup times:

- Classify each setup step as either internal or external. *Internal steps* are those done while the process is inactive. *External steps* are done while the process is operating.
- Convert internal steps to external steps.
- Reduce time for remaining internal steps.
- Eliminate adjustments.

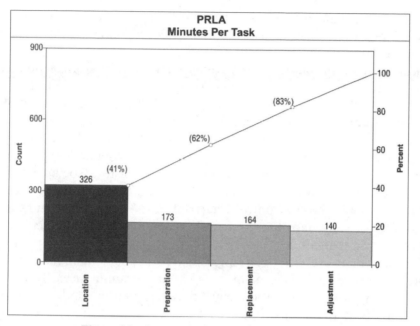

Figure 6.1 Pareto approach to setup reduction.

In converting as many internal steps as possible to external steps, the nonoperational process time is reduced. For example, if money is collected from the customers as their burgers are being cooked, rather than after they have been handed to the customer, then the total cycle time is reduced.

There are some internal steps that cannot be done while the process is operational. Efforts should concentrate on the time required to complete the steps that delay the process. Here, it is necessary to understand which activities are on the critical path, as determined using an affinity diagram. If activity times not on the critical path are decreased, there is no subsequent reduction in total process time.

Adjustments can be reduced through effective process control. Statistical process control charts and designed experiments may be used to understand the causes of process variation that precede the adjustment. These causes can then be eliminated or controlled.

Analyzing Sources of Variation

In the measure stage in Chapter 5 a process baseline was established to quantify the current process conditions. In most cases, a control chart was used to differentiate between the variation due to special causes and the variation due to common causes. This provides valuable input in analyzing the sources of variation.

Special causes of variation are evidenced by out-of-control points. The time-ordered nature of the control chart provides an indication of *when* the process was influenced by a special cause to aid in the understanding of *what* happened (in process terms). Since the control chart will not detect all shifts, nor necessarily detect shifts as soon as they occur, neighboring subgroups within the control limits could also result from the assignable (special) cause under investigation. Bear this in mind when trying to associate the timing of the special cause with possible changes in process factors. Table T.22 in the section Statistical Process Control Charts of Part 3 provides an indication of the number of subgroups that are required (on average) to detect a process shift of a given magnitude.

The common cause variation (represented by the control limits) is due to all elements of the process. These sources of variation cannot be easily associated with the point-to-point variation, since they represent a combination of factors common to all the subgroups.

Teams brainstorm to understand potential sources of variation for a process. Sources of variation are found in process *methods*, its *materials*, the *manpower* or personnel involved in the process, the *machines* or equipment used, the *measurement* techniques, and the surrounding *environment*. Collectively, these potential sources of variation are sometimes referred to as the *5Ms and E*. In service processes, the *4Ps* may be more useful: *policy, procedures, plant, and people*.

Categorizing the potential sources of variation using one of these techniques aids the team in brainstorming. Each of the categories provides a focus to ensure that potential causes are not ignored. As in any brainstorming exercise, individual responses should not be critiqued or criticized. The purpose of the brainstorming is to develop a comprehensive list of all possible sources, not just the likely ones. *The cause and effect diagram* provides a convenient fishbone format for displaying these root causes, as shown in Figure 6.2.

Once a list of potential sources has been developed, the team may use some focusing tools to reduce the list. Here, the goal is to trim the list to a manageable handful that can be included in a detailed analysis. An *interrelationship digraph* can be used to look for relationships between the causes. In this approach, each cause (an issue) is compared to each of the other causes, and the question asked: "Does issue A influence or cause issue B?" Arrows are drawn from the cause to the effect, where such a relationship is thought to exist. In this way, root causes can be determined by identifying the issues with the most arrows coming out. The items with the most arrows going

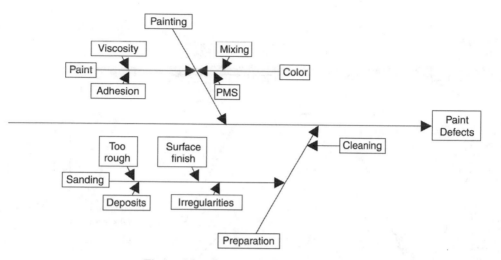

Figure 6.2   Cause and effect diagram.

into them are key outcomes. These items might be closely tied to a useful metric, or could be better descriptors for the problem. An example is shown in Figure 6.3.

The *nominal group technique* can also be used to reach consensus on the list of causes to investigate. In this approach, each team member selects and ranks their choice of the top several items. The choices with the most votes or most weighted votes are included in the subsequent analysis. Of course, if the analysis fails to attribute the variation to any of the choices, further analysis will be needed to look for other significant factors. In this case, the team will take another look at the original list of potential sources on the cause and effect diagram.

The team may collect samples from the process belonging to the populations defined by these potential sources of variation. The samples can be tested to see if they are statistically different from each other. For example, the team may question if the cycle times for product A assemblies are different from product B assemblies. A 20-piece sample of product A assemblies is randomly collected, and its average and standard deviation calculated as 11.7 and 2.2, respectively. A 10-piece sample of product B is collected, with a calculated average of 13.2 and standard deviation of 2.5. Based on these samples, are the averages of the two products different?

It is obvious that the sample averages (11.7 and 13.2) are different. However, if we were to take a second sample of product A, its average would likely be different from the first sample. So how much difference in the samples is to be expected from product A? How different does the true average of product B have to be for the difference to be detected with these samples?

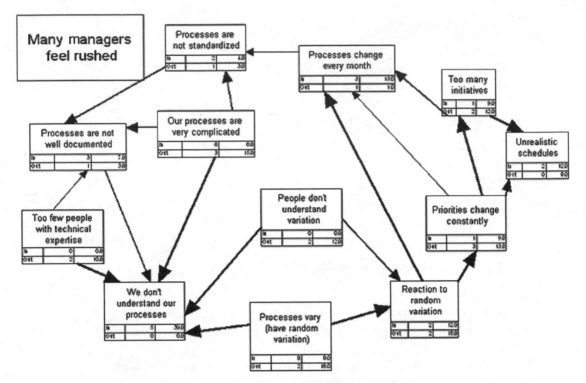

Figure 6.3   An interrelationship diagraph.

An *hypothesis test* can be performed to test whether the averages of product A and product B are identical. This hypothesis test on the mean of two samples (described in detail in Part 3) tests the null hypothesis that the mean of population A is equal to the mean of population B. A pooled standard deviation is calculated as follows:

$$S_p^2 = \frac{(n_1 - 1)S_1^2 + (n_2 - 1)S_2^2}{n_1 + n_2 - 2}$$

$$S_p^2 = \frac{(20 - 1)(2.2)^2 + (30 - 1)(2.5)^2}{20 + 30 - 2} = 5.69$$

The *t* statistic is calculated as:

$$t_0 = \frac{\overline{X}_1 - \overline{X}_2}{S_p\sqrt{\dfrac{1}{n_1} + \dfrac{1}{n_2}}} = \frac{11.7 - 13.2}{2.39\sqrt{\dfrac{1}{20} + \dfrac{1}{30}}} = -1.623$$

Since this value does not exceed the critical value of the *t* statistic for 28 degrees of freedom at a significance of 5%, we fail to reject the null hypothesis. Using these two samples, it cannot be proven that the population means are different.

There are some predictable problems that can occur with hypothesis testing that should be considered. The key assumptions of the tests, which should be validated for the samples, include:

- Samples must be random, and must be representative of the population under investigation. In surveys, low response rates would typically provide extreme value estimates (that is, the subpopulation of people who have strong opinions one way or the other).
- Samples must be from a stable population. If the population is changing over time, then estimates will be biased, with associated increases in alpha and beta risks. SPC charts provide an indication of statistical stability.
- Many of the hypothesis tests, and associated alpha and beta risks, are dependent on normality of the population. If the population is significantly non-normal, then the tests are not meaningful. Goodness of fit tests are used to verify this assumption. Nonparametric tests can be used if the populations are significantly non-normal.
- Some tests additionally require equal variance, which can be tested using equality of variance tests. If the populations do not have equal variances, then the data can be transformed (see Transformations in Part 3).
- The failure to reject is not an acceptance of the null hypothesis. Rather, it means there is not *yet* ample proof that the hypothesis should be rejected.
- The alpha risk is real!
- Consider the *power* of the samples to detect real differences.

Alpha is the probability of rejecting the null hypothesis when it is true. For example, if alpha is 0.05 (as used in the above example), then there are 5 chances in 100 of incorrectly rejecting a true null hypothesis. If *n* investigators are independently researching the issue, then the probability that at least one researcher (incorrectly) rejects the null hypothesis is $1 - (1 - \alpha)^n$. For example, the chance that 1 of 10 researchers (i.e., $n = 10$), each with an alpha risk of 0.05, will (incorrectly) reject the true null hypothesis is 40%! Consider this the next time the headlines in your newspaper report the "*surprising results of a new study.*" Would the unsurprising results of the other nine researchers warrant a headline? The alpha risk demonstrates the need for replication of analysis results.

The *beta risk* is the probability of not rejecting a false null hypothesis. Usually, the *power* of the test (the probability of correctly rejecting the false null hypothesis) is more interesting. It provides a quantitative reminder that even though the test is not rejected, the null hypothesis may still be false.

What influences the ability to correctly reject the false null hypothesis?

Larger differences between the null and alternative means make it easier to statistically detect the differences. Smaller population sigma, or larger sample sizes, cause the distributions to become more narrow, and hence there is less overlap between the null and actual mean. A large *significance level* implies that the tail regions (which may tend to overlap) will have less influence in our decision to accept or reject. This is shown in Figure 6.4.

If we fail to reject a test, larger sample sizes may be required to detect the difference, depending on the population sigma and alpha values. When the alpha value (the significance level) of the test is defined, the beta risk has (perhaps unknowingly) been defined as well. Unfortunately, the beta risk is not precisely known, since the true condition is unknown.

Operating characteristic (OC) curves (which provide beta risk) and power curves (which provide power estimates) are analogous methods to determine beta (or power) given sample size, delta (the difference), sigma, and alpha. OC and power curves are sometimes provided in statistical textbooks.

Some software (including Minitab) or online links (such as http://calculators. stat.ucla.edu/powercalc/) will provide estimates of:

- Power given sample size, delta, sigma, alpha
- Sample size to detect delta at given alpha, power
- Optimal sample size to minimize alpha, power

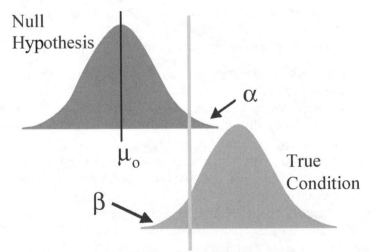

Figure 6.4   A stated alpha level defines the beta risk given the sample size, sigma, and difference between the null and the true conditions.

In the above example, the minimum sample size required (for each sample) using a t test with alpha of 0.05 and a power of 0.90 to detect a difference in population means of 1.5, assuming the standard deviation is 2.4, is 55 (using Minitab or the Web link provided above). In other words, if a minimum sample size of 55 is used for both product A and product B, then the test would detect a difference of 1.5 or more in the true means of the populations (assuming alpha and beta risks, normal distribution, and equal variance of the populations).

Nonparametric tests may also be used, particularly when distributional assumptions cannot be met. A *nonparametric test* is one in which there are no distributional requirements, such as normality, for the validity of the test. Typically, nonparametric tests require larger sample sizes than the parametric tests.

When there are more than two populations to compare, general ANOVA, or analysis of variance, techniques are applied. ANOVA provides a means of comparing the variation within each subset (or treatment) of data to the variation between the different subsets of data. The between subset variation is a reflection of the possible differences between the subset averages. The within subset variation, for each subset, is a reflection of the inherent variation observed when sampling from the subset repeatedly.

The null hypothesis tested by the ANOVA is that all the subset averages are equal. The F statistic is used to compare the mean square treatment (the average between subset variation) with the mean square error (the sum of squares of the residuals). The assumptions in the test are that the distribution for each subset is normal, and the subsets have equal variance (although their means may be different). The null hypothesis that the subset means are equal is rejected when the p value for the F test is less than 0.05, implying that at least one of the subset averages is different.

For example, using the data in Table 6.1, we can test whether the cycle times shown for the four products are equal.

The results from Microsoft Excel are shown in Table 6.2.

The low p value indicates that the null hypothesis of equal means should be rejected: one or more of the product averages are significantly different. The between group variation is much larger than the within group variation.

The techniques described in this section provide a means of determining statistical differences between sets of data. The results of these types of analysis are interesting, yet not compelling. The observational data used in the analysis may be biased, due to the manner in which it is collected, or confounded with other factors that were not measured or recorded during data collection. These confounding factors, rather than the factor under investigation which appears significant, may be the underlying cause for the statistical difference.

Table 6.1.   Example cycle time data for ANOVA.

Product A	Product B	Product C	Product D
159	180	167	174
161	174	163	182
164	180	160	171
166	184	165	176
158	177	161	179
162	178	158	175

Table 6.2.   Example results from Microsoft Excel.

SUMMARY				
Groups	**Count**	**Sum**	**Average**	**Variance**
Product A	6	970	161.6667	9.066667
Product B	6	1073	178.8333	11.36667
Product C	6	974	162.3333	11.06667
Product D	6	1057	176.1667	14.96667

ANOVA					
Source of Variation	**SS**	**df**	**MS**	**F**	**P value**	**F crit**
Between groups	1464.167	3	488.0556	42.01339	8.03E − 09	3.098393
Within groups	232.3333	20	11.61667			
Total	1696.5	23				

As a result, the findings from these analyses should serve as input to more rigorous techniques for understanding causal relationships, specifically designed experiments.

Determining Process Drivers

Designed experiments are a critical part of many successful improvement projects. While statistical process control provides a view of the past performance of the process, designed experiments provide a view of the process potential. They allow an understanding of the sources of the common and special causes of variation seen on the control chart, or the variation between subsets of a population.

In a designed experiment, each of the factors suspected of being significant is varied, several at a time over a wide range, and the process response (or responses) are measured. Manipulating the factors over a wide range provides the best chance of detecting a change in the process that may otherwise be too subtle to detect. (A detailed discussion of these techniques is presented in the Design of Experiments section in Part 3.)

How does a designed experiment differ from the traditional experiments often first taught in grade school? In traditional experiments, each factor is varied one at a time, such as shown in Table 6.3. An initial trial (trial 1) is run with each of the factors (cycle time, personalized response, and response type) set at its low level. The response (customer satisfaction) is measured, establishing a baseline.

A second trial is then run to measure the effect of cycle time. The difference between the baseline response (trial 1) and the observed response for trial 2 is assumed to be the effect of the manipulated factor. In this case, raising the cycle time from low to high results in a decrease in customer satisfaction of 14 units.

Likewise, the effect of a personalized response is estimated by comparing trials 3 and 1 and the effects of response type by comparing trials 4 and 1. In this way, the effect of the personalized response is estimated as a decrease in customer satisfaction of 7 units, and the effect of phone versus e-mail as a decrease of 8 units in customer satisfaction score.

Based on these observations, customer satisfaction is maximized by setting the factors as follows: cycle time: low; personalized response: no; response type: phone.

The problem with the traditional one-factor-at-a-time experiment is that it ignores the possible effects of interactions. The interaction plot shown in Figure 6.5 is from a designed experiment of the same process. At the high cycle

Table 6.3. Example traditional experiment.

Trial	Cycle Time	Personal Response	Response Type	Customer Satisfaction
1	Low	No	Phone	35
2	High	No	Phone	21
3	Low	Yes	Phone	28
4	Low	No	E-mail	27

time setting (shown by the line labeled 330.000), a satisfaction score of 21.0 is observed at the *no* condition of personalized response. This is trial 2 from Table 6.3. Trial 3 is shown on the line labeled 210.000 at the *yes* condition of personalized response.

On the 210.000 cycle time setting, there is very little change in the customer satisfaction score moving from a no to a yes condition of personalized response (left to right along the line). This implies that personalized response makes little difference when cycle time is low.

However, on the 330.000 cycle time setting, there is a very large change in customer satisfaction score moving from a no to a yes personalized response (left to right along the line). This implies that personalized response is a significant contributor to the change in customer satisfaction score when cycle time is high.

The estimate of the personalized response effect changes, depending on whether the effect is measured at low cycle time or high cycle time. This implies there is an *interaction* between personalized response and cycle time. This interaction is revealed by the nonparallel lines on the interaction plot, such as shown in Figure 6.5.

When interactions are ignored, improvement efforts may achieve haphazard results:

• Significant factors may appear unimportant when other factors are not manipulated at the same time, as shown in the example.
• Process improvement may only be realized when other factors remain constant. The improvement may seem to "disappear" as the process return to a prior level of performance for unknown reasons.
• The possibility of reducing the effect of a factor by minimizing variation of another will not be realized. This Taguchi approach to

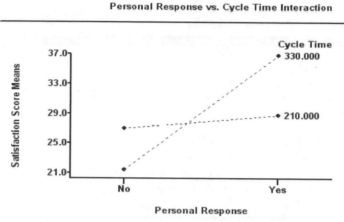

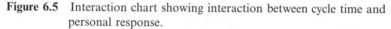

Figure 6.5   Interaction chart showing interaction between cycle time and
personal response.

robust design of processes can be seen in the example. Since the effect
of the personalized response (a significant cost driver) is negligible at
low cycle time, then reducing cycle time dampens the impact of the
personalized response.

Historical data is often analyzed with ANOVA and multiple regression
techniques to investigate patterns or significance of process factors. This so-
called *data mining* has some usefulness, but it also lacks many of the key attributes of designed experiments.

Designed experiments estimate parameter effects with less data than data
mining by using an *orthogonal array* of data. An orthogonal array is a minimum set of data conditions designed to independently estimate specific factors and their interactions. The data is collected over a relatively short period
of time, allowing the experimenters to control the conditions under which the
data is collected. Casual factors such as environmental conditions and personnel are observed or controlled, with anomalies recorded.

Historical, or happenstance, data often is incapable of detecting interactions. The effects of interactions can only be estimated when the data includes
the necessary combinations of factors, randomized to remove bias from main
effects. The data may not include sufficient variation in each factor or interaction to statistically estimate a significance of the parameter. The uncontrolled nature of the data collection may allow other factors (often
unrecorded) to contribute to noise in the data that may cloud the effects of

Table 6.4.   Example designed experiment.

Factor A	Factor B	Factor C	Factor D	Response
10	200	45	12	49
10	200	15	2	42
10	20	45	2	88
10	20	15	12	87
5	200	45	2	67
5	200	15	12	64
5	20	45	12	80
5	20	15	2	75

each factor, or be confounded with factors that seem important (as described at the end of the prior section). Since the data is not run in random order, it is possible for unrecognized factors that vary over time to bias the results.

Regression analysis may be applied to the results of the designed experiment to determine the significance of factors. In this way, a seemingly complex process with many variables can be reduced to only its few significant factors.

For example, the results of a designed experiment are shown in Table 6.4. Four main factors (A, B, C, and D) and their two factor interactions are estimated with an eight-run experiment. As discussed in Factorial Designs in Part 3, an eight-run experiment can fully estimate three factors (A, B, C) and all their interactions (AB, AC, BC, ABC), leaving one run to estimate the mean. A fourth factor can be added by aliasing it with the three-factor interaction (i.e., D = ABC). *Aliasing* allows more factors to be included in the experiment, or conversely allows a given number of factors to be estimated with less experimental runs, since a 16-run experiment would be needed to fully estimate four factors and their interactions.

The effect of aliasing factor D with the ABC interaction is that the aliased parameters are *confounded* with one another. This implies that the parameters cannot be estimated independently of one another. When factor D is aliased with the ABC interaction, then when we estimate the effect of factor D, we cannot be sure whether the effect is due to factor D, the ABC interaction, or a linear combination of D and ABC.

The intended aliasing also creates some unintended confounding between all the other possible combinations of the aliased pair. We construct the confounded pairs by moving the equal sign through the $ABC = D$ equation.

$$\text{If } ABC = D, \text{ then } A = BCD; \ B = ACD; \ C = ABD;$$
$$AB = CD; \ AC = BD; \ AD = BC$$

The eight-run experiment will estimate each of the main factors (confounded with a three-factor interaction) and the two-factor interactions (confounded with each other). The analysis provided by this experiment is scant, since there are no additional runs added for estimating error. An effects plot, shown in Figure 6.6, displays the absolute value of the (coded) effects in a Pareto chart. Larger effects have higher significance. A line of significance, such as provided in Minitab software, provides the criteria for parameter selection. A normal or half-normal plot of the effects provides similar results.

In this screening design, there were no extra runs to estimate error, so the ANOVA table is of little value. Recall that at least one run (i.e., unique design condition) is needed to estimate each parameter, including main effects (main factors), their interactions, and the overall mean (or intercept). An eight-run experiment can estimate at most seven factors and interactions. If estimates are required for only six factors and interactions, then one run is available for estimating error. There are two choices to resolve this problem: either remove one or more of the required parameters from the analysis, or add more runs to the design. For example, the interaction AC (confounded with BD) appears insignificant, so perhaps removing it from the analysis would free up a run to estimate error. Instead, the design was extended by *folding* the design.

Folding the design is a technique for extending the design by repeating one or more randomly selected runs, or by replicating the entire design. In either case, the additional trials should be run in random order, and treated as a block. Of course, each additional run increases the time and resources, and hence the cost, needed for the experiment. On the other hand, each replicate also improves the ability to detect the statistical significance of a given effect.

A design is folded by replicating the design, substituting the low levels with high levels and high values with low levels for one or more of the factors. If we fold on just one factor (i.e., substitute the plus and minus signs for one of the factors), then that factor and its two factor interactions will be free of confounding. If we substitute the plus and minus signs for the entire design,

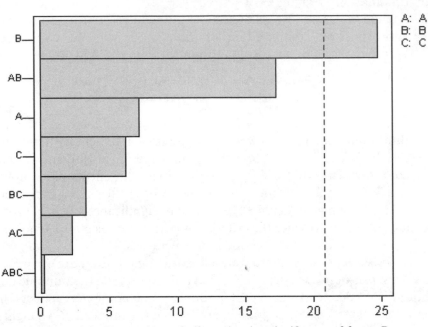

Figure 6.6   Pareto chart of effects showing significance of factor B.

then all main factors will be free of confounding with other main factors and two factor interactions.

In this case, the design was extended by folding on the entire design. The ANOVA table for the complete design is provided in Table 6.5. As described in more detail in the multiple regression section of Part 3, the ANOVA table provides an estimate of the regression significance (using the F statistic), providing there is at least one extra run to calculate error. The regression for this example is highly significant. The adjusted R^2 value is .97, which indicates that most of the variation in the data is accounted for by the regression model.

The significance of the individual parameters (main factors, interactions, and the blocking factor from the fold) can be estimated using the Student's t statistic. The graphical techniques for effects plotting just discussed should agree with these t test results. Parameters with a p value greater than 0.1 may be removed from the model. P values between 0.05 and 0.1 are marginal; these parameters may be left in the model until more data is obtained.

Table 6.5. Example ANOVA for folded DOE.

ANOVA					
	df	SS	MS	F	Significance F
Regression	8	4318.5	539.8125	65.22006	6.94E–06
Residual	7	57.9375	8.276786		
Total	15	4376.438			

The regression results for the folded design are shown in Table 6.6. Factors B and AB appear highly significant, and factor D is highly insignificant (since the p value is much greater than 0.1). As a result, factor D can be removed from the analysis, and the analysis redone to refine the model. (Recall that factors or interactions should only be removed one at a time.) Subsequent regression analysis was performed by removing BC, then AC, then finally the blocking factor (one at a time). The final analysis is shown in Table 6.7. The final adjusted R^2 value is .975.

The predicted regression model (rounded to the first decimal) is shown in the Coefficients column as:

$$Response = 68.2 - 2.4 * A - 14.6 * B + 1.6 * C - 6.9 * A * B$$

This equation can be used to predict the response at any condition within the range of the data by substituting values of factors A, B, and C. The effect of a unit change in any given factor (when all other factors remain constant) is obtained directly from the coefficients. For example, an increase of one unit in factor A causes a decrease of 1.4 units of the response.

A number of tests can be applied to the residuals (the error between the predicted model and the observed data). Any abnormality of the residuals would be cause for concern of the model. Outliers indicate problems with specific data points, and trends or dependence may indicate issues with the data collection process as a whole (as discussed in the Residuals Analysis section of Part 3).

The factors and their interactions can be further analyzed by breaking down the total error (represented by the residuals) into its components: pure error and lack of fit. *Pure error* is experimental error, the differences between repeated runs of the same condition. The remaining error is due to a poor fit of the model

Table 6.6. Regression results for folded DOE.

	Coefficients	Standard Error	t Stat	P value
Intercept	68.1875	0.719235	94.80558	3.83E − 12
A	− 2.4375	0.719235	− 3.38902	0.011615
B	− 14.5625	0.719235	− 20.2472	1.8E − 07
C	1.5625	0.719235	2.172447	0.066377
D	− 0.0625	0.719235	− 0.0869	0.933186
AB = CD	− 6.9375	0.719235	− 9.64566	2.71E − 05
AC = BD	− 0.8125	0.719235	− 1.12967	0.295833
AD = BC	0.0625	0.719235	0.086898	0.933186
Block	0.8125	0.719235	1.129672	0.295833

Table 6.7. Regression results for folded DOE (after removal of terms).

	Coefficients	Standard Error	t Stat	P value
Intercept	68.1875	0.670767	101.6559	1.04E − 17
A	− 2.4375	0.670767	− 3.6339	0.00393
B	− 14.5625	0.670767	− 21.7102	2.21E − 10
C	1.5625	0.670767	2.329421	0.03991
AB	− 6.9375	0.670767	− 10.3426	5.27E − 07

to the data. Error due to *lack of fit* is caused by either a curvature in the response surface that is not estimated with the fitted first-degree model or main factor or interaction effects that were not included in the experiment.

The ANOVA for the final model is shown in Table 6.8. The sum of square residual term (79.1875) includes both pure error and lack of fit error. Pure

Table 6.8.   ANOVA for folded DOE (after removal of terms).

	df	SS	MS	F	Significance F
Regression	4	4297.25	1074.313	149.2336	1.67E − 09
Residual	11	79.1875	7.198864		
Total	15	4376.438			

error is calculated as 68.5 using the sum of squared deviations between each observation and the mean at that condition. The lack of fit error is calculated as 10.6875 using the difference between the total (residuals) error and the pure error. The F statistic is calculated as:

$$F = \frac{SS_{LOF}/(n-p)}{SS_{PE}/(N-n)} = \frac{10.6875/(8-5)}{68.5/(16-8)} = 0.42$$

The calculated F value for the lack of fit is less than the critical value $F_{.05,3,8}$ of 4.07, so the null hypothesis that the model is adequate cannot be rejected. In this case (failing to reject that the model is adequate), the significance of the fitted model can be tested using the F statistic applied to the residuals, as in Table 6.8. If the residuals are small (as demonstrated by significance of the regression term) and pass the other general tests described in the Residual Analysis section of Part 3, then the model would seem to fit the data adequately and can be used to determine optimal combinations for the response.

If the lack of fit test is rejected, then the model should be updated with additional main factors, interactions, or higher order terms. A quick test for Surface Curvature (described in Part 3) helps rule out higher order terms.

Recall that the *power* of a statistical test is the probability of rejecting the null hypothesis when the null hypothesis is false. In this case, the null hypothesis is that the coefficients of the regression are zero; the alternative hypothesis is that at least one of the coefficients is non-zero.

Minitab provides a convenient way to test our ability to estimate effects of given magnitude, or conversely to estimate the number of design replicates needed to detect effects at a given power for a given experimental design.

For example, How many design replicates are needed to estimate an effect with a magnitude 20 for a 2-level factorial design with 5 factors, 8 corner points, and no center points when sigma is 17 (using $\alpha = \beta = .05$)?

Using Minitab's Stat/Power & Sample Size/2 Level Factorial Design function (alpha is entered using the Options button), five replicates, or 40 runs, are needed.

The various parameters can be manipulated in the Minitab dialog box to estimate their impact. For example, a larger effect, such as 25, would only require four replicates. If the power of the experiment is reduced to a 75% chance of detecting an effect with magnitude of 25, then only three replicates are needed.

The purpose of this discussion is to emphasize the limitations of an experiment. The results must be replicated before proceeding to implementation in the improve stage.

Recommended Tools

The following tools (discussed in detail in Part 3) are applicable to the analyze stage of DMAIC:

Value Stream Analysis

- *Flowcharts* and *process maps* to discover process complexities which contribute to variation or longer cycle times.
- *PERT analysis* to identify the critical path for cycle time reduction.
- *Spaghetti diagram* to identify unnecessary movement of material or personnel.
- *Velocity* to prioritize cycle time improvement opportunities.

Analyze Sources of Variation

- *Box-whisker chart* to graphically compare the location and variation of various processes or categories of products or services.
- *Cause and effect diagram* to brainstorm potential underlying process factors, which can be investigated in a designed experiment.
- *Confidence interval on mean*, *confidence interval on proportion*, and *contingency tables* to compare the mean of samples from different process conditions.
- *Failure modes and effects analysis* to define high-risk activities.
- *Hypothesis testing of two samples* and *nonparametric test on equality of means* to compare sample means from different conditions.
- SPC control charts, including *C, Np, P, U, Individual-X, X-Bar*, and *EWMA charts*, to differentiate between special and common causes of variation.

- *Multi-vari plots* to categorize variation and investigate interactions among factors.
- *Pareto charts* to focus on areas with greatest opportunity.
- *Histograms* and *stem and leaf plots* to graphically display the process output relative to the requirements.
- *Goodness of fit tests* and *probability plotting* to verify the statistical distributions assumed in the various statistical tools.
- *Work breakdown structure* to break down a problem into its potential components, to be addressed in the improve stage.

Determine Process Drivers

- *Design of experiments*, *factorial designs*, *screening designs*, and *evolutionary operations* to define efficient data collection experiments.
- *Regression analysis*, *residuals analysis*, and *scatter diagrams* to identify the significant process factors.
- *Transformations* to stabilize variance or calculate meaningful response.
- *Interaction charts* to graphically depict the relationship between two factors' effect on the mean.
- *Interrelationship digraph* to identify key process drivers (root causes) and key outcomes when potential problems can interact to cause larger problems.
- *Process decision program charts* to understand root causes of problems.

In addition, the consensus building tools noted at the end of the define stage are also applied, as needed.

Quiz for Chapter 6

1. If the cycle time of a process is predicted by cycle time $= 5.25 * $ (number of items) $+ 4.3$, with a correlation of 0.8, then the predicted cycle time for six items is:
   a. 54.1.
   b. 28.64.
   c. 35.8.
   d. Cycle time cannot be predicted with the available information.

2. Error in regression analysis is due to:
   a. Using the wrong model.
   b. Missing an independent variable.

    c. Measurement error.

    d. All of the above.

3. In the expression cycle time (in minutes) $= 3 + 1.4 *$ (number of orders) $- 2.1 *$ (number of clerks) $- .034 *$ (process distance):

    a. Removing one clerk will increase the cycle time by 2.1 minutes.

    b. Removing one clerk will decrease the cycle time by 2.1 minutes.

    c. Adding one clerk will increase the cycle time by 2.1 minutes.

    d. None of the above.

4. If an ANOVA analysis does not provide results of the F test, then:

    a. We probably did not run enough trials to estimate error.

    b. The software must be flawed.

    c. We can use the p values to determine significance of factors.

    d. We should try adding factors.

5. Which of the following is a form of waste in lean thinking? (A) Errors requiring rework. (B) Work with no immediate customer, resulting in work in progress inventory. (C) Unnecessary process steps. (D) Waiting by employees as unfinished work is completed. (E) Design of product or processes that don't meet the customer's needs.

    a. Item A.

    b. Items A and C.

    c. Items A, C, D, and E.

    d. All of the above.

6. A proper value stream analysis includes:

    a. All the steps necessary to transform the raw material to the finished good.

    b. Each of your company's processes.

    c. All the steps necessary to solve a customer's problems.

    d. Choices a and c.

7. The application of 5S in an office environment:

    a. Is generally not necessary and a waste of time.

    b. Is helpful to reduce the total cycle time.

    c. Provides a means of documenting errors.

    d. Ensures that output meets the demand.

8. In brainstorming the possible causes for a particular customer complaint, a good tool to use is:

    a. QFD.

    b. Fishbone diagram.

    c. Affinity diagram.
    d. PDPC.

9. After constructing a cause and effect diagram, the team should:
    a. Develop techniques for preventing each of the causes.
    b. Determine which of the causes are most prevalent.
    c. Exclude causes where cost to prevent exceeds their benefit.
    d. Choices a and c.

10. An abundance of decision points in a process flowchart generally indicates:
    a. Process complexity, with a potential for error.
    b. A process where the potential for human error has been minimized.
    c. A process whose cycle time has been optimized.
    d. All of the above.

7

CHAPTER

Improve Stage

After understanding the types and sources of variation in the analyze stage, the improve stage can begin to define and implement changes necessary for process improvement.

Objectives

There are several issues to be completed within the improve stage of DMAIC:

- New process operating conditions are determined.
- Benefits associated with the proposed solution are estimated by the team and approved by the sponsor.
- Failure modes for the new process are investigated and addressed.
- Process improvement is implemented and verified.

The outcome of each of these steps may cause a reconsideration of the assumptions from prior steps, forcing further analysis of the proposed improvement. This diligence is often necessary for sustained improvement.

This stage is where the rubber meets the road. It defines the improvements and cost reductions that sustain the program. It forces the team to strive for new levels of performance and become true agents of change. Management support at this point is critical, as is their buy-in. The team must work closely with their sponsor to seek direction, authority, and approval before change can be implemented.

Defining the New Process

The most obvious outcome of the improve stage is the definition of new practices to replace the current operating procedures. This change can be realized as a new process flow, or as a change in operating conditions for the existing process. In some cases, the change in operating conditions mandates a new process flow, or vice versa, so both types of change are necessary.

To truly drive a sustained reduction in process variation, process improvements must concentrate on controlling the underlying factors that predict future outcomes. This helps prevent problems before they occur. In the analyze stage, process drivers were identified that contribute to process variation. In the improve stage, these process drivers will be further investigated to define the settings necessary to achieve optimal process performance.

There are two aspects, or objectives, for optimization. Traditionally, *optimization* involves finding the best combination of factor levels to maximize (or minimize) the response. For example, it may be important to investigate the specific concentrations of reagents and temperature of reaction necessary to achieve the highest degree of product purity. In a service process, the optimal allocation of staffing and services may be needed to minimize the cycle time for a key process.

More recently, perhaps due to the influence of Taguchi, there is an increased interest in variation reduction. In this scope, optimization leads to the best combination of factor levels to produce the least variation in the response at a satisfactory average response. For example, the chemical process customer may be most interested in a consistent purity level. This is often the case when customers can make adjustments to their process over the long term, but short-term adjustments to deal with batch-to-batch variation are costly. This happens in service processes as well. An oil change service that provides a consistent two-hour service is often preferred to one that occasionally delivers with half-hour service, but sometimes makes the customer wait four hours. Consistency enhances the ability to plan, which improves resource utilization. Inconsistency mandates complexity, which comes at a cost, as is often discovered in the earlier stages of DMAIC.

When optimal solutions to problems are sought, and the process model is not clearly understood, the response surface methods are generally the most useful. *Response surface* designs are special case designed experiments that allow optimal regions to be located efficiently with usually only a few iterations. The first-order regression model developed in the analyze stage serves as the starting point. This first-order model is a good assumption, since the starting point is usually far enough away from the optimum so that it is likely to be dominated by first-order effects, and a detailed mapping of the response region far away from the optimum is not needed. Data is collected through experimentation to determine the path toward optimality using the first-order model. Tests for curvature indicate when a local minimum, maximum, or saddle point (a combination of the two) is reached.

Using three- or five-level central composite designs, the response surface can be mapped using a higher-order model. Although response surface plots such as shown in Figure 7.1 are visually appealing, the classic contour plot (such as shown in Figure 7.2) is often more useful for its direct approach. Although these plots can display only two process factors at a time, the mathematics behind the analysis extends to additional factors. Software allows these techniques to be readily applied, then verified with additional process trials.

Evolutionary operation (EVOP) offers another approach for iteratively finding an optimal solution. The advantage of EVOP is that the process does not need to be shut down, as in a designed experiment, to run conditions that would generally be outside the normal operating region for the process. Instead, the EVOP slowly moves toward an optimum by gradually extending the operating region in the direction of improvement. As such, EVOP takes many

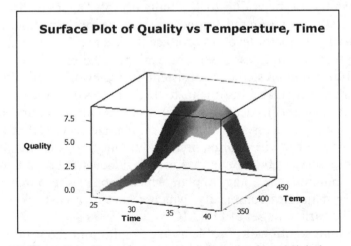

Figure 7.1   Example response surface plot from Minitab.

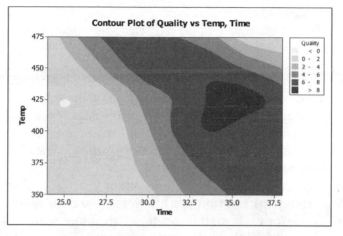

Figure 7.2   Example contour plot from Minitab.

more iterations than a response surface design to find the optimal solution, yet is simple enough to allow process personnel to make the adjustments and monitor the results as part of daily operations.

SIMULATIONS

When a process model is known, either from experimentation or by design, then process simulations can be used to find optimal solutions. While a regression model is *deterministic* in nature, in that the factors in the models are fixed values, factors in processes are random variables. Simulations provide a means of using probability estimates for the random variables to discover the impact of their joint probabilities.

Simulations have several advantages over experimentation. They are certainly cheaper in almost all cases, allowing the test of many more conditions than is practically possible with experiments. This makes them very suitable for "what-if scenarios," to test the response under worst-case circumstances. Simulations can also be used for planning, such as in a DMADV (design for Six Sigma) approach to estimate the effects of increased business activity on resources, or for new product processing.

Pyzdek (2003) lists several key uses of simulations:

- Verifying analytical solutions
- Studying dynamic situations
- Determining significant components and variables in a complex system

- Determining variables' interactions
- Studying effects of change without risk, cost, and time of experimentation
- Teaching

Simulations can be used to investigate alternative process scenarios for a given improvement strategy, allowing estimation of the solution's robustness to variation in input parameters. Proposed changes in resources, such as afforded by cross-training or staff reallocation, can be quickly analyzed with respect to cycle time. The effects of task prioritization, task order, and multitasking can also be measured.

The input parameters for the simulation include a model of the process, and a suitable probability distribution (with parameters, such as the mean, and standard deviation) for each random variable. In some cases, it will be more convenient to approximate the distribution with an alternate distribution. For example, the normal distribution provides a reasonable approximation to the binomial distribution for large samples.

The simulation, sometimes referred to as a *Monte Carlo simulation*, will generate a frequency distribution for the resulting process response. In a Monte Carlo simulation, a large number of trials (5,000 or more) are run. Each time a trial is run, a random number is generated for the response. The result is calculated and stored as the *forecast* of the result. After generating a large number of forecasts, the distributional parameters of the response may be estimated.

Of course, the outcome is only as good as the prediction model, so actual data should be used to verify the model, either at the onset (if the model is based on the current conditions) or at deployment of the improvements (if the model is developed to predict performance of a new process).

A variety of software tools are available for process simulations. Two examples will be shown in this text: the Sigma Flow software and Microsoft Excel. The Sigma Flow software will use the process map as its starting point, providing a great deal of convenience and intuition in its functionality. It can also be used to develop and store the project charter and its control plan, as well as the SIPOC, FMEA, and cause and effect analyses recommended in this book. At the time of this printing, control charts and additional statistical functionality were being added to provide a more complete solution for the Six Sigma project team.

Microsoft Excel provides a basic level of simulation when compared to general use simulation software. The simulation functionality is available in their Random Number Generation feature in the Tools/Data Analysis menu. The Data Analysis Pack is an add-on that is available on the installation CD, but not always installed by default.

Many common distributions are included within Excel's capabilities, including normal, binomial, Poisson, and more. For a given process parameter, its distribution and the distributional parameters must be specified.

Other distributions may also be modeled, such as outlined in Table 7.1. For example, random numbers from an exponential distribution may be generated by first generating a set of random numbers for a uniform distribution between 0 and 1. These results are then converted to an exponential by taking the natural log of a given number, and multiplying by -1 times the mean of the desired exponential distribution.

An example simulation may be modeled for the four steps of a critical path shown in Table 7.2. The model in this case is a simple addition of the cycle times for each of the four steps in the process. Excel generates a set of normal and uniform distributed data directly for steps 1 through 3. The exponential data for step 4 is generated from a separate set of uniform data, as described above.

The total cycle time, the sum of the cycle times for the process steps, is shown in Figure 7.3. The resulting distribution is non-normal, which can be verified using the normal probability plot and the K-S goodness of fit test. If the data is assumed to come from a controlled non-normal process, the Capability Index indicates the process will not meet the requirements for a 45-hour cycle time.

The effect of cycle time reduction for each of the process steps can then be evaluated. What is the effect of reducing the variation in step 1 by 50%? How much will total cycle time be reduced if the average cycle time for step 2 is reduced to 5 hours? If it costs twice as much to reduce the variation in step 2, is the reduction in step 1 preferred? The effect of each of these scenarios, and many more, can be easily estimated using the simulation tool.

In a similar way, the effect of process variation on more complicated regression functions can be easily estimated. The effect of tightly controlling temperature on the consistency of the product purity can be evaluated without first having to implement an expensive temperature control mechanism.

It should be clear that simulations offer a relatively simple and cost-effective method of evaluating process improvement schemes. Since the simulation is a direct reflection of the assumed model and its parameters, the results of the simulation must always be verified in realistic process conditions. Regardless, the cost of data acquisition is generally greatly reduced by the knowledge gained in the process simulations.

REDEFINING PROCESS FLOW

The results of the value stream analysis provided insight on the non-value-added activities that can be reduced or eliminated in the improve stage. The

Table 7.1   Random number generators.

DISTRIBUTION	PROBABILITY DENSITY FUNCTION	RANDOM NUMBER GENERATOR[§]
Uniform	$f(x) = \dfrac{1}{b-a}, a \le x \le b$	$x = a + (b-a)r$
Exponential	$f(x) = \lambda e^{-\lambda x}, 0 < x < \infty$	$x = -\dfrac{1}{\lambda}\ln r$
Normal	$f(x) = \dfrac{1}{\sigma\sqrt{2\pi}}\exp\left[-\dfrac{1}{2}\left(\dfrac{x-\mu}{\sigma}\right)^2\right],$ $-\infty < x < \infty$	$x_1 = [\sqrt{-2\ln r_1}\,\cos(2\pi r_2)]\sigma + \mu$ $x_2 = [\sqrt{-2\ln r_1}\,\sin(2\pi r_2)]\sigma + \mu$ [†]
Lognormal	$f(x) = \dfrac{1}{\sigma x\sqrt{2\pi}}\exp\left[-\dfrac{1}{2}\left(\dfrac{\ln x-\mu}{\sigma}\right)^2\right],$ $x > 0$	$x_1 = \exp[\sqrt{-2\ln r_1}\,\cos(2\pi r_2)]\sigma + \mu$ $x_2 = [\sqrt{-2\ln r_1}\,\sin(2\pi r_2)]\sigma + \mu$ [†]
Weibull	$f(x) = \dfrac{\beta x^{\beta-1}}{\theta^\beta}\exp\left(\dfrac{x}{\theta}\right)^\beta, x > 0$	$x = \theta(-\ln r)^{1/\beta}$
Poisson	$f(x) = \dfrac{e^{-\lambda t}(\lambda t)^x}{x!}, x = 0, 1, 2, \ldots, \infty$	$x = \begin{cases} 0, -\dfrac{1}{\lambda}\ln r > t & \ddagger \\ x, \displaystyle\sum_{i=1}^{x} -\dfrac{1}{\lambda}\ln r_i < t < \sum_{i=1}^{x+1} -\dfrac{1}{\lambda}\ln r_i \end{cases}$
Chi-square	$f(x) = \dfrac{1}{2^{v/2}\Gamma(v/2)}x^{(v/2-1)}e^{-x/2}, x > 0$	$x = \displaystyle\sum_{i=1}^{v} z_i^2 \quad z_i$ is a standard normal random deviate.
Beta	$f(x) = \dfrac{1}{B(p,q)}x^{p-1}(1-x)^{q-1},$ $0 \le x \le 1, p > 0, q > 0$	$x = \dfrac{r^{1/p}}{r^{1/p} + r^{1/q}}$
Gamma	$f(x) = \dfrac{\lambda^n}{\Gamma(\eta)}x^{(\eta-1)e^{-\lambda x}},$ $x\,?\,0, \eta\,?\,0, \lambda\,?\,0$	1. η is a non-integer shape parameter. 2. Let $\eta_1 =$ the truncated integer root of η. 3. Let $q = -\ln\displaystyle\prod_{j=1}^{\eta_1} r_j$. 4. Let $A = \eta - \eta_1$ and $B = 1 - A$. 5. Generate a random number and let $y_1 = r_j^{1/A}$. 6. Generate a random number and let $y_2 = r_{i+1}^{1/B}$. 7. If $y_1 + y_2 \le 1$ go to 9. 8. Let $i = i + 2$ and go to 5.

Table 7.1.   (*continued*)

DISTRIBUTION	PROBABILITY DENSITY FUNCTION	RANDOM NUMBER GENERATOR[§]
		9. Let $z = y_1/(y_1 + y_2)$. 10. Generate a random number, r_n. 11. Let $W = -\ln r_n$. 12. $x = (q + zW)\lambda$.
Binomial	$p(x) = (n/x)p^x(1-p)^{n-x}, x = 0, 1, \ldots, n$	$x = \sum_{i=1}^{n} y_i, \quad y_i = \begin{cases} 0, r_i > p \\ 1, r_i \le p \end{cases}$
Geometric	$p(x) = p(1-p)^{x-1}, x = 1, 2, 3, \ldots$	$\dfrac{\ln(1-r)}{\ln(1-p)} \le x \le \dfrac{\ln(1-r)}{\ln(1-p)} + 1$ [‡]
Student's t	$f(x) = \dfrac{\Gamma[(v+1)/2]}{\Gamma(v/2)\sqrt{\pi v}}\left(1 + \dfrac{x^2}{v}\right)^{-(v+1)/2},$ $-\infty < x < \infty$	$x = \dfrac{z_1}{\left(\sum_{i=2}^{v+1} \dfrac{z_i^2}{v}\right)^{1/2}}$ z_i is a standard normal random deviate.
F	$f(x) = \left(\dfrac{\Gamma[(v_1+v_2)/2](v_1/v_2)^{v_1/2}}{\Gamma(v_1/2)\Gamma(v_2/2)}\right)$ $\times \left(\dfrac{x^{v_1/2-1}}{(1+v_1x/v_2)^{(v_1+v_2)/2}}\right), x > 0.$	$x = \dfrac{v_2 \sum_{i=1}^{v_1} z_i^2}{v_1 \sum_{i=v_1+1}^{v_1+v_2} z_i^2}$ z_i is a standard normal random deviate.

[†]Two uniform random numbers must be generated, with the result being two normally distributed random numbers.
[‡]Increase the value of x until the inequality is satisfied.
[§]Statistical Software, such as MINITAB, have these functions built-in.

following techniques should be reviewed from the analyze stage for use in cycle time reduction:

- Reduce process complexity, such as through standardization.
- Remove unnecessary process steps and unnecessary movement of resources.
- Optimize the process.
- Level load the process.
- Reduce setup times.

In addition to these techniques, benchmarking can provide useful input for redesigning the process flow. *Benchmarking* is a means to evaluate the best in

Table 7.2. Example cycle time reduction.

Step	Distribution	Parameters
1	Normal	Mean $= 12.1$; Std. dev. $= 1.9$
2	Normal	Mean $= 7.3$; Std. dev. $= 0.5$
3	Uniform	Mean $= 3$
4	Exponential	Mean $= 5.1$

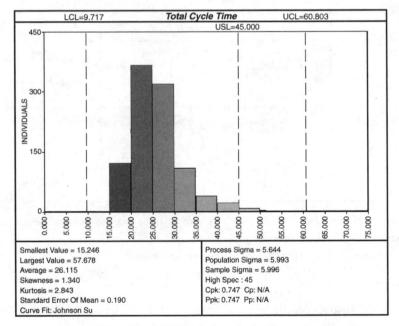

Figure 7.3 Example simulation results for cycle time.

class for particular industries, processes, or even process types. Benchmarking does not require detailed analysis of a competitor's process, on the mistaken assumption that your processes should be designed the same way as a competitor. In that case, your organization can never exceed the values provided by your competition, and never achieve recognition as an industry leader. It will also be impossible to reach breakthrough levels of improvement necessary

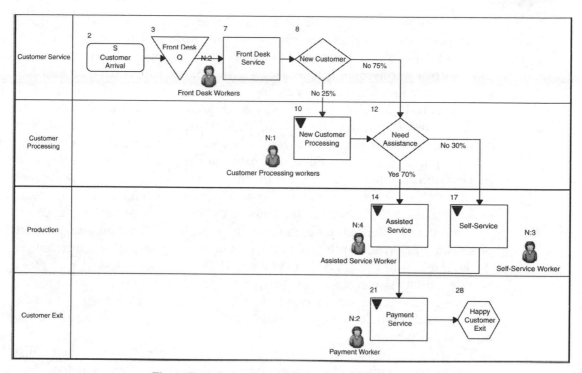

Figure 7.4   Example process map using Sigma Flow.

for Six Sigma quality. Rather, similar or even dissimilar industries may be evaluated to learn techniques new to your organization. For example, a good model for improving an assembly operation can be a fast-food restaurant specializing in rapid assembling of hamburgers.

Simulations allow the process flow to be easily revised "on paper" and evaluated for flow, bottlenecks, and cycle times. These what-if scenarios save the time and expense of actually changing the process to measure the effect. Once the process is modeled, the before and after states can be easily compared for resource allocation, costs, and scheduling issues.

The first step for using simulations to estimate the effects of cycle time improvements begins by modeling the process. The flowcharts, process maps, and SIPOC analyses introduced in the define stage are useful now to develop the flow and responsibilities for the new process. Figure 7.4 shows a process map generated by the Sigma Flow software. This example was created for a small print shop, where customers can be self-served or fully serviced by staff. Each process activity is represented in this example using a rectangle. The swim lanes (customer service, customer processing, etc.) are used to show the organizational functions associated with the process activities.

As in simpler simulations with Excel, the time required for each process activity can be specified as fixed values, or in the form of a distribution, so that the effects due to process variability can be estimated. In addition, the Sigma Flow software conveniently allows for decision paths, with relative likelihoods of occurrence for each path. For example, 25% of customers are typically new customers in Figure 7.4, while 70% of all customers require assistance.

Items flowing through the system, such as product orders, material, and customers, can also be held in queue as they wait to be processed. Queues are often required due to the differences between the arrival rates of items to a process step and the processing rate for those items. The effect of these queues can be analyzed by monitoring (in the simulation results) the number of items in the queue (WIP), as well as the amount of time items sit in the queue.

Items can be further differentiated by type, to allow multiple product processing. Priorities for the use of items in queue may also be specified, either through selection by item type, LIFO, or FIFO. In Figure 7.4, the Front Desk Service activity is preceded by a queue storage (shown by the large triangle); however, it's often easier to simply incorporate queues into a given process activity, such as indicated by the small triangle in the upper left corner of the other activity boxes.

The arrival rates at each process activity can also be specified using distributional properties. The exponential distribution is often used to model arrival rates to a process step, on the assumption that each item is independent of other items. Advanced simulation software like Sigma Flow provides many distribution choices for arrival times and processing rates, including scheduled arrivals, arrivals at set intervals, batches, and modeling based on actual data.

To run a simulation, resources must be specified for each activity. In Figure 7.4, the available resources are indicated by the worker object. For example, the Payment Service activity has two (i.e., N2) available Payment Workers, while there are four (i.e., N4) Assisted Service Workers. In this case, only one shift is operational, but in more advanced simulations the resources can be defined for each shift. Since resources must be available for work to occur, the lack of resources will act as a constraint on the process. In advanced simulation software such as Sigma Flow, resources can be specified using logic, so that the process might require a single resource to function (for example, manager must approve); two or more required resources (for example, doctor and nurse for surgical procedure); or one resource from a pooled resource (for example, customer service or technical support may answer the phone).

The input parameters for simulating the process shown above are provided in Table 7.3.

Pooled resources can be conveniently used to estimate the impact of cross-training on staff utilization and process cycle times. In some software

Table 7.3. Example input parameters for sigma flow simulation.

Objects		Model Data
Customer Entry	Interarrival Time	Exponential (5)
Front Desk	Replicate = 3	Normal (6,2)
New Customer (Decision)	25% Yes / 75% No	Fixed (0)
New Customer Processing	Replicate = 1	Normal (10,3)
Need Assistance (Decision)	70% Yes / 30% No	Fixed (0)
Assisted Service	Replicate = 5	Normal (27,8)
Self-Service	Replicate = 5	Normal (44,12)
Payment	Replicate = 3	Normal (10,3)
Resources		
Front Desk Workers		2
Cust. Processing Workers		1
Assisted Service Workers		4
Self-Service Workers		3
Payment Workers		2

(including Sigma Flow), the processing times for a given process activity can be separately specified for each class of worker within a pool, which is useful for differentiating between skill levels of the different workers. The order (or priority) for shifting each type of worker to the activity can also be specified.

Selected results from four Sigma Flow simulations are shown in Table 7.4. The Variable column provides a baseline for the process, assuming the input parameters indicated earlier. The Add Resources column provides the effects of adding three workers (one each to Assisted Service Workers, Self-Service Workers, and Payment Workers). The Average Time in System for the last step of the process (Happy Customer Exit) provides the average cycle time for the process, which has been lowered substantially by adding resources. The

Table 7.4.   Example output from sigma flow simulation.

Process Step	Results	Variable	Add Resources	Pool Resources	Pool Resources Optimized
Happy Customer Exit	Number Completed	261.0	285.0	286.0	285.0
Happy Customer Exit	Average Time in System	108.6	62.9	62.5	64.4
Happy Customer Exit	Maximum Time in System	242.1	132.6	126.1	137.5
Front Desk Workers	Utilization %	62.3	62.3	84.0	86.0
Customer Processing Workers	Utilization %	45.2	45.2	74.8	79.7
Assisted Service Workers	Utilization %	93.2	77.9	87.0	87.4
Self-Service Workers	Utilization %	82.8	65.4	54.0	53.2
Payment Workers	Utilization %	93.6	68.8	44.6	62.3
Pool Customers Facing Workers	Utilization %			68.2	76.8
Pool Production Workers	Utilization %			76.0	76.2

Number Completed indicates the throughput of the process, which has been increased. However, the utilization of the workers has gone down significantly in the areas where workers were added, indicating that the workers are waiting for new work a significant amount of time.

The Pool Resources column shows the effect of creating two new pooled resources. The Customer Facing Workers Pool is composed of the Front Desk Workers, Customer Processing Workers, and Payment Workers. The remaining workers (Assisted Service Workers and Self-Service Workers) are pooled into a group called the Production Workers. By pooling the workers, resources are shifted as needed to customers in queue. In this case, the average cycle time has been only marginally reduced for the same throughput, although the utilization for three of the five worker groups has been improved.

The Pool Resources Optimized column shows the effect of reducing the number of Payment Workers from three to two. The throughput is maintained, average cycle time only marginally increased, and utilizations improved; yet the cost of the process has been reduced. A profit and loss statement can be generated for each simulation using the random processing and queuing times associated with the process activities, allowing cost savings to be estimated for each scenario.

Assessing Benefits of Proposed Solution

It's not uncommon for a team to reach the improve stage with several possible methods of process improvement. These potential techniques must be evaluated using objective, data-driven methods to maximize buy-in of the solution and assure the stakeholders receive their optimal return on the project investment.

The *prioritization matrix* (introduced in Chapter 4) can be used to compare the proposed solutions against the criteria defined as critical in the define stage of the project.

Financial analysis tools are used to estimate the cost savings associated with the proposed solutions. To quantify financial value (and risk) associated with a proposed solution, variable costs must be differentiated from fixed costs. As shown in Figure 7.5, fixed costs (or fixed benefits) are constant regardless of volume (i.e., the number of orders filled, customers processed, units produced), such as the costs associated with building and support personnel. Variable costs and benefits depend on volume, and include items such as materials, direct labor, and shipping.

If fixed and variable costs and benefits are known, the earnings before interest and taxes (EBIT) calculation provides the potential profitability of each particular solution. The benefit of a solution is calculated as the difference between the EBIT before and the EBIT after the solution.

$$EBIT = Volume * (price\ per\ unit - variable\ cost\ per\ unit) - fixed\ cost$$

It often happens that the benefits and costs come in specific time windows, rather than in lump sums at the beginning or end of the term. A net present value (NPV) allows us to calculate the current benefit of a project for each

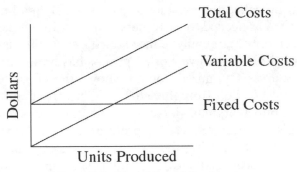

Figure 7.5 Variable and fixed costs.

window of time and over the total time period. The internal rate of return (IRR) is the equivalent interest that is gained by the project, if the net present value of the cash flow were invested for the time period. The IRR allows us to compare projects, with higher IRR associated with projects yielding a better return. MS Excel provides a convenient formula for determining NPV and IRR when the cost and benefits are tabularized.

These deterministic estimates of process savings can be further enhanced using the simulation approach outlined earlier in this chapter. The cost savings for a project can consider the distributional properties of the random variable inputs:

- *Percent reduction in defects* (*affecting material savings, capacity, and labor*). Simulate the baseline and postimprovement distributions. Calculate the difference in error rate between the results.
- *Production volume* (*affecting material savings, capacity, and labor*). Simulate effects of increasing (or decreasing) sales volume.

In this way, annualized cost savings estimates may be stated in percentiles. For example, solution A will provide a 90% likelihood of saving $500,000, and a 99% likelihood of saving $150,000.

Evaluating Process Failure Modes

Once the process flow is established, it can be evaluated for its failure modes. Understanding process failure modes allows us to define mitigation strategies to minimize the impact or occurrence of failures. These mitigation strategies may result in new process steps, optimal process settings, or process control strategies to prevent failure. In some cases, where failure cannot be economically prevented, a strategy can be developed to minimize the occurrence of the failure and contain the damage.

Cause and effect diagrams used in the analyze stage are again useful for brainstorming the potential causes of failures. This brainstorming activity will provide necessary input to process decision program charts and failure modes and effects analysis.

The process decision program chart, also known by its acronym PDPC, is a tool for identifying problems that can occur in a project or process and developing contingencies (either a solution or work-around) to deal with each problem. An example is shown in Figure 7.6.

The PDPC has the same general format as a tree diagram. For each process step shown in the first level, potential problems (what-ifs) are identified in the second level. Countermeasures provide the contingencies for each problem.

The intent of the analysis is to confront problems which otherwise might not have been addressed. Forcing the team to anticipate problems before they occur helps them uncover issues or solutions that would otherwise be ignored. Additionally, this process allows team members to discuss points that they may find troublesome, without feeling like they are being unduly negative. Once the potential problems are identified, the next step is to think of a measure to counteract this problem. When more than one countermeasure is available, note each of these and prioritize the solution(s) using the methods discussed earlier.

For instance, suppose the anticipated problem is resistance to change among the process personnel. The possible counteractive measures include an incentive program to boost morale, or an education program to inform workers of the need for change. You can then weigh the costs and benefit of each alternative in order to decide on your course of action. Of course, it is much easier to make these decisions in the calm of the planning room, rather than in the heat of the project when you suddenly discover an unanticipated problem.

Failure modes and effects analysis, also known by its acronym FMEA or failure modes, effects, and criticality analysis, is a more detailed approach to the problem. It is used to determine high risk functions or product features based on the impact of a failure and the likelihood that a failure could occur without detection. The methodology can be applied to products or processes, although the application to processes is most useful in the improve stage of DMAIC.

The FMEA process (described in detail in Part 3) begins by defining the functions for each process step. For example, the process step Enter the Product ID number for each purchased item has the function Links to the product database

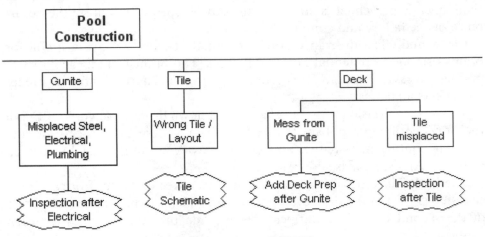

Figure 7.6   Example PDPC.

to identify the item numbers necessary for shipment of the products being purchased. For each function, the failure modes and their effect are identified, generally by posing the questions What could go wrong? or What could the customer dislike?

For example, the failure modes and their effects for the above function include:

- Failure mode 1: Product ID mistyped.
- Effect of failure mode 1: Wrong product shipped.
- Failure mode 2: Item numbers not correctly defined in database.
- Effect of failure mode 2: Wrong product items shipped.

The severity, likelihood of occurrence, detection method, and likelihood of detection are determined, and a resulting risk factor (RPN: risk priority number) calculated. The likelihood of occurrence and likelihood of detection are based on historical data, where available.

The results of the FMEA will indicate activities prone to failure, or likely to cause serious consequences if they do fail. These failure modes must be addressed, either through elimination or a mitigation strategy. Improvements in detection are stopgap measures, with increased cost of quality. Reducing the risk often demands a reduction in the rate of occurrence, such as through the process optimization techniques described earlier. Prevention methods can achieve satisfactory results, particularly in reducing the rate of occurrence of human errors.

PREVENTION OF HUMAN ERRORS

It is useful to categorize process failures according to their origin. Many failures are due to human error, particularly in service processes. While some solutions will focus on individuals' performance, most failures resulting from human error will be prevented by process or system-level solutions.

There are three main categories of human errors: inadvertent errors, technique errors, and willful errors. Inadvertent errors may be otherwise termed *mistakes*. Technique errors are related to the process procedure, and often due to poor training. Willful errors are deliberate attempts to sabotage the process.

Inadvertent errors are typically characterized by a low incidence rate, with little or no advance knowledge that a failure is coming. There is no predictable pattern to an inadvertent error.

Inadvertent errors can be prevented in a number of ways. Foolproofing, also called *poka yoke*, is one of the lean tools for preventing errors. A fundamental change is incorporated to the design of the part or the process to prevent the error from occurring.

For example, modern hypodermic needles have now been designed to prevent the needle from being used more than once to avoid possible instances of cross-contamination between patients. To prevent holes from being drilled in the wrong place on a production part, the part and the fixture used to secure the part could incorporate a pin with a mating slot so the part will not fit correctly into the fixture unless it is properly aligned.

Automation is a common way to minimize the occurrence of inadvertent errors by removing the human element. Bar code readers are simple devices used in many industries to prevent product numbers, customer information, or product data from being incorrectly typed into a database.

Another approach that has proven helpful is an ergonomic approach of improving the work environment. For example, a simpler keyboard, easily accessible to the clerk, might help reduce data entry errors.

Technique errors are characterized as being unintentional, usually confined to single characteristic or class of characteristics (for example, cracks), and isolated to a few workers.

Technique errors can be minimized using the same methods as for inadvertent errors (foolproofing, automation, and ergonomics) or through training. Training is perhaps the most common method of reducing technique errors and can be combined with visual aids and documentation at the process level for easy access by the work force.

Willful errors are characteristically nonrandom and difficult to detect. Fortunately, they usually involve only a single disgruntled worker and are extremely rare in practice. Only 100% inspection can hope to detect these types of errors, and even 100% inspection is not 100% accurate, so errors can still be undetected. An engaged and empowered work force is perhaps the best prevention.

Implementation and Verification

Once the improvement methodology and new process levels have been determined, they can be implemented. Even in the simplest of improvements, caution and diligence must be exercised at this point.

One of the most obvious, yet still overlooked, reasons for problems at this point is due to lack of communication. Previous chapters have discussed the need for regular updates with the stakeholder groups to avoid surprises at the improve stage. These updates allow the vision of the solution to be formed over time by the stakeholders, increasing the likelihood of buy-in to the solution. Through proper communication, stakeholders will understand the need for a solution in the define stage, appreciate the extent of the problem in the measure stage, and realize its complexity through the analyze stage. Exercising rigor during the improve stage brings clarity to the solution for each of the stakeholder groups.

Nonetheless, even when the solution is evident, the project team must focus on proper communication to ensure support through the implementation of the solution. Starting with the project sponsor, each step of the solution, with a contingency plan in the event of failure, must be presented in a clear and orderly fashion to the stakeholder groups. The sponsor must convey the specific authority to the project team, properly communicated through the organizational hierarchy, to implement the specific solution beginning at a specific date and time. Process personnel, and their immediate management, must be cognizant of the authority vested in the project team in implementing the solution, and provide the necessary support to ensure its proper implementation.

The process personnel must be provided with clear instructions on their new procedures, especially with regard to process failures. While the control stage includes detailed training on the new process procedures, at this point the procedures may still be somewhat in flux until the solution has been deployed. Depending on the extent of the solution, in-depth training of all personnel could be premature until the process and its procedures have been stabilized. This state of transition requires oversight by the project team and/or process personnel (under the direction of the team) to ensure the process output meets the expectations of the authorized solution. The goal is to quickly establish the merits of the solution so that the project team can move to the control stage, where in-depth training can be conducted. Until this training takes place, the project team must work closely with process personnel to communicate proper action and understanding of the process conditions.

Statistical analysis of these conditions, generally using control charts, is needed to verify the results. As discussed in Chapter 8, statistical control of the process is necessary if project success is to be measured. Hypothesis tests on the difference in means may be used to compare the process before and after implementation of the solution.

Recommended Tools

The following tools (discussed in detail in Part 3) are applicable to the improve stage of DMAIC:

Determine Operating Conditions

- *Activity network diagrams* and *PERT analysis* to verify the reduction in process critical path cycle time.
- *Five S tools* to reduce non-value-added cycle times due to movement, search time, ineffective use of floor space; to improve inventory management; or to reduce accidents and improve working conditions.
- *Level loading* to balance the flow of orders.
- *Matrix diagrams* and *prioritization matrices* to ensure that process solutions are aligned with customer needs.
- *Box-whisker charts* to graphically compare before and after states of process improvement.
- *Cause and effect diagram* to generate a list of potential failure modes that should be addressed in the solution.
- *Designed experiments, regression analysis, residuals analysis, response surface analysis, ridge analysis, factorial designs, evolutionary operations, interaction plots,* and *contour plots* to determine where a maximum or minimum response is expected within or close to the data range.

Investigate Failure Modes

- *Procession decision program charts* and *failure modes and effects analysis* to determine high-risk process activities or product features in the proposed improvement.

Implement Improvement

- *Flowcharts* and *process maps* to define the process level activities necessary.
- *Hypothesis testing of two samples* and *nonparametric test on the equality of means* to compare process averages after improvements versus baseline estimates.
- SPC control charts, including *C*, *Np*, *P*, *U*, *Individual-X*, *X-Bar*, and *EWMA charts*, and *process capability index* to verify the effects of the improvement.
- *Goodness of fit tests* and *normal probability plots* to verify the statistical distributions assumed in the various statistical tools.

In addition, the consensus building tools noted at the end of Chapter 4 are also applied, as needed.

Quiz for Chapter 7

1. A process decision program chart is useful to:
   a. Identify problems in implementing a project solution.
   b. Define the tasks required to complete a project.
   c. Develop contingency plans for problems.
   d. All of the above.

2. Of the following three types of controls, which is the most desirable?
   a. Those that prevent the cause or failure mode from occurring or reduce their occurrence.
   b. Those that detect the cause and lead to corrective action.
   c. Those that detect the failure mode.
   d. These are not design controls.

3. A reduction in the occurrence ranking in an FMEA can be achieved by:
   a. Removing or controlling one or more of the failure mode causes through a design change.
   b. An increase in design validation/verification actions.
   c. All of the above.
   d. None of the above.

4. In a process FMEA, process and/or design changes can:
   a. Reduce the probability of occurrence.
   b. Reduce the severity ranking.

    c. Increase the probability of detection.

    d. All of the above.

5. With regard to the detection of process errors:

    a. 100% inspection is a preferred approach.

    b. SPC will detect all errors that can occur.

    c. A picture or graphic of the known defects is helpful to guide process operators.

    d. It is not necessary to develop detection plans once you achieve high sigma levels.

6. We might choose to simulate a process:

    a. When the cost of experimentation is high.

    b. To test a wide variety of conditions.

    c. To generate data useful for training.

    d. All of the above.

7. A necessary prerequisite for simulation includes:

    a. Reasonable estimates of the process model and its operating conditions.

    b. A computer capable of running millions of calculations.

    c. Training on the derivation of stochastic models.

    d. All of the above.

8. Simulation results:

    a. Are usually not useful in preventing errors, but often useful to predict errors.

    b. Can be more exact than process data when real distributions are modeled.

    c. Should be verified using process data.

    d. All of the above.

9. A process critical to daily operations is in need of improvement, but management is not willing to shut the process down for investigation. A reasonable method of gaining process improvement is through:

    a. A Taguchi experiment.

    b. A classical designed experiment.

    c. Evolutionary operation.

    d. One factor at a time experimentation.

10. The *power* of an experiment refers to:

    a. The statistical significance of the effects.

    b. The ability to detect that an effect is significant.

    c. The ability to reject the alternative hypothesis when it is false.

    d. All of the above.

CHAPTER

Control Stage

The final stage of the DMAIC process improvement methodology is the control stage.

Objectives

There are several objectives to be completed within the control stage of DMAIC:

- The new methods must become standardized in practice.
- The predicted impact of the improvements, the project deliverables, must be continually verified, especially the financial return.
- Lessons learned should be documented.

Standardize on the New Methods

In the improve stage, changes are made to the process. Many times, the process procedures will be changed. The old way of doing things is replaced with new and improved methods.

Process variation may have been reduced by controlling the variation in one or more key input variables, or by redefining more appropriate levels for these parameters. These changes may result in the need for more manpower available at certain times of the day or for control of the variation in key parameters, such as room temperature, to control the size of a key dimension.

The natural response of process personnel may be to gradually, or even abruptly, return to past practices. This may occur the first time the process experiences a shift in behavior, when personnel return from vacation and fall into old habits, or when you're just not looking.

There are several practices useful for standardizing on the new process methods:

- Process control is used to monitor process variation. Some methods will ensure that variation will remain stable by precision control of the input parameters.
- Control plans are used to define the methods of control and ensure all potential sources of variation are addressed.
- Work instructions, flowcharts, and process maps are used to document the process procedures and responsibilities.
- Training is essential for process personnel to understand their new responsibilities. The communication of these methods, procedures, and responsibilities should be integrated into a training program for the process personnel.

PROCESS CONTROL

How do we prevent process from deviating from its improved state, including returning to past performance levels?

There are two main strategies for achieving process controls, stemming from the work done in the failure modes and effects analysis:

- To prevent or greatly reduce the occurrence of errors
- To detect the occurrence of the error before the customer has a chance to experience it

Of course, if the cost to implement were the same, prevention would always be preferred to detection because of the increased costs of remedying the error. Unfortunately, prevention is at least *sometimes* more costly to implement than detection, although once the cost of failure is factored in then the true cost of a detection-based control system often exceeds the cost of prevention-based control. Recall the costs associated with "hidden factories," and it is clear that control systems for a Six Sigma organization should be prevention-oriented in almost all cases.

As a result of designed experiments, we often discover input variables that drive the process output. When we apply control schemes to these variables, we can prevent errors from occurring. For example, if the number of incoming orders drives the cycle time for order shipment, then a statistically significant increase in the number of incoming orders is a clue to increase the number of personnel in shipping. In this way, the cycle time for shipping (the process output variable) is unaffected because of the previous effort.

The methods for process control include statistical process control (SPC), engineering process control (EPC), and operational procedures. *Statistical process control* refers to the statistical tools that detect process instability. SPC is used to monitor output or input variables so that any lack of stability is detected. When the process is statistically capable of meeting the require-ments, characterized by a process capability index Cpk of 1.5 or better (as defined in Part 3), a control chart of the process output will provide a means for detecting if the process output at the Six Sigma level exceeds the re-quirements. When run test rules are applied, or if the process is highly capable at or above the Six Sigma level, the control chart will also serve as a prevention tool, since it is likely to detect process shifts before out-of-control conditions are experienced.

While SPC is often applied to process output, it is much better to apply SPC to the key input variables. This was a focus for the experimentation used in the analyze and improve stages of DMAIC. Establishing and monitoring statis-tical control of the process drivers that determine the process output serves as a prevention-oriented method of controlling the process.

Engineering process control refers to automated devices designed to respond to process variation by adjusting one or more process input variables. A simple example of this approach is the thermostat found in most homes. When the air temperature inside the house reaches a set level, then the air conditioner (or heater) turns on to respond to the undesirable condition and control the temperature within a set tolerance (usually determined by the manufacturer). Although a household thermostat has rather simple programmable controls, industrial processes often use more sophisticated algorithms with multiple input parameters and even multiple outputs. The inputs are often sampled at high frequencies, and once an acceptable model is discovered the process can be controlled to a high level of precision.

Since the EPC makes changes to the process dependent on the current state of the process, the data is inherently autocorrelated, or dependent on earlier observations. This serial correlation violates the assumption of data inde-pendence required for standard SPC control charts, and must be addressed if control charts are to be used to monitor the process output. This is discussed in more detail in the Serial Correlation section in Part 3.

OPERATIONAL PROCEDURES

Like engineering process control and to some extent statistical process control, operational procedures seek to control the output of the process using operational guidelines for the human inputs to the process. Rather than automatically controlling temperature using a feedback control such as a thermostat, operational procedures would instruct a process operator to turn on the heater or air conditioner when the temperature reached a particular setting. It should be clear that the detection of the condition, as well as the response to the condition, is not as repeatable as when using the automated control. The procedures are subject to human error, such as discussed in Chapter 7.

Nonetheless, procedures offer the most cost-effective means of control for many circumstances. Particularly in transactional processes, procedures may be effectively used to:

- *Standardize the process.* For example, using flowcharts or decision trees, each of the order processing clerks will process the orders in the same fashion. Simple software can be created to facilitate the process.
- *Divert resources.* As a matter of procedure, personnel are instructed that if the wait for their service is more than five minutes, then additional resources should be immediately requested. For example, if there are more than three people in your checkout line, request additional cashiers to the front of the store.
- *Channel orders by types.* Certain customers or types of orders are routed to a standardized process line for improved efficiency. For example, at an automotive service department, the oil change customers are routed to a special line for expedited service. At a bank, an express lane is provided for merchant accounts.

Operational procedures must be documented and controlled to ensure their use. "Control" of procedures refers to revision control, where operational personnel only have access to current (not outdated) procedures that have been approved by the appropriate stakeholders. The ISO 9000 provisions for document control are an effective means of ensuring proper revision control.

Effective procedures may be documented in paragraph form, with flowcharts or process maps, with pictures, or any combination of these. The documentation method, and terminology, should be appropriate for the audience. Bear in mind the objective: to effectively communicate the proper procedure. For personnel who have a limited command of the local language, procedures in paragraph form may be completely ineffective. Simple pictures showing the correct and incorrect methods may be the most effective way to communicate the procedure to that audience, while paragraph form is used for another audience for the same procedure.

Each of these process control techniques (SPC, EPC, and operational procedures) requires a necessary standard of performance, feedback to the process, and a method of changing the process. These parameters should be specified in a control plan.

CONTROL PLANS

A control plan provides an overview of the strategies that will be used to ensure that key process or part characteristics are controlled through either detection or prevention strategies, or the combination of the two.

Key inputs to a control plan include the results of designed experiments and failure modes and effects analysis. Designed experiments are fundamental tools in determining process drivers. Robust designs in particular tell us which process factors must be controlled to reduce variation in the process response. By controlling these input factors, we can prevent errors from occurring in the process. As shown in Chapters 6 and 7, these methods can be effectively applied to transactional processes.

The failure modes and effects analysis (and its RPN, risk priority number) determines the failure modes that are the most critical to control. This is a valuable input in the construction of the control plan. The assumptions used to determine the detection level in the FMEA must be incorporated into the control plan.

A portion of a control plan is shown in Table 8.1. For each key characteristic, the following information is defined:

- *Specification*. What is the definition of "good" and "bad" for this characteristic?
- *Measurement technique*. How will the characteristic be measured? The control plan should reference more detailed measurement procedures, where needed, to instruct personnel on the proper use and interpretation of the measurement equipment.
- *Sample size*. How many measurements are required at each point in time?
- *Sample frequency*. How often should a new set of measurements be taken?

Table 8.1. Example control plan.

Characteristic	Specification	Measurement Technique	Sample Size	Sample Frequency	Analytic Tool	Reaction Rules
Finished Diameter	1.250 ± .0002	Johannson	5	1 sg/hr	X-Bar chart w/run rules	If other characteristics in control, adjust
Local Ambient Temp.	70 ± 5	Thermocouple	1	Continuous	Alarmed	Stop production; Adjust cooling control; Resume production once temp. OK
Cooling Temp.	120 ± 5	Thermocouple	1	1 per min	Alarmed	Stop production; Adjust cooling control; Resume production once temp. OK
Coolant Viscosity	.88–.94	Viscometer	1	1 per month	X Chart	Purge system

- *Analytical tool.* How are the measurements evaluated? In this case, audio alarms are installed to monitor characteristics thought to have high process capability. Other characteristics are monitored via control charts to detect process trends leading to undesirable conditions.
- *Reaction rules.* What is the proper response to the alarms (audio or from control chart)? Who should be notified?

TRAINING REQUIREMENTS

While an effective document revision and control scheme is useful for communicating new methods and procedures, it is often not sufficient, especially when procedures undergo the significant changes often resulting from the DMAIC process. Even when procedural changes are relatively narrow in scope, training is quite beneficial in communicating the changes and preventing problems or misinterpretations of the new procedures. This training can be as simple as a quick meeting with the operational personnel at their workstations or a detailed multisession training, such as may be required for new equipment or to teach customer-friendly communication skills.

Topics for training include the lessons learned during the DMAIC process, the key process factors, and their interactions, in addition to the new procedures themselves. Including these lessons learned is really helpful to the stakeholders, particularly the operational personnel, so they understand *why* the changes were necessary and how the conclusions were developed.

The training should include operational personnel, process owners, and other stakeholders (including suppliers, if appropriate). Most, if not all, of these stakeholder groups were represented on the team and included in data collection or analysis, so this part of the training will provide a good conclusion to their efforts.

For the training to be effective, it should be targeted to the current skill set of the audience, and include a means of assessing the knowledge transfer to each individual. The format of these evaluations depends on the criticality and complexity of the subject matter. In some cases, workshops are useful for employees to practice the newly acquired skills; in cases of critical safety or quality issues, employees may have to demonstrate proficiency through written or on-the-job testing.

Participants should be evaluated immediately at the end of the training and at a stipulated time later. This posttraining evaluation gauges the longer-term retention of the material and may demonstrate a need for follow-up training or a change in training format to more effectively target the audience. Of course, the best means of evaluating the impact of the training is to measure the changes in behavior resulting from the training. Are people using the new skills? To what degree?

Measure Bottom-Line Impact

A key part of the control stage is to continuously monitor the effects of the process improvement. This is a critical part of DMAIC that was often neglected in past improvement strategies.

The control plan should contain provisions for monitoring the process output either as a method of control or a sampling audit. Generally, the process owner (the operational personnel) will be responsible for the ongoing tracking of the applicable performance metric. This activity should continue for as long as necessary, as often as necessary, to establish the underlying process capability. Often sampling is fairly frequent in the beginning, and tapers off once the process has proven stable and capable of achieving the requirements. See the statistical process control charting section in Part 3 for general discussion of sampling frequency and sample sizes necessary to detect process shifts.

As part of this control stage, the Black Belt will assume responsibility for verifying the operational-level controls done by the process owners. In addition, the Black Belt will audit the process on a regular (for example, monthly) basis for the first year. The audit should include observation of process procedures and controls, as well as sampling or reviewing the results of data samples to ensure process capability.

If the process exhibits any out-of-control behavior, the Black Belt should be notified, so that a further review can be made to identify its source. In this case, the process control should be investigated, and perhaps tightened, to reduce the occurrence of further process instability. In cases of continued instability, the process should be evaluated for a new Six Sigma project, with a critical review of the initial Six Sigma project report for indication of its failings.

Just as crucial as process control is the ongoing tracking of the financial benefits, usually on a monthly basis as part of cost accounting reports. The financial reporting must include actual expenditures and savings for each of the items used for project justification in the define stage, as well as expenditures related to the project implementation, such as described in the improve stage. Savings are calculated based on methods agreed upon in the define stage, and may include actual and predicted annualized estimates. The individual responsible for tracking the cost savings should be clearly identified in the control plan.

Document Lessons Learned

The results of the Six Sigma project should be documented in a project report. The project report should include the following information:

- The project charter, as a key deliverable in the define stage, introducing the reader to the project's problem statement, objectives, and plan.
- A summary result of each stage of the DMAIC cycle, including the main objectives and results for each stage.
- Appendices containing raw data, analysis results, and a timeline of the actual activities for reference.
- A listing of the expenditures required to implement the project, including lost capacity, material, or labor.
- The cost savings received to date and projected for the next year to three years.
- The current status of the process and the control plan for the future.
- Recommendations for future projects related to the process.
- Recommendations for future project leaders and sponsors, based on lessons learned during this project.

The project report should be circulated to the finance or accounting areas for review of accuracy of the financial information. The project report (and the financial approval) must be presented to the sponsor for formal approval and project close.

In some organizations, Master Black Belt and senior management responsible for Six Sigma deployment must also sign off on the reports. It is often a good learning experience for the Black Belts to formally present the findings to management. When other senior management leaders are invited, it provides good exposure to the program and the work of the project teams.

Organizations should adopt some strategy for rewarding Six Sigma teams. Financial rewards, particularly a percent of the savings, are not necessary, nor encouraged. They send the wrong message and cultivate a culture of short-sighted profiteering or inflated savings at the expense of real improvement. Instead, teams should be recognized with ceremony and appreciation from management for a job well done. Even project failures should be celebrated for their effort, in the realization that at least some of the stretch goals sought will not be achieved.

In that vein, success stories should be communicated throughout the organization. If frustrations with a process were overcome, that speaks volumes in a language that others are anxious to hear. Project failures should also be noted for their efforts, their partial success, and the lessons learned.

Many companies have found Web-based forums on the company intranet a useful venue for sharing information. Black Belts should be given the opportunity to share, learn, and grow through one another. The use of technical skills, as well as the softer change management skills necessary for building buy-in, will grow when practitioners have a chance to see their successful application by other teams. It's truly remarkable how one team's success can be translated into other processes, even those that seem quite different. White papers, case studies, project reports, as well as chat rooms, are useful for spreading the word and institutionalizing the findings.

Recommended Tools

The following tools (discussed in detail in Part 3) are applicable to the control stage of DMAIC:

- *Flowcharts* and *process maps* to define the process level activities necessary.
- SPC control charts, including *C, Np, P, U, Individual-X, X-Bar*, and *EWMA charts*, and *process capability index* to verify the effects of the improvement.
- *Goodness of fit tests* and *probability plotting* to verify the statistical distributions assumed in the various statistical tools.
- *R&R studies* to qualify operators' proficiency on specific measurement equipment.

In addition, the consensus building tools noted at the end of Chapter 4 are also applied, as needed.

Quiz for Chapter 8

1. The control stage of a project should include which of the following objectives?
   a. Implementing methods to maintain the improvements.
   b. Measuring the financial gain associated with the improvements.
   c. Communicating the lessons learned to others in the organization.
   d. All of the above.

2. The preferred method of controlling processes is:
   a. To detect problems as soon as they occur.
   b. Using a control chart.

    c. To prevent problems from occurring.

    d. By training operators to eliminate mistakes.

3. Engineering process control is a method to:

    a. Stabilize a process by detecting process shifts.

    b. Manipulate process inputs to control process output.

    c. Correct for process autocorrelation using algorithmic logic.

    d. All of the above.

4. Statistical process control is a method to:

    a. Stabilize a process by detecting process shifts.

    b. Manipulate process inputs to control process output.

    c. Correct for process autocorrelation using algorithmic logic.

    d. All of the above.

5. Operational procedures, as a method of process control:

    a. Must consider human error.

    b. Are as repeatable as automated controls.

    c. Cannot be used unless the organization is ISO certified.

    d. All of the above.

6. Operational procedures, as a method of process control, can effectively:

    a. Standardize the process.

    b. Divert resources where needed.

    c. Channel customers for expedited service.

    d. All of the above.

7. When developing the training objectives for rolling out new process procedures:

    a. Include a discussion of the reasons for the change.

    b. Stick only to the bare essentials necessary for doing the tasks.

    c. Spend a significant amount of the time pointing out problems with the old procedures.

    d. None of the above.

8. Training plans:

    a. Are often useful, but not necessary.

    b. Should be developed solely by the training department.

    c. Need to consider the objectives of the organization.

    d. All of the above.

9. When evaluating a training session:

    a. Initial reactions are most important.

b. Initial reactions are useful, but long-term behavioral changes and results aligned with the objectives are most important.
c. Behavioral changes provide the best estimate of effective training.
d. Testing or exams to quantify the learning of each student are often not helpful.

10. After a training session has been completed, the best way to reinforce the training is:
a. To provide the opportunity to use the new tools or techniques.
b. Through financial reward for improved performance.
c. With examinations.
d. With tight supervision of the employees to ensure that they are using the techniques correctly.

Exam for Part 2

1. The nonconformance records for the Painting Department are shown in the table below, where the number reported is the number of defective units for each nonconformance type (cracked, chipped, off-color, wrong color, other):

Example Nonconformance Data.

Month	Total Shipped	Cracked	Chipped	Off Color	Wrong Color	Other
JAN	3500	7	15	21	12	200
FEB	3124	14	10	28	23	1
MAR	1245	12	5	11	17	9
APR	2020	18	9	7	11	5
MAY	1652	9	14	4	21	9
JUN	2637	11	21	26	9	13
JUL	2543	12	11	19	23	2

Example Nonconformance Data (*continued*)

Month	Total Shipped	Cracked	Chipped	Off Color	Wrong Color	Other
AUG	4042	8	12	12	18	1
SEP	1367	11	13	15	21	7
OCT	3124	21	9	13	40	7
NOV	2645	12	7	6	31	9
DEC	1200	10	4	14	17	8

Based on this information, which of the following project scope statements is best suited to maximize benefit to the company:

a. Reduce the instance of reworks due to wrong color in the Painting Department.
b. Reduce the instance of rework in the Painting Department.
c. Reduce the instance of scrap due to cracks in the Painting Department.
d. None of the above. The "other" category is the largest, and we need to understand its breakdown.

2. For the data shown in question 1, the best estimate for a baseline process defect rate related to wrong color is:
   a. 14,166 PPM
   b. 8,350 PPM
   c. 141,660 PPM
   d. 1,670 DPMO

3. The following unit costs can be applied to the data in question 1:

   Cracked: $428.25 (cost of scrap material and labor)
   Chipped: $252.15 (rework cost)
   Off color: $275.33 (rework cost)
   Wrong color: $117.53 (cost of carrying unordered product in inventory)

   Based on this information, which of the following project scope statements is best suited to maximize benefit to the company?

    a. Reduce the instance of scrap due to cracks in the Painting Department.

    b. Reduce the instance of reworks due to chips in the Painting Department.

    c. Reduce the instance of reworks due to off color in the Painting Department.

    d. Reduce the instance of reworks due to wrong color in the Painting Department.

4. In addition to the cost information shown in the preceding questions, also consider the following costs and time to deploy the proposed projects, assuming they each have an equal chance of success:

Cracked: $40,000 cost; 30 weeks
Chipped: $10,000 cost; 16 weeks
Off color: $25,000 cost; 14 weeks
Wrong color: $3,000 cost; 10 weeks

Based on this information, which of the following project scope statements is best suited to maximize benefit to the company?

    a. Reduce the instance of scrap due to cracks in the Painting Department.

    b. Reduce the instance of reworks due to chips in the Painting Department.

    c. Reduce the instance of reworks due to off color in the Painting Department.

    d. Reduce the instance of reworks due to wrong color in the Painting Department.

5. In an initial team meeting, the team should:
    a. Establish ground rules and review member responsibilities.
    b. Agree on project purpose, scope, plan, and timeline.
    c. Establish workable meeting times and locations.
    d. All of the above.

6. In a SIPOC analysis, stakeholders are usually:
    a. Suppliers.
    b. Customers.
    c. Suppliers and customers.
    d. Not considered in SIPOC.

7. In a SIPOC analysis, customers:
    a. Include anyone who receives output.
    b. Are defined as the key stakeholders of the process.

c. Are the most important part.

d. Are end-users of the product or service.

8. Two critical characteristics were inspected in a sample of 500 orders. Fifty errors were found on 25 of the orders, but 20 of these orders were reprocessed to correct the errors. The throughput yield is:

a. 90%.

b. 95%.

c. 99%.

d. 97.5%.

9. If the throughput yield is calculated as 85%, then:

a. At any given time, 15% of the units will be defective.

b. At any given time, 85% of the units will be defect-free.

c. On average, 85% of the units will have no defects.

d. Choices a and b.

10. The throughput yield for six departments processing an order in series is as follows: 99.7%, 99.5%, 95%, 89%, 92.3%, and 94%. The probability of no defects across all steps is:

a. 89%.

b. 73%.

c. 77%.

d. Approximately 30%.

11. Measurement systems analysis is needed because:

a. Measurements by different personnel using the same equipment on the same sample unit can vary.

b. Measurements by the same personnel using the same equipment on the same sample unit can vary.

c. Calibration will not remove all measurement error.

d. All of the above.

12. Residuals are:

a. The error between the actual y value and the predicted y value at each x value.

b. The difference between the observed x value and the regression line in the y direction.

c. Due to error.

d. All of the above.

13. In the expression cycle time (in minutes) $= 3 + 1.4 *$ (number of orders) $- 2.1 *$ (number of clerks) $- .034 *$ (process distance):

a. Removing one clerk will increase the cycle time by 2.1 minutes.
b. Adding 5 orders will increase the cycle time by 7 minutes.
c. Removing one clerk and adding five orders will increase the cycle time by about 9 minutes.
d. All of the above.

14. In the interaction plot below, it is evident that:
a. There is a strong interaction between moisture and fill pressure.
b. There is a weak to negligible interaction between moisture and fill pressure.
c. The effect of fill pressure on part density changes drastically as we change the moisture.
d. None of the above.

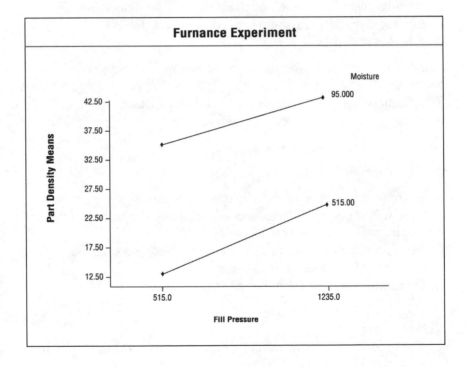

15. An ANOVA analysis provides the following p values:

Intercept $= 0.03$
Factor A $= 0.73$
Factor B $= 0.02$
Factor C $= 0.10$

Given this data, we might assume:
a. Of the three factors investigated, factor A is most significant.
b. Of the three factors investigated, factor B is most significant.
c. Of the three factors investigated, factor C is most significant.
d. None of the above.

16. In identifying which processes provide value, a company should first:
a. Evaluate key processes using a cost/benefit analysis.
b. Understand their customers' processes and needs.
c. Set up a team of internal experts that are familiar with the processes and their design.
d. Benchmark competitors' products and processes.

17. A company optimizes its processes to complement its strengths in product development. This approach:
a. Will certainly improve the company's ability to service customers.
b. Will certainly improve the company's long-term profitability.
c. All of the above.
d. None of the above.

18. In analyzing the value stream, it is observed that a bottleneck occurs in operation 4, which removes excess material from a part prior to the finishing operation. A response to this should be:
a. Operation 4 needs more personnel.
b. The operation that produces the excess material prior to operation 4 should be examined.
c. Personnel from downstream processes should be moved as needed to operation 4 to eliminate the bottleneck.
d. All of the above.

19. Screening designs are often used:
a. To conclusively prove the factors critical to process control.
b. To reduce the list of possible factors influencing a process.
c. To optimize a process.
d. All of the above.

20. We often fold a design:
a. When we can't run enough conditions in a given day.
b. To produce independent estimation of confounded terms.
c. To reduce the number of runs.
d. All of the above.

21. Inadvertent errors can be prevented by:
    a. Automation.
    b. Foolproofing.
    c. Ergonomic design.
    d. All of the above.

22. Lack of fit error may be due to:
    a. Higher order effects that are not included in the model.
    b. Main factors that are not included in the model.
    c. Interactions that are not included in the model.
    d. All of the above.

23. If we conduct a screening experiment and conclude that lack of fit error is significant:
    a. We need to throw out our data and start over.
    b. We can add center points (if we don't have them) and estimate surface curvature.
    c. We may want to extend the design to add more main factors or interactions.
    d. Both b and c.

24. Process control is most effective:
    a. When we concentrate on the process outputs.
    b. When we concentrate on the process inputs.
    c. When applied as sampling inspection of supplier material.
    d. When all process parameters are monitored.

25. When quality improvement plans are implemented, an effective control plan includes training:
    a. On the principles driving the change.
    b. To ensure the employees understand their role in the problem-solving stage of the new process.
    c. For operational employees to acquire the skills necessary to perform the new procedures or tasks.
    d. All of the above.

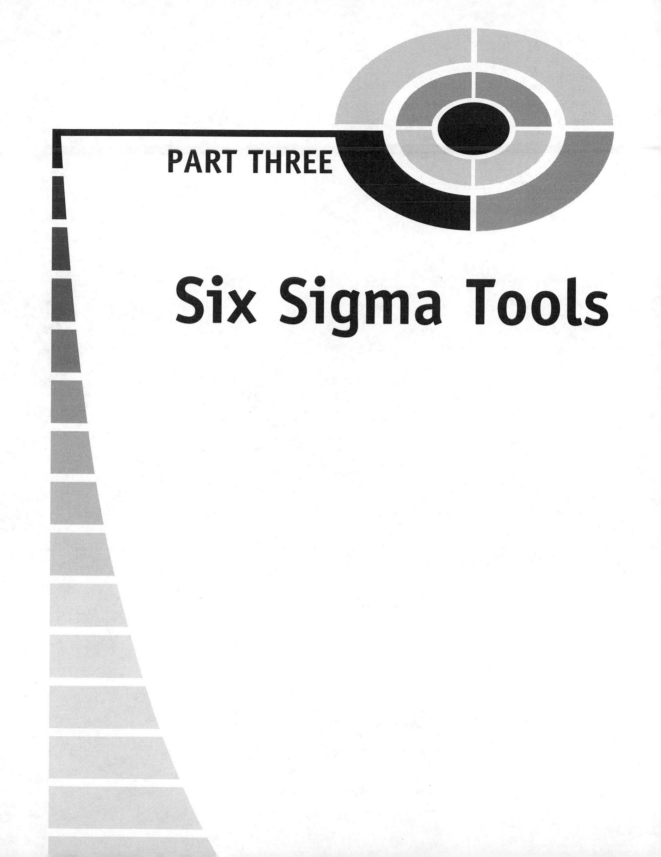

PART THREE

Six Sigma Tools

Activity Network Diagram

The activity network diagram is a tool to define the critical path for dependent tasks in a project. The *critical path* consists of all activities, in order of occurrence, required as soon as possible to keep the project on schedule. Delay in any of the critical task activities will result in slippage to the project's completion date. Tasks that are not on the critical path do not need to be completed as soon as possible: they have *slack time* associated with them. Differentiating between tasks on the critical path and those with slack time allows us to allocate our limited resources most effectively.

WHEN TO USE

Define Stage

- To identify the critical path for cycle time reduction.
- To identify project activities that determine the total project duration.

Improve Stage

- To verify the reduction in process-critical path cycle time.

METHODOLOGY

Begin by compiling a list of all the tasks that must be completed for the overall project. Arrange these tasks in a chronological order. Next, place all the tasks in a progressing line. Depending on the project, you might be able to work on some tasks simultaneously, while other tasks depend on the prior completion of tasks. Jobs that can be done simultaneously can be placed on parallel paths, whereas jobs that are dependent should be placed in series. In Figure F.1, a book revision process begins with the receipt of a final draft from the author. There are three simultaneous paths that could begin immediately: new cover design, issue new ISBN, and proof. Notice that the edit task cannot begin until both the proof and the begin layout editing tasks are complete. Likewise, the finish to printer task cannot begin until the final proof and new cover design tasks are complete.

Beginning at the first task and going forward, calculate the *earliest start* (*ES*) *time* for each task, the time at which all predecessor tasks are completed; this is calculated by summing the task times for each preceding task on the path. When more than one path meets before a task, we use the largest time as

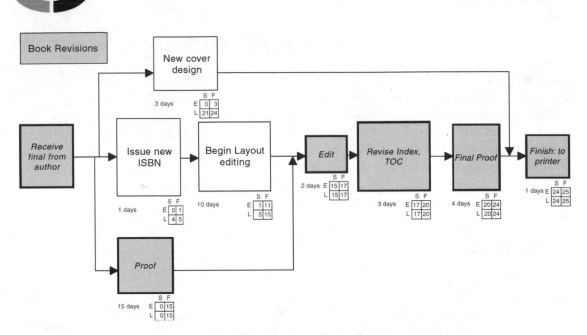

Figure F.1   Example of activity network for defining critical path.

the earliest start for the next task. For example, the earliest start time for the edit task is 15 days, since the sum of the issue new ISBN and begin new layout tasks is 11 days, while the proof task is longer at 15 days.

The *earliest finish (EF) time*, the time at which the task will be completed if it starts at the earliest possible starting time, is simply calculated by adding the task time to the earliest start time (i.e., EF = ES + task time). For example, the earliest finish for the edit task is 17 days (15 days ES plus 2 days task time).

Beginning at the last task and going backward, calculate each task's *latest finish (LF) time*, the time at which the task will be completed if it starts at the latest allowable start time. The latest finish time for the final task equals its previously calculated earliest finish time. For all other tasks, the latest finish time equals the latest start time of the task immediately following it. The latest start time for each task, the latest time at which the task can start without delaying the project completion, equals its latest finish time minus its task time.

INTERPRETATION

The activity network diagram shown uses the *activity-on-node type*, which in layman's terms means that each task is represented by a symbol. Arrows, showing the sequential ordering of the tasks, connect the symbols. Each sequentially ordered task is completed before moving on to the next task. Tasks that may be done simultaneously are represented on parallel paths. Below each task is a time schedule, indicating the earliest start, latest possible start, earliest finish, and latest finish time for that task.

The latest start indicates when the task must begin to avoid process delay. For example, if the layout editing does not begin by day 5, the process will be delayed.

In addition, this method will let you see where you can afford delays. On the critical path, shown in gray boxes, the earliest start and the latest start will always be equal. Otherwise, the difference between the ES and LS represents the slack time for the task. In Figure F.1, the begin layout editing task has an ES equal to 1 day and a LS equal to 5 days, so the slack time is 4 days. This implies that the task does not need to begin as soon as possible (day 1, the earliest start), but must begin by the latest start.

There is, by definition, no slack time on the critical path. That is, all tasks on the critical path must be completed as soon as possible (i.e., each task's earliest start time), or the project will be delayed.

PERT analysis, discussed later in Part 3, allows probabilistic estimates to be applied to a task's duration.

Affinity Diagram

Affinity diagrams are used to take a chaotic jumble of thoughts and ideas and sort them into coherent groupings. They help you to see all aspects of the problem and to figure out how these aspects are related. This method highlights trends and patterns which otherwise might have gone unrecognized. From there, you can begin to address problems meaningfully, rather than as a scattered collection of unrelated issues.

WHEN TO USE

The affinity diagram will often be your first step in a problem-solving process. Use it when you have a large number of thoughts, ideas, or facts that are not organized in any coherent manner. It is also very useful when traditional solutions to a problem have failed and you need to find new ways to approach a problem and build consensus.

Define Stage to Control Stage

- To reach consensus on issues affecting the team or the project success, such as the project's objectives, scope, or data collection strategy.
- To understand perceptions of current problems and their root causes, and then categorize to focus project's data collection.

An affinity can be used anywhere you are trying to generate ideas to reduce those ideas to a few manageable issues.

METHODOLOGY

Start with a general problem or issue which needs to be addressed. State this as the problem, objective, or goal in a simple phrase, such as "Develop a successful Six Sigma program," as shown in Figure F.2.

Have each team member write down one to three issues that contribute to the problem or prevent you from meeting the objective. Challenge them to think of different issues that affect your problem or problems that feed into it. Remember that this is a brainstorming process, which means that every idea, even the seemingly ludicrous, should be included and criticism is not allowed. The emphasis here is on getting as many ideas out as possible. Include both general ideas and nitpicky items. This all-inclusive method can lead to the discovery of problems

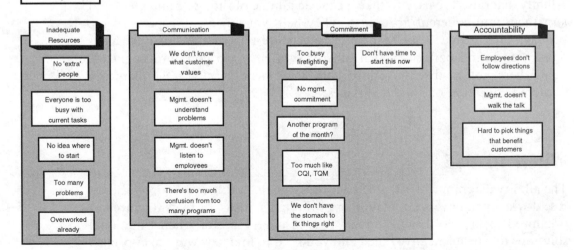

Figure F.2   Example of affinity diagram showing groupings of issues.

that might not have been mentioned otherwise. Each idea should be written down (exactly as it was suggested) onto a separate card (Post-it notes are sometimes used), represented in Figure F.2 as a square symbol by the software.

Once all the ideas are assembled, you can begin to sort them into categories of similar issues. As you might expect, it's not uncommon for there to be near replication of some of the ideas by the team members, since each team member is individually constructing the ideas. It's also common for some disagreement to occur in the grouping process. Because this is still a creative process, it's helpful to have team members individually group the issue cards, in silence. As others disagree with the grouping, allow them to change the grouping as they see fit. As one member moves a card into a particular grouping, which is yet unnamed, another member might challenge that and silently move the card into another group. The lack of verbal communication can force members to silently contemplate the choices of their comembers, a coerced empathy if you will, which can be helpful. Other times, depending on the personalities involved, it may become necessary to allow verbal communication to facilitate the grouping process.

Create header cards to describe each group. Discussion can be helpful here to generate an accurate label for the grouped ideas. These group labels then become the focal point for further analysis or discussion, perhaps as input to the prioritization matrix or nominal group technique, discussed later in Part 3.

INTERPRETATION

The end result of the affinity process is a collection of problems, grouped by main ideas. These main ideas, represented by the header cards, may provide key drivers that need to be addressed for achievement of the goal.

It's important to remember that the affinity diagram uses only subjective opinions of issues. As with any of these types of tools, we can use the tool to gain focus, but we must then substantiate these ideas with objective evidence using properly analyzed data.

In Figure F.2 the group identified 4 main issues from the 18 original issues. These issues may be further developed in other tools, such as a prioritization matrix.

ANOVA

An *ANOVA*, the acronym for the analysis of variance, is a tabular presentation of the sum of squares (SS) variance attributed to a source, the sum of squares attributed to error, and the total sum of squares from the data. F statistics on the significance of the source relative to the error are included.

WHEN TO USE

Measure Stage

- To isolate sources of measurement error, particularly when R&R studies cannot be done (such as in destructive testing).

Analyze Stage

- To look for differences between subsets of data as a source of variation in the process.
- To investigate statistical significance of a regression model to uncover potential process drivers.

METHODOLOGY

ANOVA provides a means of comparing the variation within each subset of data to the variation between the different subsets of data. The between subset variation is a reflection of the possible differences between the subset averages. The within subset variation, for each subset, is a reflection of the inherent variation observed when sampling from the subset repeatedly.

When used to test for differences in the averages between subsets of data (or treatments), the null hypothesis tested by the ANOVA (for a fixed effects model) is that all the subset averages are equal. The F statistic is used to compare the mean square treatment (the average between subset variation) with the mean square error (the sum of squares of the residuals). The assumptions in the test are that the distribution for each subset is normal and the subsets have equal variance (although their means may be different). The null hypothesis that the subsets are equal is rejected when the p value for the F test is less than 0.05, implying that at least one of the subset averages is different.

For example, using the data in the Table T.1, we can test whether the cycle times shown for the four products are equal.

INTERPRETATION

The results from Excel are shown in Table T.2.

The low p value indicates that the null hypothesis of equal means should be rejected: one or more of the product averages are significantly different. The between group variation is much larger than the within group variation.

Table T.1. Example Cycle Time Data for ANOVA.

Product A	Product B	Product C	Product D
159	180	167	174
161	174	163	182
164	180	160	171
166	184	165	176
158	177	161	179
162	178	158	175

Table T.2. Excel ANOVA Analysis.

SUMMARY				
Groups	**Count**	**Sum**	**Average**	**Variance**
Product A	6	970	161.6667	9.066667
Product B	6	1073	178.8333	11.36667
Product C	6	974	162.3333	11.06667
Product D	6	1057	176.1667	14.96667

ANOVA						
Source of Variation	**SS**	**df**	**MS**	**F**	**P-value**	**F crit**
Between Groups	1464.167	3	488.0556	42.01339	8.03E − 09	3.098393
Within Groups	232.3333	20	11.61667			
Total	1696.5	23				

Autocorrelation Charts

The autocorrelation function (ACF) is a tool for identifying dependence of current data on previous data points. It tests for correlation (in this case, autocorrelation) between observations of a given characteristic in the data set. You may notice a similarity between the formulas used for the autocorrelation function and the correlation index calculated in the scatter diagram. The scatter diagram is used to test for correlation between observations of different characteristics, while the ACF tests for correlation between observations of the same characteristic.

WHEN TO USE

Measure Stage

- To investigate process autocorrelation and its effect on baseline data.

Analyze Stage

- To analyze regression residuals for violation of independence assumption.

Control Stage

- To develop a control strategy that considers the serial dependence of the process.

Standard control charts require that observations from the process are independent of one another. Failure to meet this requirement increases the chance that the control chart will falsely indicate a process shift. Therefore, the autocorrelation function is a good tool to use to check the independence assumption. If control limits on an $\bar{X}$ chart are particularly tight, with many out-of-control points, autocorrelation should be suspected.

Many of the statistical tools, including regression, ANOVA, and general hypothesis tests, assume independence of the data observations. Failure to satisfy this assumption may result in increased Type I and Type II errors. Autocorrelation is inherent to many processes, including:

- **Chemical Processes.** Due to inertia of large batches, continuous flow of material, and/or feedback and feed-forward process control systems.

- **Service Processes.** As described in queuing theory, wait times for customers are often influenced by the wait time of previous customers.
- **Manufacturing Processes.** Due to computer controls of production equipment and downstream pooling of multiple stream processes.

METHODOLOGY

The ACF will first test whether adjacent observations are autocorrelated, that is, whether there is correlation between observations 1 and 2, 2 and 3, 3 and 4, and so on. This is known as lag one autocorrelation, since one of the pairs of tested observations lags the other by one period or sample. Similarly, it will test at other lags. For instance, the autocorrelation at lag four tests whether observations 1 and 5, 2 and 6, ... 19 and 23, and so on, are correlated.

In general, we should test for autocorrelation at lag one to lag $n/4$, where n is the total number of observations in the analysis. Estimates at longer lags have been shown to be statistically unreliable (Box and Jenkins, 1970).

Autocorrelation Function

The autocorrelation function is estimated at the given lag (m) as follows:

$$r_m = \frac{\sum_{i=1}^{n-m} (x_i - \bar{x})(x_{i+m} - \bar{x})}{\sum_{i=1}^{n} (x_i - \bar{x})^2}$$

for $m = 2, 3, 4, \ldots, n/4$, where n is the number of observations, and x-bar is the average of the observations.

Partial Autocorrelation Function

The partial autocorrelation function (PACF) is estimated at the given lag (m) as follows:

$$\Phi_{mm} = \frac{r_m - \sum_{j=1}^{m-1} \Phi_{m-1,j} r_{m-1}}{1 - \sum_{j=1}^{m-1} \Phi_{m-1,j} r_j}$$

where r_m is the autocorrelation function.

Significance Limit. The limits for the ACF (and PACF) at the stated significance level, if the true population ACF (or PACF) is zero. ACFs (or PACFs) exceeding this value should be investigated and assumed to be nonzero.

$$\text{LIMITS}_{r,\Phi} = \pm \left(\frac{k}{\sqrt{n}} \right)$$

where k is the ordinate of the normal distribution at the stated significance level (determined using Appendix 1) and n is the number of observations included in the analysis.

INTERPRETATION

If the autocorrelation is only significant at low lags (adjacent data points), you can increase the time between acquiring data points to lessen its effect. The data analyzed in the autocorrelation plot shown in Figure F.2A was sampled from a chemical process at the rate of one observation per minute. The autocorrelation is significant out to lag five, implying that revising the sampling rate to once every five minutes (or longer) will result in an independent data set.

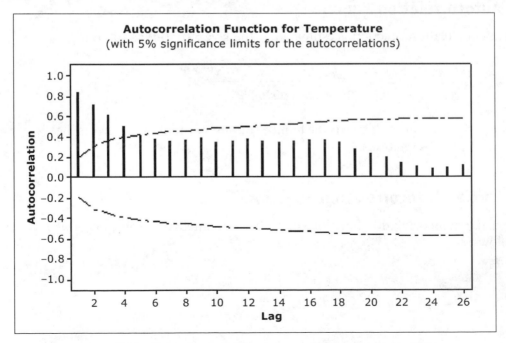

Figure F.2A   Example of significant autocorrelation out to lag five.

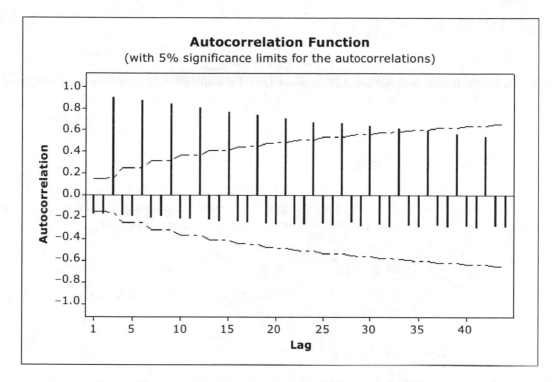

Autocorrelation Function
(with 5% significance limits for the autocorrelations)

Figure F.2B Example of autocorrelation due to mixed process streams.

Autocorrelation may also be due to sampling from multiple streams in a process. For example, when monitoring order processing times, if each data point is the time taken by each of three employees operating at a different average level, then an autocorrelation would appear at lag 3, such as shown in Figure F.2B.

In some cases, the effect of autocorrelation at smaller lags will influence the estimate of autocorrelation at longer lags. For instance, a strong lag one autocorrelation would cause observation 5 to influence observation 6, and observation 6 to influence 7. This results in an apparent correlation between observations 5 and 7, even though no direct correlation exists. The partial autocorrelation function (PACF) removes the effect of shorter lag autocorrelation from the correlation estimate at longer lags. This estimate is only valid to one decimal place.

ACFs and PACFs each vary between plus and minus one. Values closer to plus or minus one indicate strong correlation. Lags exceeding the confidence limits imply autocorrelation significantly different from zero.

Box-Whisker Chart

A *box-whisker chart* is a graphical tool used to compare summary data for multiple data sets. Each data set may be a unique characteristic, or data unique to a given condition, or any other useful category.

WHEN TO USE

In any application, box-whisker charts are *not* control charts, as they do not have statistical control limits. For that reason, they may not be used to establish statistical control of a process or to baseline a process.

Analyze Stage

- To graphically compare the location and variation of various processes or categories of products or services.

Improve Stage

- To graphically compare before and after states of process improvement.

METHODOLOGY

Figure F.3 of a box-whisker chart shows how cycle time varies with product. The cycle time data for each product is displayed in a box whose upper and lower edges are determined by the first and third quartiles of the data. (A quartile is 25% of the data, so the third quartile is at 75%.)

Protruding up and down from each box are whiskers, the lengths of which are defined by the following formula:

$$\text{Lower limit} = Q1 - 1.5 * [Q3 - Q1]$$
$$\text{Upper limit} = Q3 + 1.5 * [Q3 - Q1]$$

Note that quartiles are typically used since they are nonparametric (not dependent on the distribution of the data). If normality can be assumed, the box-whisker plot may instead use the mean and standard deviation to define the box and whisker lengths: the edges of the box defined at ± 1 sample standard deviations, with the whiskers extending to ± 3 sample standard deviations.

Extreme values may also be shown, usually as dots beyond the whiskers.

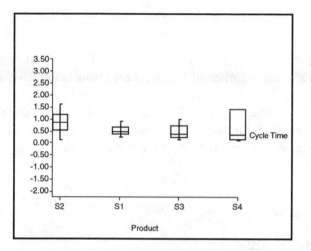

Figure F.3   Example of box-whisker chart.

INTERPRETATION

The analysis shown in Figure F.3 might be useful to understand root causes of cycle time variation. Notice how products S2 and S4 have more variation than products S1 and S3, although their median values don't appear significantly different (at least as far as we can tell from the graph). Categorizing the data in this way can sometimes be a good starting point for understanding the process dynamics and converging on suitable metrics.

As an enumerative statistical tool, care should be taken in interpretation. Unless statistical control of the underlying process is established, the statistics presented on the box-whisker chart may not be reflective of the expected process outcome.

C Chart

The C chart is one of a set of control charts specifically designed for attributes data. It monitors the number of times a condition occurs, relative to a constant sample size, when each sample can have more than one instance of the condition. For example, a specified number of transactions each month can be sampled from all the transactions that occurred. From each sample, you can track the total number of errors in the sample on the C chart.

WHEN TO USE

Measure Stage

- To estimate, using attributes data, the process baseline. Generally, we would greatly prefer the use of variables control charts for this purpose.

Improve Stage

- Since the number of errors tends to be quite small (for even very large samples), the use of attribute charts is limited in the improve stage.

METHODOLOGY

Samples are collected from the process at specific points each time. Each sample (at each point in time) has the same number of observed units, each of which may have one or more instances of the condition of interest.

Plotted statistic: the count of occurrences of a criteria of interest in a sample of items.

Centerline:

$$\bar{c} = \frac{\sum_{j=1}^{m} (count)_j}{m}$$

where m is the number of groups included in the analysis.

UCL, LCL (upper and lower control limit):

$$UCL = \bar{c} + 3\sqrt{\bar{c}}$$

$$LCL = MAX(0, \bar{c} - 3\sqrt{\bar{c}})$$

where n is the sample size and $\bar{c}$ is the average count.

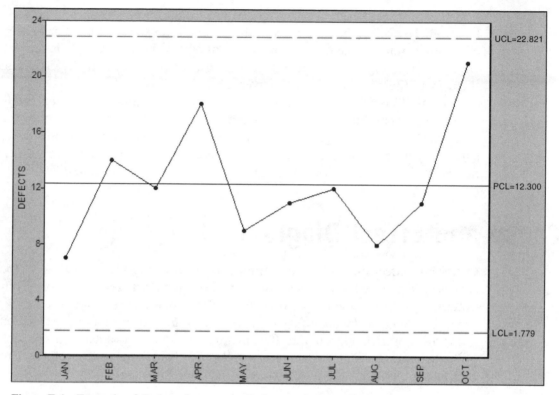

Figure F.4 Example of C chart for a controlled process (created using Quality America Green Belt XL software).

For example, we observe 500 telemarketing calls each week, and we record the total number of errors in each call, where each call may have more than one error. Ten months of data were observed, with the following number of errors in each sample: 7, 14, 12, 18, 9, 11, 12, 8, 11, 21. The control chart is shown in Figure F.4.

INTERPRETATION

The upper and lower control limits indicate the bounds of expected process behavior. The fluctuation of the points between the control limits is due to the variation that is intrinsic (built-in) to the process. This variation is due to "common causes" that influence the process. Any points outside the control limits can be attributed to a "special cause," implying a shift in the process. When a process is influenced by only common causes, then it is stable, and can be predicted.

If there are any out-of-control points, then special causes of variation must be identified and eliminated. Brainstorm and conduct designed experiments to find those process elements that contribute to sporadic changes in process location. To predict the capability of the process after special causes have been eliminated, remove the out-of-control points from the analysis. This has the effect of removing the statistical bias of the out-of-control points by dropping them from the calculations of the average and control limits.

Note that some SPC software will allow varying sample sizes for the C chart. In this case, the control limits and the average line will be adjusted for each sample. Many times, it is less confusing to use a U chart for this data, since only its control limits will vary (the average line will remain constant). See Statistical Process Control Charts later in Part 3 for more detail.

Cause and Effect Diagram

Cause and effect diagrams are graphical brainstorming tools. Listing all the causes for a given effect in a clear, organized way makes it easier to separate out potential problems and target areas for improvement. These charts are sometimes referred to as *fishbone diagrams* because of their form: causes are listed on lines which branch off from the effect in much the same way a fish's ribs branch off from its spine. They are sometimes called *Ishakawa diagrams* in reference to a Japanese engineer who popularized their usage for quality improvement.

WHEN TO USE

Analyze Stage

- To brainstorm potential underlying process factors, which can be investigated in a designed experiment.

Improve Stage

- To generate a list of potential failure modes that should be addressed in the solution.

METHODOLOGY

Begin by brainstorming the potential relationships between the process and the outcome. The outcome, or effect, is typically stated in terms of a problem rather than a desired condition, which tends to help the brainstorming.

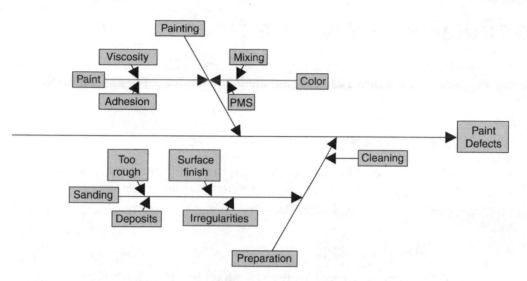

Figure F.5   Example of cause-and-effect diagram.

The major branches of the fishbone are chosen to assist in brainstorming or to categorize the potential problems afterwards. You may find it convenient to use either the 5Ms and E (manpower, machines, methods, material, measurement, environment) or 4Ps (policy, procedures, plant, people) to either categorize on the final fishbone or to ensure that all areas are considered during brainstorming. Categorizing the potential causes (as branches off the spine) can be helpful in the data collection or analysis. Subcauses (or branches) are added as needed, and it's often helpful to go down several levels of subcauses. See Figure F.5.

Bear in mind that the causes listed are *potential* causes, since there is no data at this point to support whether any of the causes really contribute to the problem. In that regard, as in all brainstorming activities, avoid judging the merits of each cause as it is offered. Only data can lead to that judgment.

INTERPRETATION

Use the cause and effect diagram to ensure that suitable potential causes are included in the data collection and analysis.

If a large majority of causes are contained in a small number of categories, consider recategorizing to break down the larger categories.

Confidence Interval on Mean

Given a sample from a population, the confidence interval around the true value of the mean can be estimated at a given confidence level.

WHEN TO USE

A key assumption is that the population has a normal distribution and is both constant (it does not change over time) and homogenous (a given sample is representative of the sample).

Measure Stage

- To estimate process average (for baseline estimates) when insufficient data exists to establish process control.

Analyze Stage

- To compare the mean of samples from different process conditions.

METHODOLOGY

There are two methods that may be used, depending on whether we have historical evidence of the population standard deviation.

Historical Standard Deviation Is Known

Calculate an average ($\bar{x}$) of n sample units.
Calculate the confidence interval as:

$$\bar{X} - Z_{\alpha/2}(\sigma/\sqrt{n}) < \mu < \bar{X} + Z_{\alpha/2}(\sigma/\sqrt{n})$$

Based on the assumption that the samples are from a population with a normal distribution, we use the normal distribution to determine the z values based on a confidence level. For a 95% confidence level, $\alpha = .05$, so $\alpha/2 = .025$ (from Appendix 1, $z_{\alpha/2} = 1.96$).

For example, the average waiting time in a doctor's office using a sample of 25 patients is 25.7 minutes. The population standard deviation is known to be 1.8 minutes. The confidence interval is calculated as:

$$\bar{X} - Z_{\alpha/2}(\sigma/\sqrt{n}) < \mu < \bar{X} + Z_{\alpha/2}(\sigma/\sqrt{n})$$
$$25.7 - 1.96(1.8/\sqrt{25}) < \mu < 25.7 + 1.96\ (1.8/\sqrt{25})$$
$$24.99 < \mu < 26.41$$

Historical Standard Deviation Is Not Known

Calculate an average ($\bar{x}$) and the sample standard deviation s of n sample units.

Calculate the confidence interval as:

$$\bar{X} - t_{\alpha/2,n-1}(s/\sqrt{n}) < \mu < \bar{X} + t_{\alpha/2,n-1}(s/\sqrt{n})$$

Based on the assumption that the samples are from a population with a normal distribution, we use the Student's t distribution to determine the t values based on a confidence level. For a 95% confidence level, $\alpha = .05$, so $\alpha/2 = .025$.

For example, the average waiting time in a doctor's office using a sample of 25 patients is 25.7 minutes. The sample standard deviation is calculated as 1.8 minutes. From Appendix 2, $t_{.025,24} = 2.064$. The confidence interval is calculated as:

$$\bar{X} - t_{\alpha/2,n-1}(s/\sqrt{n}) < \mu < \bar{X} + t_{\alpha/2,n-1}(s/\sqrt{n})$$
$$25.7 - 2.064(1.8/\sqrt{25}) < \mu < 25.7 + 2.064(1.8/\sqrt{25})$$
$$24.95 < \mu < 26.44$$

Both Excel and Minitab offer confidence interval calculations. Minitab requires the raw data. In Excel, you can use its other functions to calculate the required input parameters when using raw data.

INTERPRETATION

A 95% confidence limit on the mean, for example, indicates that in 95% of the samples the confidence interval will include the true population mean μ (pronounced "mu"). We see from the calculation that as the number of samples n increases, the confidence interval gets smaller. That is, we have more confidence in the value of the true mean when we take a larger sample.

Notice that the confidence interval when sigma is unknown (using the t tables) is wider than when sigma is known (using the z tables), since we lose some statistical confidence when we estimate the standard deviation. An additional parameter of the Student's t distribution is the degrees of freedom v (pronounced nu), which equals $n - 1$. Statistically, we say that we have lost a degree of freedom in estimating the standard deviation using the sample data.

A given sample lying within the confidence interval does *not* provide evidence of process stability, which must be verified with an SPC chart.

Confidence Interval on Proportion

When we sample from a population, and have historical evidence of the population standard deviation, we can estimate the confidence interval of the mean at a given confidence level.

WHEN TO USE

A key assumption is that population has a normal distribution and is both constant (it does not change over time) and homogenous (a given sample is representative of the sample). The normal distribution provides a good approximation to the binomial distribution when the sample size is large and when np and $n(1 - p)$ are both greater than 5.

Measure Stage

- To estimate process average error rate (for baseline estimates) when insufficient data exists to establish process control.

Analyze Stage

- To compare error rates of samples from different process conditions.

METHODOLOGY

Calculate an average error rate ($\hat{p}$) of n sample units.
Calculate the confidence interval as:

$$\hat{p} - Z_{\alpha/2}\sqrt{\frac{\hat{p}(1 - \hat{p})}{n}} \leq p \leq \hat{p} + Z_{\alpha/2}\sqrt{\frac{\hat{p}(1 - \hat{p})}{n}}$$

Based on the assumption that the samples are from a population with a normal distribution, we use the normal distribution to determine the z values

based on a confidence level. For a 95% confidence level, $\alpha = .05$, so $\alpha/2 = .025$. From Appendix 1, $z_{\alpha/2} = 1.96$.

For example, there were 14,248 orders processed during the third week of June. A sample of 100 orders processed during that week was randomly selected. Twenty-four orders in the sample were found to have one or more critical defects. The confidence interval is calculated as:

$$\hat{p} - Z_{\alpha/2}\sqrt{\frac{\hat{p}(1-\hat{p})}{n}} \leq p \leq \hat{p} + Z_{\alpha/2}\sqrt{\frac{\hat{p}(1-\hat{p})}{n}}$$

$$0.24 - 1.96\sqrt{\frac{0.24 * 0.76}{100}} \leq p \leq 0.24 + 1.96\sqrt{\frac{0.24 * 0.76}{100}}$$

$$0.16 \leq p \leq 0.32$$

INTERPRETATION

A 95% confidence limit on the error rate, for example, indicates that in 95% of the samples the confidence interval will include the true error rate. We see from the calculation that as the number of samples n increases, the confidence interval gets smaller. That is, we have more confidence in the value of the true error rate when we take a larger sample.

In the example above, how many orders with defects would we expect during the third week of June? An estimate of the number of orders with defects would range from 2,280 (16% of 14,248) to 4,559 (32% of 14,248)

A given sample lying within the confidence interval does *not* provide evidence of process stability, which must be verified with an SPC chart.

Contingency Tables

Contingency tables, also known as $R \times C$ *contingency tables*, refer to data that can be assembled into tables (of rows and columns) for comparison.

WHEN TO USE

The statistical test examines whether subsets of populations are independent. For example, we may have five healthcare plans to choose from, and wish to determine if there is a detectable difference between how these different plans are rated by hourly and salaried employees. Similarly, we may be interested to see if there is a difference between how men and women rate three different television shows, or whether the repair rate for four machines is different from shift to shift.

Analyze Stage

- To compare results of sampling from different process conditions to detect if they are independent.

METHODOLOGY

The methodology for analyzing the R rows by C columns involves using the chi-square statistic to compare the observed frequencies with the expected frequencies, assuming independence of the subsets. The null hypothesis is that the p values are equal for each column in each row. The alternative hypothesis is that at least one of the p values is different.

Construct the R × C table by separating the subsets of the population into the tested categories.

Calculate the expected values for each row/column intersection cell e_{ij}. The expected value for each row/column is found by multiplying the percent of that row by the percent of the column by the total number.

Calculate the test statistic:

$$\chi_0^2 = \sum_{i=1}^{r} \sum_{j=1}^{c} \frac{(o_{ij} - e_{ij})^2}{e_{ij}}$$

For example, consider a survey of 340 males and 160 females asking their preference for one of three television shows. The R × C contingency table is shown in Table T.3.

Table T.3. Example Data Comparing Preferences for Three Shows.

Sex	Show1	Show2	Show3	Total
Male	160	140	40	340
Female	40	60	60	160
Totals	200	200	100	500

Table T.4. Expected Preferences for Each Show Assuming Independance.

Sex	Show1	Show2	Show3	Total
Male	136	136	68	340
Female	64	64	32	160
Totals	200	200	100	500

The expected frequency for male and show1 $= e_{11} = (340/500) * (200/500) * 500 = 136$.

Similarly, the expected values for the other row/column pairs (e_{RC}) are found as $e_{12} = 136$; $e_{13} = 68$; $e_{21} = 64$; $e_{22} = 64$; $e_{23} = 32$ (and shown in Table T.4):

The test statistic is calculated as:

$$\chi_0^2 = (160 - 136)^2/136 + (140 - 136)^2/136 + (40 - 68)^2/68$$
$$+ (40 - 64)^2/64 + (60 - 64)^2/64 + (60 - 32)^2/32 = 49.63$$

INTERPRETATION

We reject the null hypothesis if $\chi_0^2 > \chi_\alpha^2$ for $(r - 1)(c - 1)$ degrees of freedom, where χ_α^2 is the chi-square value at the α level of significance.

In the example above, the critical value of the chi-square statistic at the 0.05 level of significance, with two degrees of freedom, is found from Appendix 3 as 5.991. Since the test statistic exceeds the critical value, the null hypothesis is rejected, and we assert that there is a difference between the male and female responses.

Contour Plot

A contour plot is made up of curves, each having a constant value of a fitted response. The curves have equally spaced values of the response. Additional factors are set at selected values (usually their mean).

WHEN TO USE

Improve Stage

- Use in response surface analysis to determine where a maximum or minimum response is expected within or close to the data range.

METHODOLOGY

For example, we can generate a contour plot for the model $Y = 4.5 + 0.32x_1 - 0.63x_2$. For any value of the response (Y), we can determine x_1 given x_2 or x_2 given x_1.

When $y = 5$, then $0.32x_1 - 0.63x_2 - 0.5 = 0$

If $x_1 = 0$, then $x_2 = -0.5/0.63 = -0.794$

If $x_2 = 0$, then $x_1 = 0.5/0.32 = 1.56$

Thus, the contour line for $Y = 5$ passes through the points $(0, -0.79)$ and $(1.56, 0)$. We can also easily determine for $Y = 5$ the value of x_2 when $x_1 = +1$ and $x_1 = -1$ and the value of x_1 when $x_2 = +1$ and $x_2 = -1$. In this way, we then calculate other contour lines (for different y values).

Overlaid Contour Plots

Overlaid contour techniques provide a method for evaluating joint regions of optimality for more than one response. In this technique, we lay one contour plot over the other and look for regions that provide good compromise on optimizing both responses. The overlay requires the same factors and scaling on each contour plot.

INTERPRETATION

An example of a first-order model contour plot with interaction is shown in Figure F.6. The interactions produce a curvature in the contours. When there are first-order main effects only, the contour plot will have straight, parallel lines. The response surface will be a flat plane. When interaction terms are present, the contours take on an elliptical shape, and the response surface is a twisted plane.

The direction of the path of steepest ascent or descent is indicated by a line drawn perpendicular to the contour lines.

Because contours can only involve two factors, the appearance of contour plots using different factors can vary widely.

Contour Plot for First-Order Model with Interaction

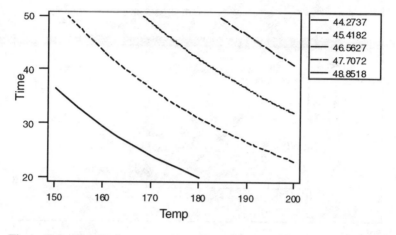

Figure F.6   First-order response surface with interaction using Minitab.

Second-Order Model Contour Plot

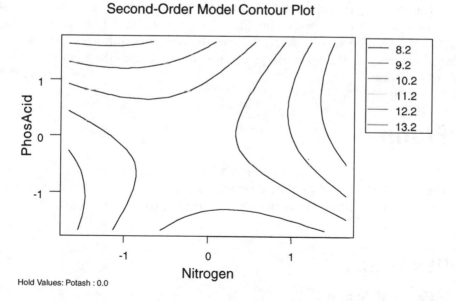

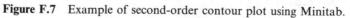

Figure F.7   Example of second-order contour plot using Minitab.

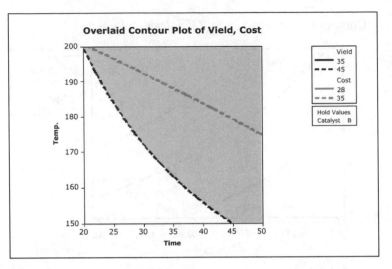

Figure F.8   Example of overlaid contour plot using Minitab.

The contour plot for the second-order model may look as shown in Figure F.7 (page 201). Note in this example how the response is a local minimum in the *y* direction (PhosAcid) and a local maximum in the *x* direction (Nitrogen), indicating a saddle point.

In Figure F.8 (above) an overlaid contour for yield and cost is shown for temperature and time, when the third factor (catalyst) is held at its high condition (A). The area between the two dashed lines indicates the region of joint optimality of the response yield and cost. See also the next tool, desirability function.

Control Plans

A control plan provides an overview of the strategies that will be used to ensure that key process or part characteristics are controlled through either detection or prevention strategies, or the combination of the two.

WHEN TO USE

Control Stage

- To document the strategy for controlling the key process variables.

METHODOLOGY

Key inputs to a control plan include the results of designed experiments and failure modes and effects analysis. The failure modes and effects analysis (and its RPN, risk priority number) determines the failure modes that are the most critical to control. The assumptions used to determine the detection level in the FMEA must be incorporated into the control plan.

For each key characteristic, the following information is defined:

- *Specification.* What is the definition of "good" and "bad" for this characteristic?
- *Measurement technique.* How will the characteristic be measured? The control plan should reference more detailed measurement procedures, where needed, to instruct personnel on the proper use and interpretation of the measurement equipment.
- *Sample size.* How many measurements are required at each point in time?
- *Sample frequency.* How often should a new set of measurements be taken?
- *Analytical tool.* How are the measurements evaluated? In this case, audio alarms are installed to monitor characteristics thought to have high process capability. Other characteristics are monitored via control charts to detect process trends leading to undesirable conditions.
- *Reaction rules.* What is the proper response to the alarms (audio or from control chart)? Who should be notified?

INTERPRETATION

An example is shown in Table T.5.

Table T.5.   Example Control Plan.

Characteristic	Specification	Measurement Technique	Sample Size	Sample Frequency	Analytic Tool	Reaction Rules
Finished diameter	$1.250 \pm .0002$	Johannson	5	1 sg/hr	$\bar{X}$ chart w/ run rules	If other characteristics in control, adjust
Local ambient temp.	70 ± 5	Thermocouple	1	Continuous	Alarmed	Stop production; Adjust cooling control; resume production once temp. OK
Cooling temp.	120 ± 5	Thermocouple	1	1 per min.	Alarmed	Stop production; Adjust cooling control; resume production once temp. OK
Coolant viscosity	.88–.94	Viscometer	1	1 per month	X Chart	Purge system

Design of Experiments (DOE)

A designed experiment consists of planned trials, where factors are set to predefined levels and one or more response variables are measured. DOE provide an understanding of the sources of variation contributing to a process.

WHEN TO USE

Measure Stage

- To estimate the effect of various conditions or equipment on measurement variation.

Analyze Stage

- To determine the process drivers, the sources of variation in a process.

Improve Stage

- To optimize a process (using response surface designs).

METHODOLOGY

Planning

In planning for a designed experiment, we should consider the following issues:

- Why should an experiment be done?
- What responses should be measured? How will they be measured?
- What factors and interactions will be investigated? What are suitable levels for each?
- When should it be scheduled, so as to minimize disruptions to the process?
- Who should specify/execute the experiment?

The project team and key stakeholders must be committed on the experimental design and its plan. Key team personnel, including the Black Belt, should be on hand to lead the experiment (although operational personnel will be responsible for operating the process). Through monitoring the course of the experiment, it is possible the Black Belt will observe conditions that lead to a better understanding of the process dynamics.

The experimental plan should include projections and allocation of resources, including costs for personnel, materials, and equipment. Don't commit all your resources to one design. A good rule of thumb is to spend no more than 20% of your total resources on any one experiment, since each successive experiment will provide information that will be confirmed or expanded on in subsequent experiments. The summarized results of each experiment should provide information on what went wrong and what to do next. Critical factors may not have been included, or were not varied sufficiently, so additional trials may be needed to collect more information.

There are several desirable characteristics of an experimental design:

- Provides distribution of information throughout the region of interest. We may begin the experimental process looking at a wide region, then narrow our focus to a particular region that looks interesting.
- Includes the necessary conditions to develop a model that predicts the response, as close as possible to the true response, at all points within the stated region of interest. This may require three or more levels of particular factors, when nonlinear models are required.
- Allows the analyst to detect a lack of fit in the model.
- May require blocking to meet the limitations of data collection or when we wish to add runs to designs (such as folding).
- Allows sequential buildup of design, such as by folding, or added axial points.
- Provides internal estimate of error variance.

The best, and most common, approach is to begin with an effective *screening design*, which will provide information on key factors and the two-factor interactions between these factors. The design can be sequentially improved with additional trials to acquire additional information.

Defining Responses

The *response* in a designed experiment is the parameter we are observing as the outcome of the experiment. For example, in a manufacturing process, we may be concerned about the density of an injection molded part. We will change a variety of conditions within the process and measure the resulting part density. In a service process, we may seek to measure the impact of process changes on customer satisfaction or cycle time.

We can often measure more than one response in an experiment. In some cases, the responses are converted or transformed during analysis to simplify the model or to uncover factors that contribute to variation in the response. See also Transformations later in Part 3.

In any event, the most useful responses are quantitative variables, rather than qualitative attributes. We need sufficient resolution on the measured variable to use the statistical regression techniques. Before conducting the experiment, we should analyze the measurement system for error in estimating the response using the measurement systems analysis (MSA) techniques. When responses are qualitative, we can sometimes convert them to quantitative scores (such as Likert scales). When conversion is not convenient or helpful, logistic regression techniques should be used for analysis.

Defining Factors

The parameters that we vary in the process to achieve changes in the response are known as *factors*. Generally, we will control these factors by setting them at specific levels for each run, or trial, of the experiment. We will run the experiment at various conditions of each of the factors, so that the effect of each factor on the response can be calculated. In an injection molding process, we may want to investigate the effect of changing furnace temperature, fill pressure, and the moisture of the raw material. Even though we cannot generally set the moisture level of the material in normal operations, we can sample and segregate the material into two or more distinct levels for the experiment. Likewise in a service process, we may choose, for the experiment, to test the effect of two different process designs, such as with and without customer follow-up.

The factors that are not generally controlled in your operations are sometimes called *subsidiary factors*. Taguchi referred to these as *noise factors*, or the *outer array*. Examples include ambient temperature, humidity, and vibration. As mentioned, it is preferred to control these factors for the experiment.

Factors are selected for the designed experiment by brainstorming among the team members. This will typically result in a long list of potential factors. For an effective yet small screening design, we'd like to limit the design to five or seven key factors. Even though this may seem "impossible" for your process, it is often the best practice. If cost and time are of little concern, then add more factors as necessary. But when cost or time is limited, the number of factors can be reduced using the nominal *group technique* or *prioritization matrix*. Alternatively, we could decide to hold some factors constant, effectively excluding them from the analysis. Factors that are neither held constant nor included are potential *lurking factors*.

Lurking factors may be a source of bias or error in the analysis. Bias causes us to confuse the effect of the factor with another factor, particularly if the lurking factor happens to be coincident with another factor. In other cases, it just limits the usefulness of the results, such as if we do not include the effects of communication skills in a customer support experiment.

We should always randomize the order of the trials to prevent any bias in the estimates. In some case, however, we cannot fully randomize the experimental trials, and instead run the experiments in blocks. Examples of *blocking factors* include the day of the week, a batch of material, a run of the furnace, an airline flight, and so on. In each of these cases, we may have multiple run conditions that can be randomized within the block, but these blocking factors cannot be randomized within the entire experiment.

Consider the baking of cookies. We might vary a number of parameters, such as the ingredients (margarine vs. butter, chocolate chips vs. M&M's), the cooking temperature, and the cooking time. While the ingredients can be varied within each batch, the time or temperature within a batch cannot be varied. In this case, time and temperature are coincident with the batch and are thus blocking factors.

In other cases, we cannot run all the sample combinations within a given batch simply because the limited size of a batch (for example, the size of the oven) permits only so many factor combinations. In this case, the batch itself becomes a blocking factor. The differences we see between the factor combinations in batch 1 and batch 2 may be due to the factor effects, or due to the batch-to-batch variation.

If we have a strong suspicion that the blocking factor would interact with a factor, we might be able to include it as a main factor. In the cookie baking example, we could treat each oven cycle as a single run of the experiment, and vary the temperature, time, and ingredients for each oven cycle. In this way, we could estimate interactions between temperature, time, and ingredients.

There are other factors, sometimes called *casual factors*, that may have an impact on our experimental response, such as temperature, humidity, time of day, and so on. If we think these factors are truly important, we should make them controllable factors for the experiment. If we can't, or choose not to since it would increase the size or cost of the experiment, we should at least measure them. We can then estimate if they are correlated with the response, which would suggest the need for additional experimental runs to analyze their effect.

Defining Factor Levels

For each factor, we must define specific levels at which to run the experimental conditions.

Factors may be either quantitative (measured) or qualitative (categorical). The qualitative factor categories are converted to coded units (such as -1 and $+1$) for regression analysis.

Qualitative factor levels may be inherent to the process or product under investigation. For example, we may have three product configurations, or we may be interested in the variation among four machining centers.

For quantitative factors, if we expect the response to be nonlinear with respect to the factor, we need at least three levels for that factor. Nonlinear effects are not addressed in initial experiments, but are instead left until we can optimize in the improve stage. Earlier experiments will be used to screen out insignificant factors, which can be done with only two levels per factor. Bear in mind that more levels lead to more experimental runs. In addition, software used for generating designs may limit the design choices when there are mixed levels for the factors.

When we define the levels for each factor, we want to span the region of interest. It's helpful to think of the expected variation we are likely to see for the factor during normal operations, but sometimes this results in factor levels being too close to measure an effect. For example, if we think temperature typically only varies from 70 to 80 degrees, we may not see much of an effect due to temperature over that 10-degree difference. It's usually better to think of "worse case scenarios," where the factor may vary considerably more. Generally, the wider the difference between the factor levels, the easier the effect will be to measure.

When we start moving far away from normal operating conditions, we can enter unknown terrain that can even be hazardous for some processes. In this case, it might be better to keep the factor levels at reasonable values and, if the factor is significant, perform additional experiments using the response surface or evolutionary operation techniques to find optimal factor levels.

Conducting the Experiment

When it comes time to implement the experimental design, some helpful guidelines include:

- *Be there!* It's important to be an active participant in the design. The data collection is a critical part of the learning process, offering opportunities to experience aspects of the process dynamics that may not have been discussed in problem solving. For this reason, and to limit potential bias in the data, process personnel should operate the process and collect the data.
- *Randomize trials.* The order of the experimental runs should be randomized across the entire design and within blocks (if blocking

factors are used). This randomization limits any potential bias introduced during the experiment.

- *Independence of runs*. When each condition is run, the process should not be influenced by prior conditions. Some processes will require their setup conditions to be torn down and reset.

INTERPRETATION

The analysis of the experiment includes the following tools discussed elsewhere in Part 3: regression analysis, interaction plots, residuals analysis.

When an experiment is run in blocks, the design isolates the effect of the blocking factor so its contribution to an ANOVA may be estimated. As a result of this design, interaction effects cannot be estimated between the blocking factor and any of the main factors. In the regression analysis, if the blocking factor is significant, its interactions with the significant main factors can be investigated with additional runs.

Desirability Function

Derringer and Suich (1980) developed an analytical approach to determining the simultaneous optima for several responses, known as a *desirability function* (Myers and Montgomery). Minitab provides calculation of desirability function given the input parameters discussed below.

WHEN TO USE

Improve Stage

- To determine simultaneous optimal conditions for multiple responses.

METHODOLOGY

For each response, we define the goal as either a minimization, a maximization, or achieving a specified target value.

Each response is weighted with respect to meeting its goal using a desirability function (d). A composite response (D) is generated as the simple geometric mean of each response desirability function as follows:

$$D = (d_1 * d_2 * d_3 * \cdots * d_m)^{1/m}$$

Minimizing the Response

The desirability function when the goal is to minimize the response (i.e., smaller is better) requires a specified target value, which is the desired minimum (where smaller values provide little improvement) and an upper bound (a point of undesirable response).

$$d = \left[\frac{\text{Response} - \text{upper bound}}{\text{Target} - \text{upper bound}} \right]^s$$

Maximizing the Response

The desirability function when the goal is to maximize the response (i.e., larger is better) requires a specified target value (the desired maximum, where larger values provide little improvement) and a lower bound (a point of undesirable response).

$$d = \left[\frac{\text{Response} - \text{lower bound}}{\text{Target} - \text{lower bound}} \right]^s$$

Target the Response

The desirability function when the goal is to achieve a target value requires a specified target value and specified lower and upper bounds. When the response is between the lower bound and the target, the desirability function is as calculated for the maximize the response case. When the response is between the upper bound and the target, the desirability function is as calculated for the minimize the response case.

Calculating the Weights

The weights s and t are determined as follows:

< 1 (min $= 0.1$): less emphasis on target; response far from target is very desirable.
$= 1$: equal importance on target and bound (linear).
> 1 (max $= 10$): high emphasis on target. Must be very close to target for desirability.

INTERPRETATION

Maximize D. Values of desirability near 1 (the maximum) indicate that all responses are in the desirable range simultaneously.

Distributions

When process and population data are fit by assumed distributions, broad predictions can be made with minimal data. Popular statistical distributions include the binomial and Poisson for discrete (count) data and the normal, exponential, and robust Johnson and Pearson distributions for continuous (measurement) data.

WHEN TO USE

Measure to Control Stages

To estimate properties of an existing or potential process or population, including its failure rate or sigma level.

Binomial Distribution

Used to estimate the number of units meeting one of two possible conditions in a process or population. For example, if the population is the total number of orders shipped in July, the condition of interest might be the number of units shipped on time. Note that there is only one other possible condition: the order is not shipped on time. It may be applied when the population is large, theoretically infinite (such as a process), or when the sample size is relatively small (less than or equal to 10%) compared to the population of interest.

Poisson Distribution

Used to estimate the number of instances a condition occurs in a process or population, where the condition may occur multiple times in a given sample unit. For example, if the population is the total number of orders shipped in July, the condition of interest might be the number of errors on the invoices. Note how this is different from the binomial estimate of the process error rate, since each invoice can have more than one error. The sample unit (for example, an invoice) is assumed to be infinitely large, providing ample opportunity for the condition of interest.

Exponential Distribution

Used for highly skewed measurement (continuous) data, such as the time between occurrences of a condition of interest. The exponential is often used to estimate the mean time between failures, which is a convenient statistic when process failures are well modeled by the Poisson distribution.

Normal Distribution

Used for measurement (continuous) data that is theoretically without bound in both the positive and negative directions, and symmetric about an average (i.e., skewness equals zero) with a defined shape parameter (i.e., kurtosis equals one). Normal distributions are perhaps the most widely known distribution: the familiar bell-shaped curve. While some statisticians would have you believe they are also nature's most widely occurring distribution, others would suggest you take a good look at one in a textbook, since you're not likely to see one occur in the "real world." Most statisticians and quality practitioners today would recognize that there is nothing inherently "normal" (pun intended) about the normal distribution, and its use in statistics is only due to its simplicity. It is well defined, so it is convenient to assume normality when errors associated with that assumption are relatively insignificant.

Pearson and Johnson Distributions

Used for measurement (continuous) data that does not fit the properties of known distributions such as the normal and exponential. Quality improvement efforts often lead to nonnormal processes, such as through narrowing or constraining the distribution or moving its location to an optimal condition. Similarly, nature itself can impose bounds on a process, such as a service process whose waiting time is physically bounded at the lower end by zero. The proper design of a service process sets the process wait time as close as economically possible to zero, causing the process mode, median, and average to move toward zero. In manufacturing, concentricity or roundness is also achieved in this manner. These processes will tend toward nonnormality, regardless of whether they are stable (in control) or unstable.

METHODOLOGY

Statistical distributions are characterized by up to four parameters:

- *Central tendency.* For symmetrical distributions (see Skewness, below) the average (or mean) provides a good description of the central tendency or location of the process. For very skewed distributions, such as incomes or housing prices, the median is a much better indicator of central tendency.

- *Standard Deviation*. The standard deviation provides an estimate of variation. In mathematical terms, it is the *second moment about the mean*. In simpler terms, it is related to the average distance of the process observations from the mean.
- *Skewness*. The skewness provides a measure of the location of the mode (or high point in the distribution) relative to the average. In mathematical terms, it is the *third moment about the mean*. Symmetrical distributions, such as the normal distribution, have a skewness of zero. When the mode is to the left of the average, the skewness is negative; to the right, it is positive.
- *Kurtosis*. The kurtosis provides a measure of the "peakedness" of a distribution. In mathematical terms, it is the *fourth moment about the mean*. The normal distribution has a kurtosis of one. Distributions that are more peaked have higher kurtosis.

If we know, or can reliably assume, the type of distribution to be applied to the process, we can estimate the necessary parameters using sample data.

The binomial, Poisson, and exponential distributions require only a known (or reliably estimated) average to define the distribution. These are one-parameter distributions, meaning that the remaining parameters (standard deviation, skewness, and kurtosis) are defined solely by its mean. The normal distribution requires two parameters (the mean and the standard deviation), since the skewness and kurtosis are defined to produce its characteristic bell shape.

The Johnson and Pearson distributions require estimates of up to four parameters for a given distribution shape. These methods are best applied using statistical software to fit the distributional curves to a set of sample data.

INTERPRETATION

Binomial Distribution

The distributional parameter, the average proportion, is assumed for a given population or is calculated by dividing the number of items in a sample that meet the condition of interest (the count) by the total number of items inspected (the sample size). We can calculate the probability of counting x items in a sample from a population with a known average proportion using MS Excel's statistical function BINOMDIST.

For example, to estimate the probability of finding exactly 3 orders with one or more errors in a sample of 50 orders, when the process mean is known to be 10%, the Excel calculation is BINOMDIST(3,50,0.1,0). The solution is 13.86%. The last parameter in the Excel formula (zero in this case) indicates whether the solution provides the cumulative result or the finite result. If we were interested in the probability of 3 or less orders, we would enter BI-NOMDIST(3,50,0.1,1) to calculate the cumulative probability (up to and including 3 errors), which equals 25.03%.

Poisson Distribution

The distributional parameter, the average number of instances per unit, is assumed for a given population or is calculated by dividing the number of instances that occur in a sample (the count) by the total number of items inspected (the sample size). We can calculate the probability of counting x instances in a sample from a population with a known average number of instances per unit using MS Excel's statistical function POISSON.

For example, to estimate the probability of finding exactly 300 typographical errors in a sample of 150 orders (i.e., 2 errors per order), when the process is known to average 4 typographical errors per order, the Excel calculation is POISSON(2,4,0). The solution is 14.65%. If we were interested in the probability of 2 or less typographical errors per order, we would enter POISSON(2,4,1), which equals 23.81%. Note that this is the sum of POISSON(0,4,0), POISSON(1,4,0), and POISSON(2,4,0).

Exponential Distribution

The distributional parameter lambda (λ) is calculated as $1/\mu$, where μ is the average time between occurrences. MS Excel's EXPONDIST function may be used to estimate the probabilities associated with an exponential process.

For example, if the time between accidents in a production plant averages 47 days (i.e., the accident rate is 13% and the plant runs 365 days a year), we can determine the probability of having an accident within the first 31 days after the last accident using the formula EXPONDIST(31,1/47,1), which equals 48.29%. Conversely, the probability of being accident-free for that period is $1 - .4829$, which equals 51.71%.

Normal Distribution

The average ($\bar{x}$) of a sample can be calculated by summing the measurements and dividing by the number of measurements (N). The standard deviation of the N sample measurements can be calculated as:

$$s = \frac{\sum_{j=1}^{N} (\bar{x} - x_i)^2}{N}$$

We calculate a z value to convert the given normal distribution into a standardized normal distribution, which has a mean of zero and a standard deviation of one.

$$z = \frac{(x - \bar{x})}{s}$$

Appendix 1 provides the cumulative percentage points of the standard normal distribution. The z value allows us to estimate the probability of being less than or greater than any given x value, such as a customer requirement. For example, if we calculate that the average cycle time of an order fulfillment process is 4.46 days and the standard deviation of the cycle time is 3.5 days, we can calculate a z value for an upper specification of 10 days as follows:

$$z = \frac{(10 - 4.46)}{2.97} = 1.86$$

From Appendix Table 1, we find that a z value of 1.58 corresponds to a cumulative probability of .9686, implying that 96.86% of the process will be within the customer requirement. Conversely, $1 - .9686$ (or 3.14%) will exceed the requirement of 10 days, assuming the process is adequately modeled by the normal distribution. This assumption is conveniently verified for a set of data using the tests discussed elsewhere in Part 3 (see "Goodness of Fit").

Pearson and Johnson Distributions

When the convenience of known distributions such as the normal or exponential cannot be applied, the more advanced curve-fitting techniques can be used to model the process data, using these basic assumptions:

1. The data is representative of the process during the period when the data was collected (i.e., measurement error is negligible, and the sampling process produced data reflective of the process conditions). This implies that the data has sufficient resolution to estimate variation among the data and that there is sufficient data to represent the common cause variation in the process.
2. The data can be represented by a single, continuous distribution. A single distribution can only be sensibly fit to the data when the process is stable (in statistical control), without any influences that may shift the process in time (special causes).
3. We cannot claim that data are distributed according to our hypothesis. We can claim only that the data may be represented by the hypothesized distribution. More formally, we can test and accept or reject, at a given confidence level, the hypothesis that the data has the same

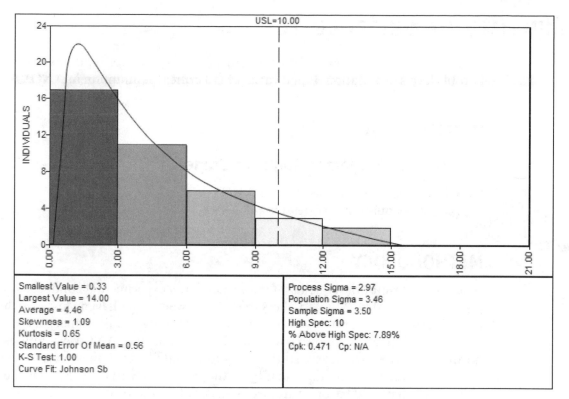

Figure F.8A Johnson distribution (created using Green Belt XL software).

distribution function as a proposed function. The Kolmogorov-Smirnov (K-S) goodness of fit statistic should be used as a relative indicator of curve fit.

For example, the K-S goodness of fit test is 0.31 for the order fulfillment cycle time data above, indicating a relatively poor fit for the normal distribution. Figure F.8A shows the Quality America Green Belt XL software's Johnson curve fit to the data. The predicted percent exceeding the upper specification limit for the Johnson distribution is 7.89%. Note that the shape of the data differs significantly from the normal assumption, with a negative skew and bound at zero. The normal distribution would incorrectly estimate that 6.7% of the process would be less than zero (i.e., $z = -1.50$), which is quite impossible for the cycle time metric.

Equality of Variance Tests

Equality of variance tests indicate whether given subsets of data have comparable levels of variation. Equal variance is a critical assumption in ANOVA.

WHEN TO USE

Analyze Stage and Improve Stage

- To test observed data used in an ANOVA.
- To test residuals in a regression analysis.

METHODOLOGY

A statistical test for the equality of the variance at a experimental conditions is provided by Bartlett. Minitab offers this test, as well as the Levene test, which is preferred if non-normality is suspected. We would generally expect the regression residuals to follow a normal distribution, and ANOVA requires normality of the parameters, so Bartlett's test is adequate in these cases.

The Bartlett test tests the equality of the treatment variances against the alternative that at least one variance is unequal to the others. The null hypothesis is that of equal variances for the subsets:

$$H_0: \sigma_1^2 = \sigma_1^2 = \sigma_2^2 = \cdots = \sigma_a^2$$

The alternative is that at least one of the subsets has an unequal variance. The null is rejected if:

$$2.3026 \; q/c > \chi^2_{\alpha, a-1}$$

where $q = (N - a)\log_{10}S_p^2 - \sum_{i=1}^{a} (n - 1)\log_{10}S_i^2$

$$c = 1 + [3(a - 1)]^{-1} * \left[\sum_{i=1}^{a} (n_i - 1)^{-1} - (N - a)^{-1} \right]$$

$$S_p^2 = (N - a)^{-1} * \sum_{i=1}^{a} (n - 1)S_i^2$$

N total observations at a conditions.

INTERPRETATION

If the condition of nonconstant variance is detected, we can transform the variable to remove its effect. See Transformations later in Part 3.

For example, summarized data for eight conditions (with 10 replicates each) is shown in Table T.6.

The pooled variance is calculated as

$$S_p^2 = (80 - 8)^{-1} * [(10 - 1) * (271.82 + 577.21 + 480.99 + 460.62 + 121.61$$
$$+ 190.4 + 174.67 + 318.1)]$$

$$S_p^2 = 324.4278$$

Bartlett's q is calculated as:

$$q = (80 - 8)\log(324.4278) - 9 * (2.43 + 2.76 + 2.68 + 2.66 + 2.08$$
$$+ 2.27 + 2.24 + 2.50)$$

$$q = 3.946$$

Bartlett's c is calculated as:

$$c = 1 + [1/21] * [(8/9) - (1/72)] = 1.041$$

Bartlett's statistic is then:

$$2.3026 \ q/c = 2.3026 * 3.946/1.041 = 8.72$$

Table T.6. Example Equality of Variance Test Data.

Average i	Std Dev i	Var i	Log (avg)	Log (Var)
816.29	16.48703194	271.8222	2.911844	2.434285
931.27	24.02521823	577.2111	2.969076	2.761335
826.18	21.93145889	480.9889	2.917075	2.682135
942.02	21.46211132	460.6222	2.97406	2.663345
581	11.02774279	121.6111	2.764176	2.084973
632.06	13.79855065	190.4	2.800758	2.279667
727.83	13.21615173	174.6667	2.86203	2.24221
832.1	17.83535814	318.1	2.920176	2.502564

The critical value of chi-square is 14.067, so the null of equal variances is rejected.

Evolutionary Operation (EVOP)

The EVOP strategy involves a series of sequential 2^k fractional factorial experiments with two or three factors. Unlike designed experiments, where we purposely manipulate factor levels to cause significant changes to the process, each of the factor levels in an EVOP represents small increments to minimize the upset to the process.

George Box proposed EVOP in 1957 as a method of routine plant operation to move toward an optimal. The techniques were further defined in Box and Draper (1969).

WHEN TO USE

Analyze Stage

- To determine significance of process factors.

Improve Stage

- To define new process factor settings resulting in an improved response.

EVOP has a number of disadvantages. A large number of repeat runs are often needed for each phase, since the factor level changes are small, with an effect that is weak relative to process noise. The repeat runs provide a reduction in the statistical error of estimating the effects.

The experiments are generally much longer term than traditional designed experiments because only two to three factors are changed at a time. In other words, it may take weeks or months to determine the significant effects compared to days for a designed experiment on the same process.

In spite of these shortcomings, EVOPs provide a number of advantages. Most importantly, during the course of the experimentation, the process continues to make usable product, unlike a designed experiment that requires the process be shut down to manipulate factors beyond their normal ranges.

Unlike happenstance data that is collected without specific purpose, EVOP data is collected at predefined operating conditions. In addition, the data may be collected as part of revised operating procedures by operational personnel.

METHODOLOGY

Definitions:

- A *cycle* refers to a collection of data at a given experimental condition. A cycle is complete when one observation has been collected at each point in the design (the replicates for that condition). A cycle is a blocking factor for the EVOP.
- A *phase* refers to a new iteration of cycles centered about a previously defined optimal condition. After several cycles, a phase is completed when the operating conditions are changed to improve the response.
- The *change in the mean*, also known as *curvature*, refers to the difference between the edge points of the 2^k experiment and their center point. If the process is centered on the current optimum, there should be a statistically significant difference between the center point and the edge points.

Juran suggests choosing two or three important factors to keep the EVOP manageable. Choose levels for each factor as "small steps" to avoid large changes in quality or operating conditions, and center the first experiment at the current "best operating condition" for the process.

- Run a 2^2 (for two factors) or 2^3 (for three factors) experiment with a center point. Repeat the experiment, and after the second cycle begin to estimate the error and the significance of effects.
- Continue with this experiment for a third cycle (i.e., third replicate), and if a factor is significant after this third cycle, then begin phase 2 with a new experiment centered on the new "best condition."
- When factors are not calculated as statistically significant, consider increasing the range of the levels for these factors, since it is possible that the levels were too similar to detect a statistical difference. Alternatively, consider replacing the nonsignificant factors with new factors, which may currently be contributing to error.
- If no factor is determined to be significant after eight cycles, then either change the factor level ranges or select new factors.
- When the optimal condition has been reached, run additional experiments with new factors or new factor level ranges to verify the optimal condition.

Consider this example chemical process to maximize yield using two process factors: temperature and reaction time. The current process setting for temperature is 150 C. Levels are chosen at 145 C and 155 C. The current process setting for reaction time is 30 minutes. Levels are chosen at 28 minutes and 32 minutes.

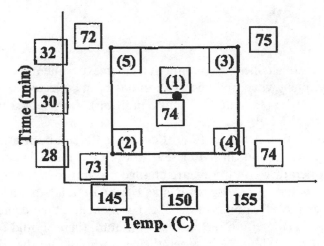

Figure F.9 Cycle 1 EVOP results.

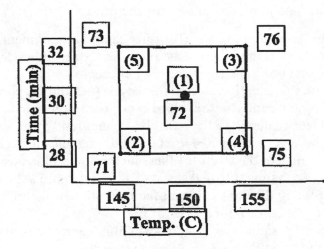

Figure F.10 Cycle 2 EVOP results.

The measured responses are shown in Figure F.9 for cycle 1 and Figure F.10 for cycle 2 at each experimental condition. The number in parentheses refers to the order of the trial. For example, the first data point of cycle 1 was run at a temperature of 150 degrees and reaction time of 30 minutes, with a resulting yield of 74%.

Table T.7. Minitab ANOVA Results for EVOP Example, Analysis of Variance for Yield (coded units).

Source	DF	Seq SS	Adj SS	Adj MS	F	P
Blocks	1	0.1000	0.1000	0.1000	0.07	0.799
Main effects	2	16.2500	16.250	8.1250	6.02	0.062
2-way interactions	1	0.1250	0.1250	0.1250	0.09	0.776
Curvature	1	0.6250	0.6250	0.6250	0.46	0.534
Residual error	4	5.4000	5.4000	1.3500		
Total	9	22.5000				

INTERPRETATION

The ANOVA results from Minitab are provided in Table T.7. Note the significance of the main effect terms.

The estimated effects and coefficients from Minitab are provided in Table T.8. Note the significance of the temperature term.

Table T.8. Minitab Effects for EVOP Example, Estimated Effects and Coefficients for Yield (coded units).

Term	Effect	Coef	SE Coef	T	P
Constant		73.6250	0.4108	179.23	0.000
Block		0.1000	0.3674	0.27	0.799
Temp	2.7500	1.3750	0.4108	3.35	0.029
Time	0.7500	0.3750	0.4108	0.91	0.413
Temp*time	0.2500	0.1250	0.4108	0.30	0.776
Ct Pt		−0.6250	0.9186	−0.68	0.534

Based on the phase 1 results, temperature is significant. Its effect on yield is positive, meaning that to obtain an increase in yield, we should increase temperature. The suggestion for phase 2 experimentation is to center the new design (the cycle replicates) around a temperature setting of 155 and a time setting of 30 minutes. Note the time factor is not changed after just two cycles. If we continue to see no significance of the time factor after eight cycles, we can either increase the factor level difference (levels such as 25 and 35 minutes) or substitute a different factor.

EWMA Charts

An exponentially weighted moving average (EWMA) chart is a control chart for variables data. It plots weighted moving average values. A weighting factor is chosen by the user to determine the relative impact of older data to more recent data on the calculated moving average value. Because the EWMA chart uses information from all samples, it detects much smaller process shifts than a normal control chart.

WHEN TO USE

Measure Stage

- To baseline a process, particularly when non-normality of the process is suspected and rational subgroup size is one.

Control Stage

- To control a process, particularly when either non-normality of the process is suspected and rational subgroup size is one, or when small shifts in the process must be detected.

EWMA charts are generally used for detecting small shifts in the process mean. They will detect shifts of a half sigma to 2 sigma much faster than Shewhart charts with the same sample size. They are, however, slower in detecting large shifts in the process mean. In addition, typical run tests cannot be used because of the inherent dependence of data points.

EWMA charts may also be preferred when the subgroups are of size $n = 1$. In this case, the alternative chart is the individual-X chart, whose standard

INTERPRETATION

We reject that the model is adequate if the calculated F statistic exceeds the critical value at the alpha level of significance:

$$F > F_{(n-p, N-n, \alpha)}$$

In the example, the calculated F value for the lack of fit is less than the critical value $F_{.05,3,8}$ of 4.07, so the null hypothesis that the model is adequate cannot be rejected. In this case (failing to reject that the model is adequate), the significance of the fitted model can be tested using the residuals. If the residuals are small (and pass the other tests described under Residual Analysis later in Part 3), then the model would seem to fit the data adequately and can be used to determine optimal combinations for the response.

If the lack of fit test is rejected, then the model should be updated with additional main factors, interactions, or higher-order terms. An F test for surface curvature (discussed next) helps rule out higher-order terms.

F Test for Significance of Second-Order Terms

When center points are available, the F statistic may be used to investigate curvature in the data, suggesting the need for a higher-order model.

WHEN TO USE

Improve Stage

- To test the significance of second-order terms in a proposed second-order model.

METHODOLOGY

Second-order models are used in response surface analysis to define the surface around a stationary point (a max, min, or saddle), and to predict the response with better accuracy than the first-order models near the optimal regions. In investigative analysis, second-order models are also used to understand the effect of current operating parameters on the response.

control limits are based on the normal distribution. When processes are severely non-normal, the individual-X chart's normal control limits may not fit the process data well. When non-normal control limits are calculated for the individual-X chart, the data is assumed to be from a controlled process as a requirement of the curve fitting. The advantage of EWMA charts is that each plotted point includes several observations, so the central limit theorem provides that the average of the points (or the moving average in this case) is normally distributed and the control limits clearly defined.

EWMA charts are also used to smooth the effect of known, uncontrollable noise in the data. Many accounting, service, and chemical processes fit into this categorization. For example, while day-to-day fluctuations in accounting processes may be large, they are not purely indicative of process instability. The choice of lambda can be determined to make the chart more or less sensitive to these daily fluctuations.

As with other control charts, EWMA charts are used to monitor processes over time. The charts' x axes are time-based, so that the charts show a history of the process. For this reason, you must have data that is time-ordered, that is, entered in the sequence from which it was generated. If this is not the case, then trends or shifts in the process may not be detected but instead attributed to random (common cause) variation.

METHODOLOGY

When choosing the value of lambda used for weighting, it is recommended to use small values (such as 0.2) to detect small shifts, and larger values (between 0.2 and 0.4) for larger shifts. A EWMA chart with lambda = 1.0 is an $\bar{X}$ chart (for subgroups larger than one) or an individual-X chart (when subgroup size equals one).

Plotted statistic:

$$z_t = \lambda_1 \bar{x}_t + (1 - \lambda_1) z_{t-1}$$

where λ is the value of the weighting factor, $\bar{x}_t$ is the subgroup average for the current subgroup at time t, and the value of z at time zero (z_0) is either a target value or the overall average of the selected subgroups.

EWMA control limits:

$$CL_{EWMA} = z_0 \pm \left(\frac{k\bar{R}}{d_2\sqrt{n}} \right) \sqrt{\frac{\lambda}{(2 - \lambda)} [1 - (1 - \lambda)^{2t}]}$$

where z_0 is the starting value (either the target value or process mean value), n is the subgroup size, d_2 is a function of n, and m is the number of subgroups selected for analysis.

The range chart ($n > 1$) or the moving range chart ($n = 1$) is generally used to monitor the process variation.

INTERPRETATION

Always look at the range chart first. The control limits on the EWMA chart are derived from the average range (or moving range, if $n = 1$), so if the range chart is out of control, then the control limits on the EWMA chart are meaningless.

On the range chart, look for out-of-control points. If there are any, then the special causes must be eliminated. Remember that the range is the estimate of the variation within a subgroup, so look for process elements that would increase variation between the data in a subgroup. Brainstorm and conduct designed experiments.

After reviewing the range chart, interpret the points on the EWMA chart relative to the control limits. Run tests are never applied to a EWMA chart, since the plotted points are inherently dependent, containing common points. Never consider the points on the EWMA chart relative to specifications, since the observations from the process vary much more than the exponentially weighted moving averages.

If the process shows control relative to the statistical limits for a sufficient period of time (long enough to see all potential special causes), then we can analyze its capability relative to requirements. Capability is only meaningful when the process is stable, since we cannot predict the outcome of an unstable process.

F Test for Lack of Fit

The F statistic may be used to test a regression model for its fit to the data.

WHEN TO USE

Analyze Stage

- To test for lack of fit in first-order models.

METHODOLOGY

Error in a regression analysis is due to two sources: pure error and lack of fit error. Pure error is experimental error, the differences between repeated runs of the same condition. The remaining error is due to a poor fit of the model to the data. Error due to lack of fit is caused by either a curvature in the response surface that is not estimated with the fitted first-degree model or main factor or interaction effects that were not included in the experiment.

An ANOVA for a proposed first-order model is shown in Table T.9. The sum of square residual term (79.1875) includes both pure error and lack of fit error. Pure error is calculated as 68.5 using the sum of squared deviations between each observation and the mean at that condition. The lack of fit error is calculated as 10.6875 using the difference between the total (residuals) error and the pure error.

The F statistic compares the sum of square variation due to lack of fit to the sum of square variation due to pure error:

$$F = \frac{SS_{LOF}/(n-p)}{SS_{PE}/(N-n)} = \frac{10.6875/(8-5)}{68.5/(16-8)} = 0.42$$

Table T.9.   ANOVA for Folded DOE (after removal of terms).

	df	SS	MS	F	Significance F
Regression	4	4297.25	1074.313	149.2336	1.67E − 09
Residual	11	79.1875	7.198864		
Total	15	4376.438			

Calculate sum of squares of the second-order terms as the difference between the sum of squares for regression for the second-order model minus the contribution from the first-order terms.

$$F = \frac{\text{SS (second-order terms)}/\text{No. of terms } (=3)}{\text{Residual mean square with second-order model}}$$

INTERPRETATION

The second-order terms are significant if the calculated F statistic exceeds the critical value $F_{(3, 4, 0.05)}$. For example, for three second-order terms (x_1^2, x_2^2, x_1x_2), if $F > F_{(3, 4, 0.05)} = 6.59$, then second-order terms are significant.

F Test for Surface Curvature

When replicated center points are available, the F statistic may be used to investigate curvature in the data, suggesting the need for a higher-order model.

WHEN TO USE

Analyze Stage

- When lack of fit is significant, test for surface curvature.

METHODOLOGY

Tests for surface curvature are useful to see if a higher-order model is needed to improve the fit approximated by a first-order model.

A simple test for curvature uses a replicate of the center point (a point in the middle of the design cube for a 2^3 design). The test compares the average response at the center with the average response at the corners.

The null hypothesis for the test of surface curvature is that the coefficients of the square terms (X_i^2) sum to zero:

$$H_0: \text{Sum of } \beta_{jj}\text{'s} = 0$$

$$H_A: \text{Sum of } \beta_{jj}\text{'s} \neq 0$$

Calculate the F statistic:

$$F = \frac{(\bar{Y}_{n_1} - \bar{Y}_{n_0})^2}{S^2 \left(\frac{1}{n_1} + \frac{1}{n_0} \right)}$$

where $\bar{Y}_{n_1}$: average of n_1 noncenter points, $\bar{Y}_{n_0}$: average of n_0 (>1) center points, s^2: sample variance of n_0 replicates at center point.

INTERPRETATION

The null is rejected if surface curvature is suspected using the F statistic, which compares the difference between the average response of the center points and noncenter points with the variance of the center points. If a significant difference is detected, then curvature in the response surface (either a maximum or minimum) exists.

Reject null (curvature suspected) if

$$F > F_{(1, \, n_0 - 1, \, \alpha)}$$

When a significant surface curvature is detected, then quadratic terms should be added to the model. Additional data may be needed to estimate the coefficients of the terms, as described in Regression Analysis later in Part 3.

Factorial Designs

Factorial designs include complete factorial designs (CFD) and fractional factorial designs (FFD). They serve as the basis for most design of experiments (DOE).

WHEN TO USE

Analyze Stage

- Use fractional factorial designs as screening designs to understand sources of variation and discover the process drivers.

Improve Stage

- Use supplement fractional factorial designs with center points to estimate curvature effects.

METHODOLOGY

Refer also to the tool Design of Experiments earlier in Part 3.

Complete Factorial Designs

Complete factorial designs are capable of estimating all factors and their interactions. We can calculate the number of experimental runs needed to estimate all of the factors and interactions using this simple formula, where b is the number of levels of each factor, and f is the number of factors:

$$\text{Number of experimental runs} = b^f$$

For example, with three factors at two levels each, we calculate that we need at least eight (2^3) experimental runs to estimate the main factors (A, B, and C), the two-factor interactions (AB, AC, and BC), and the three-factor interaction (ABC). One degree of freedom is needed to estimate the overall mean.

The complete factorial design for three factors at two levels each is presented in Table T.10. Note the pattern in the design, where a positive sign indicates the high level of the factor, and the negative sign indicates the low level of the factor. The actual run order of the design will be randomized when implemented, but the pattern is useful for seeing how the design is generated.

Graphically, the design would look as shown in Figure F.11. The trial numbers from Table T.10 are shown at the corners of the cube.

When we have five factors, we can estimate all the main factors and interactions using a 32 (2^5) run experiment. This will allow us to estimate 5 main factors (A, B, C, D, E); 10 two-factor interactions (AB, AC, AD, AE, BC, BD, BE, CD, CE, DE); 10 three-factor interactions (ABC, ABD, ABE, ACD, ACE, ADE, BCD, BCE, BDE, CDE); 5 four-factor interactions (ABCD, ABCE, ABDE, ACDE, BCDE); and 1 five-factor interaction (ABCDE).

Notice how quickly the number of runs increases as we add factors, doubling for each new factor when there are only two levels per factor. You may notice that adding a single factor at three levels would triple the number of runs required.

You may wonder: Do we really need to estimate all these three-, four-, and five-factor interactions? Fortunately, the answer is No.

Table T.10.   A Complete Factorial Design for
Three Factors.

Std. Order	Factor A	Factor B	Factor C
1	+	+	+
2	+	+	−
3	+	−	+
4	+	−	−
5	−	+	+
6	−	+	−
7	−	−	+
8	−	−	−

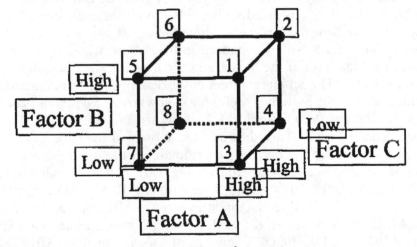

Figure F.11   A 2^3 design.

Fractional Factorial Designs

In most experiments, particularly screening experiments, we can ignore the
effects of the higher-order (larger than two-factor) interactions. It's unlikely

that these higher-order interactions are significant unless the main factors or two-factor interactions are also significant. Therefore, we can reduce the number of runs by excluding the higher-order interactions. These fractional factorial designs are constructed by *aliasing* (or substituting) the higher-order interaction terms with main factors, as shown in Table T.11. The result is a smaller design, a fraction of the original.

Consider the two-level three-factor complete factorial design constructed earlier. It had 8 runs to estimate the 3 main effects (A, B, C), the 3 two-factor interactions (AB, AC, BC), and the 1 three-factor interaction (ABC). If we assume that the ABC interaction is unlikely to be significant, then we can alias it with a fourth factor D. The result of this alias is a design half the size! Instead of requiring 16 runs, only 8 runs are needed to estimate the effect of the four factors.

The construction of the four-factor fractional factorial design is similar to the three-factor design seen earlier. The columns labeled *Factor A*, *Factor B*, and *Factor C* are identical to those shown in the CFD 2^3 design. The column labeled *Factor D* is constructed the same way that its alias, the ABC interaction, is constructed: by multiplying the factor A, factor B, and factor C columns. For example, the first row, Trial 1, is the result of multiplying $(+1) * (+1) * (+1) = (+1)$.

Table T.11. A Fractional Factorial Design for Four Factors.

Std. Order	Factor A	Factor B	Factor C	Factor D
1	+	+	+	+
2	+	+	−	−
3	+	−	+	−
4	+	−	−	+
5	−	+	+	−
6	−	+	−	+
7	−	−	+	+
8	−	−	−	−

Similarly,

Trial 2: $(+1)*(+1)*(-1)=(-1)$
Trial 3: $(+1)*(-1)*(+1)=(-1)$
Trial 4: $(+1)*(-1)*(-1)=(+1)$
And so on.

The effect of aliasing factor D with the ABC interaction is that the aliased parameters are *confounded* with one another. This implies that the parameters cannot be estimated independently of one another. For example, if factor D is aliased with the ABC interaction, then when the effect of factor D is estimated, we cannot be sure whether the effect is due to factor D, the ABC interaction, or a linear combination of D and ABC.

The intended aliasing also creates some unintended confounding between all the other possible combinations of the aliased pair. We construct the confounded pairs by moving the equal sign through the ABC = D equation.

If ABC = D, then A = BCD; B = ACD; C = ABD; AB = CD; AC = BD; AD = BC

These can be verified in Table T.11 by noticing, for example, that the results of multiplying the factor A and factor B columns provide the same result for all rows as multiplying the factor C and factor D columns. This provides evidence that the AB interaction is confounded with the CD interaction.

Fractional factorial designs have several uses. They are used commonly as screening designs to identify significant factors and their interactions and to remove insignificant factors and interactions. This allows further designs to explore the process dynamics in more detail, using fewer factors in the model.

They are also used in response surface analysis to develop the initial first-order model and its factor effect estimates needed for the steepest ascent methods. When higher-order models are suspected, the fractional factorial designs can be supplemented with axial and center points.

Saturated designs refer to special cases of fractional factorial designs where only the main factors can be estimated. In a saturated design, the minimum number of experimental conditions $(1+p)$ is used to estimate the p main factors. The main factors are all confounded with two factor interactions. See Screening Designs later in Part 3 for more detail.

INTERPRETATION

The parameter effects, the influence each factor or interaction has on the response, can be estimated for the 2^k design by calculating the difference between the average response when the parameter is set at the high level and the average response when the parameter is set at the low level. The coefficient of the parameter in the regression model is calculated as one-half the effect.

In the fractional factorial 2^{k-x} design, the effect of the aliasing is confounding between main factors and interactions. For example, if a fractional factorial design is run where factor A and interaction BC are confounded, then the calculated parameter effect may be due to either factor A, the interaction BC, or a linear combination of factor A and the interaction BC.

When the results of a screening experiment are ambiguous because of the confounding of factors, we can often *fold* the design to select additional trials to remove the confounding. A design is folded by replicating the design, substituting the low levels with high levels and high values with low levels for one or more of the factors. If we fold on just one factor (i.e., substitute the plus and minus signs for one of the factors), then that factor and its two factor interactions will be free of confounding. If we substitute the plus and minus signs for the entire design, then all main factors will be free of confounding with other main factors and two-factor interactions.

Failure Modes and Effects Analysis (FMEA)

Failure modes and effects analysis, also known by its acronym FMEA or as failure modes, effects, and criticality analysis, is used to determine high-risk process activities or product features based on the impact of a failure and the likelihood that a failure could occur without detection.

WHEN TO USE

Analyze Stage

- To prioritize process activities or product features prone to failure.

Improve or Design Stage

- To determine high-risk process activities or product features in the proposed improvement.

METHODOLOGY

The following steps are required for the FMEA:

- Define the function of each process step (or product feature, for designs). For example, in a sales process:

  Process step: Enter the product ID number for each purchased item. Function: Links to the product database to identify the item numbers necessary for the products being purchased.

- Identify the failure mode and its effect for each function. In defining failure modes and their effects, it is helpful ask: What could go wrong? or What could the customer dislike? For example:

  Function: Links to the product database to identify the item numbers necessary for the products being purchased.
  Failure mode 1: Product ID mistyped
  Effect of failure mode 1: Wrong product shipped.
  Failure mode 2: Item numbers not correctly defined in database.
  Effect of failure mode 2: Wrong product items shipped.

- Define the severity for each of the failure modes. Table T.12 provides a good means of identifying the severity for a given failure effect. Granted, defining a severity level is subjective. In the example that follows, a severity of five or seven could have been reasonable choices; the "right" answer can never be known, but consistency within a given analysis or between analyses that compete for resources is certainly important for meaningful prioritizations. For example:

  Failure mode 1: Product ID mistyped; severity = 6. From Table T.12, severity 6 is described as "Moderate disruption to operations. Some loss of product or service may occur, requiring moderate remedy. Customer will complain, product return likely."

- Define the likelihood (or probability) of occurrence. Table T.13 (AIAG, 1995) provides useful descriptions of occurrence levels from 1 to 10 based on Cpk and possible process defect rates. For example:

  Failure mode 1: Product ID mistyped; occurrence level = 5.

- Define the detection method and likelihood of detection. Table T.14 provides useful descriptions of detection levels from 1 to 10. For example:

Table T.12. Severity Table.*

Level	Description
10	May endanger personnel without warning, or violate law or regulation.
9	May endanger personnel with warning, or potentially result in violation of law or regulation.
8	Major disruption to operations. Complete loss of customer goodwill. 100% loss of product or service may occur.
7	Significant disruption to operations. Some loss of product or service will occur, requiring significant remedy, such as product sorting, rework or extra effort. Customer very dissatisfied.
6	Moderate disruption to operations. Some loss of product or service may occur, requiring moderate remedy. Customer will complain, product return likely.
5	Minor disruption to operations. Some loss of product or service may occur, requiring minor remedy. Customer's productivity reduced.
4	Marginal disruption to operations, requiring slight remedy. Customer experiences some dissatisfaction.
3	Marginal disruption to operations. No remedy required. Customer likely to be inconvenienced.
2	Slight disruption to operations. Discriminating customer notices the effect, but not impacted. Average customer doesn't notice effect.
1	No effect noticed by customer or operations.

*FMEA Severity Ratings, based on AIAG (1995) and Pyzdek (2003).

Failure mode 1: Product ID mistyped; detection = 4; detection method: accounting clerk compares the PO with the order form as the invoice is created for shipping.

- Calculate risk priority number (RPN) by multiplying the severity, occurrence, and detection levels. For example:

Table T.13.   FMEA Occurrence Rankings (AIAG, 1995).

Probable Failure	Failure Rate	Cpk	Occurrence Ranking
Very high (inevitable)	> 1 in 2 1 in 3	< 0.33 0.33	10 9
High (often)	1 in 8 1 in 20	0.51 0.67	8 7
Moderate (occasional)	1 in 80 1 in 400 1 in 2,000	.83 1.00 1.17	6 5 4
Low (isolated)	1 in 15,000	1.33	3
Very low	1 in 150,000	1.50	2
Remote (unlikely)	< 1 in 150,000	> 1.67	1

Failure mode 1: Product ID mistyped; RPN = 120 [calculated as 6 (the severity level) ∗ 5 (the occurrence level) ∗ 4 (the detection level)].

- Prioritize the failure modes based on the RPN.

INTERPRETATION

The RPN will range from 1 to 1,000, with larger numbers representing higher risks. Failure modes with higher RPN should be given priority. Some organizations use threshold values, above which preventive action must be taken. For example, the organization may require improvement for any RPN exceeding 120.

Reducing the RPN requires a reduction in the severity, occurrence, and/or detection levels associated with the failure mode. Generally:

- Reducing severity level requires a change to the design of the product or process. For example, if the process involves a manufactured part, it may be possible to alter the design of the part so that the stated failure mode is no longer a serious problem for the customer.
- Reducing detection level increases cost with no improvement to quality. In order to reduce the detection level, we must improve the detection

Table T.14. Detection Level Table.*

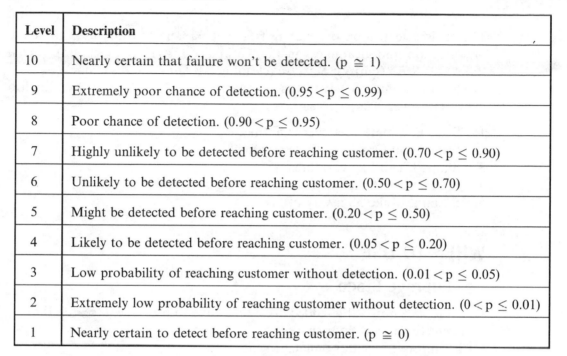

Level	Description
10	Nearly certain that failure won't be detected. ($p \cong 1$)
9	Extremely poor chance of detection. ($0.95 < p \leq 0.99$)
8	Poor chance of detection. ($0.90 < p \leq 0.95$)
7	Highly unlikely to be detected before reaching customer. ($0.70 < p \leq 0.90$)
6	Unlikely to be detected before reaching customer. ($0.50 < p \leq 0.70$)
5	Might be detected before reaching customer. ($0.20 < p \leq 0.50$)
4	Likely to be detected before reaching customer. ($0.05 < p \leq 0.20$)
3	Low probability of reaching customer without detection. ($0.01 < p \leq 0.05$)
2	Extremely low probability of reaching customer without detection. ($0 < p \leq 0.01$)
1	Nearly certain to detect before reaching customer. ($p \cong 0$)

*FMEA Detection Levels, from Pyzdek (2003).

rate. We might add process steps to inspect product, approve product, or (as in the example) to double-check a previous process step. None of these activities add value to the customer, and are "hidden factory" sources of waste to the organization.

- Reducing the occurrence level is often the best approach, since reducing severity can be costly (or impossible) and reducing the detection level is only a costly short-term solution. Reducing the occurrence level requires a reduction in process errors, which reduces cost.

Five S

The 5S is a lean tool, originating from the Japanese words used to create organization and cleanliness in the workplace [*Seiri* (organization); *Sieton* (tidiness); *Seiso* (purity); *Seiketsu* (cleanliness); *Shitsuke* (discipline)].

The traditional 5S have been translated into the following five English words (Revelle, 2000):

1. Sort: Eliminate whatever is not needed.
2. Straighten: Organize whatever remains.
3. Shine: Clean the work area.
4. Standardize: Schedule regular cleaning and maintenance.
5. Sustain: Make 5S a way of life.

WHEN TO USE

Improve Stage

- To reduce non–value-added cycle times due to movement, search time, ineffective use of floor space.
- To improve inventory management.
- To reduce accidents and improve working conditions.

METHODOLOGY

Measure a particular work station's level of 5S achievements using a rating system, such as shown below for each of the 5S criteria.

Sort

Level 1: Needed and unneeded items mixed
Level 2: Needed and unneeded items identified; unneeded items removed
Level 3: Work area clean; sources of spills removed
Level 4: Documented housekeeping assignments and schedules
Level 5: Mess prevention implemented

Straighten

Level 1: Items randomly placed
Level 2: Needed items safely stored and organized according to frequency of use

Level 3: Locations for items labeled and required quantities
Level 4: Needed items minimized and arranged for retrieval
Level 5: Needed items can be retrieved in 30 seconds with minimal steps

Shine

Level 1: Key items not identified
Level 2: Key items identified; acceptable levels documented
Level 3: Visual controls established
Level 4: Inspection, Cleaning and restocking on daily basis
Level 5: Potential problems identified; countermeasures defined

Standardize

Level 1: Work methods not followed or documented
Level 2: Documented agreements for needed items, organization, and controls
Level 3: Documented agreements on visual controls, labeling of items, and required quantities
Level 4: Reliable methods for housekeeping, inspections documented and practiced
Level 5: Reliable methods for housekeeping, inspections shared

Sustain

Level 1: No visual measurement of 5S
Level 2: Initial 5S level determined and posted
Level 3: 5S routinely monitored by work group
Level 4: Causes and frequency of problems routinely documented; CA implemented
Level 5: Root causes eliminated; preventive action deployed.

Scores from this rating can be shown on a radar chart to display a particular area's performance in the 5S rating. An example radar chart for 5S drawn using Excel's chart wizard is shown in Figure F.12. The center point designates a score of 0, and a pentagon ring is shown for scores of 1.0, 2.0, and 3.0 (the maximum score in this example). This particular work station achieved a rating of: sort 1.50; straighten 2.00; shine 1.75; standardize 3.00; sustain 2.00.

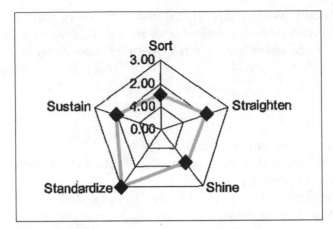

Figure F.12 A radar chart for 5S.

INTERPRETATION

These scores are useful for tracking improvement over time and identifying areas of opportunity. Higher scores demonstrate better implementation of the 5S principles.

Flowchart

A flowchart is a simple graphical tool for documenting the series of steps necessary for the activities in a process.

WHEN TO USE

Measure Stage

- Document as-is process.
- Uncover varied shareholder perceptions.

Analyze Stage

- Discover process complexities which contribute to variation or longer cycle times.

Improve Stage

- Communicate proposed changes.

Control Stage

- Document revised process.

METHODOLOGY

In the flowchart, each task is represented by a symbol. The American National Standards Institute (ANSI) provides a list of symbols which are intended primarily for computing processes but which most practitioners find useful: rectangles for most process tasks and diamonds for decision tasks. Decisions should have only two outcomes (yes or no), so decision points must be phrased in this manner.

We can use a flowchart to document the current (as-is) process. Use symbol color or shape to indicate process delays, functional responsibility for each step (for example, yellow is customer service), or points in the process where measurements are taken.

INTERPRETATION

A quick review of the as-is process using a flowchart can usually uncover complexities in the form of an excessive number of decision points and branches that may contribute to delays or even defects. When used to document the future (desired) process, we strive to make process flow uncomplicated, with the fewest symbols (tasks) and branches possible. This lack of complexity in the process will reduce the number of errors.

Figure F.13 is a rather simple flowchart. Notice how the diamond decision points have two outputs: one output continues down the main process flow, while the other diverts to a secondary path. Also note that these secondary paths may result in a jump to a later point in the process (as shown in the first decision's yes path) or to a prior point in the process (as shown in the second decision's yes path). Decision paths, as well as endpoints for processes, may also branch to other process flowcharts, as indicated by the circle in the last step of this process. In this example, the shaded symbols indicate external process steps.

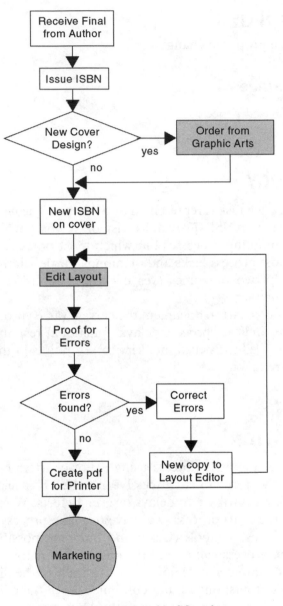

Figure F.13   Example of flowchart.

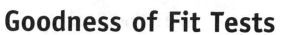

Goodness of Fit Tests

Popular goodness of fit tests include the chi-square, Kolmogorov-Smirnov (K-S), and Anderson-Darling tests.

WHEN TO USE

Measure to Control Stages

- To verify an assumed distribution to ensure validity of statistical tests, including confidence tests, hypothesis tests, and statistical control charts.

While the chi-square test is perhaps the most frequently referenced goodness of fit technique in general application statistical textbooks, its popularity in academic circles may indeed be due to its simplicity: authors can easily describe and demonstrate the test without the need for computer software. In practice, however, data is almost exclusively analyzed using computer software, allowing the use of more sophisticated techniques which are better suited for most applications, particularly in testing continuous distributions. Two of these techniques are the Kolmogorov-Smirnov test (often referred to simply as the K-S test) and the Anderson-Darling test. Each of these techniques may be used to compare the fit of assumed distributions to sample data.

METHODOLOGY

The Kolmogorov-Smirnov criterion is based on the expectation that there is likely to be a difference between a discrete distribution generated from data and the continuous distribution from which it was drawn, caused by step difference and random error. As n increases, the size of the difference is expected to decrease. If the measured maximum difference is smaller than that expected, then the probability that the distributions are the same is high.

Note that the Kolmogorov-Smirnov criterion is very demanding as n becomes large, because the K-S criterion is scaled by the square root of n, reflecting an expected decrease in the step size error. The random error and outliers then dominate, with outliers having a strong effect on the reported value for alpha (because K-S is a measure of maximum deviation).

The Anderson-Darling statistic is a modification of the Kolmogorov-Smirnov test that gives more weight to the data in the tails of the distribution. It requires a known distribution for which critical values are calculated.

INTERPRETATION

In both the Kolmogorov-Smirnov and the Anderson-Darling tests, the null hypothesis is that the data follows the specified distribution. Most statistical software reports a p value, where the null hypothesis is rejected (implying the distribution is a poor fit) if the p value is less than a predetermined alpha value (typically 0.05 or 0.10). Distributions can also be compared: the distribution with the larger p value is the more likely distributions.

Histogram

A histogram is a graphical tool used to visualize data. It is a bar chart, where the height of each bar represents the number of observations falling within a range of rank-ordered data values.

WHEN TO USE

Measure Stage and Analyze Stage

- To graphically display the data as an aid in fitting a distribution for capability analysis or to visually detect the presence of multiple distributions.

METHODOLOGY

Rank order the data from the smallest value to the largest value.

Calculate the number of bars (or cells) as approximately equal to the square root of the number of data values. The number of cells (or bars) will influence the shape of the perceived distribution, so never base it on convenience, the data resolution, or anything other than the number of data observations.

The width of each bar is calculated by dividing the range of the data (the maximum value minus the minimum value) by the number of bars.

Count the number of data observations in each bar.

The vertical axis plots the count of observations in each bar. The horizontal axis displays the data values for each bar (usually either the starting point, ending point, or midpoint). See Figure F.14.

INTERPRETATION

An advantage of the histogram is that the process location is clearly identifiable. In Figure F.14, the central tendency of the data is about 75.005. The variation is also clearly distinguishable: we expect most of the data to fall between 75.003 and 75.007. We can also see if the data is bounded or if it has symmetry, such as is evidenced in this data.

If your data is from a symmetrical distribution, such as the bell-shaped normal distribution as shown in Figure F.15A, the data will be evenly

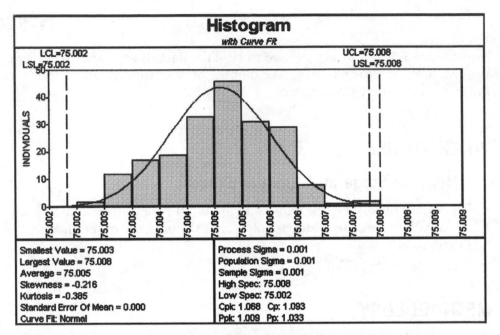

Figure F.14   Example of a histogram.

distributed about the center of the data. If the data is not evenly distributed about the center of the histogram, it is skewed. If it appears skewed, you should understand the cause of this behavior. Some processes will naturally have a skewed distribution, and may also be bounded, such as the concentricity data in Figure F.15B. Concentricity has a natural lower bound at zero, since no measurements can be negative. The majority of the data is just above zero, so there is a sharp demarcation at the zero point representing a bound.

If double or multiple peaks occur, look for the possibility that the data is coming from multiple sources, such as different suppliers or machine adjustments.

The histogram provides a view of the process as measured. The actual output over a larger sample period may be much wider, even when the process is in control. As a general rule, 200 to 300 data observations are preferred to provide a realistic view of a process distribution, although it is not uncommon to use a histogram when you have much less data. Bear in mind that less data generally implies a greater risk of error.

One problem that novice practitioners tend to overlook is that the histogram provides only part of the picture. A histogram with a given shape may be produced by many different processes, the only difference in the data being

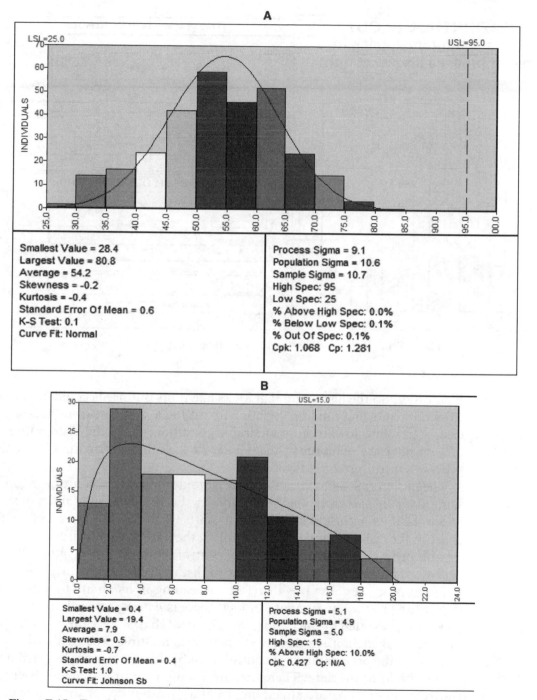

Figure F.15   Two histograms: (A) Histogram of symmetric process with normal distribution fit. (B) Histogram of skewed process with nonnormal distribution fit.

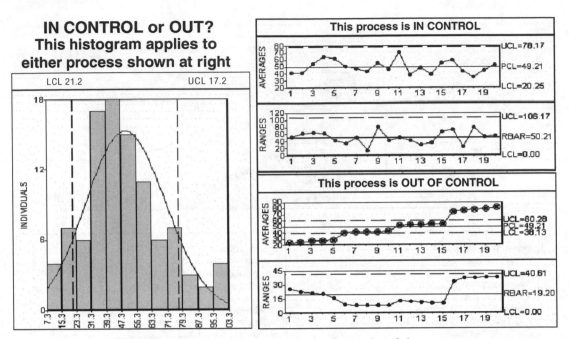

Figure F.16 This histogram conceals the time order of the process.

their order. So the histogram that looks like it fits our needs could have come from data showing random variation about the average or from data that is clearly trending toward an undesirable condition. Since the histogram does not consider the sequence of the points, we lack this information. Statistical process control provides this context.

The two sets of control charts on the right side of Figure F.16 are based on the same data as shown in the histogram on the left. The only difference between the data in the top set of control charts versus the bottom set of control charts is the order of the data. It is clear that the top set of control charts is from a stable process, while the bottom set of control charts is from an out-of-control process. The histogram by itself fails to distinguish between these two very different processes, and it is therefore misleading in its ability to graphically depict the process distribution. In fact, there is *no* single distribution for the process represented by the bottom set of control charts, since the process is out of control. By definition, then, the data is from multiple process distributions.

Thus, if the process is out of control, then by definition a single distribution cannot be fit to the data. Therefore, always use a control chart to determine statistical control before attempting to fit a distribution (or determine capability) for the data.

Hypothesis Testing on Mean of Two Samples

In this case, hypothesis tests are used to test whether the mean of two samples came from populations of equal mean.

There are many other uses of hypothesis testing. In regression analysis and designed experiments, hypothesis testing is used to determine if factors included in the analysis contribute to the variation observed in the data. This use of hypothesis testing is discussed in Regression Analysis later in Part 3.

WHEN TO USE

Key assumptions are that the population has a normal distribution and that it is both constant (it does not change over time) and homogenous (a given sample is representative of the sample). Further assuming the population variances are equal, we can calculate a pooled standard deviation using the sample standard deviations of two samples.

Analyze Stage

• To compare mean of samples from different conditions.

Improve Stage

• To compare process averages after improvements versus baseline estimates.

METHODOLOGY

State the null hypothesis Ho. The null hypothesis is what you would like to disprove by the test. That may sound funny, but if you peek down to the Interpretation section, there is a hint to the rationale for this. The conclusions that we arrive at in the result can either reject the null hypothesis or fail to reject it. In other words, we can't prove the null hypothesis, but we can disprove it. In this case, the null hypothesis would be *the mean of population 1 equals the mean of population 2.*

Specify the alternative hypothesis H_1. The alternative hypothesis must always cover the remaining options. We could, for example, test whether the mean is less than a certain value. In that case, the alternative would be that the mean is greater than or equal to that same value. Using the null hypothesis of equal mean, the alternative hypothesis would be *the mean of population 1 does not equal the mean of population 2*.

Choose a significance level (α) or the p value. The significance level, or type 1 error, is the probability of rejecting a hypothesis that is true. A significance of 0.05 is often used.

Collect samples. The sample size is related to the type 2 error (β error): the probability of accepting a false hypothesis. The value $1 - \beta$ is the power of the test.

Calculate the pooled variance, where S_1 is the calculated standard deviation for the sample of n_1 units and S_2 is the calculated standard deviation for the sample of n_2 units:

$$S_p^2 = \frac{(n_1 - 1)S_1^2 + (n_2 - 1)S_2^2}{n_1 + n_2 - 2}$$

Calculate test statistic t_0 based on sample averages:

$$t_0 = \frac{\bar{X}_1 - \bar{X}_2}{S_p \sqrt{\frac{1}{n_1} + \frac{1}{n_2}}}$$

Calculate degrees of freedom $v = n_1 + n_2 - 2$

Reject the null hypothesis based on the following conditions, where the critical region for the t statistic is found using the Student's t distribution tables in Appendix 2:

$$t_0 > t_{\alpha/2, \, n_1 + n_2 - 2} \qquad \text{or} \qquad t_0 < -t_{\alpha/2, \, n_1 + n_2 - 2}$$

In some cases, we choose to use the p value to evaluate the results of the test. The p value is the alpha value where the test statistic equals the critical value. This is sometimes more useful, since we might otherwise fail to reject a null hypothesis when we are just within the critical region, or conversely reject a null when we are just outside the critical region. Using the p value allows some flexibility in rejecting the test. Generally a p value less than 0.05 or even 0.10 may be used to reject the null hypothesis.

For example, we compare two samples, one with a mean of 15.7 from a sample of 25 units, the other with a mean of 21.2 from a sample of 100 units.

Note that the sample standard deviations are not equal, even though we assume the population standard deviations are equal when we calculate the pooled standard deviation.

The pooled variance is calculated as:

$$S_p^2 = \frac{(n_1 - 1)S_1^2 + (n_2 - 1)S_2^2}{n_1 + n_2 - 2} = \frac{24(1.8)^2 + 99(3.5)^2}{25 + 100 - 2} = 10.49$$

The test statistic (t) is calculated as:

$$t_0 = \frac{\bar{X}_1 - \bar{X}_2}{S_p\sqrt{\frac{1}{n_1} + \frac{1}{n_2}}} = \frac{15.7 - 21.2}{3.24 * \sqrt{\frac{1}{25} + \frac{1}{100}}} = -7.59$$

The critical value of the t statistic is obtained from the Student's t distribution tables in Appendix 2 as 1.96. Since the test statistic $t_0 = -7.59$ is less than -1.96, we *reject* the null hypothesis that $\mu_1 = \mu_2$.

MS Excel (in the Data Analysis menu) and Minitab (in Stat\Basic Statistics) offer other useful hypothesis tests:

- MS Excel:

  Two sample t test (equal variance)
  Two sample t test (unequal variance)
  Two sample z test (equal variance)
  Two sample F test for variances

- Minitab:

  One sample z test (equal variance)
  One sample t test (unequal variance)
  Two sample z test (equal variance)
  Two sample F test for variances

INTERPRETATION

The result of the test is to compare the calculated statistics with a test statistic. If the calculated statistic exceeds the critical value of the test statistic (based on the alpha level chosen), then we reject the null hypothesis. If not, then we fail to reject the null hypothesis. Rejecting the null hypothesis is known as a *strong conclusion:* we have disproven that the means are equal. When we fail to reject the null hypothesis, then the means may be equal, or may not be; we really can't tell based on the data. This is considered a *weak conclusion* for obvious reasons. We may want to collect larger samples to further test the hypothesis.

The key assumptions of the tests, which should be validated for the samples, include:

- Samples must be random, and we must ensure they are representative of the population we are investigating. In surveys, low response rates would typically provide extreme value estimates (that is, the subpopulation of people who have strong opinions one way or the other).
- Samples must be from a stable population. If the population is changing over time (statistically out of control), then estimates will be biased, with associated increases in alpha and beta risks.
- Many of the hypothesis tests, and associated alpha and beta risks, are dependent on normality of the population. If the population is significantly non-normal, then the tests are not meaningful. Goodness of fit tests are used to test this assumption. Nonparametric tests can be used if the populations are significantly non-normal.
- Some tests additionally require equal variance, which can be tested using equality of variance tests. If the populations do not have equal variances, then the data can be transformed (see Transformations later in Part 3).
- The failure to reject is *not* an acceptance of the null hypothesis. Rather, it means we don't have proof *yet* that the hypothesis should be rejected.
- The alpha risk is real. Consider the *power* of the samples to detect real differences. If the null hypothesis cannot be rejected, the sample size may need to be increased. These topics are discussed in Chapter 6.

Individual-X and Moving Range Charts

Individual-X and moving range charts are a set of control charts for variables data. The individual-X chart monitors the process location over time based on a subgroup containing a single observation. The moving range chart monitors the variation between consecutive subgroups over time.

WHEN TO USE

Measure Stage

- To baseline the process by quantifying the common cause level of variation inherent to the process.

Analyze Stage

- To differentiate between common and special causes of variation.

Improve Stage

- To verify the results of the process improvement on the process metric.

Control Stage

- To monitor the process to ensure the stability of the revised process and the continued benefit of the improvement.

Individual-X and moving range charts are generally used when you can't group measurements into rational subgroups or when it's more convenient to monitor actual observations rather than subgroup averages. Each subgroup, consisting of a single observation, represents a "snapshot" of the process at a given point in time. The charts' x axes are time-based, so that the charts show a history of the process. For this reason, you must have time-ordered data; that is, entered in the sequence from which the data were generated. If this is not the case, then trends or shifts in the process may not be detected, but instead attributed to random (common cause) variation.

If rational subgroups can be formed, the $\bar{X}$ charts are generally preferred, since the control limits are easily calculated using the normal distribution. When rational subgroups cannot be formed, then we must make assumptions about the distribution of the process to calculate the statistical control limits on an individual-X chart. This can be troublesome, particularly when the process distribution is very skewed or bounded.

Individual-X charts are efficient at detecting relatively large shifts in the process average, typically shifts of 2.5 to 3 sigma or larger. If X-bar charts can be used, then their larger subgroups will detect smaller shifts much quicker. (See Statistical Process Control Charts later in Part 3 for more detail.) EWMA charts can also be used at any subgroup size to increase the sensitivity to smaller process shifts.

METHODOLOGY

An important consideration for the individual-X chart is the choice of curve fit used for determining the control limits. There is a fundamental dilemma, in that a distribution should not be fit to the data unless the data is from a controlled process, yet the process distribution must be assumed to determine the control limits. Because of this limitation, you may consider using other control charts, such as the $\bar{X}$ chart or EWMA chart, to first establish process control for a set of data; then a distribution can be fit to the data.

Individual-X Chart Calculations

Plotted statistic: the observation.

Centerline: the average (normal distribution); the median of the fitted distribution (non-normal distributions).

UCL, LCL (upper and lower control limit):

$$UCL_x = \bar{x} + 3\sigma_x \quad \text{(normal distribution)}$$

$$LCL_x = \bar{x} - 3\sigma_x \quad \text{(normal distribution)}$$

where $\bar{x}$ is the average and σ_x is the process sigma.

Note: Some authors prefer to write this as:

$$UCL_x = \bar{x} + E_2\overline{MR}$$

$$LCL_x = \bar{x} - E_2\overline{MR}$$

For non-normal distributions, the UCL is defined at the 99.865 percentile of the fitted curve, and the LCL is defined at the 0.135 percentile of the fitted curve.

Moving Range Chart Calculations

Plotted statistic: the moving ranges between successive subgroups in an individual-X chart (i.e., the difference between the current observation and the observation immediately prior).

$$MR_j = |x_j - x_{j-1}|$$

Centerline:

$$\overline{MR} = \frac{1}{m-1} \sum_{j=1}^{m} MR_j$$

where m is the total number of subgroups included in the analysis and MR_j is the moving range at subgroup j.

UCL, LCL (upper and lower control limit):

$$UCL_{MR} = \overline{MR} + 3d_3\sigma_x \quad \text{(all distributions)}$$

$$LCL_{MR} = MAX(0, \overline{MR} - 3d_3\sigma_x) \quad \text{(all distributions)}$$

where $\overline{MR}$ is the average of the moving ranges, σ_x is the process sigma, and d_3 is a function of n (tabulated in Appendix 6).

Note: Some authors prefer to write this as:

$$UCL_{MR} = \overline{MR}D_4$$

$$LCL_{MR} = \overline{MR}D_3$$

INTERPRETATION

Research has shown that for processes following the normal distribution, when a special cause is detected on the moving range chart, it will also appear on the individual-X chart, thus making the moving range chart redundant.

Never adjust the process based on the observation's value relative to specifications, since this *tampering* will increase the overall variation in the process.

If there are any out-of-control points on the X chart, then the special causes must be eliminated. Brainstorm and conduct designed experiments to find those process elements that contribute to sporadic changes in process location. To predict the capability of the process after special causes have been eliminated, you should remove the out-of-control points from the analysis, which will remove the statistical bias of the out-of-control points by dropping them from the calculations of the centerline and the control limits.

Look for obviously nonrandom behavior. Use the run test rules, which apply statistical tests for trends to the plotted points.

If the process shows control relative to the statistical limits and run tests for a sufficient period of time (long enough to see all potential special causes), then we can analyze its process capability relative to requirements. Capability is only meaningful when the process is stable, since we cannot predict the outcome of an unstable process.

Interaction Plots

Interaction plots are a particular form of point-and-line charts, used to graphically show the relationship among three parameters, usually two factors and a response.

WHEN TO USE

Analyze Stage and Improve Stage

- In analyzing the results of multiple regression and designed experiments to graphically show the effect of two factor interaction on a response.

METHODOLOGY

The plot variable is assigned to the x axis, and a second variable (usually the response) to the y axis. The levels of the interaction variable are used to form the separate lines displayed on the plot.

For example, we may be interested in seeing if there is an interaction between two process factors: cycle time and personal response on the response satisfaction score, obtained from a customer survey.

We can sort the data based on cycle time as the first field and personal response as the second. In this case, there were only two conditions for cycle time (210, 330), and two conditions for personal response (yes, no). Referring to Figure F.17, we average the response data (satisfaction score) for those four conditions of cycle time, personal response [(210, yes), (210, no), (330, yes), (330, no)], and plot the average response on the interaction plot.

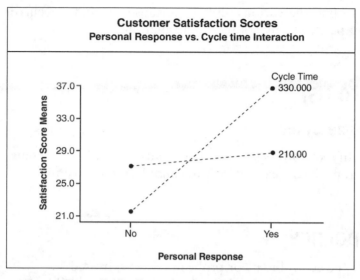

Figure F.17   Example of an interaction plot.

INTERPRETATION

In this interaction plot, there are two lines: The line for cycle time equals 210 is relatively flat, with little change in customer satisfaction as we move from the personal response (no) to the personal response (yes) condition.

The line for cycle time equals 330 is relatively steep, with a big difference in customer satisfaction between the personal response (yes) and the personal response (no) conditions.

Since the effect of cycle time on satisfaction varies depending on whether there was a personalized response or not, we say that there is an *interaction* between cycle time and personalized response. Interactions are easily spotted on an interaction plot by nonparallel lines, such as shown in the graphic.

Interrelationship Digraphs

An interrelationship digraph takes a group of items, problems, or issues, and establishes the diverse cause-and-effect relationships that exist between the group items. This allows you to uncover problems which might have seemed minor, but which in reality, feed into a great number of other problems. It also helps you to find the various underlying causes behind a recurring problem that cannot be effectively addressed in isolation.

WHEN TO USE

Analyze Stage

- To identify key process drivers (root causes) and key outcomes when potential problems can interact to cause larger problems.

METHODOLOGY

- Identify the central issue or problem to be addressed.
- Brainstorm as many related issues or subissues as possible. Your central issue should be specific enough that you do not end up with too many related items. This tool is most effective when there are between 15 and 50 items on the digraph.
- Determine the relationship of the items by considering each item in relation to every other item. If an item causes or influences the other item (even partially), then draw an arrow from the cause to its effect. Heavier lines can be used to signify stronger relationships.

INTERPRETATION

Count the number of arrows coming out of and going into each item.

In Figure F.18, the relationships were weighted using a low weight of 1, a medium weight of 3, and a high weight of 9, as indicated by the line width.

The item that has the most arrows coming out (or the highest-weighted score for outgoing arrows) is a *key driver* or *root cause*. It causes or influences others, and warrants further investigation in a problem-solving exercise. In this example, the processes vary (have random variation) issue has the highest-weighted incoming score.

The item that has the most arrows going into it (or the highest-weighted score for incoming arrows) is a *key outcome*. This item might be closely tied to a useful metric, or it could be a better descriptor for the problem. In this example, the We don't understand our processes issue has the highest weighted outgoing score.

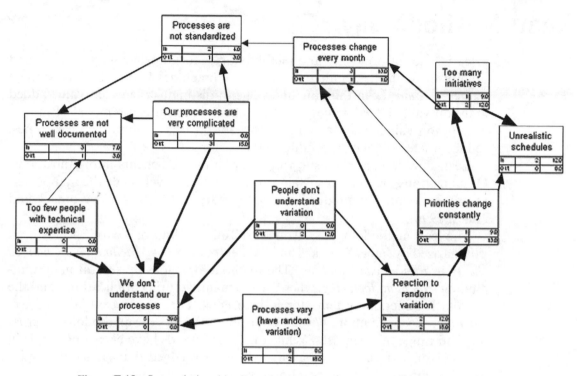

Figure F.18 Interrelationship digraph to study why many managers feel rushed.

Lean Methodology

Lean is a set of principles and methodologies for improving cycle times and quality through the elimination of waste, sometimes known by its Japanese name of *muda*. Lean thinking allows us to distinguish between value-added and non-value-added activities. The immediate result is a removal of unnecessary non-value-added activities. The objective is to improve cycle times, reduce waste, and increase value to the customer.

Lean thinking has been shown to reap dramatic benefits in organizations. Organizations are able to sustain production levels with half the manpower, improving quality and reducing cycle times from 50% to 90% (Womack and Jones, 1996).

The lean methodology is credited to Taiichi Ohno of Toyota; it has been popularized by James Womack and Daniel Jones in *The Machine That Changed the World* and *Lean Thinking*. The methodology goes by several names, including *lean manufacturing*, when used in manufacturing applications, and the Toyota Production System, due to its origins. The more recent label of *lean thinking*, used by authors Womack and Jones, applies the methodology across a broad range of businesses. While the lean methods have been a hot topic in business only since the 1970s, it is well acknowledged that Henry Ford pioneered many of these same techniques.

WHEN TO USE

Lean encompasses a variety of tools useful throughout DMAIC. Lean tools discussed elsewhere in Part 3 include 5S, level loading, process cycle efficiency, spaghetti diagrams, and velocity.

METHODOLOGY

Several of the lean methods are fairly well known in and of themselves. Just-in-time, for example, has been a buzzword within automotive manufacturing for over two decades. Other well-known methods include Kanban (Japanese for cards), Kaizen (which refers to rapid improvement), and 5S.

There may be some confusion regarding the use of lean methods and Six Sigma. Some recent practitioners of Six Sigma have struggled in their Six Sigma deployment by retaining separate functional teams responsible for lean deployment. Six Sigma is an umbrella deployment strategy for implementing value-added improvement projects aligned with an organization's business strategy. Lean provides essential methods to define *value* and *waste* to improve an organization's responsiveness to customer needs. As such, the lean methods enhance the Six Sigma strategy and can be seen as critical methods for accomplishing the Six Sigma goals.

Lean focus is on three areas: visibility, velocity, and value. *Visibility*, also known as *transparency* or *visual control*, broadens our awareness of problems. Visibility implies that problems become immediately (or very quickly) known to all stakeholders, so that action may be taken. Visibility fosters an "all hands on deck" philosophy: stakeholders stop what they're doing to help relieve the bottleneck caused by process problems.

Velocity, sometimes known as *flow*, refers to the speed of process delivery. Speed provides flexibility and improved responsiveness to customer demands. By reducing process lead times, we can quickly respond to new orders or changes required by the customer.

Value simply is the opposite of waste. Value can be defined as something for which the customer is willing to pay. If a process step does not produce value, it is a source of waste and should be removed. More detail is provided in the Value Stream Analysis section in Chapter 6.

Although it may be your initial tendency, don't limit your value stream to the walls of your organization. Fantastic sums of money have been saved by evaluating value streams as they move from supplier to customer, often because of mistaken concepts of value or attempts to achieve operational savings that diminish the customer value.

Although we often think of physical inventories of product or work in process as useful for satisfying customer demands, lean thinking challenges that assumption. Instead, we should view inventory as money spent on partial work that generates no income until it is completed. Inventories hide problems, such as unpredictable or low process yields, equipment failure, or uneven production levels. When inventory exists as work in process, it prevents new orders being processed until the WIP is completed. Although these concepts are most clearly identified with manufacturing processes, they persist in service processes, where inventory may refer to healthcare patients, hamburgers at the fast-food counter, or an unfinished swimming pool under construction.

INTERPRETATION

Visibility, velocity, and value are key focus points of lean. Visibility (or transparency) allows the organization to see progress and barriers to success. A focus on value forces resources to activities important to customers.

Improved velocity allows us to be more responsive to customer needs. Velocity can be improved by the following means:

- Increase completions per hour
- Remove unnecessary process steps
- Reduce movement of material and personnel
- Reduce process/product complexities
- Reduce errors requiring rework
- Optimize process
- Reduce waiting
- Reduce work in process

Level Loading

Level loading is a lean tool used to balance the flow of orders throughout the process.

WHEN TO USE

Improve Stage

- To balance the flow of orders through the process and reduce in-process inventories.

METHODOLOGY

Some prerequisites for successful level loading include:

- Standardization of work instructions.
- Cross-training, so employees can be shifted to meet increased demand or address process problems.
- Transparency, so operational personnel detect and respond to shifts in demand or process problems as soon as possible. Transparency, or visual control, has been found to decrease the reaction time to waste, foster responsibility, and aid in problem solving.

To balance the process steps:

- We first calculate the takt time. *Takt* is the German word for "metronome," and it is used to indicate the desired rhythm of the process.

Takt time = demand (units)/available resource (hours)

For example, if the product has an average demand of 64 units per day, and the cell works 16 hours per day (two shifts), then the takt time is calculated as 15 minutes (i.e., 4 units per hour).
- The takt time is posted at the cell, and the resources (machines, personnel) at each step within the cell are balanced so that their cycle time equals the takt time.
- While we can usually design the process and allocate standard resources for any process to meet its standard takt time, we recognize that a shift in demand will shift the takt time requirements. One way to accommodate the takt time adjustment is to shift resources.

INTERPRETATION

Level loading ensures that goods produced at each step are used immediately by the next step, ensuring a constant flow of items (or service) through the value stream. If a temporary increase in orders is received, the pace remains the same, but resources are moved to meet demand.

Linearity Analysis

Linearity analysis provides an indication of whether the bias error associated with a measurement system is constant throughout the operating range of the equipment. In other words, is the measurement system equally as accurate for large measurements as for small?

WHEN TO USE

Measure Stage

- To evaluate the accuracy of the measurement system throughout the range of measurements required for the process.

METHODOLOGY

The AIAG (Automotive Industry Action Group; *MSA Reference Manual*, February 1995) method of calculating linearity is as follows:

Choose two or more parts (product or service types) throughout the operating range of the gauge. Measure the pertinent characteristic using high-accuracy gauges, such as those used in layout inspections, to obtain a reference value.

Using the gauge to be studied, have one or more process personnel measure the characteristic multiple times. Calculate the average of these measurements for each part.

Calculate the bias for each part as the difference between the gauge average and the reference balue.

Using a scatter diagram, plot the reference value (x axis) versus the bias (y axis).

INTERPRETATION

Use the coefficient of determination R^2 to determine if the linear fit is adequate. (Usually a number like 70% or higher provides sufficient linearity.) If the fit is linear, then linearity may be calculated as:

$$Linearity = |slope| * PV$$

where $|slope|$ is the absolute value of the slope of the regression line calculated by the scatter diagram and PV is the process variation, which may be estimated as six times the process sigma value calculated from a process control chart.

Percent linearity may also be calculated using the slope:

$$\%Linearity = |slope| * 100\%$$

Matrix Diagrams

The matrix diagram is used to show the relationship between the various items in two or more groups. Matrix diagrams are tabular in format, where each cell contains a numerical score indicating the strength of the perceived relationship between the row and its intersecting column.

WHEN TO USE

Define Stage

- To select projects aligned with the company's goals and objectives.
- To understand how customer requirements are aligned with process metrics.

Improve Stage

- To ensure process solutions are aligned with customer needs.

A matrix diagram establishes pairings between two items or helps to rate an item according to its relationship to another item (or items). For instance, you might choose to make a matrix showing the relationship between all the departments in your organization and the various jobs that need to be completed. You can use the matrix to assign primary responsibility, secondary responsibility, and other levels of interest for each task. Examples of use include:

- Project deliverables versus business objectives
- Customer requirements versus internal process objectives
- Serves as foundation of quality function deployment
- Suggested projects versus project rating criteria
- Black Belt candidates versus candidate rating criteria

METHODOLOGY

First, you will need to determine what groups of items you would like to compare within your matrix. (You might want to use information collected in another tool. For instance, you could use the group headings from an affinity diagram of process issues as one group of items, and the project objectives as another.)

Each item in the group will be compared, one at a time, to each item in the other group. Using consensus decision rules, determine whether there is a relationship between the two items, and if so, whether this is a strong or weak relationship. Then mark the intersection of the two items. There are several standard systems used to denote relationships.

Plus and Minus System

A plus indicates that a relationship exists.
A minus indicates that no relationship exists.

Symbol System

A triangle indicates that a weak relationship exists.
A circle shows that some relationship exists.
A circle within a circle shows that a strong relationship exists.

Directional System

Use arrows to show that one item has an effect on another. The process of deciding which arrow to use can often lead to helpful realizations. You might have known that two things were related, but never thought about the nature of the cause and effect. Some software allows these arrows to be weighted (using bold) to show the relative strength of the relationship.

Numerical System

Analogous to the directional system, this system is intended to show the strength and direction of relationships. For example, a 10 implies a strong causal relationship, while a one-tenth shows a strong relationship in the other direction.

INTERPRETATION

An example of a prioritization matrix is shown in Figure F.19. The organization's business objectives are as follows:

- Improve profitability by 50%.
- Improve on-time delivery rate to 90%.
- Improve process efficiency (cycle time estimated to actual) to 95%.

Matrix Diagram : Project Selection Ratings (projsel.7md)							
	Financial Benefit	On-time Delivery	Process Efficiency	Quality OBA	Process Yield/Scrap	Inventor Turns	Totals
BMP Cell 12 Scrap Reduction	●	○	●	○	●	○	36
ADS Cell 2 Efficiency	○	●	○	△	△	●	26
SMT Efficiency Improvements	○	○	○	●	●	○	30
Totals	15	15	15	13	19	15	92

● (9)
○ (3)   △ (1)

Figure F.19 Example of a matrix diagram for project selection.

- Improve process yield to Six Sigma level.
- Increase number of inventory turns to 10.

Since these objectives conveniently summarized the primary concerns of their customers, shareholders, and employees, the executive staff decided to use them as prioritization criteria for the improvement projects.

A score of 1 (shown by triangle), 3 (shown by circle), or 9 (shown by filled circle) is applied to each of the projects for each of the criteria, with a score of 9 indicating that a given project is highly capable of meeting that requirement; a score of 1 indicates the project is not likely to fulfill the criteria; and a score of 3 indicates it is likely to meet the requirement.

For example, the first project (BMP cell 12 scrap reduction) was considered to be highly likely to meet the requirements of financial benefits (improve profitability by 50%), process efficiency (95% improvement in cycle time), and improved process yield, so the project received a score of 9 for each of these items. This project was likely to improve the on-time delivery rate to 90%, and inventory turns (to 10 or higher), so it received a score of 3 for these items. The sum of these scores is 36, as shown in the last column.

This score can then be compared to the score for other projects, with the highest-scored projects receiving the highest implementation priority.

The column totals shown in the last row provide an indication of how well the projects are geared to meet the criteria the organization has established. A low number indicates that few projects are likely to meet the criteria.

Multi-Vari Plots

Multi-vari plots, developed by Dorian Shainin, are used to assign variation to one of the following:

- Within piece or sample variation: For example, taper or out-of-round conditions in a manufactured part, temperature, or pH variations in a chemical sample.
- Piece-to-piece variation: what we typically think of as within subgroup process variation—the variation we see over a short term from one sample to another.
- Time-to-time variation: refers to variation changing over a period of time.

WHEN TO USE

Analyze Stage

- To categorize variation to eliminate factors.
- To investigate interactions among factors.

METHODOLOGY

First decide how data will be collected for the analysis. Are multiple measurements from the same sample available (or useful) to calculate within sample variation?

After collecting the data, construct a plot, such as shown in Figure F.20. Each sample unit will be represented with its own symbol ("batch" as shown in the figure). The symbol length (the distance between the horizontal bars on a symbol) represents the within-sample variation.

INTERPRETATION

The categorizations aid in our understanding of the types of factors that cause variation in our processes. This categorization helps to reduce the number of factors. At times, we can see the effects of interactions as they contribute to one or more of the categories of variation.

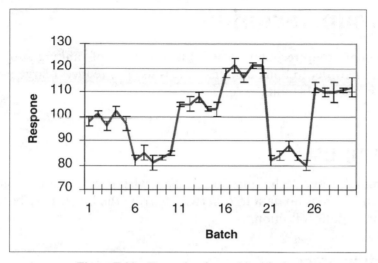

Figure F.20 Example of a multi-vari plot.

It is important to understand that the multi-vari plot is not a control chart, so it cannot be used to determine if there is a statistical instability in the process.

In Figure F.20, the plot shows both the within-batch variation and the time-to-time variation. Piece-to-piece variation (the variation between batches 1–5, 6–10, etc.) is negligible, but step changes to the process are clear between batches 5 and 6, 10 and 11, 15 and 16, and so on.

Nominal Group Technique

The nominal group technique (NGT) is a method of ranking subjective information in order to build consensus. It is used to reduce a large number of ideas into a workable number of key ideas.

WHEN TO USE

The nominal group technique can be used whenever consensus building is desired and there is no data to otherwise narrow the list. It may be used as a precursor to data collection.

Define Stage

• To reduce a large number of potential projects into a workable number of key projects.

Analyze Stage

• To reach consensus on which solution, of a large number of potential solutions, should be investigated in the initial stages of analysis.

METHODOLOGY

Start by handing out a number of index cards to each team member. For less than 20 potential options, hand out four cards per member; for 20 to 35 five options, six cards per member; and for more than 35 options, eight cards per member.

After discussion of the options, each member should choose their top N options, where N is the number of cards handed out per member. Write one option on a single card, not repeating any option, then write their rank order on each of the N cards. It's best to weight using *larger is better* criteria. For example, if there are six cards per member, then a member's top vote should be rated six and their least favorite selection (of the six) should be rated one.

Based on all the rankings from all the participants, we calculate how often an option was selected and the ranked weight for each option.

For example, six options for software implementation were evaluated by a team. Since the number of options is less than 20, each team member was

Table T.15. Nominal Group Technique.

Software Options	Bob	Jim	Tim	Jill	Times Selected	Total Score
Internal	2	1	4		3	7
Existing	1	4	2	4	4	11
Vendor A				1	1	1
Vendor B	4	3	3	2	4	12
Vendor C	3	2		3	3	8
Vendor D			1		1	1

provided four index cards. Each member selected their preferred four options, then ranked these options, with a rank of one being the least desirable option (of the four). See Table T.15.

INTERPRETATION

The result is that we can concentrate our efforts on the items selected most often or with the highest ranked weight.

In the example above, based on both the number of times an option was selected, and the total score, the "Existing" software and that from "Vendor B" are the two favored options. Note that when the two evaluation methods (total score and number of times selected) do not agree, or when the scores are close, it is usually preferred to evaluate more than one leading option.

Nonparametric Test on Equality of Means

Nonparametric tests may be used in place of traditional hypothesis tests on the equality of two means when distributional assumptions cannot be met. A nonparametric test is one in which there are no distributional requirements, such as normality, for the validity of the test. Typically, nonparametric tests require larger sample sizes than the parametric tests.

WHEN TO USE

Analyze Stage

- To compare mean of samples from different conditions, when normality cannot be assumed.

Improve Stage

- To compare process averages after improvements versus baseline estimates, when normality cannot be assumed.

METHODOLOGY

State the null hypothesis H_0, using the same reasoning discussed in Hypothesis Testing on Mean of Two Samples. In this case, the null hypothesis will be *the median of population 1 equals the median of population 2*. Nonparametric tests will typically use the median, rather than the mean, since the median is a good estimate of the central tendency regardless of the distribution. Recall that the average is not a good predictor for nonsymmetric distributions.

Specify the alternative hypothesis H_1 to cover the remaining options. In this case, the alternative hypothesis would be *the median of population 1 does not equal the median of population 2*.

Choose a significance level (α) or the *p* value. The significance level, or type I error, is the probability of rejecting a hypothesis that is true. A value of 0.05 is typical.

Collect samples. As the sample size is increased, the type II error (β error: the probability of accepting a false hypothesis) is decreased.

The simplest of the nonparametric tests for central tendency is the one sample sign test, which tests that approximately half the data is above the test level.

An enhancement of this test, known as the Wilcoxen signed rank test, includes the magnitude and sign of the difference from the median. It assumes a *symmetric*, continuous distribution, and it can be applied to differences between paired observations as well.

The Mann-Whitney test may be used for testing the equality of two medians. It assumes the distributions of the two populations have the same shape and spread. If the distributions are approximately normal, the test is 95% as efficient as a standard t test for large samples. Regardless of the distribution, the test is always at least 86% as efficient as a t test.

These tests may be performed in the Minitab or other statistical software.

INTERPRETATION

The result of the test is to compare the calculated statistics with a test statistic. For example, if the calculated statistic exceeds the critical value of the test statistic (based on the alpha level chosen), then we reject the null hypothesis. If not, then we fail to reject the null hypothesis. Rejecting the null hypothesis is known as a *strong conclusion:* we have disproven that the medians are equal. When we fail to reject the null hypothesis, then the medians may be equal, or may not be; we really can't tell based on the data. This is considered a *weak conclusion* for obvious reasons. We may want to collect larger samples to further test the hypothesis.

Np Chart

The Np chart is one of a set of control charts specifically designed for attributes data. The Np chart monitors the number of times a condition occurs, relative to a constant sample size, when each sample can either have this condition or not have this condition. For example, we could sample a set number of transactions each month from all the transactions that occurred, and from this sample count the number of transactions that had one or more errors. We would then track on the Np control chart the number of transactions with errors each month.

WHEN TO USE

Measure Stage

- To estimate, using attributes data, the process baseline. Generally, we would greatly prefer the use of variables control charts for this purpose.

Improve Stage

- Since the number of errors tends to be quite small (for even very large samples), the use of attribute charts is limited in the improve stage.

METHODOLOGY

Samples are collected from the process at specific points each time. Each sample (at each point in time) has the same number of observed units, each of which may have one or more errors.

Plotted statistic: the number of items in the sample meeting a criteria of interest.

Centerline:

$$\overline{np} = \frac{\sum_{j=1}^{m} (count)_j}{m}$$

where m is the number of groups included in the analysis.

UCL, LCL (upper and lower control limit):

$$UCL_{np} = \overline{np} + 3\sqrt{n\overline{p}(1 - \overline{p})}$$

$$LCL_{np} = MAX(0, \overline{np} - 3\sqrt{n\overline{p}(1 - \overline{p})})$$

where n is the sample size, $\overline{np}$ is the average count, and $\overline{p}$ is calculated as follows:

$$\overline{p} = \frac{\sum_{j=1}^{m} (count)_j}{m * n}$$

For example, we observe 500 telemarketing calls each week, and we record the total number of calls with one or more errors. Ten months of data are observed, with the following number of calls with errors in each sample: 7, 14, 12, 18, 9, 11, 12, 8, 11, 21. The control chart is shown in Figure F.21.

INTERPRETATION

The upper and lower control limits indicate the bounds of expected process behavior. The fluctuation of the points between the control limits is due to the variation that is intrinsic (built in) to the process. We say that this variation is due to common causes that influence the process. Any points outside the control limits can be attributed to a special cause, implying a shift in the process. When a process is influenced by only common causes, then it is stable, and can be predicted.

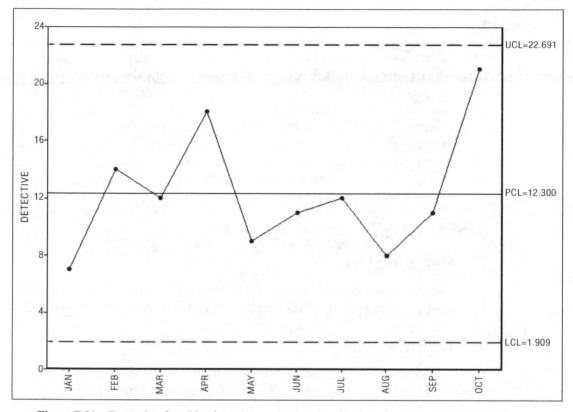

Figure F.21   Example of an Np chart (created using Quality America Green Belt XL software).

If there are any out-of-control points, then special causes of variation must be identified and eliminated. Brainstorm and conduct designed experiments to find those process elements that contribute to sporadic changes in process location. To predict the capability of the process after special causes have been eliminated, you should remove the out-of-control points from the analysis, which will remove the statistical bias of the out-of-control points by dropping them from the calculations of the average and control limits.

Note that some SPC software will allow varying sample sizes for the Np chart. In this case, the control limits and the average line will be adjusted for each sample. Many times, it is less confusing to use a P chart for this data, since only its control limits will vary (the average line will remain constant). See Statistical Process Control Charts for more detail.

P Chart

The P chart is one of a set of control charts specifically designed for attributes data. The P chart monitors the percent of samples having the condition, relative to either a fixed or varying sample size, when each sample can either have this condition or not have this condition. For example, we might choose to look at all the transactions in the month (since that would vary from month to month), or a set number of samples, whichever we prefer. From this sample, we would count the number of transactions that had one or more errors. We would then track on the P control chart the percent of transactions with errors each month.

WHEN TO USE

Measure Stage

- To estimate, using attributes data, the process baseline. Generally, we would greatly prefer the use of variables control charts for this purpose.

Improve Stage

- Since the number of errors tends to be quite small (for even very large samples), the use of attribute charts is limited in the improve stage.

METHODOLOGY

Samples are collected from the process at specific points each time. Each sample (at each point in time) has the same number of observed units, each of which may have one or more errors.

Plotted statistic: the percent of items in the sample meeting a criteria of interest.

$$p_j = \frac{(count)_j}{n_j}$$

where n_j is the sample size (number of units) of group j.

Centerline:

$$\bar{p} = \frac{\sum_{j=1}^{m}(count)_j}{\sum_{j=1}^{m} n_j}$$

where n_j is the sample size (number of units) of group j, and m is the number of groups included in the analysis.

UCL, LCL (upper and lower control limit):

$$UCL = \bar{p} + 3\sqrt{\frac{\bar{p}(1-\bar{p})}{n_j}}$$

$$LCL = MAX\left(0, \bar{p} - 3\sqrt{\frac{\bar{p}(1-\bar{p})}{n_j}}\right)$$

where n_j is the sample size (number of units) of group j, $\bar{p}$ is the average percent.

For example, we observe a varying number of telemarketing calls each week, and we record the total number of calls with one or more errors. Ten months of data are observed, with the following number of calls with errors in each sample: 7 out of 350; 14 out of 312; 12 out of 125; 18 out of 170; 9 out of 165; 11 out of 264; 12 out of 254; 8 out of 404; 11 out of 137; 21 out of 312. The control chart is show in Figure F.22.

INTERPRETATION

The upper and lower control limits indicate the bounds of expected process behavior. The fluctuation of the points between the control limits is due to the variation that is intrinsic (built in) to the process. We say that this variation is due to common causes that influence the process. Any points outside the control limits can be attributed to a special cause, implying a shift in the process. When a process is influenced by only common causes, then it is stable, and it can be predicted.

If there are any out-of-control points, then special causes of variation must be identified and eliminated. Brainstorm and conduct designed experiments to find those process elements that contribute to sporadic changes in process location. To predict the capability of the process after special causes have been eliminated, you should remove the out-of-control points from the analysis, which will remove the statistical bias of the out-of-control points by dropping them from the calculations of the average and control limits. See Statistical Process Control Charts for more detail.

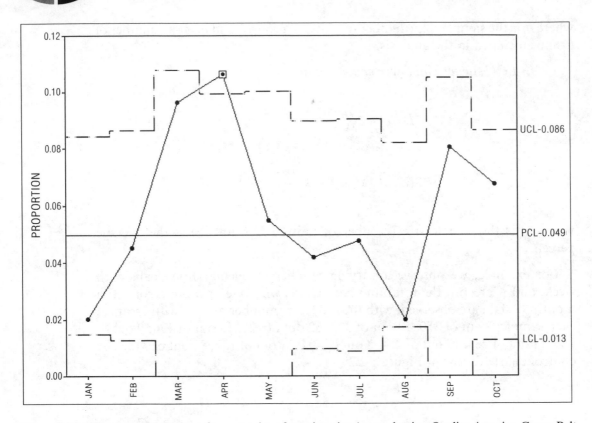

Figure F.22   Example of a P chart for examples of varying size (created using Quality America Green Belt XL software).

Pareto Chart

A Pareto chart is a vertical bar graph showing problems in a prioritized order to determine which problems should be tackled first. The categories for the vertical bars represent mutually exclusive categories of interest. The categories are sorted in decreasing order from left to right in the Pareto diagram based on the value of the metric displayed in the *y* axis, either by count or cost.

WHEN TO USE

Pareto charts provide a guide to selecting opportunities by differentiating between the vital few and the trivial many. They are typically used to prioritize competing or conflicting "problems," so that resources are allocated to the most significant areas. In general, though, they can be used to determine which of several classifications have the most "count" or cost associated with them, for instance, the number of people using the various ATMs versus each of the indoor teller locations, or the profit generated from each of 20 product lines. The important limitations are that the data must be in terms of either counts or costs. The data cannot be in terms that can't be added, such as percent yields or error rates.

Define Stage and Analyze Stage

- To focus project resources on the products, departments, issues, defects, or causes yielding the highest return.

METHODOLOGY

Choose the categories (or problem areas) to collect data for by brainstorming, or use existing data to look for these problem areas. The data you analyze must be counts (attributes data) or costs, and the data must be additive. Data as yields or percentages cannot be added, so they are inappropriate for Pareto analysis. You should also decide the time period over which the data should be collected.

The left vertical axis of the Pareto has counts or cost depending on the data used. Each vertical bar represents the contribution to the total from a given problem area. The bars are placed on the graph in rank order: the bar at the left has the highest contribution to counts or cost. The right vertical axis has percent demarcations. A cumulative line is used to add the percentages from each bar, starting at the left (highest cost or count) bar.

INTERPRETATION

The bar at the left has the highest contribution to counts or cost. Thus, we can see which categories contribute the most problems, and, with the cumulative line, determine how much of the total problem will be fixed by addressing the highest few issues.

Remember that the purpose of the Pareto is to distinguish the "vital few from the trivial many." Therefore, we would like only a few bars on the left side of the Pareto that account for most, say 80%, of the problems. Then it's clear which areas we should address. We can also look at the cumulative line to tell us if our Pareto is working well. The cumulative line should be steep, with a lot of arch to it, implying that the first few problem areas rapidly add to a high percentage of the total problems. If the cumulative line is straight, it is telling us that the contribution from each successive bar (after the first) is about even. These bars, then, should be about the same height. This says that no problems stand out as being more bothersome than the rest, which doesn't help much for problem solving.

We can get "flat" Pareto diagrams just by the way we gather our data. If we separate major problem areas into many small problem areas, then each bar won't have much in it, hence a flat shape. We might consider regrouping the problems into meaningful, larger problem areas.

The goal for the Pareto analysis is a clear identification of key categories requiring attention. A useful Pareto analysis should lead to five or fewer key categories. Note that key categories may differ for count or cost. That is, a problem that appears quite often may not be as costly as something that occurs less frequently but is more costly. It is generally most useful to consider cost data.

For key categories, we need to know whether the high count or high cost is due to common or special causes of variation, which is determined using a control chart. This distinction is important to understand our response to the high cost or occurrence: If it is due to common causes, then we must change the underlying nature of the process, whereas if it is due to a special cause of variation we can respond to that particular issue.

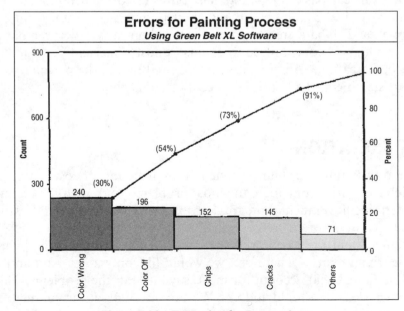

Figure F.23   Example of a Pareto chart.

The Pareto in Figure F.23 (page 282) displays the number of errors of each type of error associated with a painting process. Color Wrong represent the largest source of errors (30%), followed by Color Off (an additional 24%), and Chips (another 19%), so these categories represent the best opportunities for improvement (if all errors have the same costs).

PERT Analysis

PERT (program evaluation and review techniques) allows probabilistic estimates of activity times, such as in project scheduling or cycle time analysis.

WHEN TO USE

Define Stage

- To identify project activities that determine the total project duration.

Analyze Stage

- To identify the critical path for cycle time reduction.

Improve Stage

- To verify the reduction in process-critical path cycle time.

METHODOLOGY

Begin with activity times on the critical path, such as determined using an activity network diagram. We assume that each activity time follows a beta distribution, where:

a = an estimate for the optimistic time
b = an estimate for the pessimistic time
m = an estimate for the most likely time (usually the deterministic time applied to the activity network diagram)

The estimated duration for each activity is then calculated as:

$$\mu = (a + 4m + b)/6$$

The estimated standard deviation for each activity is calculated as:

$$\sigma = (b - a)/6$$

Based on central limit theorem, the total time for all tasks follows the normal distribution. The total duration can be calculated by summing the task times on the critical path. Likewise, the variance of the project duration can be calculated by summing the variances for the task times on the critical path. Recall that the variance is the standard deviation squared.

Total duration = sum (task times on critical path)
Variance (total duration) = sum (variances for task times on critical path)
Standard deviation (total duration) = square root [variance (total duration)]
Upper predicted limit of duration = total duration + 1.96 * standard deviation (total duration)
Lower predicted limit of duration = total duration − 1.96 * standard deviation (total duration)

In Table T.16, we used the likely times for the critical path tasks based on the earlier activity network example. Best and worst times were estimated, and from these the mean, standard deviation, and variance for each task were calculated using the previous equations. The average time of process tasks was then calculated as the sum of the mean times. The standard deviation of process tasks was calculated as the square root of the sum of the variances. In

Table T.16.   Example PERT Data.

Task	Likely Time	Best Time	Worst Time	Mean	Sigma	Variation
Proof	15	10	20	15	1.67	2.78
Edit	2	0.6	3.4	2	0.467	0.22
TOC	3	1.8	4.2	3	0.4	0.16
Final	4	3	5	4	0.333	0.11
Finish	1	.75	1.25	1	0.083	0.01

this case, the mean time is the same as calculated using the activity network diagram (25 days), but that may not always be the case.

INTERPRETATION

Use the upper and lower predicted limits of duration as best and worst case estimates of the project or process cycle time.

Prioritization Matrix

A prioritization matrix is a special type of matrix diagram designed especially to prioritize or rank options and build consensus.

WHEN TO USE

Define Stage

- To select projects aligned with company goals and objectives.
- To understand how customer requirements are aligned with process metrics.

Improve Stage

- To verify that project solutions are aligned with customer needs.

METHODOLOGY

There are two methods that you can use to make a prioritization matrix: the full analytical method and the quicker consensus criteria method.

The *full analytical method* gives you a quantitative method for deciding which criteria are the most important to your project and which options best fulfill the given criteria. It is especially useful when you are unsure which criteria are the most important.

The *consensus criteria method* is somewhat simpler than the full analytical method in that the team simply decides the importance of each criterion, then ranks the options according to their ability to meet each criterion.

Full Analytical Method

The first step in any prioritization matrix is to compile a list of your options.

Then, compile a list of all the criteria for evaluating the options. Each criterion should be stated as a goal: short period of time, low cost, ease of use, employee satisfaction, etc.

The first matrix will compare each criterion to every other criterion. The criteria will be listed across the horizontal top of the matrix as well as down the left side of the matrix. Evaluate each criterion in relation to each other criterion and assign a number designating their relative importance. Use the following number system:

$10 =$ Much more important/preferred/desirable.
$5 =$ More important/preferred/desirable.
$1 =$ Equally important /preferred/desirable.
$1/5 =$ Less important/preferred/desirable.
$1/10 =$ Much less important/preferred/desirable.

In Figure F.24 using Quality America's *GreenBelt XL* software, six criteria were defined for the selection of Black Belts: technical competence, familiarity with company systems and culture, having a positive attitude, being a risk taker, having good communication skills, and being seen as a leader by peers.

The group decided that Technical Competence was more desirable than Familiarity with Company Systems and Culture, so a value of 5 was placed in the Technical Competence row, Familiarity with Company Systems and Culture column. The software automatically filled in the complimentary cell (Familiarity with Company Systems and Culture row, Technical Competence column) with a value of one-fifth. Likewise, they considered Technical

Criteria Weighting Matrix						
	Technical Competence	Familar w/ Company Systems, Culture	Positive Attitude	Risk Taker	Good Communicator	Leader
Technical Competence	■	5	1	$\frac{1}{5}$	$\frac{1}{5}$	1
Familar w/ Company Systems, Culture	$\frac{1}{5}$	■	$\frac{1}{5}$	1	$\frac{1}{5}$	$\frac{1}{10}$
Positive Attitude	1	5	■	10	1	1
Risk Taker	5	1	$\frac{1}{10}$	■	$\frac{1}{5}$	$\frac{1}{5}$
Good Communicator	5	5	1	5	■	1
Leader	1	10	1	5	1	■

Figure F.24   Example of a criteria-weighting matrix.

Options Rating Matrix for 'Positive Attitude' ▼									
	Art	Peter	Mike	Carl	Jessie	Maria	Jerry	Adrianne	Row Totals
Art	■	$\frac{1}{5}$	$\frac{1}{5}$	$\frac{1}{5}$	$\frac{1}{5}$	$\frac{1}{5}$	1	$\frac{1}{5}$	2.2 (0.01)
Peter	5	■	1C	1C	1	1C	5	1C	51 (0.31)
Mike	5	$\frac{1}{10}$	■	1	$\frac{1}{10}$	1	5	1	13.2 (0.08)
Carl	5	$\frac{1}{10}$	1	■	$\frac{1}{10}$	1	5	1	13.2 (0.08)
Jessie	5	1	1C	1C	■	1C	1C	1C	56 (0.34)
Maria	5	$\frac{1}{10}$	1	1	$\frac{1}{10}$	■	5	1	13.2 (0.08)
Jerry	1	$\frac{1}{5}$	$\frac{1}{5}$	$\frac{1}{5}$	$\frac{1}{10}$	$\frac{1}{5}$	■	$\frac{1}{5}$	2.1 (0.01)
Adrianne	5	$\frac{1}{10}$	1	1	$\frac{1}{10}$	1	5	■	13.2 (0.08)
Column Totals	31	1.8	23.4	23.4	1.7	23.4	36	23.4	164.1

Figure F.25 Example of an options-rating matrix.

Competence to be equally important as Positive Attitude, so a 1 was placed in those two complimentary cells, and so on. The software provides an easy-to-use wizard, which prompts the user for each of these comparisons.

The full analytic method then requires you to compare each of these options for a given criteria. In Figure F.25, the options are the individuals being evaluated as Black Belt candidates. The criterion shown is "Positive Attitude." The evaluation team apparently thought Art's attitude was equal to Jerry's, but less positive than any of the other candidates. Jessie's score of 56 (the highest) shows that her attitude is perceived as more positive than any of the other candidates, with Peter a close second. The percent of total, which is shown in parentheses, will be used to calculate the final scores for all criteria.

Once the options have been compared for each of the criteria, a final weighted score can be calculated by combining the matrices. Each option's score (as a percent of total) for a given criteria is multiplied by the ranking for that criterion, summed across all criteria. The options are rank-ordered in the summary matrix, with the top row being the highest ranking (i.e., best at meeting weighted criteria). In Figure F.26, Peter, Jessie, and Adrianne are clearly distinct from the other candidates.

Consensus Criteria Method

The full analytic method can be quite time-consuming, particularly as the number of options grows. The consensus criteria method is an alternate

Summary Matrix ▼						
	Familar w/ Company Systems, Culture	Positive Attitude	Risk Taker	Good Communicator	Leader	Row Totals
Peter	0.21x0.05=0.010	0.31x0.23=0.071	0.16x0.12=0.019	0.25x0.23=0.058	0.26x0.23=0.060	0.238 (0.26)
Jessie	0.21x0.05=0.010	0.34x0.23=0.078	0.02x0.12=0.002	0.25x0.23=0.058	0.25x0.23=0.058	0.213 (0.23)
Adrianne	0.1x0.05=0.005	0.08x0.23=0.018	0.03x0.12=0.004	0.29x0.23=0.067	0.3x0.23=0.069	0.183 (0.20)
Jerry	0.13x0.05=0.007	0.01x0.23=0.002	0.37x0.12=0.044	0.07x0.23=0.016	0.02x0.23=0.005	0.081 (0.09)
Maria	0.18x0.05=0.009	0.08x0.23=0.018	0.13x0.12=0.016	0.01x0.23=0.002	0.06x0.23=0.014	0.066 (0.07)
Carl	0.11x0.05=0.006	0.08x0.23=0.018	0.25x0.12=0.03	0.03x0.23=0.007	0.01x0.23=0.002	0.064 (0.07)
Mike	0.06x0.05=0.003	0.08x0.23=0.018	0.02x0.12=0.002	0.06x0.23=0.014	0.06x0.23=0.014	0.058 (0.06)
Art	0.01x0.05=0.000	0.01x0.23=0.002	0.02x0.12=0.002	0.04x0.23=0.009	0.04x0.23=0.009	0.023 (0.02)
Column Totals	0.050	0.228	0.12	0.23	0.23	0.928

Figure F.26   Example of a summary matrix.

technique that streamlines the analysis. In this method, we again start by specifying the options and the criteria, then compare the criteria. The criteria rating is done by simply distributing 100% across the criteria, with the highest weights given to more important criteria. See Figure F.27. You may find it useful to think of distributing a hundred dollars, giving the most money to the more important criteria.

Criteria Weighting Matrix	
	Rating
Technical Competence	.15
Familar w/ Company Systems, Culture	.1
Positive Attitude	.25
Risk Taker	.05
Good Communicator	.20
Leader	.25

Figure F.27   Example of a criteria-weighting matrix for the consensus criteria method.

Options Rating Matrix for 'Leader'	
	Rating
Art	1
Peter	3
Mike	1
Carl	1
Jessie	3
Maria	2
Jerry	1
Adrianne	3

Figure F.28 Example of an options-rating matrix for the consensus criteria method.

Summary Matrix	
	Row Totals
Peter	2.95
Jessie	2.75
Adrianne	2.7
Maria	2.15
Mike	1.7
Carl	1.45
Jerry	1.35
Art	1.1

Figure F.29 Example of a summary matrix for the consensus criteria method.

Each option is then compared against the criteria with a simple weighting scale, such as 1 to 3; 1 to 5; or 1 to 10, with the largest value assigned to the best option. Figure F.28 on page 289, top. shows the options rating matrix using the 1 to 3 scale. Peter and Adrianne achieved the highest scores in this example.

The final score for each option is then obtained in the summary matrix by multiplying the scores for each criteria by the criteria weight. See Figure F.29 on page 289, bottom.

INTERPRETATION

The final weighted score indicates the prioritization you should assign to each option. The higher the score, the greater the priority.

Probability Plotting

Probability plotting is a graphical technique used to visually check that data meets distributional assumptions.

WHEN TO USE

Measure, Analyze, and Improve Stages

- To graphically test whether process data fit an assumed distribution for capability analysis.
- To detect whether population data meet the criteria of normality required for many statistical tests.

METHODOLOGY

- Rank order the data from the smallest value to the largest value.
- Assign probabilities to each value based on rank, distribution, and number of samples. The probability is calculated as $100(j - 0.5)/n$, where n is the number of data points and j is the rank order of the data point.
- Plot (value, probability) on a probability plot whose axes are scaled according to the distribution under consideration. See Figure F.30.
- Draw line of best fit through center of data.

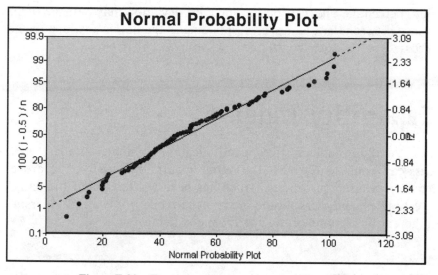

Figure F.30   Example of a normal probability chart.

INTERPRETATION

For the most part, probability plots offer only visual confirmation of goodness of fit of the data to the assumed distribution. A common method to interpret the probability plots predates the computerization of the technique. In days past, one would simply lay a fat pencil on the graph, and if the data were obscured by the pencil, then the data fit the distribution fairly well.

One useful technique for determining if there is too much data in the tail regions of the distribution is to look for patterns near the far left and far right portions of the line. Excessive data in the tails would group data above the confidence interval on the left side (small probabilities), and below the confidence interval on the right side (high probabilities).

The adequacy of the test for a given distributional fit is dependent on the stability of the process and the number of data points. Generally, two to three hundred data points are recommended for testing distributional fits, although less data can be used with less certainty in the results. If the process is not in statistical control, then no one distribution should be fit to the data.

To overcome some of the ambiguity of the probability plots, most analysts enhance their analysis with goodness of fit tests.

When normal distribution paper is used, and the data fits the distribution well, the mean of the population can be estimated as the value of the line as it crosses the 50th percentile. The distribution standard deviation may be estimated as the difference between the x values corresponding to the points at which the normal line crosses the $y = $ 50th ($z = 0$) and $y = $ 84th ($z = 1$) percentiles.

Process Capability Index

Process capability indices attempt to indicate, in a single number, whether a process can consistently meet the requirements imposed on the process by internal or external customers. Much has been written about the dangers of these estimates, and users should interpret capability only after understanding the inherent limitations of the specific index being used.

WHEN TO USE

Process capability attempts to answer the question: can we consistently meet customer requirements? Once process capability has been calculated, it can be converted into a corresponding DPMO or sigma level. It is important to remember that process capability indices are meaningless if the data is not from a controlled process. The reason is simple: process capability is a prediction, and you can only predict something that is stable. In order to estimate process capability, you must know the location, spread, and shape of the process distribution. These parameters are, by definition, changing in an out-of-control process. Therefore, only use process capability indices (and resulting DPMO and sigma level estimates) if the process is in control for an extended period.

The statistic C_p can be used when there are both and upper and lower specifications for the process. C_{pk} can be used when there is only one or the other, or both, specifications provided.

Measure Stage

• To provide a process baseline estimate for a controlled process.

Improve Stage

• To provide an estimate of the improved process and to verify that the improved process is in a state of statistical control.

Control Stage

- To continuously monitor the process to verify that it remains in a state of statistical control at the desired capability level.

METHODOLOGY

Since process capability is not valid unless the process is stable, always analyze the process using a control chart first. Once statistical control is evidenced, then process capability may be analyzed.

For normal distributions, the capability indices are calculated as:

$$C_p = \frac{HighSpec - LowSpec}{6\sigma_x}$$

$$C_{pk} = MIN(Cp_l, Cp_u)$$

$$C_{pm} = \frac{C_p}{\sqrt{1 + \frac{(\bar{\bar{x}}-T)^2}{\sigma_x^2}}}$$

where T is the process target, $\bar{\bar{x}}$ is the grand average, and σ_x is process sigma, which is calculated using the moving range (when subgroup size $= 1$) or subgroup sigma (subgroup size > 1) statistic.

$$Cp_l = -\frac{Z_l}{3} \qquad Cp_u = -\frac{Z_u}{3}$$

$$Z_l = \frac{\bar{\bar{x}} - LowSpec}{\sigma_x} \qquad Z_u = \frac{HighSpec - \bar{\bar{x}}}{\sigma_x}$$

For non-normal distributions, the capability indices are calculated as:

$$C_p = \frac{HighSpec - LowSpec}{ordinate_{0.99865} - ordinate_{0.00135}}$$

$$Z_l = Z_{normal,\ p} \qquad Z_u = Z_{normal,\ 1-p}$$

where $ordinate_{0.99865}$ and $ordinate_{0.00135}$ are the z values of the non-normal cumulative distribution curve at the 99.865 percentage point and the 0.135 percentage points, respectively; $Z_{normal,\ p}$ and $Z_{normal,\ 1-p}$ are the z values of the normal cumulative distribution curve at the p percentage point and the $1 - p$ percentage points, respectively.

Table T.17.   Capability to Sigma Level Conversion.

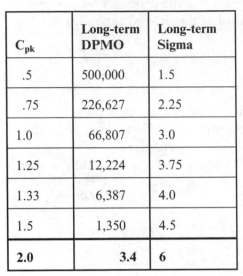

C_{pk}	Long-term DPMO	Long-term Sigma
.5	500,000	1.5
.75	226,627	2.25
1.0	66,807	3.0
1.25	12,224	3.75
1.33	6,387	4.0
1.5	1,350	4.5
2.0	3.4	6

INTERPRETATION

Compare the non-normal and normal indices. Capability indices are quite sensitive to assumptions of the distribution.

C_p provides the ratio of the tolerance (specification, or permitted amount of variation) to the process variation. A value of 1 indicates the process variation exactly equals the tolerance; values less than 1 indicate the allowable variation (the tolerance) is smaller than the process variation, an undesirable condition.

C_{pk} provides a relative indication of how both process variation and location compare to the requirements.

When C_p and C_{pk} are both available (i.e., bilateral specifications), then C_p can be used to estimate the best case process capability (assuming the target value for the process is located exactly at the center point between the specification limits).

C_{pm} is similar to the C_{pk} index, but takes into account variation between the process average and a target value. If the process average and the target are the same value, C_{pm} will be the same as C_{pk}. If the average drifts from the target value, C_{pm} will be less than C_{pk}.

A comparison of capability index with sigma values is shown here. Table T.17 provides an indication of the level of improvement effort required in a process to meet these escalating demands, where DPMO refers to the average defect level measured in parts per million.

Process Cycle Efficiency

Process cycle efficiency is a metric useful for prioritizing cycle time improvement opportunities.

WHEN TO USE

Analyze Stage

- To prioritize cycle time improvement opportunities.

METHODOLOGY

Process cycle efficiency is calculated by dividing the value-added time associated with a process by the total lead time of the process.

$$\text{Process cycle efficiency} = \text{value-added time}/\text{process lead time}$$

Little's law is used to calculate the process lead time by dividing the number of items in process by the completions per hour (George, 2002).

$$\text{Process lead time} = \text{No. items in process}/\text{completions per hour}$$

For example, if it takes 2 hours on average to complete each purchase order, then there are 0.5 completions per hour. This is the denominator of the Little law equation. If there are 10 purchase orders waiting in queue (the numerator), then Little's law says we need 10 divided by one-half equals 20 hours lead time for the process. In other words, we can't process any new orders until the 20-hour lead time has allowed the existing work in process to be completed.

INTERPRETATION

If the process consists of only value-added activities, then process cycle efficiency would reach a theoretical maximum of 100%. In practice, process cycle efficiencies will exceed 25% for processes that have been improved through the use of lean methods. Typical process cycle efficiencies are shown in Table T.18.

The key to improving (increasing) process cycle efficiency is often to reduce the lead time, the denominator of the equation. Lead time is reduced, and process efficiency increased, when work in process is reduced.

Table T.18.   Typical Process Cycle Efficiencies (George, 2002).

Process Type	Typical Efficiency	World-Class Efficiency
Machining	1%	20%
Fabrication	10%	25%
Assembly	15%	35%
Continuous	30%	80%
Transactional	10%	50%
Creative	5%	25%

The rationale is simple: new orders from customers cannot be started until work (or items) in process is completed. Thus, the activity on new items is stalled, and efficiency (from a customer's point of view) suffers. An example from a service process is a doctor's waiting room. The patients are work in process. New patients aren't seen by the doctor until those who arrived earlier are processed.

Process Decision Program Charts

Process decision program charts (PDPC) are used to delineate the required steps to complete a process, anticipate any problems that might arise in the steps, and map out a way of counteracting the problems.

WHEN TO USE

Analyze Stage

- To understand root causes of problems.

Improve Stage

- To identify potential problems with the suggested solution, so that contingency plans may be adopted for process control.

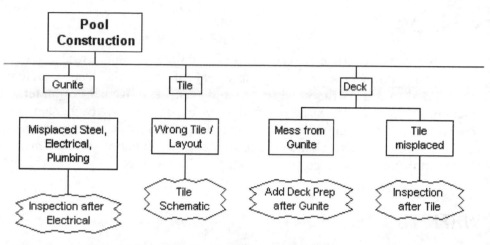

Figure F.31   Example of a process decision program chart.

METHODOLOGY

The top level is the project or process statement: for example, Pool Construction in Figure F.31. Moving from left to right in the second level are the steps required for the project or process. These steps should not be overly specific, so as to avoid cluttering the chart. A third level may be used, if necessary, to display process substep detail.

The next level contains what-if scenarios for each step, which represent the potential problems that can occur at that step. Try to think of any problems that might arise in the execution of each process step. Each step should be examined independently.

Countermeasures (such as Tile Schematic) provide the contingencies for each problem.

INTERPRETATION

In Figure F.31 a number of inspection steps have been added as well as a deck preparation step. These changes to the process flow need to be documented in the process maps discussed next. The inspection steps are not a preferred contingency, since they are not value-added from a customer perspective.

Process Maps

Similar to a flowchart, a process map is a simple graphical tool for documenting the flow (the series of steps necessary) of a process. The process map can be used to display the value stream and even the movement of materials (including information, such as in a service process), so each step and movement can be analyzed for value creation. Often, "swim lanes" can be used on a process map to indicate movement into functional departments. Cycle times may also be included to assist in the analysis.

WHEN TO USE

Define Stage

- Document top-level process.
- Identify shareholders.

Measure Stage

- Document lower levels of process.
- Uncover varied shareholder perceptions.

Analyze Stage

- Discover process complexities, responsible agents, and locations which contribute to variation or longer cycle times.

Improve Stage

- Communicate proposed changes.

Control Stage

- Document revised process.

METHODOLOGY

As in the flowchart, each task will be represented by a symbol. ANSI standard symbols may be used, but most practitioners find they use rectangles for most

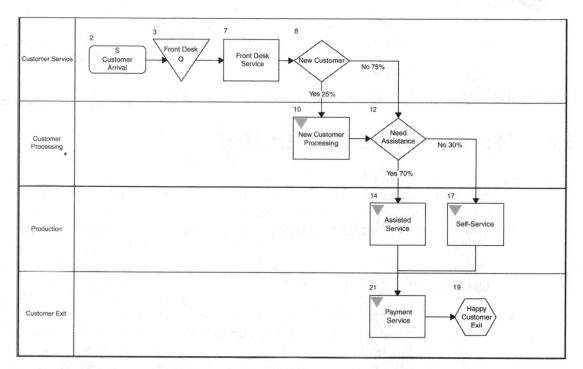

Figure F.32 Example of a process map showing stakeholder departments as swim lanes.

tasks and diamonds for decision tasks. Decisions should have only two out-comes (yes or no), so decision points must be phrased in this manner.

We can use the process map to document the current (as-is) process. See Figure F.32. We can use symbol shade or shape to indicate process delays, functional responsibility for each step (for example, the small gray inverted triangle is Customer Service), or points in the process where measurements are taken.

Location of process steps on the map is indicated by swim lanes, used to indicate physical layout, responsible department, stakeholder, schedule, or other condition for each process activity.

Figure F.32 is an example of a process map using Sigma Flow software. In this case the swim lanes provide an indication of department responsible (customer service, customer processing, or production).

INTERPRETATION

A quick review of the as-is process can usually uncover complexities in the form of an excessive number of decision points and branches that may contribute to delays or even defects. When used to document the future (desired) process, we strive to make process flow uncomplicated, with the fewest symbols (tasks) and branches possible. This lack of complexity in the process will tend to reduce the number of errors.

Process Performance Indices

Process performance attempts to answer the question: Does this sample meet customer requirements? It differs from process capability in that process performance only applies to a specific batch of material. Samples from the batch may need to be quite large to be representative of the variation in the batch.

WHEN TO USE

Process performance should only be used when statistical process control cannot be evaluated or achieved. For example, we may have insufficient data to analyze statistical process control in initial stages of product or process design; or in the measure stage we may have processes that lack statistical control.

The statistic P_p can be used when there are both and upper and lower specification for the sample. P_{pk} can be used when there is only one or the other, or both, specifications provided.

Measure Stage

• To provide a process baseline estimate for an uncontrolled process.

METHODOLOGY

For normal distributions, the performance indices are calculated as:

$$P_p = \frac{HighSpec - LowSpec}{6\sigma_x}$$

$$P_{pk} = MIN\,(Pp_l, Pp_u)$$

$$P_{pm} = \frac{P_p}{\sqrt{1 + \frac{(\bar{x}-T)^2}{\sigma_x^2}}}$$

where T is the process target, $\bar{\bar{x}}$ is the grand average, and σ_x is sample sigma.

$$P_{p_l} = -\frac{Z_l}{3} \qquad P_{p_u} = -\frac{Z_u}{3}$$

$$Z_l = \frac{\bar{\bar{x}} - LowSpec}{\sigma_x} \qquad Z_u = \frac{HighSpec - \bar{\bar{x}}}{\sigma_x}$$

For non-normal distributions, the performance indices are calculated as:

$$P_p = \frac{HighSpec - LowSpec}{ordinate_{0.99865} - ordinate_{0.00135}}$$

$$Z_l = Z_{normal, p} \qquad Z_u = Z_{normal, 1-p}$$

where $ordinate_{0.99865}$ and $ordinate_{0.00135}$ are the z values of the non-normal cumulative distribution curve at the 99.865 percentage point and the 0.135 percentage points, respectively; $Z_{normal, p}$ and $Z_{normal, 1-p}$ are the z values of the normal cumulative distribution curve at the p percentage point and the $1 - p$ percentage points, respectively.

INTERPRETATION

Process performance uses sample sigma in its calculation, so it cannot provide an estimate of process capability for the future. Since the process is not in a state of control, we cannot predict its future performance.

The calculated process performance and process capability indices will likely be quite similar when the process is in statistical control.

- A value of 1 indicates the sample variation exactly equals the tolerance.
- Values less than 1 indicate the allowable variation (the tolerance) is less than the sample variation.
- Values greater than 1 are desirable, indicating that the sample variation is less than the tolerance. Values greater than 1.3 or 1.5 are often recommended.

Use of performance indices is generally discouraged in favor of capability indices wherever possible.

Quality Function Deployment

Quality function deployment (QFD) is a detailed methodology for linking customer requirements with internal process and product requirements.

WHEN TO USE

Analyze Stage and Improve Stage

- To understand how customer requirements are translated into internal process and product requirements.

METHODOLOGY

There are four distinct stages of a proper QFD. In service organizations, the QFD can be focused on the last two stages, ensuring processes are designed and controlled to meet customer requirements (customer req.).

In the design stage, customer requirements (the *whats*) are translated into design requirements (design req.) (the *hows*). In this way, the product planning matrix provides a means of ensuring that each customer requirement is satisfied through one or more design elements. See Figure F.33.

The customer requirements are next translated into part characteristics in the part deployment matrix. This matrix thus provides insight into

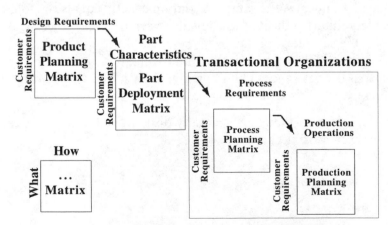

Figure F.33   QFD stages with associated matrices.

how specific qualities of the finished part will satisfy specific needs of the customer.

In the process planning matrix, the customer requirements are translated into process requirements, determining the processing methods that will be used.

Finally, in the production planning matrix, the whats of customer requirements are translated into the hows of production operations, which determine how the process will be designed and controlled.

In each matrix, the whats of the customer requirements are translated into the hows of the internal requirements.

The "house of quality" in Figure F.34 is an extended matrix used to define and rate the whats and hows at each stage. The basis for each of these elements is as follows.

We start by listing the whats in rows at the left. The whats are the customer requirements: what the customer wants or desires in the product or service, the quality attributes. If there is a natural grouping of the requirements, it's often advantageous to list them by groups. For example, convenient groups could be critical to quality, critical to schedule, or critical to cost; or perhaps aesthetics, performance, and function.

Each what is weighted for importance. A useful scale is a rating between 1 and 5, with 5 being high importance and 1 being low importance.

We then define the design requirements: the hows, depending on which matrix we are defining (product, part, process, or production), that meet the customer requirements.

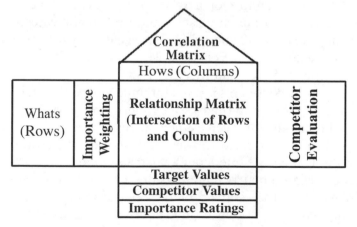

Figure F.34 House of quality.

Customer Requirements	Import.	Operational Requirements						
		No. Wait Staff	No. Cook Staff	Pre-prep	Plate Prep	Menu	Cook Training	Wait Staff Training
Service								
Wait Time	3	9	3	3	0	3	3	3
Friendliness	4	3	0	0	0	0	0	3
Order Accuracy	4	3	1	0	0	3	3	9
Culinary								
Taste	4	0	3	3	3	1	9	3
Temperature	3	3	3	1	9	0	9	3
Pricing								
Entrées<$13	3	3	3	3	0	9	0	0
Kids Menu	2	1	1	0	0	9	0	0

Figure F.35   Relationship matrix.

In the relationship matrix, we will then determine the relationship of each how to each what, recording the score in the proper intersecting cell using the following scoring index:

Strong Relationship = 9
Moderate Relationship = 3
Weak Relationship = 1
No Relationship = 0

Figure F.35 is an example of a relationship matrix. The customer requirements for a restaurant are listed for three main categories: service quality, culinary satisfaction, and pricing. Each category is broken down into more definitive requirements. For example, service quality is broken down into wait time, friendliness, and order accuracy.

Each of the subcategory items is rated for importance, shown in the column labeled *I*, using a 1 (low) to 5 (high) scale as discussed earlier.

Operational requirements, such as the number of wait staff, the number of cook staff, and so on, are rated for their influence on the customer requirements using the 1 (weak), 3 (moderate), 9 (strong) scale.

The QFD correlation matrix represents the roof of the house of quality. In this matrix, we enter the estimate of the relationships between the hows, generally using scores of 1 (low), 3 (moderate), or 9 (high).

Correlation Matrix

				0	Cook Training
			3	9	Menu
		-3	3	0	Plate Prep
	3	-3	3	0	Preprep
-3	-3	-3	9	0	No. Cook Staff
0	0	0	-1	0	9	No. Wait Staff

Operational Requirements

No. Cook Staff	Pre-prep	Plate Prep	Menu	Cook Training	Wait Staff Training

Figure F.36   Example of a correlation matrix.

Each estimate can be either positive or negative in sign. Positive values indicate a supportive relationship. In this case, the how resources can be used for multiple purposes. Negative values indicate a conflicting relationship, which will require a trade-off in resources.

In Figure F.36, the correlation matrix shown is from an Excel file. Since Excel's table structure does not permit angled cells, the shape of the roof is not triangular, as shown in the standard house of quality. Nonetheless, the inputs and results are the same.

We compare each of the hows (the operational requirements in this case) and enter the relationship, with sign, in the intersecting cell. For example, the relationship between the number of cook staff and the number of wait staff is insignificant, so a zero is entered. On the other hand, an increase in plate prep will moderately hurt the number of cook staff, so a negative 3 is entered.

Based on these entries, we can see that cook training and wait staff training will positively influence each of the other hows, whereas a more complex menu will conflict with the other operational requirements.

The competitor evaluation (on the right in Figure F.37) provides a rating of each competitor's ability to satisfy each customer requirement [i.e., the rows are the customer requirements (whats) and the columns list the competitors by name or code]. Each competitor is rated on a scale of 1 to 5, with 5 being the highest (or most likely to satisfy the customer requirements). The competitor evaluation shows where competition is strong (a challenge for you), as well as where it is weak (an opportunity).

Customer Requirements	Competitor Evaluation		
	House of Italy	*Leonardo's*	*Mama Mia*
Service Quality			
Wait Time	2	5	3
Friendliness of Staff	1	4	4
Order Accuracy	5	4	4
Culinary Satisfaction			
Taste	5	3	2
Temperature	5	4	3
Pricing			
Some Entrées <$13	1	4	3
Kids Menu	1	4	3

Figure F.37   Example of a competitor evaluation matrix.

Figure F.37 is an example of a competitor evaluation. Each of the competitors is rated for each customer requirement from 1 (low) to 5 (high).

Beneath the relationship matrix in Figure F.32 is the target row, where you will enter the desired value for the how. Conveniently listed beneath that is the competitor row for indicating a score for the competition's best solution for that how. The last row beneath the relationship matrix is the importance ratings. These are calculated by first calculating each cell's importance by multiplying each relationship score (the cell) by the importance rating for that what. We then sum these for each column to get the importance for that how. We can also rank order the hows, where a value of 1 is given to the highest importance rating, indicating the most important how.

In Figure F.38 the values provided above for both the target and competitor are defined using a common metric specific to each operational requirement. For example, the target value for number of wait staff is defined using a staff-to-table ratio (1 staff for every 2.5 tables), while the menu target is defined using an average entrée price.

The importance score for each operational requirement is also shown. We calculate the importance value for the number of wait staff using the sum of the importance times the relationship score as follows:

$$(3*9) + (4*3) + (4*3) + (4*0) + (3*3) + (3*3) + (2*1) = 71$$

Customer Requirements	Import.	Operational Requirements						
		# Wait Staff	# Cook Staff	Pre-prep	Plate Prep	Menu	Cook Training	Wait Staff Training
Service Quality								
Wait Time	3	9	3	3	0	3	3	3
Friendliness of Staff	4	3	0	0	0	0	0	3
Order Accuracy	4	3	1	0	0	3	3	9
Culinary Satisfaction								
Taste	4	0	3	3	3	1	9	3
Temperature	3	3	3	1	9	0	9	3
Pricing								
Some Entrées<$13	3	3	3	3	0	9	0	0
Kids Menu	2	1	1	0	0	9	0	0
Target Value		1:2.5	1:5	30	3	$12	40	60
Competitor Value		1:2	1:4	30	3	$11:60	40	60
Importance		71	45	33	39	70	84	78
Rank		3	5	7	6	4	1	2

Figure F.38   Example of target, competitor, and importance scores.

The importance of the other operational requirements is similarly calculated. They are rank-ordered, with the largest being the highest priority. In this example, the cook training was the most important operational requirement, followed by wait staff training. You can use the importance as input to the target value: the most important requirements might be best targeted at or better than the competitors' values, as shown in the example.

INTERPRETATION

If there are no hows (or a weak relationship of hows) for a given what, then there's an opportunity for improvement, although it may be that subsequent matrices (part, process, or operational) will address this what.

Hows unrelated to any whats are candidates for removal as non-value-added activities. We should check the customer requirements to ensure they are accurate and complete and verify this against the competitor analysis.

R&R Studies

Gage R&R (repeatability and reproducibility) analysis quantifies the error due to a measurement system.

WHEN TO USE

Measure Stage

- To quantify the measurement error's contribution to the variation (common and special causes) included in process baseline estimates.
- To verify adequate gage discrimination.

Control Stage

- To qualify operators' proficiency on specific measurement equipment.

METHODOLOGY

When conducting an R&R study, it is imperative to use production parts, or parts that are similar to production parts (such as when performing preproduction evaluations). You must not use reference standards, since the ability of the measurement system to precisely measure the standards is not a good indicator of whether the system will precisely measure parts in production. Remember the purposes of the measurement system: (1) to evaluate the suitability of given product for release to (internal or external) customers; (2) to evaluate the stability (i.e., statistical control) and capability of the process producing the parts.

Using production parts allows us to include error associated with measurement fixturing (used to hold the part or gage during measurement), as well as variation within the production pieces themselves. Each of these generally contributes to increased repeatability errors, since all the operators contend with these problems. However, it might be that select operators have improved techniques for dealing with the poor fixturing or the within-piece variation, so that their repeatability error is less than other operators'. Recognizing this, when it occurs, can lead to system improvements.

Of course, these techniques are not limited to mechanical inspections, nor to material parts. They can also be applied to optical inspections, chemical analyses, or any other measurement system. In chemical analyses, sample preparation may be a critical component of the measurement. Just as we use production parts above, this preparation should be done using actual product, so that sample preparation is done using real-world conditions.

R&R studies are conducted by obtaining a sample of parts, and having representative operators inspect each part (called a piece) multiple times (each inspection is termed a trial). A typical study involves having 3 operators measure 10 pieces with 3 trials each. The number of pieces, operators, and trials can vary from case to case, but we need multiple trials to estimate repeatability and multiple operators to estimate reproducibility. Multiple parts provide better estimates of repeatability and reproducibility, as well as part variation.

When we conduct the R&R study, keep these things in mind:

- Use production pieces (see above).
- Randomize the order of the pieces presented to each operator.
- Number each part, but try to keep this "blind" to the operator. (Some operators have astounding memories!)

Repeatability Calculations

The total variation contributed by repeatability, also known as equipment variation follows.

When the number of trials $= 10$:

$$EV = \frac{2^*(Ordinate)^* \bar{\bar{R}}}{d_2^*}$$

When the number of trials > 10:

$$EV = \frac{2^*(Ordinate)^* \bar{\bar{S}}}{c_4}$$

Where ordinate is the specified sigma level (usually 2.575 for gage R&R analysis); d_2^* is based on the sample size n (the number of trials) and the number of samples k (the number of appraisers times the number of parts). Typical values are 1.130 for 2 trials and 1.689 for 3 trials, which assumes k is large. Table for d_2^* values may be found in Appendix 7.

C_4 is based on the sample size n (the number of trials). Some authors, including AIAG, refer to the quantity $(2^*Ordinate/d_2^*)$ as K_1 (4.56 for 2 trials; 3.05 for 3 trials), and the quantity $(2^* Ordinate/c_4)$ as K_3.

$\bar{\bar{R}}$ ($\bar{\bar{S}}$) is the average of the appraisers' between trial ranges (standard deviations) for all selected parts:

$$\bar{\bar{R}} = \left(\frac{\sum_{j=1}^{\#operators} \left(\sum_{i=1}^{\#pieces} Range_{ij} \right)}{(\#operators)(\#parts)} \right)$$

Repeatability $\bar{X}$ Chart Calculations

Plotted statistic: the average of the trials for each part for each appraiser.

Centerline $(\bar{\bar{x}})$: the grand average of all the trials for all parts for all appraisers.

UCL, LCL (upper and lower control limit), based on range chart calculations
$(2 \leq number\ of\ trials \leq 10)$:

$$\bar{\bar{x}} \pm 3 \frac{\bar{\bar{R}}}{d_2^* \sqrt{\#trials}}$$

where $\bar{\bar{x}}$ is the centerline; $\bar{\bar{R}}$ is the centerline of the repeatability range chart; d_2^* is based on the sample size m (the number of trials) and number of samples g (the number of appraisers times the number of parts). A table for d_2^* values may be found in Appendix 7. Some authors, including AIAG, refer to the quantity $(3/d_2^* (SQRT(m)))$ as A_2.

UCL, LCL (upper and lower control limit), based on sigma chart calculations
(number of trials > 10):

$$\bar{\bar{x}} \pm 3 \frac{\bar{\bar{S}}}{c_4 \sqrt{\#trials}}$$

where $\bar{\bar{x}}$ is the centerline (above); $\bar{\bar{S}}$ is the centerline of the repeatability sigma chart; c_4 is based on the sample size m (the number of trials) and the number of samples g (the number of appraisers times the number of parts). Some authors refer to the quantity $(3/c_4^* (SQRT(m)))$ as A_3.

Repeatability Range Chart Calculations

Note: This chart is used when $(2 \leq number\ of\ trials \leq 10)$.

Plotted statistic: the difference between the largest and smallest trial for each part for each appraiser.

Centerline: the average range for all selected appraisers' parts.

UCL, LCL (upper and lower control limit):

$$UCL = \bar{\bar{R}} + \frac{3d_3\bar{\bar{R}}}{d_2^*}$$

$$LCL = MIN\left[0, \bar{\bar{R}} \; \frac{3d_3\bar{\bar{R}}}{d_2^*}\right]$$

where $\bar{\bar{R}}$ is the centerline of the range chart; ordinate is the specified sigma level (usually 2.575 for gage R&R analysis); d_3 is based on a subgroup size equal to the number of trials; and d_2^* is based on the sample size m (the number of trials) and the number of samples g (the number of appraisers times the number of parts). Some authors, including AIAG, refer to the quantity $(1 + 3(d_3/d_2))$ as D_4, and $(1 - 3(d_3/d_2))$ as D_3. Table for d_2^* values may be found in Appendix 7.

Repeatability Sigma Chart Calculations

Note: This chart is used when (number of trials > 10).

Plotted statistic: the sample standard deviation for each part for each appraiser, calculated using each appraiser's average for the plotted part ($\bar{x}_{oper,pc}$)

$$S_{oper,pc} = \sqrt{\frac{\sum_{i=1}^{\#trials} (x_{oper,pc,i} - \bar{x}_{oper,pc})^2}{(\#trials - 1)}}$$

Centerline: the average of the plotted statistic.

Control limits:

$$UCL = \bar{S} + 3\frac{\bar{S}}{c_4}\sqrt{1 - c_4^2}$$

$$LCL = MIN\left[0, \bar{S} - 3\frac{\bar{S}}{c_4}\sqrt{1 - c_4^2}\right]$$

where $\bar{S}$ is the centerline (above); c_4 is based on a subgroup size equal to the number of trials. Some authors, including AIAG, refer to the quantity $(1 + 3\sqrt{1 - c_4^2}/c_4)$ as B_4, and $(1 - 3\sqrt{1 - c_4^2}/c_4)$ as B_3.

Reproducibility Calculations

The variation contributed by reproducibility is also known as *appraiser variation*. It is "corrected" to remove the effects of repeatability error:

When the number of appraisers = 10:

$$AV = \sqrt{\left(\frac{2*(Ordinate)*\bar{X}_{DIFF}}{d_2^*}\right)^2 - \frac{EV^2}{(\#parts)(\#trials)}}$$

When the number of appraisers > 10:

$$AV = \sqrt{\left(\frac{2*(Ordinate)*\bar{X}_{STDDEV}}{c_4}\right)^2 - \frac{EV^2}{(\#parts)(\#trials)}}$$

where EV is the equipment variation, or repeatability; ordinate is the specified sigma level (usually 2.575 for gage R&R analysis); d_2^* is based on m (the number of appraisers) and $g = 1$ subgroups. c_4 is based on m (the number of appraisers) and $g = 1$ subgroups.

$\bar{X}_{DIFF}$ is the range between the average measurements of the selected appraisers (for all trials and all selected parts).

$\bar{X}_{STDDEV}$ is the standard deviation of the average measurements of the selected appraisers (for all trials and all selected parts).

Reproducibility $\bar{X}$ Chart Calculations

Plotted statistic: the average of all trials, all parts for each appraiser.

Centerline ($\bar{\bar{x}}$): the grand average of all the trials for all parts for all appraisers.

UCL, LCL (upper and lower control limit), based on repeatability range chart calculations (2 ≤ Number of Trials ≤10):

$$\bar{\bar{x}} \pm 3 \frac{\bar{\bar{R}}}{d_2^* \sqrt{\#trials * \#parts}}$$

where $\bar{\bar{x}}$ is the centerline; $\bar{\bar{R}}$ is the centerline of the repeatability range chart; d_2^* is based on the sample size m (the number of trials) and the number of samples g (the number of appraisers times the number of parts). Tables for d_2^* values may be found in Appendix 7. Some authors, including AIAG, refer to the quantity $(3/d_2^*(\sqrt{\#trials}))$ as A_2.

UCL, LCL (upper and lower control limit), based on repeatability sigma chart calculations (number of trials > 10):

$$\bar{\bar{x}} \pm 3 \frac{\bar{\bar{S}}}{c_4 \sqrt{\#trials * \#parts}}$$

where $\bar{\bar{x}}$ is the centerline (above); $\bar{\bar{R}}$ is the centerline of the repeatability sigma chart; c_4 is based on the sample size m (the number of trials). Some authors, including AIAG, refer to the quantity $(3/c_4^*(\sqrt{\#trials}))$ as A_3.

R&R Studies

Reproducibility Range Chart Calculations

Note: This chart is used when ($2 \leq$ number of appraisers ≤ 10).

Plotted statistic: the difference between the largest and smallest appraiser average for each part.

Centerline: the Average Range.

UCL, LCL (upper and lower control limit):

$$UCL = \bar{R} + 3d_3 \left(\frac{\bar{R}}{d_2^*} \right)$$

$$LCL = MIN \left[0, \bar{R} - 3d_3 \left(\frac{\bar{R}}{d_2^*} \right) \right]$$

where d_3 is based on a subgroup size $m =$ the number of appraisers; d_2^* is based on a subgroup size m (the number of appraisers); and g (the number of parts). A table for d_2^* values may be found in Appendix 7. Some authors, including AIAG, refer to the quantity $(1 + 3(d_3/d_2))$ as D_4, and $(1 - 3(d_3/d_2))$ as D_3.

Reproducibility Sigma Chart Calculations

Note: This chart is used when number of appraisers > 10.

Plotted statistic: the sample standard deviation of appraiser averages for each part, calculated using the average for the plotted part ($\bar{x}_{pc}$).

$$S_{\bar{x}-pc} = \sqrt{\frac{\sum_{k=1}^{\#oper} (\bar{x}_{oper,pc} - \bar{\bar{x}}_{pc})^2}{\#operators - 1}}$$

Centerline: the average of the plotted statistic.

Control limits:

$$UCL = \bar{S} + 3\frac{\bar{S}}{c_4} \sqrt{1 - c_4^2}$$

$$LCL = MIN \left[0, \bar{S} - 3\frac{\bar{S}}{c_4} \sqrt{1 - c_4^2} \right]$$

where $\bar{S}$ is the centerline (above) and c_4 is based on a subgroup size $m =$ the number of appraisers. Some authors, including AIAG, refer to the quantity $(1 + 3\sqrt{1 - c_4^2}/c_4)$ as B_4, and $(1 - 3\sqrt{1 - c_4^2}/c_4)$ as B_3.

R&R Calculations

The variation (error) contributed by both gage repeatability and reproducibility:

$$R\&R = \sqrt{EV^2 + AV^2}$$

where EV is the equipment variation, or repeatability and AV is the appraiser variation, or reproducibility.

Discrimination Calculations

The discrimination, or number of distinct categories or classes discernible by a measurement system, is obtained by determining the amount of part-to-part variation that is indistinguishable from measurement error.

$$Number\ of\ classes = \sqrt{2}\left[\frac{PV}{R\&R}\right]$$

where PV is the part variation and $R\&R$ is the gage repeatability and reproducibility error estimates.

If number of parts < 10:

$$PV = \frac{2 * Ordinate * R_{pc-avg}}{d_2^*}$$

where R_{pc-avg} is the range between the average part measurements (i.e., using the average of each part, including all selected appraisers' trials, calculate the difference between the largest average and the smallest average part size); ordinate is the specified sigma level (usually 2.575 for gage R&R analysis); d_2^* is based on the sample size $n =$ the number of parts and number of samples $k = 1$.

If number of parts ≥ 10:

$$PV = \frac{2 * Ordinate * S_{pc-avg}}{c_4^*}$$

where S_{pc-avg} is the standard deviation of the average part measurements (i.e., using the average of each part, including all selected appraisers' trials, calculate the sample standard deviation of the average part sizes); ordinate is the specified sigma level (usually 2.575 for gage R&R analysis); and c_4^* is based on a subgroup size equal to the number of parts and $k = 1$ subgroups.

INTERPRETATION

The discrimination ratio provides an estimate of the number of distinct categories or classes discernible by a measurement system. A value of 2, for instance, indicates the system is useful for only attribute analysis, since it can only effectively classify the parts as being in one group or the other (for example, good or bad). AIAG recommends a value of 3 or more, and typically a value of 8 or more is suitable for statistical analysis.

The gage R&R statistic is usually reported as either a percent of tolerance or as a percent of the total process variation.

When expressed as percent of tolerance, gage R&R indicates the relative usefulness of the gage system for determining part acceptance. Tolerance, calculated as the upper specification limit minus the lower specification limit, indicates the amount of variation that is permitted between all parts produced. As gage system error increases relative to the tolerance, then the chances increase that:

- Parts whose true value is outside specifications could be measured as being within specifications and subsequently accepted for use.
- Parts whose true value is within specifications could be measured as being outside specifications and subsequently rejected as unfit for use.

When expressed as percent of process variation, gage R&R indicates the relative usefulness of the gage system for use in control charting and process capability analysis. The calculation of statistical control limits and the estimate of process capability require a sound estimate of the process variation. Subgroups plotted on a control chart are also subject to measurement system error. As measurement error increases, so does the chance that:

- Subgroups from a controlled process will be determined to be out of control.
- Subgroups from an out-of-control process will be determined to be from an in-control process.

Typical recommendations for gage R&R, expressed as ether percent of tolerance or percent of process variation, are:

- 0 to 10%: Acceptable
- 10 to 30%: Marginal
- Over 30%: Unacceptable

Interpreting a Repeatability Control Chart

Repeatability control charts are constructed by grouping each appraiser's trials for each part into a single subgroup. Therefore, the size of the subgroup is equal to the number of trials per part. The variation within a subgroup is an estimate of the repeatability error inherent to the measurement equipment, so long as the variation is shown to be statistically stable over all parts and all appraisers. This assumption may be proved by observing the range (or sigma) chart for repeatability.

The range (or sigma) chart should be in statistical control (all the plotted groups within the control limits). Each plotted group represents the variation observed between the trials for the given part by the given appraiser. If a given part is out of control, the implication is that the variation observed between the trials for that part was larger than should be expected (based on the variation observed for the other parts). Perhaps the part had a burr or some other abnormality associated with it. That suspicion grows if the out-of-control condition is observed for the same part in more than one appraiser's measurements.

Sigma charts are used instead of range charts when the subgroup sample size (in this case, the number of trials per part) is more than 10. This is due to the decreasing efficiency of the range as an estimate of the standard deviation at larger subgroup sizes.

The $\bar{X}$ chart for repeatability is analyzed quite differently than most $\bar{X}$ charts. The plotted statistic, $\bar{X}$, is the average of each subgroup (in this case, the average of each appraiser's trials for a given part). These $\bar{X}$ variations are an indication of part-to-part variation. The control limits, however, are calculated using the average range between trials for each part, which provides an indication of measurement equipment error. It is desirable that the measurement system detects real part differences in the presence of this measurement error. For that reason, the variation that is observed from subgroup to subgroup (i.e., part-to-part fluctuations) should be larger than the measurement errors (i.e., control limits), meaning that many subgroups should be out of control on the $\bar{X}$ chart for repeatability. AIAG recommends that at least half the subgroups exceed the $\bar{X}$ control limits.

The repeatability control charts are available in two formats: combined and per appraiser. The combined charts are those typically used to analyze statistical stability of the measurement system across selected appraisers and parts. The per-appraiser charts are provided to estimate each appraiser's repeatability independently. Appraiser's repeatability may then be compared to indicate possible training benefits.

Interpreting a Reproducibility Control Chart

The $\bar{X}$ chart for reproducibility analyzes whether each appraiser's average for the selected parts is within the expected variability of these averages. In other words, it detects whether the differences between appraiser averages are an indication of appraiser bias or an expected variation due to equipment.

If the equipment error, as represented on the combined appraiser repeatability range (or sigma) chart, is in control, then σ_{repeat} is an appropriate estimate of the variation from trial to trial. As long as there are no outside influences affecting the trial measurements, such as appraiser bias, trial averages should fall within the variability reflected by:

$$\sigma_{repeat}/\sqrt{\# \ trials}$$

This is the basis for the reproducibility $\bar{X}$ control chart.

The range chart for reproducibility analyzes the variability in appraiser averages for each part. As such, it may be used to identify whether the reproducibility is in a state of statistical control. If control is not exhibited, then the estimate of reproducibility may not be valid. Out-of-control points indicate that the variability in average measurements between appraisers is affected by part bias.

Sigma charts are used instead of range charts when the subgroup sample size (in this case, the number of appraisers) is more than 10, because of the decreasing efficiency of the range as an estimate of the standard deviation for larger subgroup sizes.

Regression Analysis

Regression analysis is used to determine if a dependent variable can be adequately predicted by a set of one or more independent variables.

WHEN TO USE

Measure Stage

- Assess linearity of measurement system.

Analyze Stage

- Investigate relationship of process factors to metrics.

Improve Stage

- Verify relationship of process factors to metrics after improvement.

Simple linear regression analysis is often applied as part of the analysis done with a scatter diagram.

Multiple regression is used when there is more than one factor that influences the response. For example, cycle time for a sales process may be impacted by the number of items purchased and the time of day. In this case, there are two independent variables: (1) number of items purchased and (2) time of day. We can also estimate the interaction between these factors. For example, perhaps the effect of time of day varies depending on the number of items purchased. It may be that when only a few items are purchased, the time of day makes a big difference in cycle time variation, yet when many items are purchased, time of day makes little difference to cycle time variation.

METHODOLOGY

Simple Linear Regression

The regression model used for simple linear regression is that of a straight line. You might recall this equation as y equals m times x plus b, where y is the dependent variable, x is the independent variable, m is the slope, and b is the value of y when x equals zero (b is sometimes called the intercept).

$$Y = \beta_0 + \beta_1 X + \text{error}$$

Another way to write this is using the Greek letter beta, as shown above. β_0 (beta naught) is used to estimate the intercept, and β_1 (beta one) is used to indicate the slope of the regression line. We show the equation using the Greek letters as most statistical textbooks use this notation.

In order to define the equation, we need to estimate the two parameters: slope and intercept. The statistical technique most often used is known as the *method of least squares*, which will find values for β_0 and β_1 such that the fitted line has a minimum squared distance from each of the experimental data values.

The error term is an acknowledgment that even if we could sample all possible values there would most likely be some unpredictability in the outcome. This unpredictability could be due to many possibilities, including measurement error in either the dependent or independent variable, the effects of other unknown variables, or nonlinear effects.

Multiple Regression First-Order Model

Multiple regression is used when there is more than one factor that influences the response. For example, the cycle time for a sales process may be impacted by the number of cashiers, the number of floor clerks, and the time of day. In this case, there are three independent variables: (1) number of cashiers, (2) number of floor clerks, and (3) time of day.

Multiple regression requires additional terms in the model to estimate each of the other factors. If we have enough data, of the right conditions, we can also estimate the interaction between these factors. For example, perhaps the effect of time of day varies depending on the number of cashiers, such that when only a few floor clerks are working, the time of day has a big effect toward cycle time variation, yet when many floor clerks are working, time of day has little effect on cycle time variation.

The first-order model for this example is of the form shown:

$$Y = \beta_0 + \beta_1 X_1 + \beta_2 X_2 + \beta_3 X_3 + \beta_{12} X_{12} + \beta_{13} X_{13} + \beta_{23} X_{23} + \text{error}$$

where:

X_1 is the number of cashiers.
X_2 is the number of floor clerks.
X_3 is the time of day.
X_{12} is the interaction between the number of cashiers and the number of floor clerks.
X_{13} is the interaction between the number of cashiers and the time of day.
X_{23} is the interaction between the number of floor clerks and the time of day.

The error is assumed to have zero mean and a common variance (for all runs). The errors are independent and normally distributed. These assumptions will be tested in the *residuals analysis* of the model in the next tool.

The first-order model produces a plane when viewed in three dimensions of two significant factors and the response. Interaction effects between the two factors cause a twisting, or flexing, of the plane.

First-order models work well for a great number of cases. They are often used in Six Sigma projects because so much can be learned about reducing process variation, with little data. We only need to identify significant factors and two factor interactions, and may have little use for precisely defining the model or a higher-order curvilinear response surface. Over limited regions, it is not uncommon for linear effects to dominate, so higher-order models are not necessary.

Multiple Regression Higher-Order Models

Higher-order terms, such as squares (the second power), cubes (the third power), and quadratics (the fourth power), may also be added. These higher-order terms generate curvilinear response surfaces, such as peaks (maximums) and valleys (minimums). In order to estimate these higher-order terms, we need at least three or more experimental levels for the factor, since two-level designs can only estimate linear terms.

The full model includes p parameters for k main factors, where p is calculated as:

$$p = 1 + 2k + k*(k-1)/2$$

For example, two factors includes $1 + 4(\beta_1 X_1 + \beta_2 X_2 + \beta_{11} X_1^2 + \beta_{22} X_2^2) + 1(\beta_{12} X_1 X_2) = 6$ terms. Three factors includes $1 + 6(\beta_1 X_1 + \beta_2 X_2 + \beta_3 X_3 + \beta_{11} X_1^2 + \beta_{22} X_2^2 + \beta_{33} X_3^2) + 3(\beta_{12} X_1 X_2 + \beta_{13} X_1 X_3 + \beta_{23} X_2 X_3) = 10$ terms.

In order to estimate each of these terms, we need at least p distinct design points and three levels for each factor to estimate the quadratic terms.

Often, we count on the fact that the effect of higher-order terms is generally small, unless the main factors themselves are important. In this way, we can often do initial experiments looking for only main factors (X_1, X_2, X_3, etc.) and their interactions (X_{12}, X_{13}, X_{23}, etc.) and ignore the effect of the higher-order terms. If main factors or interactions look significant, we may decide to look for higher-order effects with additional experiments.

The shape of the resulting response surface is highly dependent on the region analyzed and determined by the signs and magnitudes of the model, particularly the pure quadratic (the squared terms) and the interaction terms. You should always bear in mind that the shape of the surface is *estimated* subject to errors inherent with the model-building process.

In spite of their limitations, second-order models are widely used because of their flexibility in mapping a variety of surfaces, including simple maximums (peaks) or minimums (valleys), stationary ridges (such as in a mountain range), rising ridges (a ridge that increases in height), or saddles (also known as minimax, where a minimum in one factor meets a maximum in the other). Second-order models are used in response surface analysis to define the surface around a stationary point (a max, min, or saddle), and to predict the response with better accuracy than the first-order models near the optimal regions.

In investigative analysis, second-order models are also used to understand the effect of current operating parameters on the response.

INTERPRETATION

Simple Linear Regression

The statistical methods used to develop the regression model include an ANOVA table. *Analysis of Va*riation is a statistical tool for partitioning error among terms. For simple linear regression, the ANOVA table provides an indication of the statistical significance of the regression by partitioning the variation into two components:

Variability accounted for by regression line: regression sum of squares

$$SS_R = \sum_{i=1}^{n} (\hat{y}_i - \bar{y})^2$$

Variability *not* accounted for by regression line: error sum of squares

$$SS_E = \sum_{i=1}^{n} (y_i - \hat{y}_i)^2$$

The ANOVA table uses the F statistic to compare the variability accounted for by the regression model with the remaining variation due to error. The null hypothesis is that the slope of the regression line is zero: there is no statistical correlation between the two variables. If we reject the null hypothesis, the alternative hypothesis is that the slope is non-zero, implying that there is correlation between the two variables.

Although we could use the F-statistic tables in Appendices 4 and 5 to determine whether to accept or reject the hypothesis, most statistical software will provide a *p* value for the F statistic to indicate the relevance of the model. Most times we will reject the null hypothesis, and assert that the calculated linear regression model is significant, when the *p* value is less than 0.10.

Bear in mind that statistical significance may or may not indicate physical significance. If we measure statistical significance of a given factor to a response, it does not necessarily mean that the factor is in fact significant in predicting the response. Factors may happen to vary coincident with other factors, some of which may be significant. For example, if we estimate that shoe size is statistically significant in understanding the variation in height, it does not mean that shoe size is a good predictor, nor should it imply that increasing shoe size causes increased height.

In Figure F.39 we've used the *Green Belt XL* software to calculate the regression model for a set of data. The regression model is shown in the analysis as *y* equals minus 0.023 plus 0.055 times *x*.

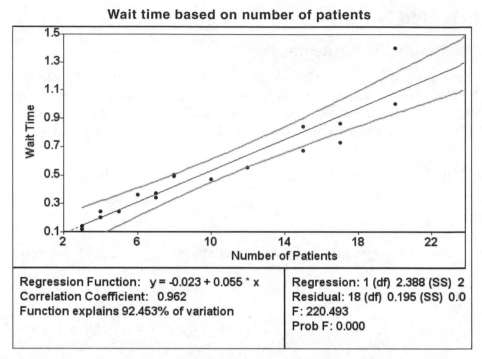

Figure F.39   Example of a first-order regressive model.

The regression model represents our best estimate of future values of y based on given values of x. For example, when there are 10 patients (i.e., x equals 10), the best guess for the wait time y is:

$$\text{Wait time} = -.023 + .055 * 10 = 0.527 \text{ hour}$$

Similarly, we could calculate values of y for any value of x. Recall, however, that extrapolation beyond our data region should be done with caution.

In this example, the calculated p value is 0.000, so the null hypothesis that the slope is zero is rejected.

Another useful statistic provided by the ANOVA table is the coefficient of determination (R^2), which is the square of the Pearson correlation coefficient R. R^2 varies between zero and 1, and indicates the amount of variation in the data accounted for by the regression model. In Figure F.39, the correlation coefficient is calculated as 0.962. Squaring that value provides an R^2 value of 0.925: approximately 93% of the variation in the response is explained by the regression function (in this case, our linear equation). R^2 values near 0.7 or higher are generally considered acceptable.

A large R-squared value does *not* imply that the slope of the regression line is steep, that the correct model was used, or that the model will accurately predict future observations. It simply means that the model happens to account for a large percent of the variation in this particular set of data.

Once we have constructed a model, there are a variety of ways to check the model, especially through the use of *residuals analysis* (discussed next) to look for patterns.

Confidence Intervals on Regression

A confidence interval for the regression line is also shown in Figure F.39. The width of the confidence interval provides an indication of the quality of the fitted regression function. The fact that the confidence lines diverge at the ends, and converge in the middle, may be explained in one of two ways:

1. The regression function for the fitted line requires estimation of two parameters: slope and y intercept. The error in estimating intercept provides a gap in the vertical direction. The error in estimating slope can be visualized by imagining the fitted line's rotating about its middle. This results in the hourglass-shaped region shown by the confidence intervals.
2. The center of the data is located near the middle of the fitted line. The ability to predict the regression function should be better at the center of the data; hence the confidence limits are narrower at the middle. The ability to estimate at the extreme conditions is much less, resulting in a wider band at each end.

Don't confuse the confidence interval on the line with a prediction interval for new data. If we assume that the new data is independent of the data used to calculate the fitted regression line, then a prediction interval for future observations is dependent on the error that is built into the regression model, plus the error associated with future data. While our best estimate for the y value based on a given x value is found by solving the regression equation, we recognize that there can be variation in the actual y values that will be observed. Thus, the shape of the prediction interval will be similar to that seen in the confidence interval, but wider.

Multiple Regression Models

The analysis method is somewhat similar when there are multiple factors to consider. The ANOVA table uses the F statistic to compare the variation predicted by the regression model with the remaining variation, which must be due to error in the model.

In calculating the F statistic, we need to know how much data was needed to calculate the regression model and how much was left over for calculating the error. The numerator of the F statistic is based on the sum of squares of the regression, which uses 1 degree of freedom for each of the k terms in the model, plus 1 additional degree of freedom for β_0. For example, if we estimate β_0, β_1, β_2, and β_{12} in our model, then there are 4 degrees of freedom used by the regression model. If there are 12 data points in the experiment (i.e., $n = 12$), then that leaves $n - k - 1 = 12 - 3 - 1 = 8$ degrees of freedom for estimating the error term.

The null hypothesis H_0 in the multiple regression is that the coefficients β_i are equal to zero. That is, that there is no significant relationship between the response and the factors. The alternative hypothesis is that at least 1 of the β_i are not equal to zero. Rejecting the null hypothesis implies that there is at least 1 significant term in the model. We use the p value of .05 or less to reject the null. (When using a small number of data points, we may decide to use a p value of .10 to reflect the uncertainty in the data.)

Each coefficient β_i indicates the predicted change in y for a unit change in that x, when all other terms are constant. For example, $\beta_2 = -3.5$ implies that cycle time goes down by 3.5 minutes for each additional floor clerk.

Generally, the magnitude of the beta coefficients does not provide an indication of the significance or the impact of the factor. In the example equation below, we cannot say that the time of day is more critical than the number of cashiers or number of floor clerks simply because β_3 is larger than β_2 or β_1, since the scaling (or unit of measure) of each factor is different.

$$\text{Cycle time} = 2.7 - .87 * (\text{number of cashiers}) - 1.3 * (\text{number of floor clerks})$$
$$+ 2.3 * (\text{time of day})$$

However, some software will provide the regression function in coded form, in which case the coefficients are applied to coded values of the factors (such as -1 and $+1$), allowing direct comparison to estimate the factors' effect.

Recall from simple linear regression that R^2 (the coefficient of multiple determination) is used to estimate how much of the variation in the data is accounted for by the model. In multiple regression, the Pearson correlation coefficient R^2 approaches 1 as the number of factors approaches the number of data values. That is, if we have 5 factors and 8 data values, R^2 may be close to 1 regardless of whether the fit is good or not. R^2 always increases as factors are added, whether the factors are significant or not.

Table T.19.

	Coefficients	Standard Error	t Stat	P value
Intercept	30.47639512	14.14030711	2.155285234	0.0521
Personalized response	8.683251781	5.952910922	1.458656428	0.1703
Complexity	− 18.9432843	5.947821126	− 3.184911564	0.0078
Response time	0.011754508	0.048737915	0.241177907	0.8135

For these reason, an adjusted value Ra^2 is calculated for multiple regression models that adjusts based on the number of parameters in the model. Ra^2 will always be less than the R^2 value, but provides a better approximation of the amount of variation accounted for by the model.

In Table T.19 first we code the data, so that the no/yes and low/high factors have numerical values of 0 and 1. This allows us to calculate statistics based on the data conditions.

Using MS Excel's tools \ Data Analysis \ Regression function, ANOVA is found as shown in Table T.20.

In this case, there are 3 degrees of freedom for the regression model (one for each of the factors in the data: Personalized Response, Complexity, and Response Time). Since there are 16 data points total, there are $16 - 3 - 1$ degrees of freedom left over to estimate the error (or residual) of the regression model. Excel calculates the sum of squares variation for the model and the

Table T.20.

ANOVA					
	df	SS	MS	F	Significance F
Regression	3	1736.381891	578.7939638	4.0918	0.032439879
Residual	12	1697.415484	141.4512903		
Total	15	3433.797375			

error. The mean square error (MS) is calculated by dividing each sum of square (SS) by its degree of freedom. The F statistic is calculated by dividing the MS of the regression by the MS of the error term.

Appendices 4 and 5 contain F tables for alpha values of 5% and 1%. You'll notice that the critical value of F for 3 degrees of freedom in the numerator and 12 degrees of freedom in the denominator is 3.49 for alpha equals 5% and 5.95 for alpha equals 1%. The calculated F statistic of 4.09 falls between these two values. An F statistic of 4.09 (based on the given degrees of freedom) coincides with an alpha equals 3.2%, as shown in the Excel results. Since this value is less than 0.05, we reject the null hypothesis that the coefficients are zero and assert that at least one of the coefficients appears non-zero.

Note that the total sum of squares (SS) is equal to the SS accounted for by the regression plus the SS due to error. The regression SS is composed of the sum of squares due to each of the model parameters.

Excel also provides a more detailed analysis of the model testing each parameter of the regression model using a t test, as shown previously in Table T.19. The table provides the coefficient of each term in the model. In this example, the calculated regression model is as follows:

Satisfaction $= 30.47 + 8.68 *$ (Personalized response) $- 18.94 *$ (Complexity) $+ 0.011 *$ (Response time)

A t test is performed on each of the model parameters, with a resulting p value provided. If the p value is less than 5%, then it is likely to be significant and should be retained in the model. (In some cases, such as when we have limited data from an initial study, we may choose a higher threshold, such as 0.10).

In this example, it would appear that only Complexity is significant. The adjusted R^2 of 0.38 indicates a relatively poor fit, implying that the model may be missing terms. In Excel, we can create new columns for the interaction terms. For example, the AB interaction is simply the product of the factor A and the factor B columns. We repeat the analysis, including the two-factor interaction terms (AB, AC, BC) in the model.

In the revised model, using interaction terms, the adjusted R^2 value is now 0.82, which is much better. Values in the range of 0.6 or higher are usually good starting points. In addition, the regression model shows high significance (or low p value of .0007), so the null hypothesis is again rejected.

We now examine the results of the t tests on the individual parameters, and we see that the main factors B and C are highly significant, with factor A being perhaps significant (since its p value is greater than 0.05 but less than 0.1). Furthermore, the AC and BC interactions are significant. See Table T.21.

Table T.21.

	Coefficients	Standard Error	t Stat	p value
Intercept	87.89545138	13.219105	6.64912252	9.3833E − 05
A: Personalized response	− 30.9826101	15.122148	− 2.0488233	0.0707483
B: Complexity	− 96.3499185	15.257884	− 6.3147628	0.00013854
C: Response time	− 0.19764873	0.0474831	− 4.1625026	0.00243863
AB Interaction	4.853094312	6.4983773	0.74681633	0.47423139
AC Interaction	0.138973228	0.0538671	2.57992673	0.02970019
BC Interaction	0.279313827	0.0536613	5.20512133	0.00056021

Removing Terms from the Multiple Regression Model

When reviewing the t tests for the individual factors, we are considering whether the individual factors should be removed from the model. When we remove terms from the model, we must be careful to remove only one term at a time, since the error is partially reapportioned among the remaining parameters when a parameter is removed.

It is recommended to remove higher-order terms (such as third-order, second-order, then higher-order interactions) first. In fact, we often don't include higher-order terms in initial studies so we can eliminate the factors which are not significant using less data. Factors with borderline significance, such as a p value between 0.05 and 0.10, are best left in the model, particularly at the early stages.

There are two considerations for modeling. The first is *paucity*, which means that the best model is the one with the fewest number of significant parameters with the highest adjusted R^2 value. Basically, paucity implies doing more with less: the best model explains the data with only a few simple terms. The opposite of paucity is *overmodeling:* adding lots of terms that help the model explain all of the variation in the data. This sounds great, until you collect more data and discover that there is a random component that cannot be explained by your earlier model. When we overmodel we tend to have a poorer fit when new data is analyzed. This means there is no predictive value in the model, so it is of little practical purpose.

When considering terms for a statistical model, it is helpful to recall the infamous words of George Box: "All models are wrong, but some models are useful."

The other consideration is that of *inheritance:* if a factor is removed from the model because it is nonsignificant, then all its interactions should also be removed from the model. Likewise, if the interaction is significant, then all its main factors should be retained. In our example, we saw that the AC interaction was significant. Recall that the main factor A was borderline. In that case, it would be best to leave both A and AC in the model.

When interactions are significant, and one or more of their main factors are insignificant, then we should consider whether the interaction may be confounded with another interaction or main factor, or perhaps even a factor we did not include. *Confounding* means that the factors move together, often because of the way in which the data were collected. Randomizing the data collection helps to reduce the instances of confounding.

We now repeat the analysis, removing the AB column from the data. In this case, the regression is still highly significant, as is each factor and interaction in the model.

Stepwise regression is a set of techniques for automating the removal of terms in the model based on statistical consideration. There are three basic types of stepwise regression:

- *Forward Selection.* Begins with no parameters; adds them one at a time based on partial F statistic. In this case, factors are not revisited to see the impact of removing them after other terms have been added.
- *Backward Elimination.* Begins with all parameters; removes one at a time based on partial F statistic. This is basically what we did manually after adding the interaction terms.
- *Stepwise.* Combination of forward selection and backward elimination.

Minitab provides each of these stepwise regression techniques in the Stat\Regression\Stepwise mcnu. In our example, the backward elimination method removed the AB interaction on the second pass, the forward selection removed the AB Interaction on the fifth pass, and the stepwise regression option removed the AB interaction on the fifth pass.

To further test the fitted model, we should conduct residuals analysis (discussed next in this Tools section). In this case, since the data is not time-based, we can test for normality of the residuals using a normal probability plot. Excel will generate the standardized residuals as an option within its regression function.

The normal probability plot (generated using the *Green Belt XL* software) for the example is shown in Figure F.40. The K-S test of 0.922 indicates that the standardized residuals fit approximately a normal distribution, supporting the premise that the regression model fits the data.

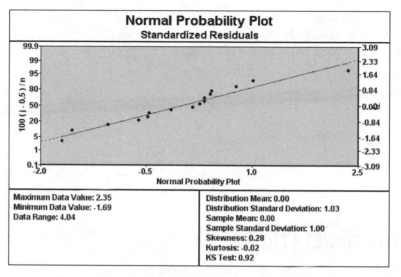

Figure F.40   Normal probability plot of residuals data.

Residuals Analysis

Residuals analysis refers to a collection of techniques used to check the regression model for unnatural patterns, which may be indicative of an error in the model.

WHEN TO USE

Analyze Stage and Improve Stage

- To check regression models for unnatural patterns.

METHODOLOGY

A *residual* is calculated as the difference between the observed value of a response (the dependent variable) and the prediction for that response based on the regression model and the actual value of the dependent variables.

$$e_i = y_i - \hat{y}_i$$

Statisticians often use either a standardized or a studentized residual. The effect of standardizing the residuals is to scale the error to achieve a variance of one, which helps make outliers more prominent.

Standardized residual:

$$= e_i / \sqrt{s^2}$$

Studentized residual:

$$= e_i \Big/ \sqrt{s^2 \left[1 - \left(\frac{1}{n} + \frac{(x_i - \bar{x})^2}{S_{xx}}\right)\right]}$$

INTERPRETATION

There are a number of tools (discussed elsewhere in this Tools section) useful for finding patterns in residuals.

- *Normality test for residuals.* If the error between the model and the data is truly random, then the residuals should be normally distributed with a mean of zero. A normal probability plot or goodness of fit test will allow us to see departures from normality, indicating a poor fit of the model to particular data.
- *Residuals versus independent variable (x).* We shouldn't see any pattern, or any significant correlation, when we analyze the residuals (on the y axis) and the independent variable (on the x axis) using a scatter diagram. If patterns exist, that would imply that the model changes as a function of the x variable, meaning that a separate model for particular values of x (or higher-order terms in x) should be considered.
- *Residuals versus fitted response.* A pattern here would suggest the model does not fit well over the range of the response. When we have repeated runs at each experimental condition, we can also look for nonconstant variance of the response (shown in Figure F.41). If nonconstant variance of the response is suspected, then Bartlett's equality of variance test can be used to test for the condition. Reasons for nonconstant variance include an increase in measurement error for larger responses (such as when error is a fixed percentage of the measured value) and the distributional properties of the response (such as for skewed distributions where the variance is a function of the mean).

If the Data can be ordered in a time-based manner (meaning that for each data you have a unit of time at which it occurred), then we can do some additional analysis of the model.

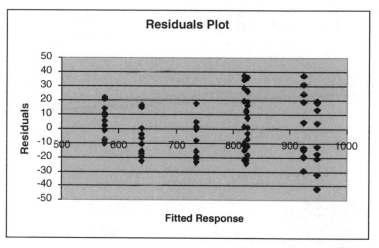

Figure F.41   Example of residuals plot.

- *Control chart of residuals.* A control chart of the residuals would indicate if the error changes over the time in which the data occurred. An out-of-control condition (or run test violation) on this chart implies that another factor (that changes over time) is influencing the response.
- *Test for autocorrelation of residuals.* Significant autocorrelation of the residuals (which may be detected using the autocorrelation function) implies that the error at one period in time is influenced by earlier error. In this case, it's likely we are missing a factor that varies over time. We can use the autocorrelation function or the Durbin-Watson test for independence of consecutive residuals.

Outliers

We can also look for outliers in the data. Data far removed from the "middle" of the data may have a large influence on the model parameters (the beta coefficients R_a^2 and the mean square error terms). Two statistics that help us find outliers are the standardized residuals and Cook's distance:

- If standardized residuals are greater than 2.0 for any point, we should consider them outliers which should be investigated.
- Cook's distance provides a measure of the squared distance between the β estimate with and without the observation. Minitab provides an estimate of Cook's distance.

When outliers are found, it is best to remove them from the analysis and regenerate the model.

Response Surface Analysis

Response surface analysis (RSA) refers to techniques to determine the optimal value of the response. For example, we may be interested in finding the specific concentrations of reagents and temperature of the reaction to achieve the highest degree of product purity. In a service process, we may seek optimal allocation of staffing and services to minimize the cycle time for a key process.

WHEN TO USE

Improve Stage

- To map the response surface in the region of interest, to provide prediction of the change in the response as factor settings vary.
- To optimize the response, such as a maximum or minimum response or minimum variation in the response, to achieve improved process capability and yield for existing processes or best performance for new products or processes.
- To select operating conditions to meet desired specifications, such as when there are multiple specifications (one for each response) that must be simultaneously met.

METHODOLOGY

The general technique for response surface analysis, sometimes referred to the *Sequential RSA Technique*, involves two phases (phase 1 and phase 2), and a prerequisite (phase 0) (Myers and Montgomery, 1995).

Phase 0 is the use of screening designs to narrow the list of potential factors down to a critical set of significant factors and develop a first-order regression model. Response surface analysis should not be started until this work has been completed.

In phase 1, the steepest ascent methodology is used to define the current operating region and determine the direction of optimality. Phase 1 uses the first-order model generated earlier because of its economy of data collection. The first-order model is a good assumption, since the starting point is usually far enough away from the optimum that it is likely to be dominated by first-order effects, and we are not interested in a detailed mapping of the response region far away from the optimum.

Phase 2 will use a second-order model and ridge analysis techniques within a small region to locate the optimal conditions. This technique is discussed next in Ridge Analysis.

Steepest Ascent Methodology

Using the first-order model developed in phase 0, create a contour plot of the response versus two significant main factors (on the x and y axes). Draw a line perpendicular to the contour lines to define the path of steepest ascent (to obtain a maximum) or steepest descent (to obtain a minimum).

Collect data (either single data points or replicated runs) along the path of steepest ascent, using the regression equation. Start at the design center: the point where, in coded units, $(x_1, x_2) = (0, 0)$. For example, in the model $y = 4.5 + .32 x_1 - .63 x_2$, if the levels of x_1 and x_2 are, in real terms, (0, 100) pounds and (500, 1000) milligrams, respectively, then the design center is (50 pounds, 750 milligrams). This will be our first test condition.

The path of steepest ascent is a simultaneous move of β_1 (the coefficient of the x_1 term: 0.32) coded units in the x_1 direction for every β_2 (the coefficient of the x_2 term: 0.63) coded units in the x_2 direction. Given a specified change in x_1, when x_1 and x_2 are in coded units, we can calculate the appropriate change in x_2 as:

$$\text{Change in } x_2 = \beta_2/\beta_1(\text{change in } x_1)$$

Since the difference between the -1 x_1 level and the $+1$ x_1 level is two coded units, then one x_1 unit in real terms is 50 pounds and one x_2 unit in real terms is 250 milligrams (half the difference between the maximum and minimum design levels). If we decide to run our trials along the path of steepest ascent with intervals of 25 pounds (half of a coded unit) in x_1, then the change in x_2 in coded units is calculated as:

$$\text{Change in } x_2 = -.63/.32(.5) = -.984$$

This equates to a decrease of 246 milligrams ($= .984 * 250$ milligrams) for each 25 pound increase in x_1.

Our path (or design conditions) is then calculated as:

- Starting Point 1: (50 pounds, 750 milligrams)
- Point 2: (75 pounds, 504 milligrams)
- Point 3: (100 pounds, 258 milligrams)

We can also consider steepest ascent subject to constraints imposed by the physical limitations of the system. For example, consider in the previous example if the x_2 factor could not be less than 500 milligrams. When one or more factors are constrained, we will proceed along the path of steepest ascent until the constraint is hit, then proceed along its path (i.e., all subsequent data has x_2 factor set at 500 milligrams).

INTERPRETATION

We determine local maximum conditions by observing when the response decreases. Data preceding an observed decrease in the response is likely to be near a maximum condition.

We then conduct another experiment near the assumed maxima. It is sufficient to run a suitable design to obtain a first-order model with center points and enough degrees of freedom to calculate the F test for lack of fit (discussed earlier in Part 3).

If the lack of fit is not significant, then determine a new path of steepest ascent by varying the starting point, intervals, or direction along the first-order model. If lack of fit is significant, and curvature is present, then this suggests you are near a stationary point, which may be a local maximum, minimum, or saddle point (a maximum in one factor, minimum in another). At this point, stop the steepest ascent methodology and proceed to phase 2 Ridge Analysis next.

Ridge Analysis

Ridge analysis techniques are phase 2 of a sequential response surface analysis. They are used to locate a set of coordinates (factor conditions) for the optima and the predicted response at the optima.

WHEN TO USE

Improve Stage

- After response surface analysis has narrowed the range for the optimal conditions.

METHODOLOGY

The graphical method for ridge analysis is as follows:

- Use a central composite design near the optima (defined in the previous tool Response Surface Analysis) to generate a second-order regression model.
- Generate contour plots and response surface plots for each pair of factors.
- Determine the stationary point from the plots. A *stationary point* is the point where the slope of the second-order response surface model with respect to each of the factors is zero. A stationary point may be either a maximum, a minimum, or a saddle point (also known as a *minimax*). In *n* dimensions, a saddle point is a point where one or more parameters are at a maximum and one or more parameters are at a minimum. The stationary point may lie well outside the data range, in which case it is useful for direction only.
- Calculate the predicted response at the optima using the second-order regression model.
- Collect new data in the region of the optima to verify the model.

Optimizing Multiple Responses

In practice, most processes must achieve optimality with respect to more than one response. For example:

- Cost and yield in chemical, manufacturing, and healthcare processes
- Cost and customer satisfaction in service process
- Efficacy of drug and minimal side effect in pharmaceutical process
- Timeliness of service and cost in service process

For multiple responses, overlaid contour plots (see the Contour Plot tool) or desirability functions can be used.

Analytical Method

The analytical method of ridge analysis provides greater certainty than the graphical method. The analytical method converts the regression model for coded factors to one using new variables W_1 and W_2, whose axes represent the principal axes of the response surface with their origin at the stationary point. This new model is known as the *canonical form:*

$$\hat{Y} = Y_0 + \lambda_1 W_1^2 + \lambda_2 W_2^2$$

$\hat{Y}$ provides the predicted value of the response for given values of W_1 and W_2. The intercept Y_0 is the predicted response at the stationary point. The coefficients λ_1 and λ_2 are the eigenvalues of the symmetric matrix. They provide a means of understanding the nature of the stationary point.

INTERPRETATION

In some cases, the ridge analysis can be inconclusive.

When the stationary point is outside the experimental region, the experimental region should be expanded with new data, where possible. When new data cannot be generated because the stationary point lies in a region where the factors cannot exist, then we can use the steepest ascent techniques with constrained optimization.

When the stationary point is a saddle point, we can also use the steepest ascent with constrained optimization techniques.

Analytical Method

Use the coefficients λ_1, λ_2, etc. (the eigenvalues of the symmetric matrix), to understand the nature of the stationary point:

- When the coefficients are all negative, then the stationary point is a *maximum* response.
- When the coefficients are all positive, then the stationary point is a *minimum* response
- When the coefficients are mixed signs (positive and negative), then the stationary point is a *saddle point* response.

Run Test Rules

The Western Electric run test rules add sensitivity to the control chart. These run tests, developed by Western Electric with some improvements by statistician Lloyd Nelson, apply statistical tests to determine if there are any patterns or trends in the plotted points.

WHEN TO USE

Use tests 1–8 on $\bar{X}$ and individual-X control charts; use tests 1–4 on attribute (P, U, Np, and C) charts. Run tests cannot be applied when the underlying data or the plotted statistic is autocorrelated, such as in EWMA charts.

METHODOLOGY

The *Western Electric Statistical Quality Control Handbook* defined zones using the sigma levels of the normal distribution, as shown in Figure F.42.

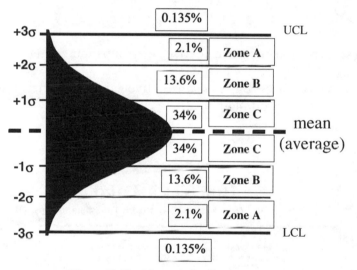

Figure F.42   Normal distribution zones.

Run Test 1 (Western Electric): One subgroup beyond three sigma, an indication that the process mean has shifted. See Figure F.43.
Run Test 2 (Nelson): Nine consecutive subgroups on the same side of the average (Note: Western Electric uses eight consecutive points same side of average). See Figure F.43.

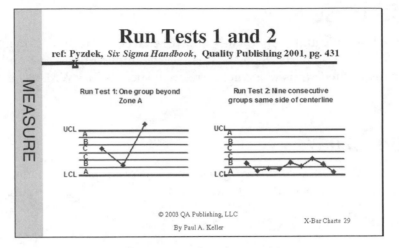

Figure F.43   Run Tests 1 and 2.

Run Test 3 (Nelson): Six consecutive subgroups increasing or decreasing. See Figure F.44.
Run Test 4 (Nelson): Fourteen consecutive subgroups alternating up and down. See Figure F.44.

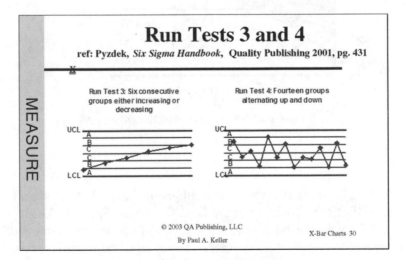

Figure F.44   Run Tests 3 and 4.

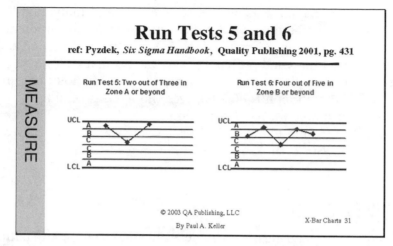

Figure F.45   Run Tests 5 and 6.

Run Test 5 (Western Electric): Two out of three consecutive subgroups beyond two sigma. See Figure F.45.

Run Test 6 (Western Electric): Four out of five consecutive subgroups beyond one sigma. See Figure F.45.

Run Test 7 (Western Electric): Fifteen consecutive subgroups between plus one sigma and minus one sigma. See Figure F.46.

Run Test 8 (Western Electric): Eight consecutive points beyond plus one sigma and minus one sigma (both sides of center). See Figure F.46.

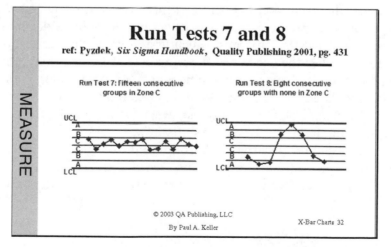

Figure F.46   Run Tests 7 and 8.

The run tests are applied as written to $\bar{X}$ charts and individual-X charts when the normal distribution is used. When non-normal distributions are used for individual-X charts, the average is replaced with the median, and zones are defined to provide the same probabilities as the normal curve at the stated sigma level. For example, run test 1 is interpreted as any point in the .135% tails (99.73% within the control limits), even though this would probably not be ±3 sigma for a non-normal distribution.

Run tests 1, 2, 5, and 6 are applied to the upper and lower halves of the chart separately. Run Tests 3, 4, 7, and 8 are applied to the whole chart.

INTERPRETATION

The run tests apply statistical tests to determine if there are any patterns or trends in the plotted points. Run tests 1, 2, 3, 5, 6 provide an indication that the process mean has shifted, while the others tell us something about sampling errors, inconsistent with the base premise of rational subgrouping.

Run Test 4: an indication of sampling from multistream process (subgroups alternate between two or more process levels).

Run Test 7: an indication of stratification in sampling (multistream sampling within a subgroup).

Run Test 8: an indication of sampling from a mixture (multistream sampling, subgroups on each side of center from separate distributions).

The statistical basis of the run tests is simply that if the subgroups are truly from the stated distribution, and independent of one another, then there will not be any pattern to the points. The run tests increase the power of the control chart (the likelihood that shifts in the process are detected with each subgroup), but also provide an increased (yet minimal) false alarm rate.

Keep in mind that the subgroup which first violates the run test does not always indicate when the process shift occurs. For example, when run test 2 is violated, the shift may have occurred nine points (or more, or less) prior to the point which violated the run test. As another example, a process may be in control and not in violation of any run tests for a period of time, say 50 subgroups. Then the process average shifts upward. As more and more subgroups are added at the new level, subgroups in the original 50 subgroups will start violating run tests or control limits, since these points now show an unnatural pattern relative to the combined distributions of the two process levels.

Scatter Diagrams

A scatter diagram is an *X–Y* plot used to investigate the correlation of one variable to another.

WHEN TO USE

Analyze Stage

- To investigate the correlation of one variable to another.

METHODOLOGY

The *x* axis is used to measure the scale of one characteristic (called the *independent variable*), and the *y* axis measures the second (called the *dependent variable*). To collect data, independently change values in *x*, and observe values of the *y* variable.

For example, we are interested in understanding the relationship between cooking time and the amount (or percent) of popcorn effectively cooked. We observe a cooking time of one and a half minutes produces a 76% kernel conversion rate in a bag of popcorn, so we plot a point at an *x* value of 1.5 minutes and a *y* value of 76. We conduct additional trials at other cooking times, measure the resulting conversion rate, then plot the (*x,y*) paired values. The collected data is shown in Table T.22, with the resulting scatter diagram shown in Figure F.47.

There are a few general suggestions to keep in mind when working with scatter diagrams:

- Vary the *x* value over a sufficient range so that we have data over the entire region of interest.
- It is best to only work with data that is specifically collected for the analysis. Other so-called *happenstance data* may include data that is mixed over several populations. These separate populations may indicate a hidden variable, or interaction, which is difficult to detect after the fact.

INTERPRETATION

Correlation implies that as one variable changes, the other also changes. Although this may indicate a cause and effect relationship, this is not always

Table T.22.   Example Paired Data for Scatter Diagram.

x: Cooking Time	y: Kernel Conversion Rate
1.5	76
1.3	85
1.1	75
1.6	84
2	88
1.75	90

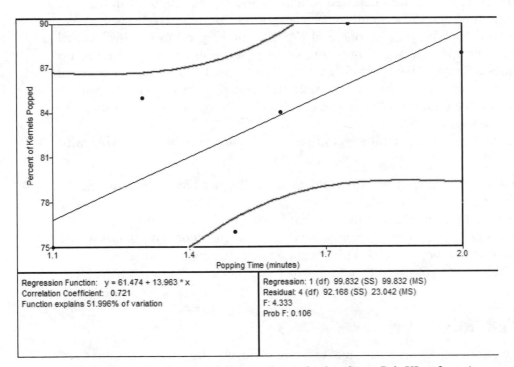

Regression Function: y = 61.474 + 13.963 * x
Correlation Coefficient: 0.721
Function explains 51.996% of variation

Regression: 1 (df) 99.832 (SS) 99.832 (MS)
Residual: 4 (df) 92.168 (SS) 23.042 (MS)
F: 4.333
Prob F: 0.106

Figure F.47   Example of a scatter diagram (created using Green Belt XL software).

the case, since there may be a third characteristic (or many more) that actually cause the noted effect of both characteristics.

Sometimes, though, if we know that there is good correlation between two characteristics, we can use one to predict the other, particularly if one characteristic is easy to measure and the other isn't. For instance, if we prove that weight gain in the first trimester of pregnancy correlates well with fetus development, we can use weight gain as a predictor. The alternative would be expensive tests to monitor the actual development of the fetus.

If the two characteristics are somehow related, the pattern formed by plotting them in a scatter diagram will show clustering in a certain direction and tightness. The more the cluster approaches a line in appearance, the more the two characteristics are likely to be linearly correlated.

The relative correlation of one characteristic to another can be seen both from how closely points cluster the line and from the correlation coefficient. Values near 1 imply very high correlation between the dependent and independent variables, meaning that a change in one characteristic will be accompanied by a change in the other characteristic. Weak correlation means the variation in the independent variable is not well explained by the changes in the dependent variable. This lack of correlation implies that other variables (including measurement error) may be responsible for the variation in y.

Positive correlation means that as the independent variable increases, so does the dependent variable, and this is shown on the scatter diagram as a line with positive slope. Negative correlation implies that as the independent variable increases, the dependent variable decreases, and a negative slope is seen on the scatter diagram.

Regression analysis (discussed earlier in Part 3) provides a prediction model for the relationship between the two variables.

Be careful not to extrapolate beyond the data region, since you have no experience upon which to draw. Extrapolation should be done with great caution, as the relationship between the two variables may change significantly. For example, the size of a balloon will increase as we pump more air into it, but only to a point! Once we pass this point, the outcome will change dramatically.

When we suspect there are hidden variables, we can stratify our data to see if we can detect the effect of the interactions, as shown in the Figure F.48. In this case, there is no clear correlation between the two variables. However, if we recognize that there is a third variable, then we notice three distinctly different patterns. In investigating the effect of cooking time on kernel conversion, suppose each of the three series, shown in the graph in Figure F.48 as squares, triangles, and circles, represented different cooking temperatures. Series one, displayed with diamonds, shows a positive correlation. Series two, in squares, shows a negative correlation. Series three, in triangles, shows less correlation. By

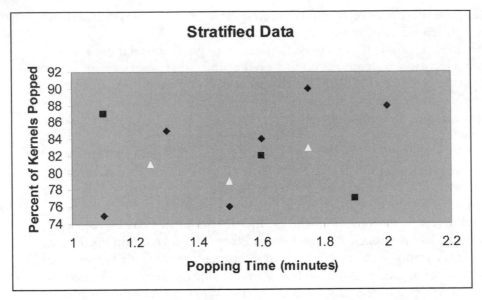

Figure F.48   Data that appears to be uncorrelated may be stratified.

looking for these hidden patterns, we may find other key variables that impact our resultant *y*. We would want to verify these suspicions using additional investigative techniques discussed elsewhere in Part 3, such as multiple regression analysis and design of experiments.

Screening Designs

A screening design is a designed experiment that uses a minimal number of run conditions to determine the most significant factors, usually so additional experimentation can be done concentrating on this reduced list of possible factors.

WHEN TO USE

Analyze Stage

- Use screening designs to understand sources of variation and discover the process drivers.

METHODOLOGY

Refer also to Design of Experiments earlier in Part 3 for introductory material.

The purpose of screening designs is to reduce the number of critical factors and interactions. We often start with many factors, brainstorm to a manageable number of key factors, then run a relatively small screening design to reduce the number of factors and interactions even further.

Although fractional factorial designs (see Factorial Designs) may be used as screening designs, saturated designs, augmented with one or more additional runs, are often the most economical starting point.

Saturated designs refer to special cases of fractional factorial designs where only the main factors can be estimated. In a saturated design, the minimum number of experimental conditions $(1 + p)$ is used to estimate the p main factors. For example, use a 2^{3-1} design to estimate 3 factors in 4 runs; a 2^{7-4} design to estimate 7 factors in 8 runs; a 2^{15-11} design to estimate 15 factors in 16 runs. In saturated designs, the main factors are all confounded with two factor interactions. In addition, we have no "extra" runs to estimate error, so we cannot determine which parameters are significant to the regression. We can only calculate the parameter effects, which provide the coefficients of the regression equation.

Generally, we will add at least one additional run (a degree of freedom) to the saturated design, resulting in $p + 2$ runs. This will allow an estimate of experimental error, which can be used to estimate significance of the terms. A center point (where each factor is set to the midpoint between its high $(+1)$ and low (-1) condition) can be used to provide a rough estimate.

When we take replicates of the center point, we can test for surface curvature. *Surface curvature* occurs when the response surface between the low and high levels of a factor is nonlinear, implying a higher-order effect of the factor, which can be either a local maximum or minimum across the surface. If the cost of the data is not prohibitive, a center point with a replicate is a useful addition to a screening design, providing both estimates of curvature as well as estimates of error. Unfortunately, meaningful center points cannot be defined for quantitative (categorical) factors, such as process type or supplier.

In this way, saturated designs (augmented with at least one additional run) are useful as screening designs. It should be clear that the fewer parameters we need to estimate, the less costly the experiment will be to run. Often, at least one factor in a design is statistically insignificant. If, after collecting and analyzing the data, we can remove that factor from the analysis, we are left with a replicated data set which provides an estimate of error and better estimates of the remaining factors.

If confounded factors are found to be significant, we may choose to extend the design by adding specific runs to estimate the confounded factor, or run a subsequent *foldover* design in which one or more of the significant factors' signs (the plus and minuses in the standard construction) are switched. A design is folded by replicating the design, substituting the low levels with high levels and high values with low levels for one or more of the factors. If we fold on just one factor (i.e., substitute the plus and minus signs for one of the factors), then that factor and its two-factor interactions will be free of confounding. If we substitute the plus and minus signs for the entire design, then all main factors will be free of confounding with other main factors and two-factor interactions.

INTERPRETATION

We use the general techniques discussed in the design of experiments tool to analyze the experimental results.

The two-levels per factor (2^k) designs used for screening can only provide a first-order model. When saturated designs have been augmented with one or more additional runs, we can estimate the error in the model and significance of parameters using ANOVA techniques. If the additional runs include a center point, we can investigate the need for a higher-order model by testing for curvature.

The next step after successful analysis of the screening experiment depends on the objectives of the experimental process. If we are trying to control the process, then the successful experiment has differentiated between the significant and insignificant sources of variation. We should verify this by replicating the experiment, then implement control mechanisms on the significant factors as part of the improve stage.

If we also need to define a precise model for prediction purposes, then we should run a central composite design. It's possible our screening design can be extended with just a few experimental conditions to satisfy this requirement.

If we need to optimize the process by moving it to a region of maximum yield, we can proceed to response surface analysis or evolutionary operation techniques, both of which were discussed earlier Part 3.

SIPOC

SIPOC, an acronym standing for suppliers, inputs, process, outputs, and customers, refers to the technique of analyzing a process relative to these parameters to fully understand its impact. In this context, each element of SIPOC is defined as follows.

Suppliers: those who provide inputs for process.
Inputs: the data, knowledge, and resources necessary for process to generate desired output.
Process: the activity that transforms inputs to outputs.
Outputs: the result of process (deliverables).
Customers: the person, persons, or function receiving outputs.

WHEN TO USE

Define Stage

• Document the top-level process, its transactions, and its stakeholders.

METHODOLOGY

We begin a SIPOC analysis by focusing on the process. We map the process using either a flowchart or a process map.

We then define the outputs for the process. These include all the outcomes and results of the process, including the value-added products or services provided as well as documentation, inputs to other processes, and payments. A complete list of outputs will enhance the definitions of customers, inputs, and suppliers, so spend some time making sure you are complete at this point.

Once the outputs are defined, we can list the customers. A customer is anyone who receives an output from the process, and so may include internal as well as external customers.

We then identify the inputs to the process. Consider all the resources necessary for the process. Look particularly at decision points in the process, since the information needed to make decisions is a necessary input.

Finally, once we've identified the inputs, we define the source of the input as the supplier.

Table T.23 is a SIPOC example from a publishing company. The process is shown here in text for simplicity, but a process map could also be used. The SIPOC was developed following the guidelines presented above.

Table T.23. SIPOC for a Publisher.

Suppliers	Input	Process	Output	Customers
Legal	ISBN	Receive draft	ISBN	Printer
Author	Final draft	Issue ISBN	New cover	Reader
Graphic design	Cover design	Cover	Error list	Marketing
Layout editor	Quark files	Edit layout	Correspondence with editor	
		Proof for errors	PDF files	
		Create PDF for printer		
		Send to marketing		

INTERPRETATION

The results of the SIPOC will assist in the proper definition of the project. The process team should have representatives from each of the key customer and supplier groups (collectively, the stakeholders). The inputs and outputs to the process provide a check on the process map, and they can assist in project scope definition, as well as general problem solving of sources of variation.

Spaghetti Diagram

A spaghetti diagram, as shown in Figure F.49, is a graphical tool used to indicate the movement of material or personnel.

WHEN TO USE

Analyze Stage

• To identify unnecessary movement of material or personnel.

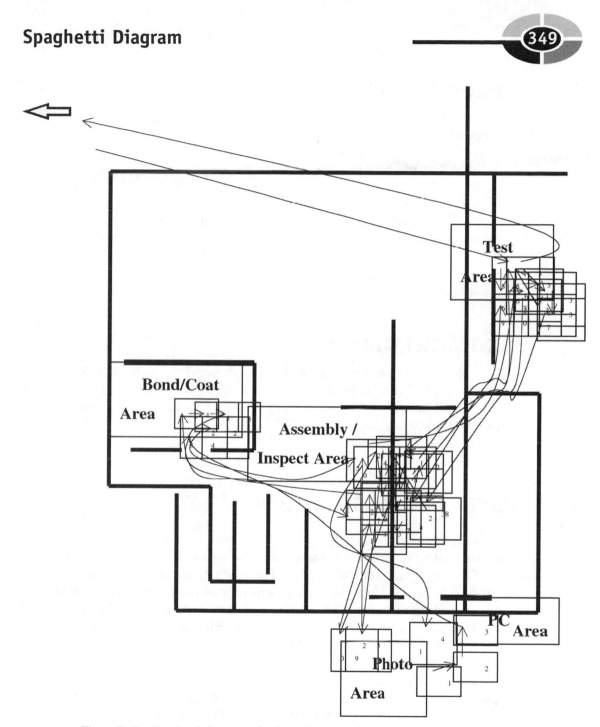

Figure F.49 Spaghetti diagram of a floor plan showing poor use of physical space.

METHODOLOGY

Begin with a floor plan, layout, or map of the physical area utilized by the process.

Write a number 1 at the physical location where the process begins, then a number 2 at the next physical location where the material or personnel will move to. Draw a line from number 1 to number 2. Repeat for all subsequent movements of the material or personnel.

An example of a spaghetti diagram is shown in Figure F.49. The floor plan for the process provides the background, complete with walls and doors. The flow of the process is superimposed to show the flow of personnel and material as the process activities are undertaken.

INTERPRETATION

Look for opportunities to move necessary process steps closer in location to one another. Notice in the example the scrambled mess, resembling the tangles of cooked spaghetti, resulting from excessive movement and poor use of physical space.

Statistical Process Control Charts

Walter Shewhart, working for AT&T's Bell Laboratories, developed the concept of statistical process control in the 1920s. Statistical process control, or SPC as it is commonly called, uses data from prior observations of a process to predict how the process will vary in the future. Shewhart offered this definition of statistical control: "A phenomenon is said to be in statistical control when, through the use of past experience, we can predict how the phenomenon will vary in the future."

The element of time, which is lacking in enumerative statistical tools (including histograms, confidence intervals, and hypothesis tests), is a critical parameter for investigating process characteristics, since processes are by definition occurring over the course of time. Enumerative tools pool the data from the past into single estimates of the average and standard deviation: the time element is lost! An enumerative analysis of this nature is only valid when we can assume that all the prior data is from a single distribution.

In contrast, SPC uses the element of time as one of its principal components. Its control charts can be used to verify that the process is stable, implying that the data is from a single distribution.

WHEN TO USE

Measure Stage

- To baseline the process, by quantifying the common cause level of variation inherent to the process.
- As part of measurement systems analysis, to evaluate repeatability and reproducibility.

Analyze Stage

- To differentiate between common and special causes of variation.

Improve Stage

- To verify the results of the process improvement on the process metric.

Control Stage

- To monitor the process to ensure the stability of the revised process and the continued benefit of the improvement.

A fundamental benefit of control charts is their ability to identify the common cause operating level of the process. The region between the upper and lower control limits defines the variation that is expected from the process statistic. This is the variation due to common causes: sources of variation that contribute to all the process observations.

W. Edwards Deming demonstrated the principles behind SPC with his red bead experiment, which he regularly conducted during his seminars. In this experiment, he used a bucket of beads, or marbles. Most of the beads were white, but a small percentage (about 10%) of red beads were thoroughly mixed with the white beads in the bucket. Students volunteered to be process workers, who would dip a sample paddle into the bucket and produce a day's "production" of 50 beads for the White Bead Company. Other students would volunteer to be inspectors, who counted the number of white beads in each operator's daily production. The white beads represented usable output that could be sold to the White Bead Company's customers, while the red beads

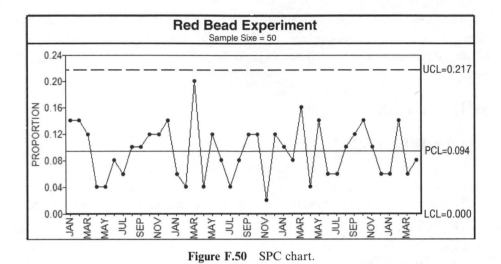

Figure F.50   SPC chart.

were scrap. These results were then reported to a manager, who would invariably chastise operators for a high number of red beads. If the operator's production improved on the next sample, she was rewarded; if the production of white beads went down, more chastising.

Figure F.50 shows a control chart of the typical white bead output. It's obvious from the control chart that there was variation in the process observations: each dip into the bucket yielded a different number of white beads. Has the process changed? No! No one has changed the bucket, yet the number of white beads is different every time. The control limits tell us that we should expect anywhere between 0% and 21% red beads on a given sample of 50 beads.

When the process is in control, we can use the control limits to predict the future performance of the process. For example, we might use the chart to predict the error levels, which tell us something about the cost to produce the product or deliver the service. If the process variable is the time to deliver the product or service, we can use the chart to plan resources, such as in a doctor's office, or deliver product, such as in a warehouse.

Another fundamental benefit of a control chart is its ability to provide an operational definition of a special cause. Once we accept that every process exhibits some level of variation, we might consider how much variation is natural for the process. If a particular observation seems large, is it unnaturally large, or should an observation of this magnitude be expected? The control limits remove the subjectivity from this decision, and define this level of natural process variation.

When a sample subgroup is beyond the control limits, we say that it is a result of a special cause of variation. In other words, something unexpected happened at this point in time (or just prior to this point in time) to influence the process differently than we've seen before.

Although we may not be able to immediately identify the special cause in process terms (for example, cycle time increased due to staff shortages), we have statistical evidence that the process has changed. This process change can occur as a change in process location or a change in process variation.

A change in process location is sometimes simply referred to as a *process shift*. For example, the average cycle time may have changed from 19 days to 12 days. Process shifts may result in process improvement (for example, cycle time reduction) or process degradation (for example, an increased cycle time). Recognizing this as a process change, rather than just random variation of a stable process, allows us to learn about the process dynamics, reduce variation, and maintain improvements.

The variation in the process may also increase or decrease. This is evidenced by a change in the width of the control limits. Generally, a reduction in variation is considered a process improvement, since the process is then easier to predict and manage.

In the absence of control limits, we assume that an arbitrarily "different" observation is due to a shift in the process. In our zeal to reduce variation, we adjust the process to return it to its prior state. For example, we sample the value highlighted in the leftmost distribution in Figure F.51 from a process that (unbeknown to us) is in control. We feel this value is excessively large, so assume the process must have shifted. We adjust the process by the amount of deviation between the observed value and the initial process average. The process is now at the level shown in the center distribution in the figure. We sample from this distribution and observe several values near the initial average, then sample a value such as is highlighted in the center distribution. We adjust the process upward by the deviation between the new value and the initial mean, resulting in the rightmost distribution shown in the figure. As we continue this process, we can see that we actually increase the total process variation, which is exactly the opposite of our desired effect.

Responding to these arbitrary observation levels as if they were special causes is known as *tampering*. This is also called "responding to a false alarm," since a false alarm is when we think that the process has shifted when it really hasn't. Deming's funnel experiment demonstrates this principle. In practice, tampering occurs when we attempt to control the process to limits that are within the natural control limits defined by common cause variation. Some causes of this include:

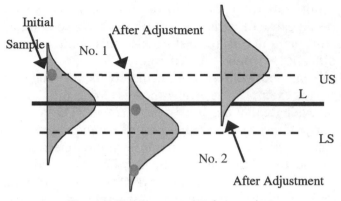

Figure F.51   An example of tampering.

- We try to control the process to specifications, or goals. These limits are defined externally to the process, rather than being based on the statistics of the process.
- Rather than using the suggested control limits defined at ± 3 standard deviations from the centerline, we use limits that are tighter (or narrower) than these on the faulty notion that this will improve the performance of the chart. Using limits defined at ± 2 standard deviations from the centerline produces narrower control limits than the ± 3 standard deviation limits, so it would appear that the ± 2 sigma limits are better at detecting shifts. Assuming normality, the chance of being outside of a ± 3 standard deviation control limit is 0.27% if the process has not shifted. On average, a false alarm is encountered with these limits once every 370 (1/0.0027) subgroups. Using ± 2 standard deviation control limits, the chance of being outside the limits when the process has not shifted is 4.6%, corresponding to false alarms every 22 subgroups! If we respond to these false alarms, we tamper and increase variation.

METHODOLOGY

In an SPC analysis, we collect samples over a short period of time. Each of these samples is referred to as a *subgroup*. Each subgroup tells us two things about the process: its current location and its current amount of variation.

Once we've collected enough subgroups over a period of time, we can use these short-term estimates to predict where the process will be (its location) and how much the process is expected to vary over a longer time period.

Control charts take many forms, depending on the process that is being analyzed and the data available from that process. All control charts have the following properties:

- The x axis is sequential, usually a unit denoting the evolution of time.
- The y axis is the statistic that is being charted for each point in time. Examples of plotted statistics include an observation, an average of two or more observations, the median of two or more observations, a count of items meeting a criteria of interest, or the percent of items meeting a criteria of interest.
- Limits are defined for the statistic that is being plotted. These control limits are statistically determined by observing process behavior, providing an indication of the bounds of expected behavior for the plotted statistic. They are never determined using customer specifications or goals.

The key to successful control charts is the formation of rational subgroups. Control charts rely upon rational subgroups to estimate the short-term variation in the process. This short-term variation is then used to predict the longer-term variation defined by the control limits.

Nelson (1988) describes a *rational subgroup* as simply "a sample in which all of the items are produced under conditions in which only random effects are responsible for the observed variation." Another way of stating this is that the causes of *within* subgroup variation are equivalent to the causes of *between* subgroup variation.

A rational subgroup has the following properties:

- The observations comprising the subgroup are independent. Two observations are independent if neither observation influences, or results from, the other. When observations are dependent on one another, we say the process has *autocorrelation*, or *serial correlation*. (These terms mean the same thing.)
- The subgroups are formed from observations taken in a time-ordered sequence. In other words, subgroups cannot be arbitrarily constructed by taking multiple samples, each equal to the subgroup size, from a set of data (or a box of parts). Rather, the data comprising a subgroup must be a "snapshot" of the process over a small window of time, and the order of the subgroups would show how those snapshots vary in time (like a movie). The size of the "small window of time" is determined on an individual process basis to minimize the chance of a special cause occurring in the subgroup (which, if persistent, would provide the situation described immediately below).

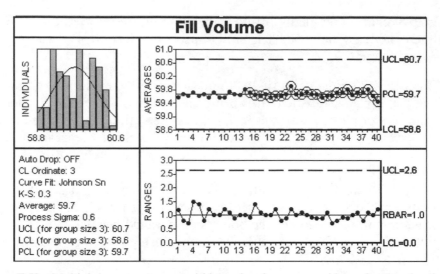

Figure F.52   Multiple process streams within each subgroup provide an irrational estimate of process variation.

- The observations within a subgroup are from a single, stable process. If subgroups contain the elements of multiple process streams, or if other special causes occur frequently within subgroups, then the within subgroup variation will be large relative to the variation between subgroup averages. This large within subgroup variation forces the control limits to be too far apart, resulting in a lack of sensitivity to process shifts.

In Figure F.52 you might suspect that the cause of the tight grouping of subgroups about the $\bar{X}$ chart centerline was a reduction in process variation. But the range chart fails to confirm this theory.

This data, provided by a major cosmetic manufacturer, represents the fill weight for bottles of nail polish. The filling machine has three filling heads, so subgroups were conveniently formed by taking a sample from each fill head. The problem is that the heads in the filling machine apparently have significantly different average values. This variation between filling heads causes the within subgroup variation (as plotted on the range chart) to be much larger than the variation in the subgroup averages (represented graphically by the pattern of the plotted points on the $\bar{X}$ chart). The $\bar{X}$ chart control limits, calculated based on the range chart, are thus much wider than the plotted subgroups.

The underlying problem then is that the premise of a rational subgroup has been violated: we tried to construct a subgroup out of apples and oranges. But all is not lost (fruit salad isn't so bad) because we've learned something about our process. We've learned that the filler heads are different and that we could reduce overall variation by making them more similar. Note the circles that highlight subgroups 16 and on in Figure F.52. The software has indicated a violation of run test 7, which was developed to search for this type of pattern in the data. (See the Run Test Rules earlier in Part 3.)

This type of multistream behavior is not limited to cosmetic filling operations. Consider the potential for irrational subgroups in these processes:

- A bank supervisor is trying to reduce the wait time for key services. She constructs a control chart, using subgroups based on a selection of five customers in the bank at a time. Since she wants to include all the areas, she makes sure to include loan applications as well as teller services in the subgroup.
- An operator finish grinds 30 parts at a time in a single fixture. He measures 5 parts from the fixture for his subgroup, always including the two end pieces. His fixture is worn, so that the pieces on the two ends differ substantially.

Most likely, each of these examples will result in an irrational subgroup due to multistream processes.

Sampling Considerations

Many times, the process will dictate the size of the rational subgroup. For example, the rational subgroup size for service processes is often equal to one. A larger subgroup, taken over a short interval, would tend to contain dependent data; taken over a longer interval, the subgroup could contain special causes of variation.

The safest assumption for maintaining a rational subgroup is to use a subgroup size of one. Since data usually has some cost associated to it, smaller subgroups are generally cheaper to acquire than larger subgroups. Unfortunately, smaller subgroup sizes are less capable of detecting shifts in the process.

As seen in Figure F.53, it is easier to detect larger process shifts than to detect smaller process shifts. The larger shift, shown by the k equals 3 sigma shift on the far right, has much more area outside the control limits, so is easier to detect than the k equals 1 sigma shift.

Table T.24 shows the average number of subgroups necessary to detect the shift of size k (in standard deviation units) based on the subgroup size n. For example, if we observe the process a large number of times, then on average a subgroup of size $n = 3$ will detect a $k = 1$ sigma shift in 9 subgroups. As you can see from the table, small subgroups will readily detect relatively large

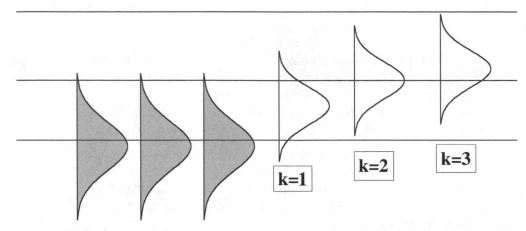

Figure F.53   Larger shifts are easier to detect, since there is a larger percentage of the process outside the control limits.

Table T.24.   Average Number of Subgroups to Detect Shift.

n/k	0.5	1	1.5	2	2.5	3
1	155	43	14	6	3	1
2	90	17	5	2	1	1
3	60	9	2	1	1	1
4	43	6	1	1	1	1
5	33	4	1	1	1	1
6	26	3	1	1	1	1
7	21	2	1	1	1	1
8	17	2	1	1	1	1
9	14	1	1	1	1	1
10	12	1	1	1	1	1

shifts of two or three sigma, but are less capable of readily detecting smaller shifts. This demonstrates the power of the X-bar chart.

Defining Control Limits

To define the control limits, we need an ample history of the process to define the level of common cause variation. There are two issues here:

1. Statistically, we need to observe a sufficient number of data observations before we can calculate reliable estimates of the variation and (to a lesser degree) the average. In addition, the statistical "constants" used to define control chart limits (such as d_2) are actually variables and only approach constants when the number of subgroups is "large." For a subgroup size of five, for instance, the d_2 value approaches a constant at about 25 subgroups (Duncan, 1986). When a limited number of subgroups are available, short-run techniques may be useful.

2. To distinguish between special causes and common causes, you must have enough subgroups to define the common cause operating level of your process. This implies that all types of common causes must be included in the data. For example, if we observe the process over one shift, using one operator and a single batch of material from one supplier, we are not observing all elements of common cause variation that are likely to be characteristic of the process. If we define control limits under these limited conditions, then we will likely see special causes arising due to the natural variation in one or more of these factors.

Control Chart Selection

There are many control charts available for our use. One differentiator between the control charts is the type of data that will be analyzed on the chart:

• *Attribute data* (also known as *count data*). Typically, we will count the number of times we observe some condition (usually something we don't like, such as a defect or an error) in a given sample from the process.
• *Variables data* (also known as measurement data). Variables data is continuous in nature, generally capable of being measured to enough resolution to provide at least 10 unique values for the process being analyzed.

Attribute data has less resolution than variables data, since we only count if something occurs, rather than taking a measurement to see how close we are to the condition. For example, attributes data for a manufacturing process might include the number of items in which the diameter exceeds the specification, whereas variables data for the same process might be the measurement of that part diameter. In a service process, we may measure the time it takes to process an order (variables data) or count the number of times the order processing time exceeds a predefined limit (attributes data).

Attributes data generally provides us with less information than variables data would for the same process. Attributes data would generally not allow us to predict if the process is trending toward an undesirable state, since it is already in this condition. As a result, variables data is considered more useful for defect *prevention*.

There are several attribute control charts, each designed for a slightly different use:

- *np* chart: for monitoring the number of times a condition occurs.
- *p* chart: for monitoring the percent of samples having the condition.
- *c* chart: for monitoring the number of times a condition occurs, when each sample can have more than one instance of the condition.
- *u* chart: for monitoring the percent of samples having the condition, when each sample can have more than one instance of the condition.

There are also several variables charts available for use. The first selection is generally the subgroup size. The subgroup size is the number of observations, taken in close proximity of time, used to estimate the short-term variation. Although subgroups of size one provide some estimate of the process location, we sometimes choose to collect data in larger subgroups since we obtain a better estimate of both the process location and the short-term variation at that point in time.

Control charts available for variables data include:

- Individual-X chart (also known as *individuals chart*, *I chart*, *IMR chart*): Used for subgroup size equal to one.
- $\bar{X}$ charts: Used for subgroup size two and larger.
- EWMA (exponentially weighted moving average) chart: Used for subgroups of size one or larger. Suitable for non-normal data or increased sensitivity to small process shifts.

Figure F.54 shows selection criteria for control charts.

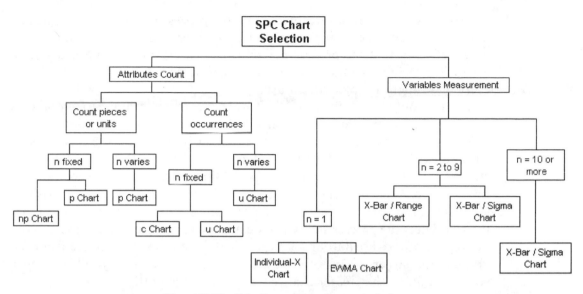

Figure F.54 Selection criteria for control charts.

INTERPRETATION

When evaluating the results of a control chart, we must realize that reacting to special causes is one of the key reasons for using a control chart. Out-of-control points provide valuable information about the process.

The control charts are designed to detect shifts with a minimal chance of a *false alarm*. That is, there is a negligible chance that the process has not changed when a special cause has been identified. Conversely, there is overwhelming evidence that the process has changed, and by removing this *special cause*, we will reduce the overall variability of the process. Therefore, whenever a special cause is present, we must not ignore it but learn from it.

When we encounter special causes of variation, we must determine (in process terms) the cause of the process shift. For example, if the control chart indicates that service times are now below the lower control limit, indicating that they were improved, the cause might be that we had *changed the method of customer service by routing clients to more experienced personnel*.

Once we have identified the special cause, we can statistically recalculate the control chart's centerlines and control limits without including the data known to be affected by the special cause. If the process shift is sustained, such as when a new procedure replaces the old process procedures, then we simply calculate new control limits for the new, improved process.

As discussed earlier in this topic, when the process is in control, subgroups have only an extremely small chance of being outside the control limits. If we incorrectly say that the process has shifted, then we have committed a false alarm. The chance of a false alarm in most control charts is about 1 in 370: for every 370 subgroups plotted, on average one subgroup would be falsely estimated to be out of control. Since we often experience real changes to our process in less time that that, this is considered to be appropriately insignificant.

We start the process of variation reduction by isolating the instances of variation due to special causes. We can use the time-ordered nature of the control chart to understand what happened (in process terms) at each point in time that represents special causes. When the process does undergo a shift, such as is shown in the three distribution curves on the right of Figure F.53, then we detect the process shift when we happen to sample subgroups from the tail region of the distribution that exceeds the limits. As we can see from the graphic, the larger the process shift, the more tail area is beyond the upper control limit, so the greater chance we will detect a shift.

An important point to remember is that a control chart will not detect all shifts, nor necessarily detect shifts as soon as they occur. Notice in Figure F.53 that even though there was a large tail area outside the upper control limit, the majority of the subgroup samples will be within the control limits.

For this reason, we should be suspect of neighboring points, even those within the control limits, once an assignable cause has been detected.

Furthermore, we should realize that there are often choices we can make to improve the detection of special causes, including the type of control chart, its options, the use of run test rules, and the method by which we sample from the process.

Once we have differentiated between the variation due to special causes and the variation due to common causes, we can separately reduce the variation due to each. To reduce the variation due to common causes, we look to all elements of the system and process for clues to variation. We can generally ignore the point-to-point variation, since it represents a combination of factors that is common to all the subgroups. We'll typically use designed experiments and multiple regression analysis to understand these sources of variation.

Stem and Leaf Plot

A stem and leaf plot is a simple data analysis tool used in exploratory data analysis (EDA) to display the data patterns. It is similar in this regard to a histogram, but rather than simply grouping the data as in a histogram, the stem and leaf shows the actual data values.

WHEN TO USE

Measure Stage

- To depict the data pattern, as an aid in understanding the underlying distribution, or distributions, of the data.

METHODOLOGY

The data is first rank-ordered from smallest to largest data value, then grouped into equal width ranges.

The first column in Figure F.55 displays the cumulative count of the data, up to the median value of the data. The second column displays the leading digit or digits of data (the stem), and the third column displays the trailing digit of the data (the leaf). There is one digit for each recorded value.

In the example shown, the data ranges from 90 to 109. The data is grouped so that each row has two values. The value of 90 occurs twice, as represented

Stem & Leaf Example

MEASURES		
2	9	00
5	9	333
11	9	444455
21	9	6666777777
(18)	9	888888888899999999
21	10	00011111
13	10	22233
8	10	444
5	10	6667
1	10	9

© 2003 QA Publishing, LLC
By Paul A. Keller

Measure Tools
& Objectives 30

Figure F.55   Example of a stem and leaf plot.

by the two zeroes shown in the third column of the first row. The stem of the value 90 is 9, and is displayed in the second column of the first row.

The second row has three observations, so the cumulative count of data is now five, as shown in the first column. There are three occurrences of the value 93 in this row.

The third row has four occurrences of 94 and two occurrences of 95. These six observations increase the cumulative count to 11 (which equals the previous count of 5 plus the 6 observations in this row).

The median value for the data is 98. That is, half the data is above or equal to that value, and half is below or equal to that value. We can easily see the median in the stem and leaf because the cumulative counts stop at that row. Below the median row, the first column displays a cumulative count that starts in the last row and increases moving upward (until the median row).

INTERPRETATION

Look for patterns in the data that may hint at multiple distributions, which would indicate multiple stream processes. For example, cycle time for a purchase order may be very different depending on the product ordered.

Transformation

Transformation creates a new variable using one or more original variables, usually to make an analysis more useful.

WHEN TO USE

Analyze Stage

- To stabilize variance to meet the assumptions required for ANOVA techniques (a constant level of variance at each response level).
- To calculate parameters based on a measured response or responses. For example, cost may be the preferred response, even though labor time was measured. The effect of the parameter on process variation can also be calculated when there are repeat runs at each operating condition.

METHODOLOGY

Variance Stabilization

Once the condition of nonconstant variance is detected using equality of variance tests (discussed earlier in Part 3), we can plot the log of the standard deviation at each experimental condition with the log of the mean of the experimental condition. The resulting slope of the line will provide an indication of a useful transformation, as shown in Table T.25 (Box, Hunter, and Hunter, 1978). Note that slopes lying between those indicated in Table T.25 should be rounded up or down to the levels provided.

For example, a plot of the log of the averages (of the replicated trials) versus the log of the standard deviation (of the replicated trials) indicates a slope of 1.462 in Figure. F.56. Since this is close to 1.5, a reciprocal square root transformation will be applied, so that the transformed $y_t = 1/$square root (y).

Box and Cox developed an iterative approach for determining an optimal lambda that minimizes the sum of squares error term. Myers and Montgomery provide an example of this approach. A sample Minitab output using the previous example's data is shown in Figure F.57.

In this case, the Box-Cox plot suggests an optimal lambda at $-1/2$. This is the same value suggested by the plot of log (StdDev$_i$) versus log (Mean$_i$).

Since the confidence interval does not include the value 1 (the lambda for no transformation), a transformation would be helpful to stabilize the variance.

Table T.25.   Suggested Transformations Based on Slope of VAR.

Slope	$\lambda = 1 - \alpha$	Transform	Useful for
0	1	None	
1/2	1/2	Square root	Poisson data
1	0	Log	Log normal data
3/2	$-1/2$	Reciprocal Square root	
2	-1	Reciprocal	

Calculated Parameters

Simple calculated responses occur frequently when a response is measured and then converted to a response with more general interest. For example, the labor required to assemble a piece of furniture may be measured in labor hours, then converted to labor cost, since that more directly relates to profitability. Measurement equipment may output a resistance that can be converted to a more meaningful temperature response.

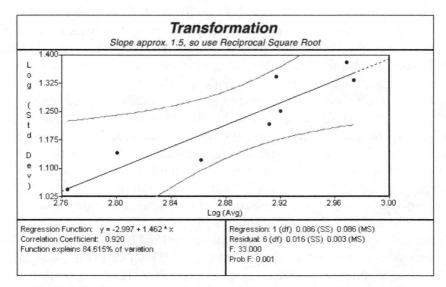

Figure F.56   Use of scatter diagram to estimate transformation technique.

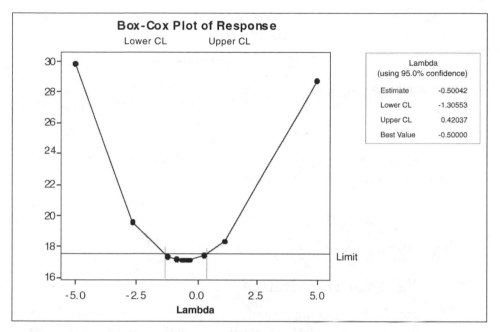

Figure F.57   Example of a Box-Cox plot.

We can also convert multiple responses to a single response. A simple example is the calculation of density based on measured displaced volume and mass. We may similarly calculate utilization based on usage and availability (such as "bed days" in healthcare).

Finally, we may calculate statistics based on the grouping of repeated runs to better understand how a factor influences the process variation. Taguchi's signal to noise ratios are one example of this.

Classical experiments often investigated effects of a parameter on the mean response. Taguchi popularized investigating parameter effects on the variation of the response, using signal-to-noise ratios. Estimating the effects on variation is often useful for designing processes that are robust to parameter variation, or in some cases to reduce common cause variation.

The estimation of the variance requires grouping of responses based on multiple observations at each condition, such as with replication or repeat runs (during the running of the experiment), or after insignificant terms have been discarded.

Taguchi's signal-to-noise ratio is a grouped response that considers both the variation of replicated measurements and the proximity of the average response to a specified target value. Taguchi defined over 70 signal-to-noise ratios, three of which are most common:

- *Smaller is better*. Used when the target value for the response is zero. The signal-to-noise ratio is calculated as:

$$S/N \text{ ratio} = -10 \ \log[\text{SUM}(y_i^2)/n]$$

- *Larger is better*. Used when the target value for the response is infinity. The signal-to-noise ratio is calculated as:

$$S/N \text{ ratio} = -10 \ \log[\text{SUM}(1/y_i^2)/n]$$

- *Nominal is better*. Used to minimize the variability of the response. The signal-to-noise ratio is calculated as:

$$S/N \text{ ratio} = 10 \ \log[\text{SUM}(\bar{y}^2)/s^2]$$

INTERPRETATION

Variance Stabilization

The transformed response should be checked for constant variance using the equality of variance test. If the transformed response passes the tests for constant variance, then the ANOVA for the transformed response is acceptable for use.

In the example above, the Bartlett's test for equality of variance is not rejected for the transformed response, so the regression analysis is redone using the transformed response.

Calculated Parameters

Generally, calculated parameters will be analyzed using the same techniques discussed elsewhere in this book.

Taguchi's signal-to-noise ratios may be interpreted as follows:

- *Smaller is better*. The goal of the process improvement is to minimize the responses, which equates to a maximization of the signal-to-noise ratio.
- *Larger is better*. The goal of the process improvement is to maximize the responses, which equates to a minimization of the inverse of the responses and a maximization of the signal-to-noise ratio.
- *Nominal is better*. As the variability of the response (*s* squared) decreases relative to the average response, the signal-to-noise ratio increases. The goal of the process improvement is to maximize the signal-to-noise ratio.

A simple criticism of the signal-to-noise ratios is that they are confusing. A more detailed criticism of the ratios is that they confuse variation of the response with the average response in a single metric, which tends to obscure information. This is particularly dangerous in cases where the variation changes as a function of the average response. A preferred approach is to consider the average and variance of the response as separate metrics (or responses), each to be maximized, minimized, or targeted as necessary (Note: Usually a minimized variance is desirable).

More detailed analysis of the signal-to-noise ratios may be found in Box (1988) and Pignatiello and Ramberg (1985).

U Chart

U charts are one of a set of control charts specifically designed for attributes data. The U chart monitors the percent of samples having the condition, relative to either a fixed or varying sample size, when each sample can have more than one instance of the condition. For example, we might choose to look at all the transactions in the month (since that would vary month to month) or a set number of samples, whichever we prefer. From this sample, we track the total number of errors in each month.

WHEN TO USE

Measure Stage

- To estimate, using attributes data, the process baseline. Generally, we would greatly prefer the use of variables control charts for this purpose.

Improve Stage

- Since the number of errors tends to be quite small (for even very large samples), the use of attribute charts is limited in the improve stage.

METHODOLOGY

Samples are collected from the process at specific points each time. Each sample (at each point in time) has the same number of observed units, each of which may have one or more errors.

Plotted statistic: the average count of occurrences of a criteria of interest in sample of items.

$$u_j = \frac{(count)_j}{n_j}$$

where n_j is the sample size (number of units) of group j.

Centerline:

$$\bar{u} = \frac{\sum_{j=1}^{m} (count)_j}{m}$$

where n_j is the sample size (number of units) of group j, and m is the number of groups included in the analysis.

UCL, LCL (upper and lower control limit):

$$UCL = \bar{u} + 3\sqrt{\frac{\bar{u}}{n_j}}$$

$$LCL = MAX\left(0, \bar{u} - 3\sqrt{\frac{\bar{u}}{n_j}}\right)$$

where n_j is the sample size (number of units) of group j and $\bar{u}$ is the average percent.

For example, we observe 500 telemarketing calls each week, and record the total number of errors in each call, where each call may have more than one error. Ten months of data are observed, with the following number of errors in each sample: 7 out of 350; 14 out of 312; 12 out of 125; 18 out of 170; 9 out of 165; 11 out of 264; 12 out of 254; 8 out of 404; 11 out of 137; 21 out of 312. The control chart is show in Figure F.58.

INTERPRETATION

The upper and lower control limits indicate the bounds of expected process behavior. The fluctuation of the points between the control limits is due to the variation that is intrinsic (built-in) to the process. We say that this variation is due to common causes that influence the process. Any points outside the control limits can be attributed to a special cause, implying a shift in the process. When a process is influenced by only common causes, then it is stable, and can be predicted.

If there are any out-of-control points, then special causes of variation must be identified and eliminated. Brainstorm and conduct designed experiments to find those process elements that contribute to sporadic changes in process location. To predict the capability of the process after special causes have been eliminated, you should remove the out-of-control points from the analysis, which will remove the statistical bias of the out-of-control points by dropping them from the calculations of the average and control limits. See the Statistical Process Control Charts tool for more detail.

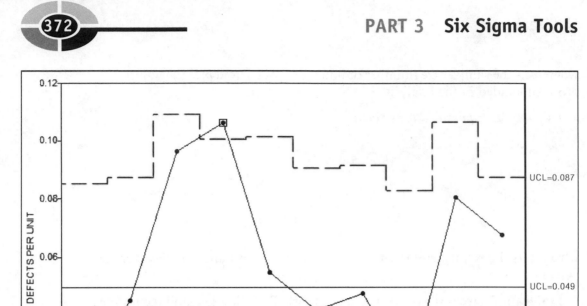

Figure F.58   Example of a U chart for varying sample size (created using Quality America Green Belt XL software).

Velocity

Velocity is a lean metric useful for prioritizing cycle time improvement opportunities.

WHEN TO USE

Analyze Stage

- To prioritize cycle time improvement opportunities.

METHODOLOGY

Velocity is calculated by dividing the number of value-added steps by the process lead time.

$$\text{Velocity} = \text{number of value-added steps/process lead time}$$

Little's law is used to calculate the process lead time by dividing the number of items in process by the completions per hour (George, 2002).

$$\text{Process lead time} = \text{number items in-process/completions per hour}$$

For example, if it takes two hours on average to complete each purchase order, then there are 0.5 completions per hour. This is the denominator of the Little law equation. If there are 10 purchase orders waiting in queue (the numerator), then Little's law says we need 10 divided by one-half equals 20 hours lead time for the process. In other words, we can't process any new orders until the 20-hour lead time has allowed the existing work in process to be completed.

If there are five value-added process steps in this process, then the velocity may be calculated as 5 divided by 20 equals 0.25 steps per hour.

A process observation log (see Table T.26) is a useful tool for analyzing velocity of the process.

For each step in the process:

- Classify the step as value-added (VA), non-value-added but necessary (NVA-type 1), or non-value-added and unnecessary (NVA-type 2).
- Calculate the measured distance from the previous process step location to this process step's location.

Table T.26. Process Observation Log.

Step Description	VA/NVA Type	Distance from Last Step	Average Task Time	Average Queue Time	Average No. Items in Queue

- Estimate the average time to complete the process step. This is best determined using a control chart for task time.
- Estimate the average time that the product or customer waits in queue for this process step. This is best determined using a control chart for queue time.
- Estimate the average number of items in queue, as determined through control charting.

After summing the averages, we can use Little's law to calculate the process lead time and the velocity.

INTERPRETATION

The velocity of the process represents the responsiveness or flexibility of the process to customer demand. A long lead time results in slow velocity.

Lead time is reduced, and velocity increased, when work in progress is reduced.

The rationale is simple: New orders from customers cannot be started until work (or items) in process is completed. Thus, the activity on new items is stalled. An example from a service process is a doctor's waiting room. The patients are work in process. New patients aren't seen by the doctor until those who arrived earlier have been seen.

There are two general methods for increasing velocity, both of which reduce the process lead time: The first method to reduce lead time is to increase the Little law denominator, the *completions per hour*. Completions per hour can be increased by reducing the amount of time necessary for each item to be completed. The second method to reduce lead time is to reduce the numerator of Little's Law, the work in process.

Work Breakdown Structure

A work breakdown structure (WBS) is a tree diagram used to break down problems or projects into their components. It reduces "big and complex" issues down to "tiny and manageable" issues that a single project can address.

By breaking the process down into its components, we can recognize that there are really several subprocesses that would each require separate improvement strategies. Limiting our project to one or only a few closely related categories will lead to a better chance of project success. We will need to understand the potentials for each of these subprocesses in financial terms to justify a given project proposal.

WHEN TO USE

Define Stage

- To categorize the problems so the project can focus on one or more key areas (used in conjunction with Pareto analysis).
- To reduce the scope of the project to ensure completion in a reasonable time frame.

Analyze Stage

- To break down a problem into its potential components, to be addressed in the improve stage.

METHODOLOGY

At each level of the tree, brainstorm on categories for each element: How many different ways can this element occur?

For example, a project was developed to reduce the cycle time for a purchase order. A work breakdown structure was used to understand the process dynamics. In this case, the process can be broken down into approved and unapproved vendors, then by classification of the purchased items.

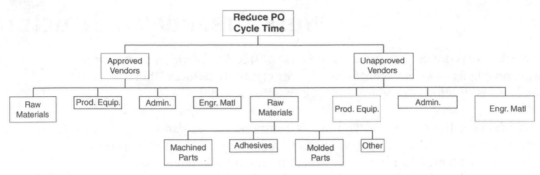

Figure F.59   Example of a work breakdown structure used to isolate the potential project issues.

INTERPRETATION

The output of the WBS will provide input into other tools, generally data collection tools like the Pareto diagram. In Figure F.59, after breaking down the elements of the purchase order process into the different types of products ordered, we would then want to consider which of these types are in most critical need for improvement.

X-Bar Charts

An X-bar chart, or $\bar{X}$ chart, is a control chart useful for variables data. The X-bar chart monitors the process location over time, based on the average of a collection of observations, called a subgroup.

X-bar charts are used with an accompanying chart for monitoring variation between observations in the subgroup over time: either the range chart or the sigma chart.

WHEN TO USE

Measure Stage

- To baseline the process by quantifying the common cause level of variation inherent to the process.
- As part of measurement systems analysis to evaluate repeatability and reproducibility.

Analyze Stage

- To differentiate between common and special causes of variation.

Improve Stage

- To verify the results of the process improvement on the process metric.

Control Stage

- To monitor the process to ensure the stability of the revised process and the continued benefit of the improvement.

X-bar charts are used when you can rationally collect measurements in groups (subgroups) of more than two observations. Each subgroup represents a "snapshot" of the process at a given point in time. The charts' x axes are time-based, so that the charts show a history of the process. For this reason, you must have data that is time-ordered, that is, entered in the sequence from which it was generated. If this is not the case, then trends or shifts in the process may not be detected, but instead attributed to random (common cause) variation.

For subgroup sizes greater than 10, use sigma charts in place of the range chart for monitoring process variation, since the range statistic is a poor estimator of process sigma for large subgroups. In fact, the subgroup sigma is always a better estimate of subgroup variation than subgroup range. The popularity of the range chart is only due to its ease of calculation, dating to its use before the advent of computers. For subgroup sizes equal to 1, an individual-X/moving range or EWMA chart can be used.

Averages are more sensitive to process shift than individual data observations. The distribution of subgroup averages for a given set of data is shown in the top distribution curve in Figure F.60. For the same data, the distribution of the observations making up the averages is shown in the bottom distribution curve. We can see that as we drift from the target, the distribution of the average moves from the target value more quickly, increasing our ability to detect the shift.

In fact, as seen by comparing the equations for each distribution (see below), the distribution of the averages is smaller than the distribution of the observations by a factor of 1 over the square root of n, the subgroup size. So for subgroups of size n equals 5, the distribution of the averages is 45% of the width of the distribution of the observations. This is a good reason to *never* show process specifications on an averages chart: the specifications apply to the observations, yet the distribution of the plotted averages will be much tighter even when there

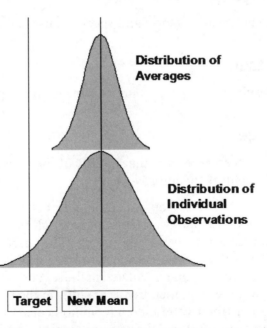

Figure F.60   Comparison of the distribution of process observations with that of the averages calculated from the observations.

are observations outside the specifications. Thus, the averages and the specifications are apples and oranges that cannot be directly compared.

$$\sigma_{\bar{x}} = \frac{\bar{R}}{d_2\sqrt{n}}$$

$$\sigma_x = \frac{\bar{R}}{d_2}$$

The sensitivity of X-bar charts to process shifts can be improved with the proper selection of subgroup size. The larger the subgroup, the more sensitive the chart will be to shifts, providing a rational subgroup can be formed.

Table T.27 shows the average number of subgroups necessary to detect the shift of size k (in standard deviation units) based on the subgroup size n. For example, if we observe the process a large number of times, then on average a subgroup of size $n = 3$ will detect a 1-sigma shift in 9 subgroups. As you can see from the table, small subgroups will readily detect relatively large shifts of

Table T.27. Average Number of Subgroups Required to Detect Shift of k Sigma with Subgroup Size of n.

n/k	0.5	1	1.5	2	2.5	3
1	155	43	14	6	3	1
2	90	17	5	2	1	1
3	60	9	2	1	1	1
4	43	6	1	1	1	1
5	33	4	1	1	1	1
6	26	3	1	1	1	1
7	21	2	1	1	1	1
8	17	2	1	1	1	1
9	14	1	1	1	1	1
10	12	1	1	1	1	1

Table T.28. Efficiency of Range of Statistic Relative to Sigma Statistic.

Subgroup Size (n)	Relative Efficiency
2	1.000
3	0.992
4	0.975
5	0.955
6	0.930
10	0.850

2 or 3 sigma, but are less capable of readily detecting smaller shifts. For more sensitivity to smaller process shifts, at a given subgroup size, a EWMA chart may be used.

Because it attempts to estimate the variation within the subgroup using only two of the observations in the subgroup (the smallest and largest), the range estimate of process variation is not as precise as the sigma statistic. The range chart should not be used for subgroup sizes larger than 10 due to its poor performance, as shown in Table T.27. Its popularity is largely due to its ease of use in days preceding the advent of computers. As seen in Table T.28, the sigma chart is a more efficient estimator of the standard deviation whenever the subgroup size is greater than 2 (Montgomery, 1991).

METHODOLOGY

After selecting a rational subgroup size and sampling frequency, as discussed in Statistical Process Control, we construct the X-bar and range charts (or X-bar and sigma charts) using the calculations shown below.

X-Bar Chart Calculations

Plotted statistic: subgroup average.

Centerline: grand average.

UCL, LCL (upper and lower control limit):

$$UCL_{xbar} = \bar{\bar{x}} + 3\left(\frac{\sigma_x}{\sqrt{n}}\right)$$

$$LCL_{xbar} = \bar{\bar{x}} - 3\left(\frac{\sigma_x}{\sqrt{n}}\right)$$

where $\bar{\bar{x}}$ is the grand average and σ_x is process sigma, which is calculated using the subgroup range or subgroup sigma statistic.

Note: Some authors prefer to write this as:

$$UCL_x = \bar{x} + A_2\bar{R}$$
$$LCL_x = \bar{x} - A_2\bar{R}$$

where $\bar{R}$ is the average range, or

$$UCL_x = \bar{x} + A_3\bar{S}$$
$$LCL_x = \bar{x} - A_3\bar{S}$$

where $\bar{S}$ is the average sigma.

Range Chart Calculations

Plotted statistic:

$$\text{Range}_j = \text{MAX}(x_1, x_2, \ldots, x_n) - \text{MIN}(x_1, x_2, \ldots, x_n)$$

where $x_1, x_2, \ldots$ are the n observations in the subgroup j

Centerline: average range.

UCL, LCL (upper and lower control limit):

$$UCL_R = \bar{R} + 3d_3\sigma_x$$
$$LCL_R = \max(0, \bar{R} - 3d_3\sigma_x)$$

where $\bar{R}$ is the average range, d_3 is a function of n (tabulated in Appendix 6), and σ_x is process sigma, which is calculated using the average range as $\bar{R}/d_2$.

Note: Some authors prefer to write this as:

$$UCL_R = \bar{R}D_4$$
$$LCL_R = \bar{R}D_3$$

where D_3 and D_4 are a function of n (tabulated in Appendix 6).

Sigma Chart Calculations

Plotted statistic: the subgroup standard deviation:

$$S_j = \sqrt{\frac{\sum_{i=1}^{n}(x_i - \bar{x}_j)^2}{n-1}}$$

where x_i are the observations in subgroup j, $\bar{x}_j$ is the subgroup average for subgroup j, and n is the subgroup size.

Centerline: average sigma.

UCL, LCL (upper and lower control limit):

$$UCL_S = \bar{S} + 3\left(\frac{\bar{S}}{c_4}\right)\sqrt{1 - c_4^2}$$

$$LCL_S = MIN\left(0, \bar{S} - 3(\bar{S}/c_4)\sqrt{1 - c_4^2}\right)$$

where $\bar{S}$ is the average sigma, c_4 is a function of n (tabulated in Appendix 6).

Note: Some authors prefer to write this as:

$$UCL_S = \bar{S}B_4$$
$$LCL_S = \bar{S}B_3$$

where B_3 and B_4 are a function of n (tabulated in Appendix 6).

INTERPRETATION

Always look at the range (or sigma) chart first. The control limits on the X-bar chart are derived from the average range (or average sigma), so if the range (or sigma) chart is out of control, then the control limits on the X-bar chart are meaningless.

Interpreting the Range (or Sigma) Chart

On the range (or sigma) chart, look for out-of-control points. If there are any, then the special causes must be eliminated. Brainstorm and conduct designed experiments to find those process elements that contribute to sporadic changes in variation. To predict the capability of the process after special causes have been eliminated, you should remove the out-of-control points from the analysis, which will remove the statistical bias of the out-of-control points by dropping them from the calculations of the average range (or sigma), the range (or sigma) control limits, and the X-bar control limits.

Also on the range (or sigma) chart, there should be more than five distinct values plotted, and no one value should appear more than 25% of the time. If values are repeated too often, then you have inadequate resolution of your measurements, which will adversely affect your control limit calculations. In this case, you'll have to look at how you measure the variable and try to measure it more precisely.

Once you've removed the effect of the out-of-control points from the range (or sigma) chart, the X-bar chart can be analyzed.

Interpreting the X-Bar Chart

After reviewing the range (or sigma) chart, interpret the points on the X-bar chart relative to the control limits and run test rules. Never consider the points on the X-bar chart relative to specifications, since the observations from the process vary much more than the subgroup averages.

If there are any out-of-control points on the X-bar chart, then the special causes must be eliminated. Brainstorm and conduct designed experiments to find those process elements that contribute to sporadic changes in process location. To predict the capability of the process after special causes have been eliminated, you should remove the out-of-control points from the analysis, which will remove the statistical bias of the out-of-control points by dropping them from the calculations of X-doublebar and the X-bar control limits.

Look for obviously nonrandom behavior. Use the run test rules, which apply statistical tests for trends to the plotted points.

If the process shows control relative to the statistical limits and run tests for a sufficient period of time (long enough to see all potential special causes), then we can analyze its capability relative to requirements. Capability is only meaningful when the process is stable, since we cannot predict the outcome of an unstable process.

Appendices

Appendix 1

Area Under the Standard Normal Curve

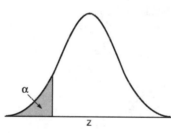

z	0.00	0.01	0.02	0.03	0.04	0.05	0.06	0.07	0.08	0.09
− 3.4	0.0003	0.0003	0.0003	0.0003	0.0003	0.0003	0.0003	0.0003	0.0003	0.0002
− 3.3	0.0005	0.0005	0.0005	0.0004	0.0004	0.0004	0.0004	0.0004	0.0004	0.0003
− 3.2	0.0007	0.0007	0.0006	0.0006	0.0006	0.0006	0.0006	0.0005	0.0005	0.0005
− 3.1	0.0010	0.0009	0.0009	0.0009	0.0008	0.0008	0.0008	0.0008	0.0007	0.0007
− 3.0	0.0013	0.0013	0.0013	0.0012	0.0012	0.0011	0.0011	0.0011	0.0010	0.0010

Continued on next page . . .

Continued...

z	0.00	0.01	0.02	0.03	0.04	0.05	0.06	0.07	0.08	0.09
−2.9	0.0019	0.0018	0.0018	0.0017	0.0016	0.0016	0.0015	0.0015	0.0014	0.0014
−2.8	0.0026	0.0025	0.0024	0.0023	0.0023	0.0022	0.0021	0.0021	0.0020	0.0019
−2.7	0.0035	0.0034	0.0033	0.0032	0.0031	0.0030	0.0029	0.0028	0.0027	0.0026
−2.6	0.0047	0.0045	0.0044	0.0043	0.0041	0.0040	0.0039	0.0038	0.0037	0.0036
−2.5	0.0062	0.0060	0.0059	0.0057	0.0055	0.0054	0.0052	0.0051	0.0049	0.0048
−2.4	0.0082	0.0080	0.0078	0.0075	0.0073	0.0071	0.0069	0.0068	0.0066	0.0064
−2.3	0.0107	0.0104	0.0102	0.0090	0.0096	0.0094	0.0091	0.0089	0.0087	0.0084
−2.2	0.0139	0.0136	0.0132	0.0129	0.0125	0.0122	0.0119	0.0116	0.0113	0.0110
−2.1	0.0179	0.0174	0.0170	0.0166	0.0162	0.0158	0.0154	0.0150	0.0146	0.0143
−2.0	0.0228	0.0222	0.0217	0.0212	0.0207	0.0202	0.0197	0.0192	0.0188	0.0183
−1.9	0.0287	0.0281	0.0274	0.0268	0.0262	0.0256	0.0250	0.0244	0.0239	0.0233
−1.8	0.0359	0.0351	0.0344	0.0336	0.0329	0.0322	0.0314	0.0307	0.0301	0.0294
−1.7	0.0446	0.0436	0.0427	0.0418	0.0409	0.0401	0.0392	0.0384	0.0375	0.0367
−1.6	0.0548	0.0537	0.0526	0.0516	0.0505	0.0495	0.0485	0.0475	0.0465	0.0455
−1.5	0.0668	0.0655	0.0643	0.0630	0.0618	0.0606	0.0594	0.0582	0.0571	0.0559
−1.4	0.0808	0.0793	0.0778	0.0764	0.0749	0.0735	0.0721	0.0708	0.0694	0.0681
−1.3	0.0968	0.0951	0.0934	0.0918	0.0901	0.0885	0.0869	0.0853	0.0838	0.0823
−1.2	0.1151	0.1131	0.1112	0.1093	0.1075	0.1056	0.1038	0.1020	0.1003	0.0985
−1.1	0.1357	0.1335	0.1314	0.1292	0.1271	0.1251	0.1230	0.1210	0.1190	0.1170
−1.0	0.1587	0.1562	0.1539	0.1515	0.1492	0.1469	0.1446	0.1423	0.1401	0.1379
−0.9	0.1841	0.1814	0.1788	0.1762	0.1736	0.1711	0.1685	0.1660	0.1635	0.1611
−0.8	0.2119	0.2090	0.2061	0.2033	0.2005	0.1977	0.1949	0.1922	0.1894	0.1867
−0.7	0.2420	0.2389	0.2358	0.2327	0.2296	0.2266	0.2236	0.2206	0.2177	0.2148
−0.6	0.2743	0.2709	0.2676	0.2643	0.2611	0.2578	0.2546	0.2514	0.2483	0.2451
−0.5	0.3085	0.3050	0.3015	0.2981	0.2946	0.2912	0.2877	0.2843	0.2810	0.2776
−0.4	0.3446	0.3409	0.3372	0.3336	0.3300	0.3264	0.3228	0.3192	0.3156	0.3121
−0.3	0.3821	0.3783	0.3745	0.3707	0.3669	0.3632	0.3594	0.3557	0.3520	0.3483
−0.2	0.4207	0.4168	0.4129	0.4090	0.4052	0.4013	0.3974	0.3936	0.3897	0.3859
−0.1	0.4602	0.4562	0.4522	0.4483	0.4443	0.4404	0.4364	0.4325	0.4286	0.4247
−0.0	0.5000	0.4960	0.4920	0.4880	0.4840	0.4801	0.4761	0.4721	0.4681	0.4641
0.0	0.5000	0.5040	0.5080	0.5120	0.5160	0.5199	0.5239	0.5279	0.5319	0.5359
0.1	0.5398	0.5438	0.5478	0.5517	0.5557	0.5596	0.5636	0.5675	0.5714	0.5753
0.2	0.5793	0.5832	0.5871	0.5910	0.5948	0.5987	0.6026	0.6064	0.6103	0.6141
0.3	0.6179	0.6217	0.6255	0.6293	0.6331	0.6368	0.6406	0.6443	0.6480	0.6517
0.4	0.6554	0.6591	0.6628	0.6664	0.6700	0.6736	0.6772	0.6808	0.6844	0.6879

Continued on next page...

Continued...

z	0.00	0.01	0.02	0.03	0.04	0.05	0.06	0.07	0.08	0.09
0.5	0.6915	0.6950	0.6985	0.7019	0.7054	0.7088	0.7123	0.7157	0.7190	0.7224
0.6	0.7257	0.7291	0.7324	0.7357	0.7389	0.7422	0.7454	0.7486	0.7517	0.7549
0.7	0.7580	0.7611	0.7642	0.7673	0.7704	0.7734	0.7764	0.7794	0.7823	0.7852
0.8	0.7881	0.7910	0.7939	0.7967	0.7995	0.8023	0.8051	0.8078	0.8106	0.8133
0.9	0.8159	0.8186	0.8212	0.8238	0.8264	0.8289	0.8315	0.8340	0.8365	0.8389
1.0	0.8413	0.8438	0.8461	0.8485	0.8508	0.8531	0.8554	0.8577	0.8599	0.8621
1.1	0.8643	0.8665	0.8686	0.8708	0.8729	0.8749	0.8770	0.8790	0.8810	0.8830
1.2	0.8849	0.8869	0.8888	0.8907	0.8925	0.8944	0.8962	0.8980	0.8997	0.9015
1.3	0.9032	0.9049	0.9066	0.9082	0.9099	0.9115	0.9131	0.9147	0.9162	0.9177
1.4	0.9192	0.9207	0.9222	0.9236	0.9251	0.9265	0.9279	0.9292	0.9306	0.9319
1.5	0.9332	0.9345	0.9357	0.9370	0.9382	0.9394	0.9406	0.9418	0.9429	0.9441
1.6	0.9452	0.9463	0.9474	0.9484	0.9495	0.9505	0.9515	0.9525	0.9535	0.9545
1.7	0.9554	0.9564	0.9573	0.9582	0.9591	0.9599	0.9608	0.9616	0.9625	0.9633
1.8	0.9641	0.9649	0.9656	0.9664	0.9671	0.9678	0.9686	0.9693	0.9699	0.9706
1.9	0.9713	0.9719	0.9726	0.9732	0.9738	0.9744	0.9750	0.9756	0.9761	0.9767
2.0	0.9772	0.9778	0.9783	0.9788	0.9793	0.9798	0.9803	0.9808	0.9812	0.9817
2.1	0.9821	0.9826	0.9830	0.9834	0.9838	0.9842	0.9846	0.9850	0.9854	0.9857
2.2	0.9861	0.9864	0.9868	0.9871	0.9875	0.9878	0.9881	0.9884	0.9887	0.9890
2.3	0.9893	0.9896	0.9898	0.9901	0.9904	0.9906	0.9909	0.9911	0.9913	0.9916
2.4	0.9918	0.9920	0.9922	0.9925	0.9927	0.9929	0.9931	0.9932	0.9934	0.9936
2.5	0.9938	0.9940	0.9941	0.9943	0.9945	0.9946	0.9948	0.9949	0.9951	0.9952
2.6	0.9953	0.9955	0.9956	0.9957	0.9959	0.9960	0.9961	0.9962	0.9963	0.9964
2.7	0.9965	0.9966	0.9967	0.9968	0.9969	0.9970	0.9971	0.9972	0.9973	0.9974
2.8	0.9974	0.9975	0.9976	0.9977	0.9977	0.9978	0.9979	0.9979	0.9980	0.9981
2.9	0.9981	0.9982	0.9982	0.9983	0.9984	0.9984	0.9985	0.9985	0.9986	0.9986
3.0	0.9987	0.9987	0.9987	0.9988	0.9988	0.9989	0.9989	0.9989	0.9990	0.9990
3.1	0.9990	0.9991	0.9991	0.9991	0.9992	0.9992	0.9992	0.9992	0.9993	0.9993
3.2	0.9993	0.9993	0.9994	0.9994	0.9994	0.9994	0.9994	0.9995	0.9995	0.9995
3.3	0.9995	0.9995	0.9995	0.9996	0.9996	0.9996	0.9996	0.9996	0.9996	0.9997
3.4	0.9997	0.9997	0.9997	0.9997	0.9997	0.9997	0.9997	0.9997	0.9997	0.9998

Appendix 2

Critical Values of the t Distribution

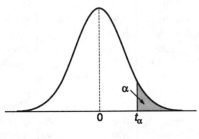

df	α				
	0.1	0.05	0.025	0.01	0.005
1	3.078	6.314	12.706	31.821	63.657
2	1.886	2.920	4.303	6.965	9.925
3	1.638	2.353	3.182	4.541	5.841
4	1.533	2.132	2.776	3.747	4.604
5	1.476	2.015	2.571	3.365	4.032

Continued on next page . . .

Continued...

df	α				
	0.1	0.05	0.025	0.01	0.005
6	1.440	1.943	2.447	3.143	3.707
7	1.415	1.895	2.365	2.998	3.499
8	1.397	1.860	2.306	2.896	3.355
9	1.383	1.833	2.262	2.821	3.250
10	1.372	1.812	2.228	2.764	3.169
11	1.363	1.796	2.201	2.718	3.106
12	1.356	1.782	2.179	2.681	3.055
13	1.350	1.771	2.160	2.650	3.012
14	1.345	1.761	2.145	2.624	2.977
15	1.341	1.753	2.131	2.602	2.947
16	1.337	1.746	2.120	2.583	2.921
17	1.333	1.740	2.110	2.567	2.898
18	1.330	1.734	2.101	2.552	2.878
19	1.328	1.729	2.093	2.539	2.861
20	1.325	1.725	2.086	2.528	2.845
21	1.323	1.721	2.080	2.518	2.831
22	1.321	1.717	2.074	2.508	2.819
23	1.319	1.714	2.069	2.500	2.807
24	1.318	1.711	2.064	2.492	2.797
25	1.316	1.708	2.060	2.485	2.787
26	1.315	1.706	2.056	2.479	2.779
27	1.314	1.703	2.052	2.473	2.771
28	1.313	1.701	2.048	2.467	2.763
29	1.311	1.699	2.045	2.462	2.756
∞	1.282	1.645	1.960	2.326	2.576

Appendix 3

Chi-Square Distribution

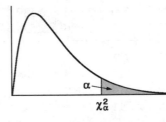

	α									
γ	0.995	0.99	0.98	0.975	0.95	0.90	0.80	0.75	0.70	0.50
1	0.00004	0.000	0.001	0.001	0.004	0.016	0.064	0.102	0.148	0.455
2	0.0100	0.020	0.040	0.051	0.103	0.211	0.446	0.575	0.713	1.386
3	0.0717	0.115	0.185	0.216	0.352	0.584	1.005	1.213	1.424	2.366
4	0.207	0.297	0.429	0.484	0.711	1.064	1.649	1.923	2.195	3.357
5	0.412	0.554	0.752	0.831	1.145	1.610	2.343	2.675	3.000	4.351

Continued on next page . . .

Continued...

γ	α									
	0.995	0.99	0.98	0.975	0.95	0.90	0.80	0.75	0.70	0.50
6	0.676	0.872	1.134	1.237	1.635	2.204	3.070	3.455	3.828	5.348
7	0.989	1.239	1.564	1.690	2.167	2.833	3.822	4.255	4.671	6.346
8	1.344	1.646	2.032	2.180	2.733	3.490	4.594	5.071	5.527	7.344
9	1.735	2.088	2.532	2.700	3.325	4.168	5.380	5.899	6.393	8.343
10	2.156	2.558	3.059	3.247	3.940	4.865	6.179	6.737	7.267	9.342
11	2.603	3.053	3.609	3.816	4.575	5.578	6.989	7.584	8.148	10.341
12	3.074	3.571	4.178	4.404	5.226	6.304	7.807	8.438	9.034	11.340
13	3.565	4.107	4.765	5.009	5.892	7.042	8.634	9.299	9.926	12.340
14	4.075	4.660	5.368	5.629	6.571	7.790	9.467	10.165	10.821	13.339
15	4.601	5.229	5.985	6.262	7.261	8.547	10.307	11.037	11.721	14.339
16	5.142	5.812	6.614	6.908	7.962	9.312	11.152	11.912	12.624	15.338
17	5.697	6.408	7.255	7.564	8.672	10.085	12.002	12.792	13.531	16.338
18	6.265	7.015	7.906	8.231	9.390	10.865	12.857	13.675	14.440	17.338
19	6.844	7.633	8.567	8.907	10.117	11.651	13.716	14.562	15.352	18.338
20	7.434	8.260	9.237	9.591	10.851	12.443	14.578	15.452	16.266	19.337
21	8.034	8.897	9.915	10.283	11.591	13.240	15.445	16.344	17.182	20.337
22	8.643	9.542	10.600	10.982	12.338	14.041	16.314	17.240	18.101	20.337
23	9.260	10.196	11.293	11.689	13.091	14.848	17.187	18.137	19.021	22.337
24	9.886	10.856	11.992	12.401	13.848	15.659	18.062	19.037	19.943	23.337
25	10.520	11.524	12.697	13.120	14.611	16.473	18.940	19.939	20.867	24.337
26	11.160	12.198	13.409	13.844	15.379	17.292	19.820	20.843	21.792	25.336
27	11.808	12.879	14.125	14.573	16.151	18.114	20.703	21.749	22.719	26.336
28	12.461	13.565	14.847	15.308	16.928	18.939	21.588	22.657	23.647	27.336
29	13.121	14.256	15.574	16.047	17.708	19.768	22.475	23.567	23.577	28.336
30	13.787	14.953	16.306	16.791	18.493	20.599	23.364	24.478	25.508	29.336

Continued on next page...

Continued...

γ	α									
	0.30	0.25	0.20	0.10	0.05	0.025	0.02	0.01	0.005	0.001
1	1.074	1.323	1.642	2.706	3.841	5.024	5.412	6.635	7.879	10.828
2	2.408	2.773	3.219	4.605	5.991	7.378	7.824	9.210	10.597	13.816
3	3.665	4.108	4.642	6.251	7.815	9.348	9.837	11.345	12.838	16.266
4	4.878	5.385	5.989	7.779	9.488	11.143	11.668	13.277	14.860	18.467
5	6.064	6.626	7.289	9.236	11.070	12.833	13.388	15.086	16.750	20.515
6	7.231	7.841	8.558	10.645	12.592	14.449	15.033	16.812	18.548	22.458
7	8.383	9.037	9.803	12.017	14.067	16.013	16.622	18.475	20.278	24.322
8	9.524	10.219	11.030	13.362	15.507	17.535	18.168	20.090	21.955	26.124
9	10.656	11.389	12.242	14.684	16.919	19.023	19.679	21.666	23.589	27.877
10	11.781	12.549	13.442	15.987	18.307	20.483	21.161	23.209	25.188	29.588
11	12.899	13.701	14.631	17.275	19.675	21.920	22.618	24.725	26.757	31.264
12	14.011	14.845	15.812	18.549	21.026	23.337	24.054	26.217	28.300	32.909
13	15.119	15.984	16.985	19.812	22.362	24.736	25.472	27.688	29.819	34.528
14	16.222	17.117	18.151	21.064	23.685	26.119	26.873	29.141	31.319	36.123
15	17.322	18.245	19.311	22.307	24.996	27.488	28.259	30.578	32.801	37.697
16	18.418	19.369	20.465	23.542	26.296	28.845	29.633	32.000	34.267	39.252
17	19.511	20.489	21.615	24.769	27.587	30.191	30.995	33.409	35.718	40.790
18	20.601	21.605	22.760	25.989	28.869	31.526	32.346	34.805	37.156	42.312
19	21.689	22.718	23.900	27.204	30.144	32.852	33.687	36.191	38.582	43.820
20	22.775	23.828	25.038	28.412	31.410	34.170	35.020	37.566	39.997	45.315
21	23.858	24.935	26.171	29.615	32.671	35.479	36.343	38.932	41.401	46.797
22	24.939	26.039	27.301	30.813	33.924	36.781	37.659	40.289	42.796	48.268
23	26.018	27.141	28.429	32.007	35.172	38.076	38.968	41.638	44.181	49.728
24	27.096	28.241	29.553	33.196	36.415	39.364	40.270	42.980	45.559	51.179
25	28.172	29.339	30.675	34.382	37.652	40.646	41.566	44.314	46.928	52.620
26	29.246	30.435	31.795	35.563	38.885	41.923	42.856	45.642	48.290	54.052
27	30.319	31.528	32.912	36.741	40.113	43.195	44.140	46.963	49.645	55.476
28	31.391	32.620	34.027	37.916	41.337	44.461	45.419	48.278	50.993	56.892
29	32.461	33.711	35.139	39.087	42.557	45.722	46.693	49.588	52.336	58.301
30	33.530	34.800	36.250	40.256	43.773	46.979	47.962	50.892	53.672	59.703

Appendix 4

F Distribution ($\alpha = 1\%$)

$$F_{.99}\ (n_1, n_2)$$
n_1 = degrees of freedom for numerator n_2 = degrees of freedom for denominator

n_2 \ n_1	1	2	3	4	5	6	7	8	9	10
1	4052	4999.5	5403	5625	5764	5859	5928	5982	6022	6056
2	98.50	99.00	99.17	99.25	99.30	99.33	99.36	99.37	99.39	99.40
3	34.12	30.82	29.46	28.71	28.24	27.91	27.67	27.49	27.35	27.23
4	21.20	18.00	16.69	15.98	15.52	15.21	14.98	14.80	14 66	14.55
5	16.26	13.27	12.06	11.39	10.97	10.67	10.46	10.29	10.16	10.05
6	13.75	10.92	9.78	9.15	8.75	8.47	8.26	8.10	7.98	7.87
7	12.25	9.55	8.45	7.85	7.46	7.19	6.99	6.84	6.72	6.62
8	11.26	8.65	7.59	7.01	6.63	6.37	6.18	6.03	5.91	5.81
9	10.56	8.02	6.99	6.42	6.06	5.80	5.61	5.47	5.35	5.26
10	10.04	7.56	6.55	5.99	5.64	5.39	5.20	5.06	4.94	4.85
11	9.65	7.21	6.22	5.67	5.32	5.07	4.89	4.74	4.63	4.54
12	9.33	6.93	5.95	5.41	5.06	4.82	4.64	4.50	4.39	4.30
13	9.07	6.70	5.74	5.21	4.86	4.62	4.44	4.30	4.19	4.10
14	8.86	6.51	5.56	5.04	4.69	4.46	4.28	4.14	4.03	3.94

Continued on next page . . .

Continued...

$$F_{.99}(n_1, n_2)$$

$n_1 = $ degrees of freedom for numerator $n_2 = $ degrees of freedom for denominator

n_2 \ n_1	1	2	3	4	5	6	7	8	9	10
15	8.68	6.36	5.42	4.89	4.56	4.32	4.14	4.00	3.89	3.80
16	8.53	6.23	5.29	4.77	4.44	4.20	4.03	3.89	3.78	3.69
17	8.40	6.11	5.18	4.67	4.34	4.10	3.93	3.79	3.68	3.59
18	8.29	6.01	5.09	4.58	4.25	4.01	3.84	3.71	3.60	3.51
19	8.18	5.93	5.01	4.50	4.17	3.94	3.77	3.63	3.52	3.43
20	8.10	5.85	4.94	4.43	4.10	3.87	3.70	3.56	3.46	3.37
21	8.02	5.78	4.87	4.37	4.04	3.81	3.64	3.51	3.40	3.31
22	7.95	5.72	4.82	4.31	3.99	3.76	3.59	3.45	3.35	3.26
23	7.88	5.66	4.76	4.26	3.94	3.71	3.54	3.41	3.30	3.21
24	7.82	5.61	4.72	4.22	3.90	3.67	3.50	3.36	3.26	3.17
25	7.77	5.57	4.68	4.18	3.85	3.63	3.46	3.32	3.22	3.13
26	7.72	5.53	4.64	4.14	3.82	3.59	3.42	3.29	3.18	3.09
27	7.68	5.49	4.60	4.11	3.78	3.56	3.39	3.26	3.15	3.06
28	7.64	5.45	4.57	4.07	3.75	3.53	3.36	3.23	3.12	3.03
29	7.60	5.42	4.54	4.04	3.73	3.50	3.33	3.20	3.09	3.00
30	7.56	5.39	4.51	4.02	3.70	3.47	3.30	3.17	3.07	2.98
40	7.31	5.18	4.31	3.83	3.51	3.29	3.12	2.99	2.89	2.80
60	7.08	4.98	4.13	3.65	3.34	3.12	2.95	2.82	2.72	2.63
120	6.85	4.79	3.95	3.48	3.17	2.96	2.79	2.66	2.56	2.47
∞	6.63	4.61	3.78	3.32	3.02	2.80	2.64	2.51	2.41	2.32

Continued on next page...

Continued...

$$F_{.99} (n_1, n_2)$$

$n_1 =$ degrees of freedom for numerator $n_2 =$ degrees of freedom for denominator

n_2 \ n_1	12	15	20	24	30	40	60	120	∞
1	6106	6157	6209	6235	6261	6287	6313	6339	6366
2	99.42	99.43	99.45	99.46	99.47	99.47	99.48	99.49	99.50
3	27.05	26.87	26.69	26.60	26.50	26.41	26.32	26.22	26.13
4	14.37	14.20	14.02	13.93	13.84	13.75	13.65	13.56	13.46
5	9.89	9.72	9.55	9.47	9.38	9.29	9.20	9.11	9.02
6	7.72	7.56	7.40	7.31	7.23	7.14	7.06	6.97	6.88
7	6.47	6.31	6.16	6.07	5.99	5.91	5.82	5.74	5.65
8	5.67	5.52	5.36	5.28	5.20	5.12	5.03	4.95	4.86
9	5.11	4.96	4.81	4.73	4.65	4.57	4.48	4.40	4.31
10	4.71	4.56	4.41	4.33	4.25	4.17	4.08	4.00	3.91
11	4.40	4.25	4.10	4.02	3.94	3.86	3.78	3.69	3.60
12	4.16	4.01	3.86	3.78	3.70	3.62	3.54	3.45	3.36
13	3.96	3.82	3.66	3.59	3.51	3.43	3.34	3.25	3.17
14	3.80	3.66	3.51	3.43	3.35	3.27	3.18	3.09	3.00
15	3.67	3.52	3.37	3.29	3.21	3.13	3.05	2.96	2.87
16	3.55	3.41	3.26	3.18	3.10	3.02	2.93	2.84	2.75
17	3.46	3.31	3.16	3.08	3.00	2.92	2.83	2.75	2.65
18	3.37	3.23	3.08	3.00	2.92	2.84	2.75	2.66	2.57
19	3.30	3.15	3.00	2.92	2.84	2.76	2.67	2.58	2.49
20	3.23	3.09	2.94	2.86	2.78	2.69	2.61	2.52	2.42
21	3.17	3.03	2.88	2.80	2.72	2.64	2.55	2.46	2.36
22	3.12	2.98	2.83	2.75	2.67	2.58	2.50	2.40	2.31
23	3.07	2.93	2.78	2.70	2.62	2.54	2.45	2.35	2.26
24	3.03	2.89	2.74	2.66	2.58	2.49	2.40	2.31	2.21
25	2.99	2.85	2.70	2.62	2.54	2.45	2.36	2.27	2.17
26	2.96	2.81	2.66	2.58	2.50	2.42	2.33	2.23	2.13
27	2.93	2.78	2.63	2.55	2.47	2.38	2.29	2.20	2.10
28	2.90	2.75	2.60	2.52	2.44	2.35	2.26	2.17	2.06
29	2.87	2.73	2.57	2.49	2.41	2.33	2.23	2.14	2.03
30	2.84	2.70	2.55	2.47	2.39	2.30	2.21	2.11	2.01
40	2.66	2.52	2.37	2.29	2.20	2.11	2.02	1.92	1.80
60	2.50	2.35	2.20	2.12	2.03	1.94	1.84	1.73	1.60
120	2.34	2.19	2.03	1.95	1.86	1.76	1.66	1.53	1.38
∞	2.18	2.04	1.88	1.79	1.70	1.59	1.47	1.32	1.00

Appendix 5

F Distribution ($\alpha = 5\%$)

$$F_{.95}(n_1, n_2)$$

n_1 = degrees of freedom for numerator n_2 = degrees of freedom for denominator

n_2 \ n_1	1	2	3	4	5	6	7	8	9	10
1	161.4	199.5	215.7	224.6	230.2	234.0	236.8	238.9	240.5	241.9
2	18.51	19.00	19.16	19.25	19.30	19.33	19.35	19.37	19.38	19.40
3	10.13	9.55	9.28	9.12	9.01	8.94	8.89	8.85	8.81	8.79
4	7.71	6.94	6.59	6.39	6.26	6.16	6.09	6.04	6.00	5.96
5	6.61	5.79	5.41	5.19	5.05	4.95	4.88	4.82	4.77	4.74
6	5.99	5.14	4.76	4.53	4.39	4.28	4.21	4.15	4.10	4.06
7	5.59	4.47	4.35	4.12	3.97	3.87	3.79	3.73	3.68	3.64
8	5.32	4.46	4.07	3.84	3.69	3.58	3.50	3.44	3.39	3.35
9	5.12	4.26	3.86	3.63	3.48	3.37	3.29	3.23	3.18	3.14
10	4.96	4.10	3.71	3.48	3.33	3.22	3.14	3.07	3.02	2.98
11	4.84	3.98	3.59	3.36	3.20	3.09	3.01	2.95	2.90	2.85
12	4.75	3.89	3.49	3.26	3.11	3.00	2.91	2.85	2.80	2.75
13	4.67	3.81	3.41	3.18	3.03	2.92	2.83	2.77	2.71	2.67
14	4.60	3.74	3.34	3.11	2.96	2.85	2.76	2.70	2.65	2.60

Continued on next page . . .

Continued...

$$F_{.95}(n_1, n_2)$$

n_1 = degrees of freedom for numerator n_2 = degrees of freedom for denominator

n_2 \ n_1	1	2	3	4	5	6	7	8	9	10
15	4.54	3.68	3.29	3.06	2.90	2.79	2.71	2.64	2.59	2.54
16	4.49	3.63	3.24	3.01	2.85	2.74	2.66	2.59	2.54	2.49
17	4.45	3.59	3.20	2.96	2.81	2.70	2.61	2.55	2.49	2.45
18	4.41	3.55	3.16	2.93	2.77	2.66	2.58	2.51	2.46	2.41
19	4.38	3.52	3.13	2.90	2.74	2.63	2.54	2.48	2.42	2.38
20	4.35	3.49	3.10	2.87	2.71	2.60	2.51	2.45	2.39	2.35
21	4.32	3.47	3.07	2.84	2.68	2.57	2.49	2.42	2.37	2.32
22	4.30	3.44	3.05	2.82	2.66	2.55	2.46	2.40	2.34	2.30
23	4.28	3.42	3.03	2.80	2.64	2.53	2.44	2.37	2.32	2.27
24	4.26	3.40	3.01	2.78	2.62	2.51	2.42	2.36	2.30	2.25
25	4.24	3.39	2.99	2.76	2.60	2.49	2.40	2.34	2.28	2.24
26	4.23	3.37	2.98	2.74	2.59	2.47	2.39	2.32	2.27	2.22
27	4.21	3.35	2.96	2.73	2.57	2.46	2.37	2.31	2.25	2.20
28	4.20	3.34	2.95	2.71	2.56	2.45	2.36	2.29	2.24	2.19
29	4.18	3.33	2.93	2.70	2.55	2.43	2.35	2.28	2.22	2.18
30	4.17	3.32	2.92	2.69	2.53	2.42	2.33	2.27	2.21	2.16
40	4.08	3.23	2.84	2.61	2.45	2.34	2.25	2.18	2.12	2.08
60	4.00	3.15	2.76	2.53	2.37	2.25	2.17	2.10	2.04	1.99
120	3.92	3.07	2.68	2.45	2.29	2.17	2.09	2.02	1.96	1.91
∞	3.84	3.00	2.60	2.37	2.21	2.10	2.01	1.94	1.88	1.83

Continued on next page...

Continued...

$F_{.99}(n_1, n_2)$

n_1 = degrees of freedom for numerator n_2 = degrees of freedom for denominator

$n_2 \backslash n_1$	12	15	20	24	30	40	60	120	∞
1	243.9	245.9	248.0	249.1	250.1	251.1	252.2	253.2	254.3
2	19.41	19.43	19.45	19.45	19.46	19.47	19.48	19.49	19.50
3	8.74	8.70	8.66	8.64	8.62	8.59	8.57	8.55	8.53
4	5.91	5.86	5.80	5.77	5.75	5.72	5.69	5.66	5.63
5	4.68	4.62	4.56	4.53	4.50	4.46	4.43	4.40	4.36
6	4.00	3.94	3.87	3.84	3.81	3.77	3.74	3.70	3.67
7	3.57	3.51	3.44	3.41	3.38	3.34	3.30	3.27	3.23
8	3.28	3.22	3.15	3.12	3.08	3.04	3.01	2.97	2.93
9	3.07	3.01	2.94	2.90	2.86	2.83	2.79	2.75	2.71
10	2.91	2.85	2.77	2.74	2.70	2.66	2.62	2.58	2.54
11	2.79	2.72	2.65	2.61	2.57	2.53	2.49	2.45	2.40
12	2.69	2.62	2.54	2.51	2.47	2.43	2.38	2.34	2.30
13	2.60	2.53	2.46	2.42	2.38	2.34	2.30	2.25	2.21
14	2.53	2.46	2.39	2.35	2.31	2.27	2.22	2.18	2.13
15	2.48	2.40	2.33	2.29	2.25	2.20	2.16	2.11	2.07
16	2.42	2.35	2.28	2.24	2.19	2.15	2.11	2.06	2.01
17	2.38	2.31	2.23	2.19	2.15	2.10	2.06	2.01	1.96
18	2.34	2.27	2.19	2.15	2.11	2.06	2.02	1.97	1.92
19	2.31	2.23	2.16	2.11	2.07	2.03	1.98	1.93	1.88
20	2.28	2.20	2.12	2.08	2.04	1.99	1.95	1.90	1.84
21	2.25	2.18	2.10	2.05	2.01	1.96	1.92	1.87	1.81
22	2.23	2.15	2.07	2.03	1.98	1.94	1.89	1.84	1.78
23	2.20	2.13	2.05	2.01	1.96	1.91	1.86	1.81	1.76
24	2.18	2.11	2.03	1.98	1.94	1.89	1.84	1.79	1.73
25	2.16	2.09	2.01	1.96	1.92	1.87	1.82	1.77	1.71
26	2.15	2.07	1.99	1.95	1.90	1.85	1.80	1.75	1.69
27	2.13	2.06	1.97	1.93	1.88	1.84	1.79	1.73	1.67
28	2.12	2.04	1.96	1.91	1.87	1.82	1.77	1.71	1.65
29	2.10	2.03	1.94	1.90	1.85	1.81	1.75	1.70	1.64
30	2.09	2.01	1.93	1.89	1.84	1.79	1.74	1.68	1.62
40	2.00	1.92	1.84	1.79	1.74	1.69	1.64	1.58	1.51
60	1.92	1.84	1.75	1.70	1.65	1.59	1.53	1.47	1.39
120	1.83	1.75	1.66	1.61	1.55	1.50	1.43	1.35	1.25
∞	1.75	1.67	1.57	1.52	1.46	1.39	1.32	1.22	1.00

Appendix 6

Control Chart Constants

CHART FOR AVERAGE			CHART FOR STANDARD DEVIATIONS					
Factors for Control Limits			Factors for Central Line		Factors for Control Limits			
A	A_2	A_3	c_4	$1/c_4$	B_3	B_4	B_5	B_6
2.121	1.880	2.659	0.7979	1.2533	0	3.267	0	2.606
1.732	1.023	1.954	0.8862	1.1284	0	2.568	0	2.276
1.500	0.729	1.628	0.9213	1.0854	0	2.266	0	2.088
1.342	0.577	1.427	0.9400	1.0638	0	2.089	0	1.964
1.225	0.483	1.287	0.9515	1.0510	0.030	1.970	0.029	1.874
1.134	0.419	1.182	0.9594	1.0423	0.118	1.882	0.113	1.806
1.061	0.373	1.099	0.9650	1.0363	0.185	1.815	0.179	1.751
1.000	0.337	1.032	0.9693	1.0317	0.239	1.761	0.232	1.707
0.949	0.308	0.975	0.9727	1.0281	0.284	1.716	0.276	1.669
0.905	0.285	0.927	0.9754	1.0252	0.321	1.679	0.313	1.637
0.866	0.266	0.886	0.9776	1.0229	0.354	1.646	0.346	1.610
0.832	0.249	0.850	0.9794	1.0210	0.382	1.618	0.374	1.585
0.802	0.235	0.817	0.9810	1.0194	0.406	1.594	0.399	1.563
0.775	0.223	0.789	0.9823	1.0180	0.428	1.572	0.421	1.544

The "Observations in Sample, n" column values are: 2, 3, 4, 5 (first group); 6, 7, 8, 9, 10 (second group); 11, 12, 13, 14, 15 (third group).

Continued on next page . . .

Continued...

CHART FOR AVERAGE				CHART FOR STANDARD DEVIATIONS					
Observations in Sample, n	Factors for Control Limits			Factors for Central Line		Factors for Control Limits			
	A	A_2	A_3	c_4	$1/c_4$	B_3	B_4	B_5	B_6
16	0.750	0.212	0.763	0.9835	1.0168	0.448	1.552	0.440	1.526
17	0.728	0.203	0.739	0.9845	1.0157	0.466	1.534	0.458	1.511
18	0.707	0.194	0.718	0.9854	1.0148	0.482	1.518	0.475	1.496
19	0.688	0.187	0.698	0.9862	1.0140	0.497	1.503	0.490	1.483
20	0.671	0.180	0.680	0.9869	1.0133	0.510	1.490	0.504	1.470
21	0.655	0.173	0.663	0.9876	1.0126	0.523	1.477	0.516	1.459
22	0.640	0.167	0.647	0.9882	1.0119	0.534	1.466	0.528	1.448
23	0.626	0.162	0.633	0.9887	1.0114	0.545	1.455	0.539	1.438
24	0.612	0.157	0.619	0.9892	1.0109	0.555	1.445	0.549	1.429
25	0.600	0.153	0.606	0.9896	1.0105	0.565	1.435	0.559	1.420

Continued on next page...

Continued...

| Observations in Sample, n | CHART FOR RANGES | | | | | | | X CHARTS |
| | Factors for Central Line | | | Factors for Contral Limits | | | | |
	d_2	$1/d_2$	d_3	D_1	D_2	D_3	D_4	E_2
2	1.128	0.8865	0.853	0	3.686	0	3.267	2.660
3	1.693	0.5907	0.888	0	4.358	0	2.574	1.772
4	2.059	0.4857	0.880	0	4.698	0	2.282	1.457
5	2.326	0.4299	0.864	0	4.918	0	2.114	1.290
6	2.534	0.3946	0.848	0	5.078	0	2.004	1.184
7	2.704	0.3698	0.833	0.204	5.204	0.076	1.924	1.109
8	2.847	0.3512	0.820	0.388	5.306	0.136	1.864	1.054
9	2.970	0.3367	0.808	0.547	5.393	0.184	1.816	1.010
10	3.078	0.3249	0.797	0.687	5.469	0.223	1.777	0.975
11	3.173	0.3152	0.787	0.811	5.535	0.256	1.744	0.945
12	3.258	0.3069	0.778	0.922	5.594	0.283	1.717	0.921
13	3.336	0.2998	0.770	1.025	5.647	0.307	1.693	0.899
14	3.407	0.2935	0.763	1.118	5.696	0.328	1.672	0.881
15	3.472	0.2880	0.756	1.203	5.741	0.347	1.653	0.864
16	3.532	0.2831	0.750	1.282	5.782	0.363	1.637	0.849
17	3.588	0.2787	0.744	1.356	5.820	0.378	1.622	0.836
18	3.640	0.2747	0.739	1.424	5.856	0.391	1.608	0.824
19	3.689	0.2711	0.734	1.487	5.891	0.403	1.597	0.813
20	3.735	0.2677	0.729	1.549	5.921	0.415	1.585	0.803
21	3.778	0.2647	0.724	1.605	5.951	0.425	1.575	0.794
22	3.819	0.2618	0.720	1.659	5.979	0.434	1.566	0.786
23	3.858	0.2592	0.716	1.710	6.006	0.443	1.557	0.778
24	3.895	0.2567	0.712	1.759	6.031	0.451	1.548	0.770
25	3.931	0.2544	0.708	1.806	6.056	0.459	1.541	0.763

Appendix 7

Table of d_2^* Values

		m = repeat readings taken						
		2	3	4	5	6	7	8
g = # parts × # inspectors	1	1.41	1.91	2.24	2.48	2.67	2.83	2.96
	2	1.28	1.81	2.15	2.40	2.60	2.77	2.91
	3	1.23	1.77	2.12	2.38	2.58	2.75	2.89
	4	1.21	1.75	2.11	2.37	2.57	2.74	2.88
	5	1.19	1.74	2.10	2.36	2.56	2.73	2.87
	6	1.18	1.73	2.09	2.35	2.56	2.73	2.87
	7	1.17	1.73	2.09	2.35	2.55	2.72	2.87
	8	1.17	1.72	2.08	2.35	2.55	2.72	2.87
	9	1.16	1.72	2.08	2.34	2.55	2.72	2.86
	10	1.16	1.72	2.08	2.34	2.55	2.72	2.86
	11	1.16	1.71	2.08	2.34	2.55	2.72	2.86
	12	1.15	1.71	2.07	2.34	2.55	2.72	2.85
	13	1.15	1.71	2.07	2.34	2.55	2.71	2.85
	14	1.15	1.71	2.07	2.34	2.54	2.71	2.85
	15	1.15	1.71	2.07	2.34	2.54	2.71	2.85
	>15	1.128	1.693	2.059	2.326	2.534	2.704	2.847

Continued on next page . . .

Continued . . .

| | | m = repeat readings taken | | | | | | |
		9	10	11	12	13	14	15
	1	3.08	3.18	3.27	3.35	3.42	3.49	3.55
	2	3.02	3.13	3.22	3.30	3.38	3.45	3.51
	3	3.01	3.11	3.21	3.29	3.37	3.43	3.50
	4	3.00	3.10	3.20	3.28	3.36	3.43	3.49
	5	2.99	3.10	3.19	3.28	3.35	3.42	3.49
	6	2.99	3.10	3.19	3.27	3.35	3.42	3.49
	7	2.99	3.10	3.19	3.27	3.35	3.42	3.48
	8	2.98	3.09	3.19	3.27	3.35	3.42	3.48
	9	2.98	3.09	3.18	3.27	3.35	3.42	3.48
g = # parts × # inspectors	10	2.98	3.09	3.18	3.27	3.34	3.42	3.48
	11	2.98	3.09	3.18	3.27	3.34	3.41	3.48
	12	2.98	3.09	3.18	3.27	3.34	3.41	3.48
	13	2.98	3.09	3.18	3.27	3.34	3.41	3.48
	14	2.98	3.08	3.18	3.27	3.34	3.41	3.48
	15	2.98	3.08	3.18	3.26	3.34	3.41	3.48
	> 15		3.078		3.258		3.407	
		2.970		3.173		3.336		3.472

Appendix 8

Sigma Level to DPMO Conversion

For a given sigma level, the defects per million opportunities (DPMO) is provided, assuming normality and a 1.5 sigma shift. Note that below approximately 3 sigma defects are included from both tails of the normal distribution.

Sigma	DPMO	Sigma	DPMO	Sigma	DPMO
1	697672	2.7	115083	4.4	1866
1.1	660083	2.8	96809	4.5	1350
1.2	621378	2.9	80762	4.6	968
1.3	581815	3	66811	4.7	687
1.4	541694	3.1	54801	4.8	483
1.5	501350	3.2	44567	4.9	337
1.6	461140	3.3	35931	5	233
1.7	421428	3.4	28717	5.1	159
1.8	382572	3.5	22750	5.2	108
1.9	344915	3.6	17865	5.3	72
2	308770	3.7	13903	5.4	48
2.1	274412	3.8	10724	5.5	32
2.2	242071	3.9	8198	5.6	21
2.3	211928	4	6210	5.7	13
2.4	184108	4.1	4661	5.8	9
2.5	158687	4.2	3467	5.9	5
2.6	135687	4.3	2555	6	3.4

Appendix 9

Estimating Sigma Using Long-Term DPMO (from Field Data)

For a given defects per million opportunities (DPMO), the sigma level is provided, assuming normality and a 1.5 sigma shift. Note that below approximately 3 sigma, the sigma levels are slightly inaccurate, since only one tail of the normal distribution was included for simplicity in the calculation.

DPMO	Sigma	DPMO	Sigma	DPMO	Sigma	DPMO	Sigma
300,000	2.02	6,000	4.01	90	5.25	3	6.03
200,000	2.34	5,000	4.08	80	5.28	2	6.11
100,000	2.78	4,000	4.15	70	5.31	1	6.25
90,000	2.84	3,000	4.25	60	5.35	0.9	6.27
80,000	2.91	2,000	4.38	50	5.39	0.8	6.30
70,000	2.98	1,000	4.59	40	5.44	0.7	6.33
60,000	3.05	900	4.62	30	5.51	0.6	6.36
50,000	3.14	800	4.66	20	5.61	0.5	6.39
40,000	3.25	700	4.69	10	5.77	0.4	6.44
30,000	3.38	600	4.74	9	5.79	0.3	6.49
20,000	3.55	500	4.79	8	5.81	0.2	6.57
10,000	3.83	400	4.85	7	5.84	0.1	6.70
9,000	3.87	300	4.93	6	5.88	0.09	6.72
8,000	3.91	200	5.04	5	5.92	0.08	6.74
7,000	3.96	100	5.22	4	5.97	0.07	6.77

Final Exam

1. A six sigma level of quality:
   a. Implies 99.73% of the output will meet customer requirements.
   b. Equates to a capability index of 1.33.
   c. Represents 3.4 defects per million opportunities.
   d. Provides half the defects of a three sigma level of quality.

2. Project sponsors:
   a. Ensure that the Six Sigma projects are defined with clear deliverables.
   b. Help clear roadblocks encountered by the project team.
   c. Are generally members of management.
   d. All of the above.

3. The "house of quality" is produced by which of the following methods?
   a. TQM
   b. Quality function deployment
   c. Affinity diagrams
   d. ISO 9000

4. The "hows" section of a house of quality for design:
   a. Lists the customer requirements.
   b. Lists the product design requirements.
   c. Defines the customer ratings for the requirements.
   d. Lists the technical importance of the requirements.

						Correlation Matrix		
							0	Cook Training
						3	9	Menu
					-3	3	0	Plate Prep
				3	-3	3	0	Pre-Prep
			-3	-3	-3	9	0	# Cook Staff
		0	0	0	-1	0	9	# Wait Staff

Customer Requirements	Import.	Operational Requirements							Competitor Eval.		
		# Wait Staff	# Cook Staff	Pre-prep	Plate Prep	Menu	Cook Training	Wait Staff Training	House of Italy	Leonardo's	Mama Mia
Service Quality											
Wait Time	3	9	3	3	0	3	3	3	2	5	3
Friendliness of Staff	4	3	0	0	0	0	0	3	1	4	4
Order Accuracy	4	3	1	0	0	3	3	9	5	4	4
Culinary Satisfaction											
Taste	4	0	3	3	3	1	9	3	5	3	2
Temperature	3	3	3	1	9	0	9	3	5	4	3
Pricing											
Some Entrées <$13	3	3	3	3	0	9	0	0	1	4	3
Kids Menu	2	1	1	0	0	9	0	0	1	4	3
Target Value		12.5	15	30	3	$12	40	60			
Competitor Value		12	14	30	3	$11.60	40	60			
Importance		71	45	33	39	70	84	78			
Rank		3	5	7	6	4	1	2			

Figure F.61

5. The QFD matrix shown in Figure F.61 indicates that:
   a. Cook Training is strongly related to Wait Time.
   b. Cook Training is strongly related to Order Accuracy.
   c. Cook Training is strongly related to Taste.
   d. None of the above.

6. The QFD matrix shown in Figure F.61 (question 5) indicates that:
   a. The customer places a strong value on Kids Menu.
   b. Internal management thinks Friendliness of Staff is important.
   c. Plate Prep is a key process requirement.
   d. Wait Staff Training is a key issue for meeting important customer requirements.

7. The QFD matrix shown in Figure F.61 (question 5) indicates that:
   a. Pre-prep is critical to meeting the Temperature demands of the customers.
   b. The most important operational requirement for Culinary Satisfaction is the Menu offerings.
   c. The most important operational requirement for Culinary Satisfaction is the Cook Training.
   d. None of the above.

8. The QFD matrix shown in Figure F.61 (question 5) indicates that:
    a. The House of Italy provides a good benchmark for Culinary Satisfaction.
    b. The House of Italy is preferred to Mama Mia's for pricing.
    c. The House of Italy is preferred to Mama Mia's for staff friendliness.
    d. All of the above.

9. Comparing the Number of Cook Staff with Cook Staff Training in the QFD matrix shown in Figure F.61 (question 5):
    a. Number of Cook Staff is more important in meeting customer demands.
    b. Cook Staff Training is more important in meeting customer demands.
    c. Number of Cook Staff is not correlated with any key customers demands.
    d. None of the above.

10. In deciding which projects should be pursued, the management team has defined a set of criteria. Unfortunately, the team does not think the criteria have equal weights. A tool that can be helpful in choosing projects is:
    a. The project decision program chart (PDPC).
    b. The prioritization matrix.
    c. The matrix diagram.
    d. Force field analysis.

11. To effectively plan improvement strategies for the organization:
    a. We must understand the little ys that drive the organizational metrics.
    b. Regression analysis is a useful tool.
    c. We must understand which process variables influence the critical dashboard metrics.
    d. All of the above.

12. A particular project has many stakeholder groups. In an attempt to keep the team size at a reasonable level, some of the nonkey stakeholder groups were not included in the team. As a result:
    a. The team leader can boost buy-in from these groups by bringing credible group members into the problem solving as ad hoc team members.
    b. The team leader should also restrict the distributed progress reports to only the key groups represented in the team to prevent confusion and interference on the part of the nonkey groups.

    c. The sponsor should ensure that the concerns of the nonkey groups are met by the team recommendations.

    d. All of the above.

13. Joan is a Black Belt and project team leader. Her team includes, among other members, a manager and a clerk from different departments. Early in today's team meeting, after the clerk had offered an idea during a brainstorming session, the manager made a joke about the feasibility of the idea. Just now, the manager has stifled the clerk's comments by asserting the clerk lacked the experience to suggest potential causes of the problem under investigation. Joan should:

    a. Wait until the end of the meeting and discuss the issue separately with the clerk and the manager.

    b. Immediately remind the manager of the team ground rule of "respectful communication" and the general rules for brainstorming.

    c. Give it some time and allow personalities to jell. Perhaps the manager is having a bad day and will be more agreeable in future meetings.

    d. Do nothing. The manager should be given respect for his or her position in the company, and the point is well-taken on the clerk's experience. Furthermore, the earlier joke really gave the team something to chuckle about, easing tension.

14. Bill's team is having a hard time agreeing on a plan for data gathering. There are three general suggestions that have been offered: one by a process expert and two by other team members. To decide which plan to deploy, the team should:

    a. Accept the idea offered by the process expert. Doing otherwise is an insult to his or her expertise.

    b. Vote on the different proposals, with the plan receiving the highest number of votes being deployed.

    c. Develop new plans that take the best parts of the proposed plans, with compromises on the conflicting aspects of the various plans. Vote on the resulting plans.

    d. Try to reach a compromise on the various plans, with a resulting plan that everyone can live with, even if it's not perfect to any of the parties.

15. A conflict has developed with a team member regarding a proposed solution. Joan, the team leader, should:

    a. Insist that the team members behave and stop disagreeing.

b. Allow all members to explain their point of view, then take a vote to see which proposal wins.

c. Use problem-solving tools to determine the true causes of dissension, then use that information to guide the solution.

d. All of the above.

16. A team has so many ideas of where to start that they are lost. A good tool for them to start understanding how these ideas are related is:

a. QFD.

b. Fishbone diagram.

c. Affinity diagram.

d. PDPC.

17. In a SIPOC analysis, inputs include:

a. Data.

b. Output from other processes.

c. Products from suppliers.

d. All of the above.

18. In a SIPOC analysis, outputs include:

a. Data.

b. Results, value-added products or services, payments, documentation, input to other processes.

c. Results, value-added products or services.

d. Results, value-added products or services, resources.

The following data describing the operations (with cycle times) needed to release a customer order to production is used for questions 19 through 24, which follow the data:

(1) Define bill of materials: 2 days.

(2a) Order and receive materials: 10 days (can be done concurrently with 2b).

(2b1) Schedule job in production: 3 days (can be done concurrently with 2a, but must be before 2b2 and 2b3).

(2b2) Define quality plan for product: 1 day (can be done concurrently with 2a, but must be after 2b1 and before 2b3).

(2b3) Enter schedule and quality requirements into scheduling software: 1 day (can be done concurrently with 2a, but must be after 2b1 and 2b2).

(3) Release to production.

19. A project to reduce the time it takes to schedule jobs in production (step 2b1) is proposed, with the expectation that it would reduce

the time from 3 days to 1 day. In defining the benefits to the company:

a. The capacity of the process will be improved, with a potential to handle increased sales.

b. The cost savings due to cycle time improvement are difficult to determine, but the project will improve the total delivery time so is beneficial.

c. All of the above.

d. None of the above.

20. It is proposed to break step 1 into two steps: verify bill of materials (step 1a) and enter bill of material into production software (step 2b0). Step 1a replaces step 1 as the initial step of the process, requiring 1 day. Step 2b0, requiring one day, must take place before step 2b1, but can be done concurrent with step 2a. The net effect of this change on the total cycle time is:

a. No change.

b. Reduction of one day.

c. Reduction of two days.

d. Increase of one day.

21. The total cycle time for the process shown in the previous example is:

a. 17 days.

b. 12 days.

c. 7 days.

d. Cannot be determined with the information provided.

22. To reduce the total cycle time for the process:

a. Reduce the cycle time for step 1.

b. Reduce the cycle time for step 2a.

c. Reduce the cycle time for step 1 or step 2a.

d. Reduce the cycle time for any of the process steps.

23. The earliest start time for step 2b2 is:

a. 5 days.

b. 6 days.

c. 12 days.

d. 15 days.

24. The latest start time for step 2b2 is:

a. 5 days.

b. 6 days.

    c. 10 days.
    d. 11 days.

25. If we don't define the critical path for a process:
    a. We can't effectively reduce defect levels.
    b. We may reduce cycle times of noncritical path activities, which won't have as much of an impact on total cycle time.
    c. We may reduce cycle times of noncritical path activities, which will have no impact on total cycle time.
    d. All of the above.

26. The advantage of a probabilistic approach to PERT analysis is:
    a. It properly considers that processes are not deterministic.
    b. It assumes that there is variation in activity times.
    c. It could provide a more realistic estimate of project completion times.
    d. All of the above.

27. If the optimistic, pessimistic, and most likely times for step 1 of a process is (2 days, 9 days, 5 days) and for step 2 it is (4 days, 13 days, 8 days), then the best estimate for the total cycle time for the two steps is:
    a. 13 days.
    b. 13.34 days.
    c. 8 days.
    d. 22 days.

28. If the optimistic, pessimistic, and most likely times for step 1 of a process is (2 days, 9 days, 5 days) and for step 2 it is (4 days, 13 days, 8 days), then the best estimate for the standard deviation of the total cycle time for the two steps is:
    a. 3.6 days.
    b. 2.67 days.
    c. 1.9 days.
    d. 1.5 days.

29. Process flowcharts can be used to:
    a. Uncover differences in stakeholders' perceptions of the process.
    b. Communicate process changes.
    c. Discover process complexities that contribute to variation or longer cycle times.
    d. All of the above.

30. The prime use of a control chart is to
    a. Detect assignable causes of variation in the process.
    b. Detect nonconforming product.
    c. Measure the performance of all quality characteristics of a process.
    d. Detect the presence of random variation in the process.

31. An invoicing process is the same for products A and B, yet the average time required to process the invoice for product A is twice that of B. Generally, there are only 10 to 15 orders per month of each product type. In establishing the statistical control of the invoice process, you should:
    a. Use separate control charts for products A and B.
    b. Use the same control chart for products A and B.
    c. Use the same control chart for products A and B, after standardizing the observations.
    d. Calculate the pooled standard deviation of products A and B, and establish control limits based on this estimate.

32. An invoicing process is the same for products A and B, yet the average time required to process the invoice for product A is twice that of B. Generally, there are only 10 to 15 orders per month of each product type. In establishing the statistical control of the invoice process:
    a. Use a subgroup size of 1.
    b. Use a subgroup size of 5, which is generally the best size.
    c. Use a subgroup size of 10.
    d. Use a subgroup size of 15.

33. To demonstrate compliance to a requirement that the C_{pk} index be at least 1.33 based on a $\pm 3\square$ spread, the quality engineer computed C_{pk} from 50 units selected at random from the production lot before it was delivered to the customer. Which of the following statements describes this approach to capability analysis?
    a. It is invalid because no rational subgroup was used.
    b. It is an acceptable method of computing C_{pk}.
    c. It is invalid because the process may be out of control, which would not be detected with this approach.
    d. All of the above except b.

34. Which of the following is the correct control chart for the waiting time for customers in a bank; each individual customer's waiting time will be plotted.

    a. U chart
    b. Individual-X/moving range
    c. $\bar{X}$ and s
    d. Np chart

35. A process shows statistical control using an individual-X chart. Assuming the implementation cost of a different chart is negligible, but the cost of sampling is significant, the most economical method for increasing the sensitivity of the chart to small process shifts is:
    a. Increase the subgroup size.
    b. Use an EWMA or CuSum chart.
    c. Use the $\bar{X}$/range chart.
    d. All of the above.

36. The EWMA statistic:
    a. Has historical use in financial applications.
    b. Is useful in chemical processes where the data is dependent.
    c. Is used for autocorrelated processes.
    d. All of the above.

37. When are control charts for individuals' data necessary?
    a. The rational subgroup size is one.
    b. There is only one characteristic to be monitored.
    c. It is always the best choice for control charting.
    d. All of the above.

38. A disadvantage of control charts for individuals' data is:
    a. There is less data to collect.
    b. The chart is less sensitive to process shifts than larger subgroups.
    c. It only works for autocorrelated processes.
    d. All of the above.

39. An advantage of using control charts for individuals data is:
    a. There is less data to collect.
    b. The control limits can be directly compared to the specifications.
    c. It costs less than larger subgroup sizes.
    d. All of the above.

40. An individual-X chart with limits at ± 3 standard deviations:
    a. Uses the moving range statistic to estimate short-term process variation.
    b. Is useful unless the process distribution is very non-normal.
    c. Plots the individual values instead of subgroup averages.
    d. All of the above.

41. When an observation is observed beyond the three sigma limits on the individual-X chart:
    a. You should wait to see if more observations go beyond the limits, since there is a chance that subgroups will be out of control when the process has not shifted.
    b. You should respond immediately, since the chance of an out-of-control point is very small unless the process has shifted.
    c. You should see if the point also fails run test rules before responding.
    d. You should only respond if the characteristic is critical to the customer.

42. When a process is extremely non-normal:
    a. An individual-X chart with three sigma limits may predict control limits that don't match the process.
    b. An EWMA or moving average chart may be useful, since the plotted points assume normality.
    c. You should understand why the process is so distributed.
    d. All of the above.

43. When the cost of collecting samples is high:
    a. You shouldn't use control charts, since sampling inspection is cheaper.
    b. Subgroups of size five are always best, but they increase the time between samples.
    c. A control chart using a subgroup size of one is preferred.
    d. You should ignore the cost, since the control chart is always value-added.

44. When process data occurs infrequently, subgroups containing more than one observation:
    a. Might include special causes of variation.
    b. Generally are not rational subgroups.
    c. Are poor indicators of short-term variation.
    d. All of the above.

45. It is appropriate to use the sample standard deviation to define control limits on an individual-X chart in which of the following cases?
    a. When the process may drift.
    b. When the process is highly capable.
    c. Always.
    d. Never.

Table T.29.

Month	Total Shipped	Cracked	Chipped	Off Color	Wrong Color	Other
JAN	3500	7	15	21	12	200
FEB	3124	14	10	28	23	1
MAR	1245	12	5	11	17	9
APR	2020	18	9	7	11	5
MAY	1652	9	14	4	21	9
JUN	2637	11	21	26	9	13
JUL	2543	12	11	19	23	2
AUG	4042	8	12	12	18	1
SEP	1367	11	13	15	21	7
OCT	3124	21	9	13	40	7
NOV	2645	12	7	6	31	9
DEC	1200	10	4	14	17	8

46. Based on Table T.29, a reasonable goal for a Six Sigma improvement project is:
    a. To improve the sigma level related to Wrong Color from 3.9 to 4.1.
    b. To improve the sigma level related to Wrong Color from 3.9 to 6.0.
    c. To decrease the ppm defects related to Wrong Color from 8000 to 800.
    d. To improve the process sigma level from 3.3 to 5.0.

47. Gage R&R studies are best done using:
    a. Calibration standards.
    b. Actual samples from the process.

    c. Vendor samples.

    d. Only the best operators.

48. When trying to evaluate the error due to a piece of automated test equipment, a gage R&R study:

    a. Is usually not worth doing, since the error in the electronics is likely to be small.

    b. Should be replaced by a gage linearity study.

    c. Can detect differences due to sample preparation or equipment set-up.

    d. Can only detect variation between the test operators.

49. Gage R&R studies may be used to:

    a. Understand and reduce common causes of variation in a process.

    b. Ensure that process personnel can take process measurements with minimal error.

    c. Compare the performance of new test equipment.

    d. All of the above.

50. When using a $\bar{X}$/range chart for evaluating gage repeatability:

    a. The range chart indicates the variation between operators.

    b. The $\bar{X}$ chart should be out of control.

    c. The $\bar{X}$ chart is scaled using the process variation.

    d. All of the above.

51. A criterion for acceptance of gage R&R is:

    a. The calculated R&R should be less than 10% of process variation.

    b. The calculated R&R should be less than 10% of process tolerances.

    c. The calculated discrimination should be more than 8 or 10.

    d. All of the above.

52. Histograms:

    a. Give us a graphical view of process location and variation.

    b. Provide of quick means of checking process control.

    c. Detect subtle trends in the process.

    d. All of the above.

53. When using process capability estimates:

    a. C_p may be acceptable and C_{pk} unacceptable.

    b. C_p tells us how the actual variation compares to the acceptable variation.

c. C_{pk} is better to use than C_p since C_{pk} considers process location.
d. All of the above.

54. When using process capability estimates:
   a. The process must be in control or the estimate is misleading.
   b. Always estimate the process using sample sigma.
   c. We should sort the data prior to analysis.
   d. All of the above.

55. When using process capability estimates:
   a. A C_{pk} value of 1.0 is perfect.
   b. A C_{pk} value greater than 1.3 is usually preferred.
   c. Smaller values of C_{pk} are best.
   d. C_p values must not exceed the C_{pk} value.

56. When reporting how well we meet our customer requirements:
   a. A histogram showing our data and the specification limits is the preferred graphical tool to use.
   b. We should remove outliers.
   c. We should use C_{pk} if the process is in control and P_{pk} if the process is not in control.
   d. All of the above.

57. A 90% confidence interval for the mean is from 13.8067 to 18.1933. This means that
   a. There is a 90% probability that the true mean lies between 13.8067 and 18.1933.
   b. 90% of all values in the population lie between 13.8067 and 18.1933.
   c. 90% of all the sample values in the population lie between 13.8067 and 18.1933.
   d. None of the above

58. Some useful purposes for model transformations include:
   a. To calculate parameters that are not easily measured directly.
   b. To understand the effect of parameter settings on process variation.
   c. To stabilize the variance to improve parameter estimates.
   d. All of the above.

59. To detect nonconstant variance in the response:
   a. We need replicated observations at each level of the response.
   b. We need multiple responses.

    c. We need replicated observations at multiple experimental conditions.

    d. All of the above.

60. When transforming data to stabilize the variance:

    a. We can plot the log of the standard deviation at each experimental condition against the log of the mean of the experimental condition to determine a suitable transform function.

    b. We should verify that the transformed data has a stabilized variance.

    c. We will use the transformed response in place of the original response when estimating significance of factors or the model.

    d. All of the above.

61. In constructing a scatter diagram, it is customary to put the dependent variable on:

    a. The x axis.

    b. The y axis.

    c. All of the above.

    d. None of the above.

62. On a scatter diagram, attempting to predict beyond the region of the data is known as:

    a. Interpolation.

    b. Bipolarization.

    c. Multiple regression.

    d. Extrapolation.

63. Positive correlation implies that:

    a. The dependent variable improves as the independent variable increases.

    b. The dependent variable decreases as the independent variable increases.

    c. The dependent variable increases as the independent variable increases.

    d. The independent variable decreases as the dependent variable increases.

64. Negative correlation implies that:

    a. The dependent variable improves as the independent variable decreases.

    b. The dependent variable decreases as the independent variable increases.

c. The dependent variable increases as the independent variable increases.

d. The independent variable decreases as the dependent variable decreases.

65. Strong correlation implies:
    a. The dependent variable improves as the independent variable increases.
    b. There is little error between the predicted response and the actual response of the dependent variable increases.
    c. The dependent variable increases rapidly as the independent variable increases.
    d. All of the above.

66. Weak correlation implies:
    a. The dependent variable is not well predicted by the model.
    b. There is one or more unexplained source of variation, preventing good prediction of the response of the dependent variable increases.
    c. It might be useful to stratify the data.
    d. All of the above.

67. In linear correlation analysis, if the slope of the line is low, then:
    a. The dependent variable is not well predicted by the model.
    b. There is weak correlation between the variables.
    c. As the independent variable changes, there is a small change in the dependent variable.
    d. All of the above.

68. In estimating correlation, we should vary the independent variable over a sufficient range so that:
    a. A sufficient amount of variation in the dependent variable is experienced.
    b. We can predict the dependent variable over a wide range.
    c. We don't need to extrapolate.
    d. All of the above.

69. If the cycle time of a process is predicted by cycle time $= 5.25 \times$ (number of items) $+ 4.3$, with a correlation of 0.8, then the slope of the line is:
    a. 5.25.
    b. 4.3.

c. 35.8.

d. 0.8.

70. If the cycle time of a process is predicted by cycle time $= 5.25 \times$ (number of items) $+ 4.3$, with a correlation of 0.8, then it is fair to say:

a. We can predict cycle time with no error.

b. Only the number of items influences the predicted cycle time.

c. Cycle time is definitely influenced by the number of items.

d. None of the above.

71. Larger correlation implies:

a. Less error in the predicted response.

b. Larger slope of the line.

c. A greater increase in the response given a certain increase in the independent variable.

d. None of the above.

72. If the correlation coefficient R is 0.9 for a simple linear regression, then:

a. 90% of the variation in y is explained by the regression model.

b. 81% of the variation in y is explained by the regression model.

c. 90% of the variation in y is explained by the variation in x.

d. Approximately 95% of the error is explained by the variation in x.

73. An R-squared value of 0.20 indicates:

a. For every unit increase in x, there is a 20% increase in y.

b. There are probably other variables that contribute to the variation in the response.

c. 20% of the time we will predict y correctly.

d. All of the above.

74. Confidence intervals about the regression line are flared at the ends because:

a. We can't predict the y values at the extremes with as much certainty.

b. There are fewer data at the endpoints.

c. The error in predicting the slope causes greater uncertainty at the extremes.

d. All of the above.

75. All of the following statements are true *except:*

a. In multiple regression, extrapolation beyond the region of observations can lead to erroneous predictions.

b. At least three variables are involved in multiple regression.
c. Multiple regression involves one independent and two or more dependent variables.
d. None of the above statements are true.

76. Multiple regression techniques may be used to:
   a. Determine which of many factors are significant contributors to the effect.
   b. Mine data to investigate potential relationships between observed conditions and responses.
   c. Investigate potential relationships among customer responses in a survey.
   d. All of the above.

77. Assuming the coefficients in the expression
   $Y = \beta_0 + \beta_1 X_1 + \beta_2 X_2 + \beta_3 X_3$ are non-zero:
   a. There are three factors influencing the response.
   b. The β_0, β_1, β_2, and β_3 terms are constants.
   c. As X_1 changes we expect to see a change in y.
   d. All of the above.

78. In the expression cycle time (in minutes) = $3 + 1.4 \times$ (Number of Orders) $- 2.1 \times$ (Number of Clerks) $- .034 \times$ (Process Distance):
   a. The number of clerks is most important.
   b. The process distance is least important.
   c. The cycle time is about 5 minutes when number of orders equals 5, number of clerks equals 2, and process distance equals 14.
   d. All of the above.

79. In the expression Cycle Time (in minutes) = $3 + 1.4 \times$ (Number of Orders) $- 2.1 \times$ (Number of Clerks) $- .034 \times$ (Process Distance):
   a. There is an interaction between the number of orders and the number of clerks.
   b. The number of orders goes down as the number of clerks goes up.
   c. The number of orders stays constant as the number of clerks goes up.
   d. None of the above.

80. In the interaction plot in Figure F.62, it is evident that:
   a. There is an interaction between furnace temperature and fill pressure.
   b. At higher furnace temperature, an increase in fill pressure has more effect on part density.

c. The effect of fill pressure on part density changes as we change the furnace temperature.

d. All of the above.

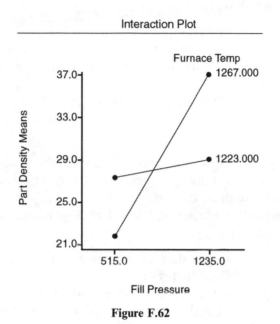

Figure F.62

81. Considering only the interaction plot in Figure F.62, it is evident that:
    a. If furnace temperature is difficult to control, we should run the process at high fill pressure to minimize the variation in part density.
    b. If fill pressure is difficult to control, we should run the process at low furnace temperature to minimize the variation in part density.
    c. Running the process at high furnace temperature and high fill pressure gives us the best conditions.
    d. None of the above.

82. A model of the form $Y = \beta_0 + \beta_1 X_1 + \beta_2 X_2 + \beta_{12} X_{12}$:
    a. Will result in a surface that is nonlinear.
    b. Requires experimental trials where x is set to at least three distinct levels.
    c. Includes an interaction term.
    d. All of the above.

83. A model of the form $Y = \beta_0 + \beta_1 X_1 + \beta_{11} X_1^2 + \beta_2 X_2 + \beta_{12} X_{12}$:
   a. Will result in a surface that is nonlinear.
   b. Requires experimental trials where x_1 is set to at least three distinct levels.
   c. Includes an interaction term.
   d. All of the above.

84. To estimate the regression model $Y = \beta_0 + \beta_1 X_1 + \beta_2 X_2 + \beta_{12} X_{12}$:
   a. Using four experimental trials allows for no estimation of error.
   b. Requires experimental trials where X_1 is set to at least three distinct levels.
   c. We can always use the F statistic to estimate significance of the parameters.
   d. All of the above.

85. If an ANOVA analysis does not provide results of the F test, then:
   a. We probably did not run enough trials to estimate error.
   b. The software must be flawed.
   c. We can remove a factor with an effect close to zero to free up trials.
   d. Choices a and c.

86. A 3^2 experiment means that we are considering:
   a. Two levels of three factors.
   b. Two dependent variables and three independent variables.
   c. Two go/no-go variables and three continuous variables.
   d. Three levels of two factors.

87. Which of the following purposes are served by replicating an experiment?
   i. Provide a means for estimating the experimental error.
   ii. Increase the number of treatments included in the experiment.
   iii. Improve the precision of estimates of treatment effects.
   a. Purposes i and ii only.
   b. Purposes i and iii only.
   c. Purposes ii and iii only.
   d. Purposes i, ii, and iii.

88. An assembly process is receiving the incorrect pieces for assembly. To ensure that only the correct pieces are sent, the parts tub is redesigned so that only the correct pieces (at their correct number) can fit into the tub. This is an application of:
   a. Kanban.
   b. *Poka yoke*.

    c. Visual factory.

    d. 5S.

89. In evaluating an RPN:

    a. A high number indicates high risk.

    b. A high number indicates low risk.

    c. A remote detection ability minimizes the RPN.

    d. A high occurrence minimizes the RPN.

90. Which of the following experimental designs typically has the largest number of replications?

    a. Taguchi.

    b. Plackett-Burman.

    c. Response surface.

    d. EVOP.

91. How can you determine if main effects are confounded with interactions?

    a. Interaction plots.

    b. Interaction designs.

    c. Interaction logs.

    d. None of the above.

92. First-order models are often used:

    a. To determine optimal conditions for a process.

    b. To narrow down a list of suspected factors influencing a process.

    c. To emphatically prove which factors need to be controlled.

    d. All of the above.

93. If the fitted model is a good approximation to the data, then:

    a. The residuals will have a mean close to zero.

    b. The residuals will have constant variance.

    c. The residuals will be normally distributed.

    d. All of the above.

94. A good reason to begin with screening designs and a first-order model includes:

    a. Less data is necessary, so time and money are saved.

    b. Over limited regions of interest, a first-order model is often a good approximation.

    c. We can often eliminate factors from the experiment.

    d. All of the above.

95. In a two-level experiment, when factor A is run at its high level, factor B at its low level, and factor C at its high level:
    a. The interaction AB will be at its low level.
    b. The interaction AC will be at its low level.
    c. The interaction ABC will be at its middle level.
    d. All of the above.

96. If we alias a factor F with the ABCD interaction, then:
    a. Interaction BF is confounded with ACD.
    b. We may not be able to distinguish between a measured response due to CF and ABD.
    c. We may not be able to distinguish between a measured response due to F and ABCD.
    d. All of the above.

97. When we fold an entire design:
    a. We double the total number of experimental runs.
    b. All main factors will be free of confounding with other main factors and two factor interactions.
    c. We may find we have extra runs useful for estimating error.
    d. All of the above.

98. In a normal probability plot of the effects of a designed experiment:
    a. Points close to the line should be further evaluated for relevance.
    b. Points below (but close to) the line are almost significant; those above (and close to) the line are most significant.
    c. Points far from the line indicate significance.
    d. Both a and b.

99. Defect detection as a means for process control:
    a. Is preferred so long as the detection occurs prior to customer receipt of the product or service.
    b. Provides an effective method of improving quality.
    c. Is usually not as economical in the long run as a preventive approach.
    d. All of the above.

100. When calculating the benefits of training, we should seek to quantify which of the following?
    a. Improved customer satisfaction.
    b. Lower employee turnover.
    c. Improved efficiency.
    d. All of the above.

Answers to Quizzes and Exams

Chapter 1: Deployment Strategy

1. Choice d.
2. Choice d.
3. Choice b.
4. Choice c.
5. Choice d. Although a DPMO of 20,000 equates to (approximately) a 3.5 sigma level (Appendix 3), the best answer is choice d (all of the above), since the reported cost of quality would indicate a much better sigma level (Figure 1.3). When the cost of quality is under-reported, then a "hidden factory" is at work masking those activities.
6. Choice d. Joseph Juran included the concept of breakthrough in his *Quality Control Handbook*, first published in 1951.
7. Choice a.
8. Choice c.
9. Choice b.
10. Choice d.

Chapter 2: Personnel Requirements

1. Choice b.
2. Choice a.
3. Choice c.
4. Choice d.
5. Choice c.
6. Choice a.
7. Choice d.
8. Choice b.
9. Choice c.
10. Choice b. Green Belts generally retain their operational role, so they do not act full-time doing Six Sigma projects. They typically receive much less training in statistical methods than Black Belts.

Chapter 3: Focusing the Development

1. Choice c.
2. Choice a.
3. Choice b.
4. Choice d.
5. Choice d. Each of these levels of quality is included in the Kano model.
6. Choice c.
7. Choice b.
8. Choice d. Customer satisfaction is a value judgment made by a customer regarding their total experience with your product or service. Quality is an absence of defects and the presence of desirable product or service features. Quality is one of many factors evaluated by customers when arriving at a satisfaction judgment.
9. Choice d.
10. Choice c.

Part 1 Exam

1. Choice d.
2. Choice d. Choice a is not the best answer since a successful deployment will emphasize training projects that will realize benefits greatly exceeding the first year training expenses.
3. Choice b.
4. Choice a.
5. Choice d.

6. Choice c.
7. Choice d.
8. Choice d.
9. Choice b.
10. Choice d.
11. Choice b.
12. Choice c.
13. Choice a.
14. Choice a.
15. Choice d. Prevention is the focus, rather than detection. Understanding customer needs is critical to this effort.
16. Choice c. Choice b is incorrect. Reducing time to market is a key element of customer satisfaction.
17. Choice c. Complaints are not prevented, but detected at this point. There may be many other problems that customers don't bother to report.
18. Choice b.
19. Choice c.
20. Choice b. Project B has the highest weighted score. Using a prioritization matrix, the weighted score for each project is determined as follows:

    Project A $= (120 * 0.3) + (140 * 0.5) + (30 * 0.2) = 112$
    Project B $= (80 * 0.3) + (200 * 0.5) + (25 * 0.2) = 129$
    Project C $= (100 * 0.3) + (100 * 0.5) + (45 * 0.2) = 89$
    Project D $= (140 * 0.3) + (70 * 0.5) + (65 * 0.2) = 90$

21. Choice c. In choice a, profitability is increased. In choice b, a benefit is provided to the customer, potentially enhancing the marketability of the product or service.
22. Choice d.
23. Choice d. The costs associated with rework include labor, WIP carrying costs, increased equipment maintenance, and improved cycle time.
24. Choice d.
25. Choice b. Choices a and d are not generally realistic in a single short-term project. Choice c represents a 50% reduction, while choice b represents a reduction to one-tenth of the current defect rate. Reasonable criteria, used by General Electric for establishing goals for Six Sigma projects, are:
    Sigma Level < 3 Sigma: $10 \times$ reduction in defects
    Sigma Level > 3 Sigma: 50% reduction in defects.

Answers to Quizzes and Exams

Chapter 4: Define Stage

1. Choice b. Projects should be broken down to manageable projects lasting three to six months. Projects lasting longer than this are likely to lose support and team members, greatly reducing their chance of success.
2. Choice c.
3. Choice d. A properly defined project charter should include each of these elements, which help boost buy-in from stakeholders.
4. Choice c. The affected department is one of the stakeholders that should have been identified and included in the problem solving, if not the team itself. Involving the sponsor should be a last resort. The team needs to satisfy the department's legitimate concerns and help them understand why the proposed solution is the best course (if in fact it is, given the department's concerns).
5. Choice b. Replacing team members or asking for intervention from a sponsor would be last resorts after considerable time has been spent on more productive means of resolving the problems. The problems could most likely be best handled by the ideas listed in choice b.
6. Choice c. Choice c best represents the concept of consensus decision making, which is preferable to voting or mandating decisions.
7. Choice d. The four stages of team development are forming, storming, norming, and performing. Option a refers to typical behavior in the forming stage, and options b and c refer to the storming phase.
8. Choice b. This type of conduct is not uncommon during the storming stage of team development. The team leader should allow the team to become independent.
9. Choice c. Jane is acting as an information and opinion seeker, critical roles in the group that must be met for the group to be productive. The other team members are being nonproductive and disruptive with their nonverbal disapproval of Jane's questions.
10. Choice c. Excluding one of the key stakeholder groups (choice a) will reduce the chance of team success. Choice b is an incorrect use of a sponsor, as well as a neglect of Jim's role as change agent. Choice d will not improve the chances of the team meeting its goals.

Chapter 5: Measure Stage

1. Choice a. The menu is not a deliverable of the process in question, so satisfaction with the menu offerings is not a good baseline for this process.
2. Choice b. Choice a ignores the rework, which is often a significant cost of quality. Choice c is incorrect.

3. Choice c. The traditional yield calculation defined above ignores the hidden factory rework and waste, and does not consider the number and severity of defect types.
4. Choice b. The normalized yield is $Y_n = (Y_{rt})^{1/n} = (.95)^{1/4} = .987$
5. Choice d.
6. Choice b.
7. Choice a.
8. Choice d.
9. Choice b.
10. Choice a.

Chapter 6: Analyze Stage

1. Choice c.
2. Choice d.
3. Choice a. A given coefficient indicates the change in the response for each unit change in its factor.
4. Choice a.
5. Choice d. Womack and Jones offer each of these as types of waste.
6. Choice d. Womack and Jones define a value stream as the "set of all specific actions required to bring a specific product (or service or combination of two) through the three critical management tasks of any business: problem-solving task, information management task, and the physical transformation task." Choice a refers to the physical transformation task; choice c refers to the problem-solving task. Choice b is vague and includes processes that may not be part of the value stream.
7. Choice b.
8. Choice b. The fishbone diagram, aka the cause and effect diagram, is a useful tool to brainstorm and visualize the potential causes of problems.
9. Choice b. The brainstorming process will generate a list of possible causes, without regard to the true causes of the observed problems. Data must be used to define which causes are most prevalent.
10. Choice a.

Chapter 7: Improve Stage

1. Choice d. The PDPC is developed by defining the tasks required, identifying the problems that can occur at each step, and developing contingency plans for each problem.
2. Choice a.

3. Choice a. An increase in design validation/verification actions will result in a reduction in the detection ranking only.
4. Choice d.
5. Choice c.
6. Choice d.
7. Choice a.
8. Choice c.
9. Choice c. Choices a and b require the process be taken off line. Choice d is not recommended.
10. Choice b.

Chapter 8: Control Stage

1. Choice d.
2. Choice c.
3. Choice b.
4. Choice a.
5. Choice a.
6. Choice d.
7. Choice a.
8. Choice c.
9. Choice b. Behavioral changes are most important, but they may not provide the best measure because they are dependent on so many other things, such as management systems that encourage the new behavior.
10. Choice a.

Part 2 Exam

1. Choice a. The "other" category is only the highest because of a single month with an exceptionally large nonconformance. This illustrates the inadequacy of Pareto charts alone for highlighting problem areas, since the Pareto cannot determine if the problem area represents a common occurrence (i.e., a common cause) or an anomaly (i.e., a special cause). Special causes of variation may not reoccur, so can't offer the same financial savings as elimination of common causes of variation. The special cause noted in January for the category other has yet to be repeated over the course of the year, and may have already been addressed as an operational issue. The wrong color category is next highest on the Pareto based on count, so is the best choice for a project based on the information provided. Choice b is inadequate in defining what will be addressed.

2. The total defect rate for wrong color during the time period is calculated as the total number of wrong color defects (243) divided by the number of shipped items (29,099). The result is 0.8351%, or approximately 8,350 parts per million defects.

3. Choice a. Cracks represent a better financial payback (in the absence of data comparing the cost to deploy the different improvement projects, and assuming a constant percentage of defect reduction across all projects). The cost to the company for the year given was as follows:

   Cracked: $62,096.25
   Chipped: $32,779.50
   Off color: $48,458.08
   Wrong color: $28,559.79

4. Choice d. The PPI for each project is cracked: 0.05; chipped: 0.20; off color: 0.13; wrong color: 0.95. The wrong color project has the highest PPI, so is preferred. In this case, it also has the lowest cost/benefit ratio, the highest payback (benefit less cost), and the highest payback per week (of project time), making it the most attractive by those criteria as well.

5. Choice d.

6. Choice c.

7. Choice a.

8. Choice a. The defects per unit is calculated as:
   $$DPU = 50 \text{ defects}/500 \text{ orders} = 0.1$$
   The throughput yield is calculated as:
   $$Yt = (1 - DPU) = (1 - 0.10) = 0.90 = 90\%$$

9. Choice c.

10. Choice b. The rolled throughput yield is calculated as the product of the individual throughput yields.

11. Choice d.

12. Choice a.

13. Choice d. A given coefficient indicates the change in the response for each unit change in its factor.

14. Choice b.

15. Choice b. The P-value provided for Factor A would indicate low significance. Factor C is marginal, but factor B appears highly significant based on this data.

16. Choice b. A key aspect of lean thinking is to define value in customer terms. A set of internal experts is not the best solution, nor is benchmarking.

17. Choice d. Providing products or services based on your strengths will not necessarily meet customers' demands or needs. Rather,

identifying customer value and optimizing processes to meet that definition improve a company's ability to service its customers and to remain profitable in the long term.

18. Choice b. Choice b is an issue that should be investigated. It's possible that operation 4 could be entirely removed from the process if the upstream operation (including a supplier process) could be modified. Choice a is a quick fix which adds little value to the customer and increases costs. We don't know enough about the flow of the downstream processes to recommend movement of personnel from downstream processes, but moving personnel from the processes immediately upstream may increase the capacity of the process.
19. Choice b.
20. Choice b.
21. Choice d.
22. Choice d.
23. Choice d.
24. Choice b.
25. Choice d.

Final Exam

1. Choice c.
2. Choice d.
3. Choice b.
4. Choice b.
5. Choice c.
6. Choice d.
7. Choice c.
8. Choice a. Choices b and c are incorrect. A negative interaction implies that as one requirement decreases, the other increases.
9. Choice b. Cook Staff Training has a higher Importance than Number of Cook Staff. Choice c is incorrect since Number of Cook Staff has a moderate relationship with Taste, which has a Customer Importance of 4.
10. Choice b.
11. Choice d.
12. Choice a. Choice b is incorrect. In order to boost buy-in from these groups, it is recommended to include them on progress reports, so they can appreciate the concerns and choices of the project team. While the sponsor provides a useful checkpoint to raise concerns about team recommendations, the sponsor is not usually in a position to adequately present a stakeholder's concerns.

13. Choice b. The manager needs to conduct him- or herself within the acceptable rules of conduct. Ground rules such as mentioned in choice b are typical, as is a rule that employees' rank in the organization should not influence the team dynamics. A public reminder of the ground rules, done quickly and respectfully, shows the team that no one is above these rules. By addressing this concern immediately, the chance of future instances is reduced.

14. Choice d. Choice d best represents the concept of consensus decision making, which is preferred to voting or mandating decisions.

15. Choice c. Conflict is necessary for ideas to be generated and discussed and should not be discouraged. Voting is not a preferred way to settle conflict. Conflicts should be resolved using consensus.

16. Choice c. The affinity diagram involves grouping the ideas into meaningful categories to further understand the issues.

17. Choice d.

18. Choice b.

19. Choice d. Step 2b1 is not on the critical path, so any improvement will not improve capacity, nor will it improve the total delivery time.

20. Choice b. Step 1a will remain on the critical path. The effect of moving step 2b0 to run concurrent with step 2a is to move it off the critical path, so the cycle time for the critical path is reduced by one day.

21. Choice b.

22. Choice c.

23. Choice a.

24. Choice c.

25. Choice c.

26. Choice d.

27. Choice b. The average expected time for step 1 is $(2 + (4 * 5) + 9)/6 = 5.17$, and the average expected time for step 2 is $(4 + (4 * 8) + 13)/6 = 8.17$. The sum of the two steps is then 13.34 days.

28. Choice c. The expected standard deviation of the cycle time for step 1 is $(9 - 2)/6 = 1.17$, and the expected standard deviation of the cycle time for step 2 is $(13 - 4)/6 = 1.5$. The sum of the variances of the two steps is then $(1.17^2) + (1.5^2) = 3.6$. The standard deviation of the two steps is the square root of $3.6 = 1.9$ days.

29. Choice d.

30. Choice a. Walter Shewhart's main reason for inventing the control chart technique was to detect assignable causes of variation in the process.

31. Choice c. Separate control charts are not desirable given the limited number of data. Standardizing the observations is the technique employed used in short run processes to define control charts.

32. Choice a. Subgroups larger than one would include samples taken over too long a period, increasing the chance of including special causes.
33. Choice d.
34. Choice b.
35. Choice b. Although increasing the subgroup size will increase the sensitivity of the chart to small process shifts, it comes at the cost of increased sampling and measurement.
36. Choice d.
37. Choice a.
38. Choice b.
39. Choice d.
40. Choice d.
41. Choice b.
42. Choice d.
43. Choice c.
44. Choice d.
45. Choice d.
46. Choice a. A reasonable criterion, used by General Electric for establishing goals for Six Sigma projects, is: sigma level < 3 sigma: $10 \times$ reduction in defects; sigma level > 3 sigma: 50% reduction in defects. Choices b through d are not generally realistic in a single short term project.
47. Choice b.
48. Choice c.
49. Choice d.
50. Choice b.
51. Choice d.
52. Choice a.
53. Choice d.
54. Choice a.
55. Choice b.
56. Choice c.
57. Choice a.
58. Choice d.
59. Choice d.
60. Choice d.
61. Choice b.
62. Choice d.
63. Choice c.
64. Choice b.

65. Choice b.
66. Choice d.
67. Choice c.
68. Choice d.
69. Choice a.
70. Choice d.
71. Choice a.
72. Choice b.
73. Choice b.
74. Choice d.
75. Choice c. The multiple regression model has one dependent variable and two or more independent variables.
76. Choice d.
77. Choice d.
78. Choice c. Choices a and b are incorrect because we cannot determine significance directly from the coefficients.
79. Choice d. There is no interaction between the number of orders and the number of clerks. Changing one has no effect on the other.
80. Choice d. Each of the statements is true.
81. Choice b. When furnace temperature is low (the 1223 line), then the variation in part density is smallest. Choice c is incorrect since we have not defined "best conditions."
82. Choice c.
83. Choice d. Note the X_1^2 term.
84. Choice a. Choice b is incorrect as there are no higher order terms. Choice c may not be correct if there are no extra runs (degrees of freedom) to calculate error, as when only four trials are used.
85. Choice d. F tests cannot be performed on the regression when there are insufficient degrees of freedom (unique trials or experimental conditions) to estimate error. Often, factors can be removed from the regression to free up trials for error estimation.
86. Choice d. Standard notation for designed experiments where there are n factors all at L levels is L^n.
87. Choice b. Increasing the number of observations by replicating an experiment provides the benefits described by 1 and 3. Note that 2 is untrue and that only choice b doesn't have 2.
88. Choice b.
89. Choice a.
90. Choice d. Taguchi and Plackett Burman designs are screening designs that involve a large number of factors with a small number of trials. Response surface designs attempt to fit a nonlinear

equation to the response surface. This requires more degrees-of-freedom than a screening experiment. EVOP (Evolutionary Operation) is used to make gradual improvements over time. A large number of trials are made; then very small changes are made in the factor levels.

91. Choice a. If an interaction plot does not yield parallel lines, then an interaction is present.
92. Choice b.
93. Choice d.
94. Choice d.
95. Choice a. The interaction AB will be at its low level, AC at its high level, and ABC at its low level.
96. Choice d.
97. Choice d.
98. Choice c.
99. Choice c.
100. Choice d.

GLOSSARY

Alias

Factors or interactions are aliased or confounded when an independent estimate cannot be made for a parameter that is the alias of another parameter. See also *Factorial Designs* in Part 3.

Attributes Data

Attributes data is also known as "count" data. Typically, we will count the number of times we observe some condition (usually something we don't like, such as an error) in a given sample from the process. This is different from measurement data in its resolution. Attribute data has less resolution, since we only count if something occurs, rather than taking a measurement to see how close we are to the condition. For example, attributes data for a health-care process might include the number of patients with a fever, whereas variables data for the same process might be the measurement of the patients' temperature.

Attributes data generally provides us with less information than measurement (variables) data would for the same process. Using attributes data, we will generally not be able to predict if the process is trending toward an undesirable state, since it is already in this condition.

Average

The average, sometimes called *X-bar*, is calculated for a set of *n* data values as:

$$\bar{x} = \frac{1}{n}\sum_{i=1}^{n} x_i$$

Simply, the sum of each observation (x_i) is divided by the number of observations *n*. An example of its use is as the plotted statistic in an X-bar chart. Here, the n is the subgroup size, and $\bar{x}$ indicates the average of the observations in the subgroup.

When dealing with subgrouped data, you can also calculate the overall average of the subgroups. It is the average of the subgroups' averages, so is sometimes called *X-doublebar*.

$$\bar{\bar{x}} = \frac{1}{m*n} \sum_{j=1}^{m} \sum_{i=1}^{n} x_i$$

where n is the subgroup size and m is the total number of subgroups included in the analysis.

When the subgroup size is 1, this equation simplifies to:

$$\bar{\bar{x}} = \frac{1}{m} \sum_{j=1}^{m} x_j$$

Average Range
The average of the subgroup ranges (R-bar).

$$\bar{R} = \frac{1}{m} \sum_{j=1}^{m} R_j$$

where R_j is the subgroup range of subgroup j and m is the total number of subgroups included in the analysis.

Average Sigma
The average of the subgroup sigma (S-bar).

$$\bar{S} = \frac{1}{m} \sum_{j=1}^{m} S_j$$

where S_j is the subgroup sigma of subgroup j and m is the total number of subgroups included in the analysis.

Backward Elimination
Regression by backward elimination involves an interactive series of regressions, starting with the initial model (the interaction array). At each step the significance of the t statistic for each remaining parameter is compared to the specified probability criterion. The lowest (poorest comparison) parameter is discarded and the regression run again until all remaining parameters meet the criterion. See Regression Analysis in Part 3.

Balance

Balance in a designed experiment is used in two contexts. First, the levels in a design may be balanced; second, the data may be distributed in a balanced way. When a design is balanced, each column of the design array has the same number of levels of that parameter. When the data is balanced, the data points are distributed over the experimental region so that they have an equal contribution to the parameter estimates. Although many designs satisfy both criteria, some, such as central composite designs, forgo design balance in favor of data balance. Balance of both kinds is often forfeited in favor of adding points to better estimate the experimental error. At times it may be preferable to void the balance by removing runs to make a smaller design that can meet a time or resource constraint.

Bias

Also known as *accuracy*, bias is an estimate of the error in the measurement system. Bias is estimated by taking repeat samples of a part or standard using the measurement system, and comparing the average of these measurements with a measurement taken of the same piece using equipment with higher accuracy.

$$\text{Bias} = \text{average of measurements} - \text{reference value}$$
$$\%\text{bias} = (\text{bias/process variation}) * 100\%$$

Process variation may be estimated as six times the process sigma value calculated from a control chart.

Blocking Factor

When all runs cannot be completed under the same environment (homogeneous conditions), exclusive of the factors themselves, blocking may be necessary. The maximum block size may be limited by such constraints as the number of runs that can be done in one day or shift. Blocking factors may not interact with main factors. Blocking factors are evaluated as random factors in an ANOVA.

Box-Behnken Design

A Box-Behnken design (named for the authors who originally proposed it) uses a selection of corner, face, and central points to span an experimental space with fewer points than a complete factorial design. It is similar in intent to a central composite design, but it differs in that no corner or extreme points are used. It has no extended axial points, so it uses only three-level factors. They usually require fewer runs than a three-level

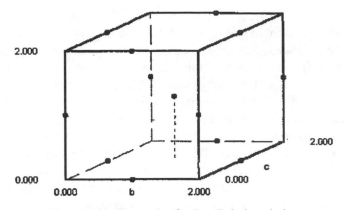

Figure F.63   Example of a Box-Behnken design.

fractional factorial design, and they are useful to avoid the extreme factor level combinations that central composite designs might require.

An example is shown in Figure F.63. Notice that instead of corner points, factors are run midpoints and center on the cube.

Casual Factor

Also known as random variable or covariate. Occasionally, an experimental factor will be present that is not controllable for an experimental run. Such a factor cannot be included in a design, but can be recorded and included in the experimental data: for example, outside air temperature, run sequence, and day of the week. A poor fit of the data to the model is sometimes an indicator of the presence of a significant casual factor.

Central Composite Design

A central composite design (CCD) spans a set of quantitative factors with fewer points than a standard fractional factorial multilevel design, without a large loss in efficiency. Central composite designs consist of central points, corner points (as in the fractional factorial design), and either face-centered points or extended axial points. Central composite designs with face points require three levels; with extended axial points, five levels are required.

These three-level designs are often used for response surface analysis, to map out the shapes of the quadratic surfaces. The center and axial points allow estimates of quadratic terms. (Recall that two-level designs can only be used to estimate linear surfaces.) Repeat center points provide an estimate of pure error.

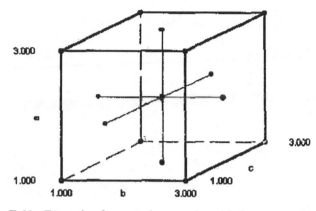

Figure F.64 Example of a central composite with face-centered points.

An example of a face-centered central composite design is shown in Figure F.64. Note the points on the face of the cube. In this case, a standard 2^3 fractional factorial design is supplemented with the six face centered points and two center points.

Figure F.65 is an example of a central composite design with axial points. In this case, a standard 2^3 fractional factorial design is supplemented with the six axial points and two center points.

The location of the axial points (or more precisely, the levels of the factors) is often determined to achieve a *rotatable* design. A design is rotatable if the variance of the predicted response is constant at all points

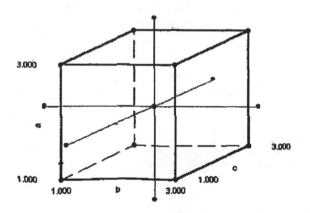

Figure F.65 Example of a central composite design with axial points.

Table T.30.

k	2	3	4	5
α	1.414	1.682	2.00	2.378

equidistant from the center of the design. Most design generation software will define the axial points to achieve rotatable designs. For example, with $k = 2$ factors, design points are equally spaced at plus and minus 1.414, as shown in Table T.30.

For central composite designs, it is not uncommon for the data to be collected in blocks, due to the size of the experiment. For example, we may begin with a screening fractional factorial, then add center and axial points.

Recall that *orthogonal* designs are designs which allow all parameters to be independently estimated. Orthogonal blocking implies that the block effects do not affect the ability to estimate parameters independently. In a blocked central composite design, the choice of the axial point locations and the number of center point replicates affect orthogonal blocking.

The recommendations suggested for central composite designs with blocking are shown in Table T.31. The last column refers to a half fractional design for five factors.

Coefficient
The multiplicative term preceding each parameter in the regression equation. For example, in the regression equation response $= 3.5$ (factor A) $+ 4.2$ (factor B) $+ 1.6$ (factor AB) $+ 25.64$, 3.5 is the coefficient of factor A and 25.64 is the coefficient of the mean term (i.e., in simple linear regression, the y intercept).

Coefficient of Determination R Squared
The coefficient of determination (COD) indicates how much of the total variation in the dependent variable can be accounted for by the regression function. For example, a COD of .70 implies that 70% of the variation in y is accounted for by the regression equation. Most statisticians consider a COD of .7 or higher for a reasonable model.

$$COD = R^2$$

where R is the correlation coefficient.

Table T.31.

Number factors		2	3	4	5(1/2)
Blocks within cube	Points in cube	4	8	16	16
	Blocks in cube	1	2	2	1
Center point replicates in each block		3	2	2	6
Axial block	Axial points	4	6	8	10
Center point replicates		3	2	2	1
Total observations (N)		14	20	30	33
α		1.414	1.633	2.0	2.0

Coefficient of Determination, Adjusted

The coefficient of determination, corrected for the number of terms in the regression equation. It is typically lower and more stable than R-squared when there is more than one independent variable.

$$R^2_{\text{Adjusted}} = 1 - c(1 - R^2)$$
where $c = (n - 1)/(n - p - 1)$
$\quad n$ = number of runs
$\quad p$ = number of parameters estimated by regression.

Complete Factorial Design

A complete factorial design (CFD) consists of all combinations of all factor levels. A CFD is capable of estimating all factors and their interactions. For example, a complete factorial design of three factors, each at two levels, would consist of $2^3 = 8$ runs. *See* Factorial Designs in Part 3.

Confounding

Confounding exists in a multiple regression when two or more factors cannot be estimated independently of one another. Usually this means that there are not enough of the proper runs to form the required estimates for each factor. Confounding may result when runs are removed from a designed experiment without changing the parameter requirements.

An extended design may be generated to add runs to eliminate the confounding. See Factorial Designs in Part 3.

Correlation Coefficient R

A measure of how much linear relationship exists between the values for the two variables. The correlation coefficient can range between $+1$ and -1. Positive values indicate a relationship between X and Y variables so that as X increases so does Y. Negative values imply the relationship between X and Y is such that as values for X increase, values for Y decrease. A value near zero means that there is a random, nonlinear relationship between the two variables.

$$R = \frac{S_{xy}}{S_{xx} * S_{yy}}$$

$$S_{yy} = \sigma_y^2(N-1)$$

$$S_{xx} = \sigma_x^2(N-1)$$

$$S_{xy} = \sum_{j=1}^{N} (x_j - \bar{\bar{x}})(y_j - \bar{\bar{y}})$$

where N is the total number of observations, $\bar{\bar{x}}$ and $\bar{\bar{y}}$ are the averages of x and y, respectively, and σ_x and σ_y are the sample sigma of the x and y values, respectively.

Critical Path

Those tasks which, if not completed in the minimum amount of time, will cause subsequent tasks to be delayed and upset the entire project (or process) completion schedule. See Activity Network Diagram in Part 3.

Degrees of Freedom

A measure of how many runs are used to form an estimate of the parameter. Each parameter estimate absorbs one degree of freedom from the total number of degrees of freedom available. Before any estimates are made, the number of degrees of freedom available equals the number of independent data values.

F Statistic

Provides an indication of the lack of fit of the data to the estimated values of the regression.

$$F = \frac{MS_{reg}}{MS_E}$$

where the mean square regression is $MS_{reg} = SS_{reg} = \beta_1 S_{xy}$

(note: the degrees of freedom for the regression $= 1$),

and the mean square error (residual) is: $MS_E = \frac{SS_E}{df_E} = \frac{S_{yy} - \beta_1 S_{xy}}{N-2}$

$$S_{yy} = \sigma_y^2(N-1)$$

$$S_{xy} = \sum_{j=1}^{N} (x_j - \bar{\bar{x}})(y_j - \bar{\bar{y}})$$

where N is the total number of observations, $\bar{\bar{x}}$ and $\bar{\bar{y}}$ are the averages of x and y, respectively, and σ_y is the sample sigma of the y values.

Several examples of *F Tests* are presented in Part 3.

Fixed Effects
Fixed effects are factors chosen at specific levels of interest, spanning a region of interest, for which a systematic effect on the model response is expected. In a separate context, factors are said to be fixed when held at a constant level during an experiment. The alternative to a fixed effect is a *random effect*.

Fractional Factorial Design
A fractional factorial design is a design that is a regular fraction (1/2, 1/4, 1/8, ...; 1/3, 1/9, 1/27, ...; 1/5, 1/25, ...), a 3/4 fraction, or an irregular unbalanced fraction of a complete factorial design. See Factorial Designs in Part 3.

Gage
An instrument or scale used to measure a process parameter.

Interactions
When the influence of one parameter upon a response is dependent upon the setting of another parameter, this suggests that the interaction of the two parameters may be significant.

In practice, it is often found that only two-factor interactions have a significant effect. The effect of quadratic terms (A^2, B^2, etc.) depends on the process. Some processes are inherently nonlinear with respect to the factor values used in the model. If the data can be fitted only by using many higher-order terms or is not well fitted even with all possible linear and quadratic terms, it may indicate that the process is oscillating over the range of one or more factors. It may also mean that the factor levels or the response should be transformed. Quadratic terms for qualitative factors are often very difficult to interpret and should generally be avoided.

The decision to include or exclude interactions between main factors is extremely important. A screening experiment, which allows for no interactions, may be useful when there is little understanding of the process and no interactions are believed to exist. During the analysis of a screening experiment, it may be found that some main factors are unimportant. If that is the case, the effect of some unplanned interactions may be estimated. There is, however, no assurance that important interactions will not remain confounded with main factors. A better choice is to use a resolution IV design instead of the screening (resolution III) design. The R-IV design will assure no confounding between main effects and two-factor interactions, although the two-factor interactions cannot be estimated.

During the analysis of an experiment planned with interactions, it is often possible to eliminate one or more main factors and to add unplanned interactions to the analysis. See Factorial Designs in Part 3.

John's 3/4 Designs

John's 3/4 designs are 3/4 fractions of regular fractional factorial designs. For example, designs can be constructed of 12 runs (3/4 of 16 run) and 24 runs (3/4 of 32 runs). Conditions are chosen to maximize the number of interactions independently estimated. In this way the designs are constrained by the interactions.

Usually, for the same number of runs, the John's 3/4 designs can accommodate more interactions than a Placket Burman or fractional factorial design. See Factorial Designs in Part 3.

K-S Statistic

The Kolmogorov-Smirnov (K-S) statistic can be used as a relative indicator of curve fit. See Goodness of Fit Tests in Part 3.

Kurtosis

A measure of the flatness or peaked-ness of a distribution. Kurtosis is 0 for a normal distribution. Values greater than 0 imply the distribution has more of a peak than a normal distribution. Values less than 0 imply the distribution is flatter than a normal distribution.

$$kurtosis = \left[\frac{N(N+1)}{(N-1)(N-2)(N-3)} \sum_{j=1}^{N} \frac{(x_j - \bar{\bar{x}})^4}{\sigma_x^4} \right] - \frac{3(N-1)^2}{[(N-2)(N-3)]}$$

where x_j is the observation j, N is the total number of observations, $\bar{\bar{x}}$ is the average, and σ_x is the sample sigma.

Glossary

Lack of Fit

The difference between the total sum of squares of the residuals and the pure error sum of squares, that is, a measure of lack of fit between the data and the fitted response. An F test is used to express the significance of the lack of fit, which is expected to be non-significant for a well-fitted model. See F Test for Lack of Fit in Part 3.

Median

The 50th percentile. The median of a sample of data is found by rank-ordering the data from smallest to largest value, then selecting the data value that is in the middle of the sample. It will have an equal number of data values greater than it and less than it. When there are an even number of data values, use the average of the two central values.

For normal distributions, the median value occurs at the average of the distribution. This is also where the mode, or high point (most frequently occurring value), of the distribution occurs.

For distributions skewed left, both the median and mode occur to the left of (are smaller than) the distribution's average.

For distributions skewed right, both the median and mode occur to the right of (are larger than) the distribution's average.

Minimum Detectable Effect

A design's minimum detectable effect (MDE) refers to the minimum main effect that can be detected at a specified alpha-significance and beta-confidence. The MDE is measured in units of standard deviation. A MDE of 2.6 or less is recommended.

Mixed Level Designs

Mixed level designs have factors in which at least one factor has a different number of levels than another factor. For example, a 2-factor design in which one factor has 2 levels and another has 3 levels is a mixed level design; so is a design consisting of a 2-level factor, a 3-level factor, and a 12-level factor. Mixed level designs are generated using pseudo-factors.

To determine the number of runs required to estimate each possible factor and interaction in a mixed level design, multiply the number of runs calculated separately for each fixed level case. For example, a design with five 2-level factors and one 3-level factor would require $2^5 * 3^1 = 32 * 3 = 96$ runs. See Factorial Designs in Part 3.

Mixture Design

Formulations, blends, combinations, compounds, amalgams, and recipes are designs in which the sum of the factor levels in each run either all sum to a fixed quantity (volume, charge, load) or are restricted to a range of quantities.

Mixture designs differ from ordinary fractional factorials because the levels for the factors in a run cannot be chosen independently of one another. Each factor level must be measurable in some common unit of measure; the common measure need not be the experimental factors units of measure. The common unit may be cubic feet, with factor measures in gallons, pounds, and cubic inches. A factor level may have a minimum or maximum; in addition, the sum of all the factor levels in a run may be specified to not fall below some minimum or exceed some maximum quantity. Standardized designs are based on a nondimensional unit, which may have upper and lower bounds on the sum of all factor levels in a run or which may have upper or lower bounds on the levels for each factor.

Mixture designs are usually special forms of response surface designs except for screening designs that have no center or other interior points. Mixture designs are usually constructed to estimate linear interactions only; that is, they estimate interactions such as AB or ABC but cannot estimate AB^2, A^2B^2 or higher interaction forms.

Noise Factors

See Subsidiary Factor.

Normalization

Normalizing is one of several useful transformation techniques. The effect is to transform the values of the variable to a -1 to $+1$ range when the experimental array is balanced, so the parameters (factors or response) are in a common range. This allows the effects (the relative importance of any factor or interaction) to be identified more clearly. It improves the numerical accuracy of the regression and the computation of significance. Often, the parameters to be retained or discarded are thus identified more easily. Usually either all or none of the quantitative factors to be used in a particular regression run are normalized. Normalizing has no useful purpose for qualitative factors.

Where the experimental situation is nonlinear, the linear model will not fit well and normalizing is of limited value, except as a first step in screening out factors or interactions that have minimal effect on the response. After an initial determination of significant parameters, a regression may be done on transformed experimental values. Often, it's convenient to do a final analysis with the experimental values so that the results in plotting are displayed in conventional units.

$$\text{Normalized value} = (\text{value} - \text{mean of value})/(0.5 \times \text{range of values})$$

Orthogonality

Orthogonality refers to the property of a design that assures that all specified parameters may be estimated independently of any other.

The degree of orthogonality is measured by the normalized value of the determinant of the information matrix. An orthogonal design matrix having one row to estimate each parameter (mean, factors, and interactions) has a measure of 1. It's easy to check for orthogonality: if the sum of the factors' columns in standard format equal 0, then the design is orthogonal.

Some writers lump orthogonality with balance, which is different. *Balance* implies that the data is properly distributed over the design space. It implies a uniform physical distribution of the data, and an equal number of levels of each factor.

Designs do not necessarily need balance to be good designs. Rather, some designs (such as central composite designs) sacrifice balance to achieve better distribution of the variance or predicted error. Balance may also be sacrificed by avoiding extreme combinations of factors, such as in the Box-Behnken design.

For example, a complete factorial design is both orthogonal and balanced if in fact the model that includes all possible interactions is correct. Such a design, although both balanced and orthogonal, would not be a recommended experimental design because it cannot provide an estimate of experimental error. When an additional point (row) is added (which for a complete factorial design must be a repeated run), the design is still orthogonal but unbalanced. If the complete interaction model were not correct, then the design is balanced but the distribution of data is not balanced for the parameters to be estimated.

Fractional factorial and Plackett-Burman designs are normally constructed to have both orthogonality and balance; however, they may have more rows than are required for estimating parameters and error. In such cases, appropriate rows may be trimmed so that orthogonality is preserved but balance is lost. Central composite designs are orthogonal in that all the parameters for the central composite model may be estimated, but the design itself is unbalanced. A greater or lesser number of center points are used to achieve an estimating criterion and an error estimate.

PCL

The PCL, or process centerline, is the average when a normal distribution is assumed for the control chart statistic, or it is typically the median of the distribution for non-normal distributions.

Plackett-Burman Designs

Plackett-Burman (PB) designs are quite useful as screening designs. Plackett-Burman designs are generated in steps of 4 runs, from 4 to 100 runs.
The number of runs n must be at least $k + 1$, where k is the number of parameters. For example, a design can be constructed in 12 runs to estimate 11 parameters.

When the number of runs are a power of two (i.e. 2^x, such as 8-, 16-, or 32-run experiments), the design is the same as a standard fractional factorial. When the number of runs equals a factor of four (such as 12-, 20-, or 24-run experiments), the design can be more efficient than the fractional factorial.

Usually, for the same number of runs, the John's 3/4 designs can accommodate more interactions.

Process Sigma

An estimate of the standard deviation of a controlled process.
Based on the Moving Range Chart (when subgroup size $n = 1$)

$$\sigma_x = \frac{\overline{MR}}{d_2}$$

where $\overline{MR}$ is the average moving range and d_2 (available in Appendix 6) is based on $n = 2$.

Based on the Range Chart (when subgroup size $n > 1$) *Note*: This is the standard deviation of the observations, *not* the standard deviation of the subgroup averages, which may be calculated by dividing this estimate by the square root of n.

$$\sigma_x = \frac{\bar{R}}{d_2}$$

where $\bar{R}$ is the average range and d_2 (available in Appendix 6) is a function of n.

Based on the Sigma Chart (when subgroup size $n > 1$) *Note*: This is the standard deviation of the observations, *not* the standard deviation of the subgroup averages, which may be calculated by dividing this estimate by the square root of n.

$$\sigma_x = \frac{\bar{S}}{c_4}$$

where $\bar{S}$ is the average sigma and c_4 (available in Appendix 6) is a function of n.

Population Sigma

The standard deviation of the population from which the sample was drawn.

$$\sigma_x = \sqrt{\frac{\sum_{j=1}^{N} (x_j - \bar{\bar{x}})^2}{N}}$$

where N is the total number of observations, x_j is the observation at time j, and $\bar{\bar{x}}$ is the average.

Pure Error

Experimental error, the differences between repeated runs of the same condition. The total error includes both pure error and lack of fit error.

We can estimate pure error as the variation between the repeat runs using the sum of squared deviations between each observation and the average at that design condition. To estimate pure error, we need to repeat at least one of the run conditions.

In some cases, we may even have a full design replicate, such as when we remove a factor from the analysis if it is not statistically significant. For example, if we ran a two-level complete factorial design for three factors (2^3) and determined the ABC interaction was insignificant, we would have a replicated 2^{3-1} design.

We can also extend designs to estimate error. See Factorial Designs in Part 3.

Qualitative Factors

Qualitative factors are those that are not assigned measurable levels, such as on/off or blue/green/red. The levels of a qualitative factor are nominal; they do not have a natural order or a measure of separation between them. Qualitative factors often exist in a few discrete categories only. When numerical calculations are made using qualitative data, a numerical value must be assigned to each factor category for regression analysis.

Quantitative Factors

Quantitative factors have a natural order that may be quantified, such as weight or distance. Often they are referred to as continuous variables or variable data. Quantitative factors may be measured as an interval between levels or with respect to some common origin. In some cases, qualitative information may be expressed quantitatively for the purposes of analysis, such as setting slow = 0, medium = 7, and fast = 10. Such quantification need not be related to any recognized scale, but it should be spaced realistically. Quantitative factors can describe a specific response curve or surface, whereas the shape of the response to qualitative factors depends on an arbitrary factor ordering.

Random Effects

Random effects result from factors having levels that are representative of a larger set of levels. An assumption is made that the random levels included in the design are representative because they are chosen randomly from a population having normally distributed effects. They are included in a design as a nonsystematic source of variation. Blocking factors are used as random effect factors. Random factors are often nuisance parameters; they may be a source of variation, but they are generally not useful for control. They are often included in a design with the hope, if not the expectation, that they will be found to be nonsignificant.

Rational Subgroups

Most control charts, including the X-bar and individual-X charts, rely upon rational subgroups to estimate the short-term variation in the process. This short-term variation is then used to predict the longer-term variation defined by the control limits. But what is a rational subgroup?

A rational subgroup is simply "a sample in which all of the items are produced under conditions in which only random effects are responsible for the observed variation" (Nelson, 1988). As such, it has the following properties:

1. The observations comprising the subgroup are independent. Two observations are independent if neither observation influences, or results from, the other. When observations are dependent on one another, we say the process has autocorrelation, or serial correlation. (These terms mean the same thing). Many processes are subject to autocorrelation. Examples include:

• *Chemical Processes*. When dealing with liquids, particularly in large baths, samples taken close together in time are influenced by one another. The liquid retains the effect of the first observation, such as temperature, which carries over into subsequent temperature observations for a period of time. Subgroups formed over a small time frame from these types of processes are sometimes called homogenous subgroups, since the observations within the subgroups are often nearly identical (except for the effect of measurement variation).

• *Service processes*. Consider the wait time at a bank. The wait time of any person in the line is influenced by the wait time of the person in front of him or her.

• *Discrete part manufacturing*. Although this is the "classic" case of independent subgroups, when feedback control is used to change a process based upon past observations, the observations become inherently dependent.

When observations within a subgroup are autocorrelated, the within-subgroup variation is often quite small, and not a reflection of the between-subgroup process variation. The small within-subgroup variation forces the control limits to be too narrow, resulting in frequent out-of-control conditions. This leads to tampering.

2. The observations within a subgroup are from a single, stable process. If subgroups contain the elements of multiple process streams, or if other special causes occur frequently within subgroups, then the within-subgroup variation will be large relative to the variation between subgroup averages. This large within-subgroup variation forces the control limits to be too far apart, resulting in a lack of sensitivity to process shifts. Run test 7 (15 successive points within one sigma of centerline) is helpful in detecting this condition.

3. The subgroups are formed from observations taken in a time-ordered sequence. In other words, subgroups cannot be randomly formed from a set of data (or a box of parts); instead, the data comprising a subgroup must be a "snapshot" of the process over a small window of time, and the order of the subgroups would show how those snapshots vary in time (like a movie). The size of the "small window of time" is determined on an individual process basis to minimize the chance of a special cause occurring in the subgroup.

Replicated Designs
Replicated designs are designs in which all or almost all of the main factor design is repeated a few or several times. Replication allows an estimate of

variance for each run of the main factor design, thereby allowing for an analysis of variation over the full range of the experiment.

Regression Function

The equation of the least square fit line through the data, used to estimate values of the dependent variable (the y axis) for given values of the independent variable (the x axis) or variables (X_1, X_2, etc.).

Residuals

A residual is the difference between the observed response and the value calculated from the regression model (the fitted response) for that combination of factor levels. The residual includes the effect of both experimental error (pure error) and the lack of fit between the assumed model and the true model.

Resolution

Resolution provides an indication of the interaction types that can be independently estimated with the design. Recall that when factors and interactions are confounded, they cannot be independently estimated.

Resolution, as a way of describing performance of a design, is most useful when complete sets of interactions are required.

• *Resolution III*. At least one main factor may be confounded with an interaction. These are typically useful only as a preliminary screening design.
• *Resolution IV*. Main factors are not confounded with two-factor interactions, but may be confounded with higher-order interactions. Two-factor interactions may be confounded with one another and with higher-order interactions.
• *Resolution V*. Main-factor and two-factor interactions are not confounded with one another but may be confounded with higher-order interactions. Three-factor and higher-order interactions may be confounded.
• *Resolution VI*. Main-factor and two-factor, interactions are not confounded with each other or with three-factor interactions. Three-factor and higher-order interactions may be confounded with one another.
• *Resolution VII designs*. Main-factor, two-factor, and three-factor interactions are not confounded with one another but may be confounded with higher-order interactions. Four-factor and higher-order interactions may be confounded.

Resolution V or VI designs provide the most detail needed for first-order models.

As the resolution increases, the number of trials also increases, quite dramatically with the number of factors.

Mixed resolution designs are also possible. That is, we may not need estimates of all the three-factor interactions or even all the two-factor interactions. This often happens with mixture experiments (where the levels of the individual factors contribute to the whole of the factors) as well as for response surfaces (where quadratic effects may only exist for some factors).

Reducing designs, by eliminating extraneous runs, can produce mixed-resolution designs.

Sample Sigma

The standard deviation of the samples drawn from the population.

$$\sigma_x = \sqrt{\frac{\sum_{j=1}^{N} (x_j - \bar{\bar{x}})^2}{N - 1}}$$

where x_j is the observation at time j, N is the total number of observations, and $\bar{\bar{x}}$ is the average.

Screening Designs

Screening designs are initial designs with a minimum number of runs (design conditions, trials) used to eliminate factors from subsequent designs. Screening designs often do not estimate interactions. Regular and irregular Plackett-Burman designs may be used for screening. Screening designs may satisfy resolution III or IV. See Factorial Designs in Part 3.

Skewness

A measure of the symmetry of a distribution around its mean. Positive values indicate a shift or tail to the right; negative values indicate a shift or tail to the left. Skewness is 0 for a normal distribution.

$$skewness = \frac{[(N - 1)(N - 2)]}{N} \sum_{j=1}^{N} \frac{(x_j - \bar{x})^3}{\sigma_x^3}$$

where x_j is the observation j, N is the total number of observations, $\bar{x}$ is the average, and σ_x is the sample sigma.

Slack Time

The amount of time that a particular task may be delayed without delaying the completion of the entire project. The latest start time minus the earliest start time on the time schedule is equal to the slack time. See Activity Network Diagram in Part 3.

Standard Error of Mean
Used as an indication of the reliability of the average as an estimate of the mean of the population. Smaller numbers mean the estimate of the population average has less variability.

$$\text{Standard error} = \frac{\sigma_x}{\sqrt{N}}$$

where x_j is the observation j, N is the total number of observations, and σ_x is the sample sigma.

Standardized Short-Run p Statistic
The p statistic can be standardized for use in short-run processes as follows. Once standardized, the data can be plotted on a p chart.

$$z_i = \frac{p_i - \bar{p}_r}{\sqrt{\frac{1}{n}(\bar{p}_r(1 - \bar{p}_r))}}$$

where n is the sample size, and $\bar{p}_r$ is a constant based on prior data or a desired value.

When based on prior data, $\bar{p}_r$ may be calculated as:

$$\bar{p}_r = \frac{\sum_{j=1}^{r} (count)_j}{\sum_{j=1}^{r} n_j}$$

Standardized Short-Run u Statistic
The u statistic can be standardized for use in short-run processes as follows. Once standardized, the data can be plotted on a u chart.

$$z_i = \frac{u_i - \bar{u}_r}{\sqrt{(\bar{u}_r)(1/n)}}$$

where n is the sample size, and $\bar{u}_r$ is a constant based on prior data or a desired value.

When based on prior data, $\bar{u}_r$ may be calculated as:

$$\bar{u}_r = \frac{\sum_{j=1}^{r} (count)_j}{r}$$

Standardized Short-Run c Statistic

The c statistic can be standardized for use in short-run processes as follows. Once standardized, the data can be plotted on a c chart:

$$z_i = \frac{c_i - \bar{c}_r}{\sqrt{\bar{c}_r}}$$

where n is the sample size, and $\bar{c}_r$ is a constant based on prior data or a desired value.

When based on prior data, $\bar{c}_r$ may be calculated as:

$$\bar{c}_r = \frac{\sum_{j=1}^{r} (count)_j}{r}$$

Standardized Short-Run np Statistic

The np statistic can be standardized for use in short-run processes as follows. Once standardized, the data can be plotted on a np chart.

$$z_i = \frac{np_i - n\bar{p}_r}{\sqrt{n\bar{p}_r(1 - \bar{p}_r)}}$$

where n is the sample size, and $n\bar{p}_r$ is a constant based on prior data or a desired value.

When based on prior data, $n\bar{p}_r$ may be calculated as:

$$n\bar{p}_r = \frac{\sum_{j=1}^{r} (count)_j}{r}$$

Standardized Short-Run Observations

Observations can be standardized for use in short-run processes as follows. Once standardized, the data can be plotted on any variables control chart.

For use as nominal control charts:

$$z_i = x_i - nominal$$

where x_i is the observation and nominal is a constant based on prior data or a desired value.

For use as stabilized control charts:

$$z_i = \frac{x_i - nominal}{\sigma}$$

where x_i is the observation, σ is the standard deviation of the observations, and nominal is a constant based on prior data or a desired value.

Stationary Point

The point (if it exists) on a response surface which may be located at a maximum, minimum, or saddle. The stationary point may be outside the experimental range. When the stationary point is far from the data region, it should be used only to indicate a general direction, requiring additional data for validation. See Ridge Analysis in Part 3.

Studentized Residual

See Residuals Analysis in Part 3.

Subsidiary Factor

Subsidiary factors are factors that may be contributors to the response but are not controlled in normal operations; however, they must be controlled for the experiment. When not included in the design, they contribute to error. If the effect of a subsidiary factor is suspected of being strong, it should be included as a main factor so its interaction effects can be properly estimated.

Taguchi uses the labels *inner array* for main factors and *outer array* for subsidiary factors. Taguchi's *noise* factors refer to factors that cannot usually be controlled in practice. In classical design literature, these factors are often referred to as *subsidiary factors*. Many times we fail to recognize these process variables, and their effect contributes to experimental error.

Taguchi defined three types of noise:

- *External*: such as temperature, dust, or vibration
- *Internal*: such as material wear or aging
- *Unit-to-Unit*: such as time of day for order arrival, material composition

Attempts to control these process variables are often costly. Instead, it is often preferred to determine optimal regions for the process or product which minimizes the impact of these uncontrollable factors. Designing processes and products in this way is known as a robust design.

The effect of interaction between a subsidiary factor and a main factor cannot be estimated. When subsidiary factors are incorporated in a design, they are usually considered as random effects during the analysis, or as noise factors.

When subsidiary (or noise) factors are included in an experiment, we can construct a subsidiary design (Taguchi's outer array). We can specify interaction among the subsidiary factors, but the subsidiary factors cannot interact with any of the main factors (or their interactions). The final design repeats each run of the main design for each subsidiary design trial. For example, a 16-run main design, coupled with a 4-run subsidiary design created for two noise factors results in a final design of $16 \times 4 = 64$ trials.

If the analysis indicates significance of a noise factor, then it is possible that main and noise factors interact. If interaction is suspected, it is best to run additional experimental trials treating the significant noise factors as main factors and look for interaction between the noise and (original) main factors. For this reason, it is always better to try to incorporate a subsidiary factor as a main factor in the initial design.

Taguchi Designs

Taguchi designs are fractional factorial designs, with the order of the factors or rows revised from the standard order. In this way, Taguchi did not develop any new designs. Some practitioners feel his design construction is more complicated, obscuring the interactions or factor effects.

Instead, Taguchi's contributions to design were in his recommendations for screening designs to include the effect of variance. Taguchi emphasized the use of replicates, including subsidiary (or noise) factors, to estimate variance.

Tampering

Tampering with a process occurs when we respond to variation in the process (such as by "adjusting" the process) when the process has not shifted. In other words, it is when we treat variation due to common causes as variation due to special causes. This is also called "responding to a false alarm," since a false alarm is when we think that the process has shifted when it really hasn't.

In practice, tampering generally occurs when we attempt to control the process to limits that are within the natural control limits defined by common cause variation. Some causes of this include:

- We try to control the process to specifications, or goals. These limits are defined externally to the process, rather than being based on the statistics of the process.
- Rather than using the suggested control limits defined at ± 3 standard deviations from the centerline, we instead choose to use limits that are tighter (or narrower) than these (sometimes called *warning limits*). We might do this based on the faulty notion that this will improve the performance of the chart, since it is more likely that subgroups will plot outside of these limits. For example, using limits defined at ± 2 standard deviations from the centerline would produce narrower control limits than the ± 3 standard deviation limits. However, you can use probability

theory to show that the chance of being outside of a ± 3 standard deviation control limit for a normally distributed statistic is .27% if the process has not shifted. On average, you would see a false alarm associated with these limits once every 370 subgroups ($= 1/.0027$). Using ± 2 standard deviation control limits, the chance of being outside the limits when the process has not shifted is 4.6%, corresponding to false alarms every 22 subgroups!

Deming showed how tampering actually increases variation. It can easily be seen that when we react to these false alarms, we take action on the process by shifting its location. Over time, this results in process output that varies much more than if the process had just been left alone. See Statistical Process Control Charts in Part 3.

Taguchi Ratios
See Transformations in Part 3.

Variance Analysis Ratio
A plot of the variance analysis ratio may be used to select a transform of the response. Transforms are sometimes used to stabilize the variance over the range of the data. See Transformations in Part 3.

REFERENCES

AIAG (1995). *Potential Failure Modes and Effects Analysis Reference Guide.* Automotive Industry Action Group.

———. (1995). *MSA Reference Manual.* Automotive Industry Action Group.

Box, G. E. P. (1988). "Signal-to-Noise Ratios, Performance Criteria and Transformations." *Technometrics* 30, 1–40.

Box, G. E. P. and Cox, D. R. (1964). "An Analysis of Transformations," *Journal of the Royal Statistical Society, Series B* 26, pp. 211–246.

Box, G. E. P. and Draper, N. R. (1969). *Evolutionary Operation: A Statistical Method for Process Improvement.* New York: John Wiley & Sons.

Box, G. E. P., Hunter, W. G., and Hunter, J. S. (1978). *Statistics for Experimenters.* New York: John Wiley & Sons.

Box, G. E. P. and Jenkins, G. M. (1970). *Time Series Analysis, Forecasting and Control.* San Francisco: Holden-Day.

Breyfogle, F. W. III (1999). *Implementing Six Sigma.* New York: John Wiley & Sons.

Breyfogle, F. W. III, Cupello, J. M., and Meadows, B. (2001). *Managing Six Sigma,* New York: John Wiley & Sons.

Burr, I. W. "Control Charts for Measurements with Varying Sample Sizes." *Journal of Quality Technology* 1.3 (July 1969), pp. 163–167.

Carlzon, J. (1989). *Moments of Truth.* New York: HarperCollins.

Deming, W. E. (1986). *Out of the Crisis.* Cambridge, MA: MIT Press.

Derringer, G. and Suich, R. (1980). "Simultaneous Optimization of Several Response Variables." *Journal of Quality Technology* 12, pp. 214–219.

Duncan, A. J. (1986) *Quality Control and Industrial Statistics.* 5th ed. Homewood: Richard D. Irwin.

Eckes, G. (2001) *The Six Sigma Revolution.* New York: John Wiley & Sons.

Forum Corporation (1996). Annual Report.

General Electric (1997–2000). Annual Reports to Shareholders.

George, M. L. (2002). *Lean Six Sigma,* New York: McGraw-Hill.

Hahn, G. J. and Shapiro, S. S. (1967). *Statistical Models in Engineering.* New York: John Wiley & Sons.

Harry, M. and Schroeder, R. (2000). *Six Sigma*. New York: Doubleday.

Johnson, N. L. and Kotz, S. eds. (1983). *Encyclopedia of Statistical Sciences*. pp. 303–314. New York: John Wiley & Sons.

Juran, J. M. and Gryna, F. M. (1988) *Juran's Quality Control Handbook,* 4th ed. New York: McGraw-Hill.

Keller, P. A. "Demystifying SPC: Choosing X Over X-Bar Charts." *PI Quality* May–June 1993, p. 26.

———. "Demystifying SPC, Part II: Sampling Period and Autocorrelation." *PI Quality*, July–August 1993, pp. 34–35.

———. "Demystifying SPC, Part III: EWMA Makes It Easy." *PI Quality*, September–October 1993, pp. 50–52.

———. (2001). *Six Sigma Deployment*. Tucson: QA Publishing, LLC.

Kohler, H. (1988). *Statistics for Business and Economics*. Glenview, IL: Scott, Foresman.

Massey, F. J., Jr. "The Kolmogorov-Smirnov Test for Goodness of Fit." *Journal of the American Statistical Association* 46 (1951), pp. 68–78.

Montgomery, D. C. (1991). *Introduction to Statistical Quality Control*. New York: John Wiley & Sons.

Montgomery, D. C. and Runger, G. C. (1994). *Applied Statistics and Probability for Engineers*. 1st ed. New York: John Wiley and Sons.

Myers, R. H. and Montgomery, D. C. (1995). *Response Surface Methodology*. New York: John Wiley and Sons.

Nelson, Lloyd S. "The Shewhart Control Chart—Tests for Special Causes." *Journal of Quality Technology* 16.4 (October 1984), pp. 237–239.

———. "Control Charts: Rational Subgroups and Effective Applications." *Journal of Quality Technology* 20.1 (January 1988), pp. 73–75.

Pignatiello, J. J., Jr. and Ramberg, J. S. (1985). "Discussion of Off-Line Quality Control, Parameter Design and the Taguchi Method by R.N. Kackar." *Journal of Quality Technology* 17, pp. 198–206.

Pyzdek, T. (1990). *Pyzdek's Guide to SPC, Volume One: Fundamentals*. Milwaukee: ASQC Press.

———. "Johnson Control Charts." *Quality,* February 1991a, p. 41.

— —. (1992) *Pyzdek's Guide to SPC Volume Two: Applications and Special Topics*. Milwaukee: ASQC Press.

———. "Process Control for Short and Small Runs." *Quality Progress*, April 1993, p. 51.

———. (2003). *Six Sigma Handbook,* 2nd ed. New York: McGraw-Hill.

Revelle, J. (2000). *What Your Quality Guru Never Told You*. Tucson, AZ: QA Publishing.

Slater, R. (1999). *Jack Welch and the GE Way*. New York: McGraw-Hill.

———. (2000). *The GE Way Fieldbook*. New York: McGraw-Hill.

Snee, R. D. "The Project Selection Process." *Quality Progress*, September 2002, pp. 78–80.

References

Taguchi, G. (1986). *Introduction to Quality Engineering*. Tokyo: Asian Productivity Organization.

Western Electric Company. (1958). *Statistical Quality Control Handbook*. 2nd ed. New York: Western Electric Company.

Womack, J. P. and Jones, D. T. (1996). *Lean Thinking*. New York: Simon & Schuster.

INDEX

About the Author

Paul A. Keller is Vice President and Senior Consultant with Quality America. He has developed and implemented successful Six Sigma and quality improvement programs in service and manufacturing applications. He is the author of *Six Sigma Deployment: A Guide for Implementing Six Sigma in Your Organization*, providing a practical "how to" approach for management deployment of Six Sigma. He has written numerous articles and book chapters on quality improvement and Six Sigma methods, and has developed and led well-received training and consulting programs on Six Sigma and related topics to numerous clients in diverse industries, including Boeing, Dow Corning, Arris, Los Alamos National Labs, Parker Hannifan Fuel Products, Warner Lambert, University of Arizona, Bell Atlantic, Ford Motor Company, and many others.

Before launching Quality America's training and consulting business in 1992, Paul specialized in quality engineering in the masters program at the University of Arizona. He later served as a quality manager for a consumer goods manufacturer and as an SPC Director at an industrial products manufacturer. In these roles, he developed company-wide quality systems to meet the demands of a diverse customer base, including the automotive and aerospace industries. He is currently active in Six Sigma training and consulting through Quality America. Paul may be reached via e-mail at: pkeller@qualityamerica.com